Front Cover Photograph By

Sherry G. Mangum

Flagstaff, Arizona

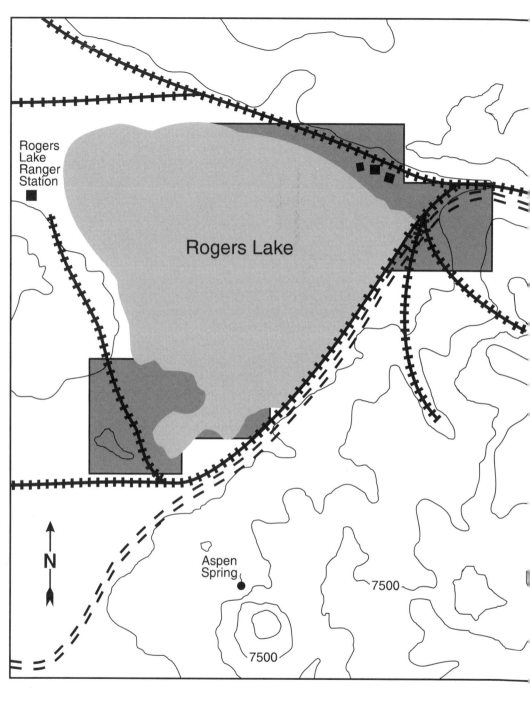

Rogers Lake Ranger Station

Rogers Lake

N

Aspen Spring

7500

7500

Map by Cynthia Gross

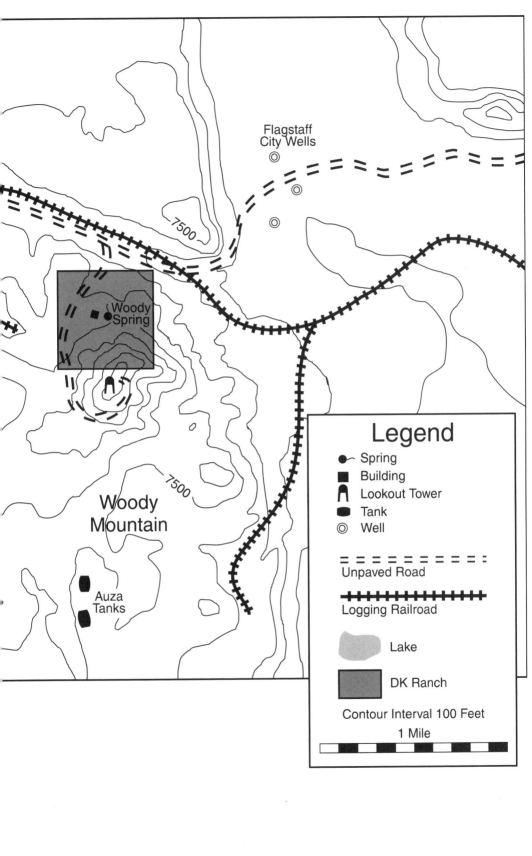

W oody Mountain, a modest lava cone that stands on the horizon eight miles southwest of Flagstaff, Arizona, has for a moment in its long existence been entangled with the lives of explorers, pioneers, loggers, ranchers, scientists, lookouts, and rangers, and with the lives of people in the nearby town that grew along the railraod at the base of an old volcano. The history of the west touched at one lilluminating point, the tale is full of informaiton previously hidden in government, university, and private archives. Biography of a Small Mountain *is a unique addition to the literatuve of Arizona history and, in the wider significance of the story, to the human literature of the West.*

Biography of a
Small Mountain

Donna Ashworth

Small Mountain Books
Flagstaff, Arizona

Small Mountain Books
1109 S. Plaza Way #380
Flagstaff, Arizona 86001

Library of Congress Catalog Card Number: 91-91288

Library of Congress Cataloging-in-Publication Data
Ashworth, Donna
    Biography of a Small Mountain/by Donna Ashworth
    p.   cm.   Includes index and bibliographical references

1. Arizona—History
2. Woody Mountain, Arizona
3. Flagstaff (Arizona)—History
4. Coconino National Forest (Arizona)—History
5. United States—Forest Service—Coconino National Forest
I. Title

ISBN 0-9630364-4-0

979.133
A831b

Permission to quote from A Westerly Trend : Being a Veracious Chronicle of More than Sixty Years
of Joyous Wanderings Mainly in Search of SPACE AND SUNSHINE by Godfrey Sykes and "Scraps
from the Past" by Glenton Sykes was granted by the Sykes heirs Jocelyn Cushman, Diane Boyer, and
Dr. Georgiana S. Boyer.

There is no history; there is only biography.
Ralph Waldo Emerson

to John Irwin
partner in the search

Special thanks to
Virginia Rose
for several excellent reasons

Historical research can be a lonely trail. The many people who were aid and welcome compnay along the way are listed in page 323–339 under the headings of Correspondence and Conversations. Six of them turned help into friendship.

John Irwin
Flagstaff City—Coconino County Public Library

Lois Leman
Special Collections and Archives Department
Cline Library, Northern Arizona University

Henry Giclas
Lowell Observatory

Stanton Wallace
US Forest Service

Louise Black

and
Timothy Allen Riordan

Mary Beth Green was a scrupulous copy editor and a friend.

Table of Contents

List of Illustrations

Foreword

This is much more than a story about a mountain. While Woody Mountain, from earliest geologic time to the present, is the underlying recurrent theme, the story introduces the reader to a unique cross-section of Flagstaff history. Through these pages the reader becomes intimately acquainted with many of Flagstaff's pioneers and gains an insight into the beginning of controlled use of our forest resources. it will be difficult, too, for a reader not to share and appreciate the deep love the author has for this mountain and its relationship to our present day problems of conservation.

After reading about the first white men to appear near the mountain in 1851, known to be the Lieutenant Sitgreaves expedition (which contributed the first known local casualty, a Mexican herder), one meets Charles T. Rogers who ran cattle in the area to the west some twenty years later and for whom Rogers Lake was named. The first land surveyor makes his appearance in 1878. It is about this time that John Woody arrives at the spring on the north side of the mountain and establishes his first headquarters there and the mountain receives its name. There follow many interesting accounts of early Flagstaff citizens and their social life in connection with Ella Woody, John's wife, who comes alive as a personality you will be happy to know.

An interesting saga of western cattle and sheep raising introduces the several Millers who made use of the area and identifies the present family of Duane Miller and the DK outfit. Then there is an account of early day logging of the forest by railroad, with an introduction by T.A. Riordan family. Along with this develops an excellent documented account of the beginning of the Forest Service, Exemplified by the struggles of the first Flagstaff ranger, Col. Fred Breen.

Chapter VI includes the establishment of the Southwest Experimental Forest Station at Fort Valley with its controversial first director, Gus Pearson, whose research the author credits making the reforestation of the mountain possible. To introduce the presence of the well fields that flank Woody Mountain today there is a compelling account of the evolution and development of water for the city of Flagstaff from early times. Chapter VIII explains how the forest lookout towers came into being and describes many of the people who have served on Woody Mountain since 1910. This more or less brings the status of the mountain up to date.

The reader will find this is a remarkable book for its wealth of history, factual information, and insight into why conditions in our forest are what they are today. It is presented in a warm and understanding way with many lovely digressions that make very enjoyable reading and that would surely have been stricken as irrelevant if the manuscript had been edited by a professional historian.

Henry L. Giclas
Flagstaff, 1991

Preface

E very morning while sunlight still came low and flickering through the trees, I started up the stairs of the fire tower, carrying a Forest Service radio, ready to begin the day's work. "Sept. 1936" was scratched into the concrete slab at the bottom step, but I gave it slight attention as I climbed through summer sunrise at eight thousand feet, emerging above tree tops into wind and weather and the possibility of smoke in a hundred miles of spreading landscape. Old writing on concrete was just a detail on the ground. I was in service on Woody Mountain southwest of Flagstaff, in the company of the trees of the Coconino National Forest, one of the sixty full-time fire lookouts left in Arizona. My tower was seven feet square, about the dimensions of a large bed.

Imagine standing around on your bed eight hours a day, and you'll have an idea of the confines of my job. Don't feel sorry for me.you probably can't see for a hundred miles from your bed; I could from my tower. After fifteen years of trying to teach English to teenagers, I treated isolation as freedom. One morning in 1985 I said, "If those numbers in the concrete are the date of construction, the tower is one year older than the Golden Gate Bridge, and the fiftieth anniversary is coming up. There must be stories to tell." I asked at the district ranger station, but no one seemed to know much. Fifty years is a longer working life than most people have.

I had been alone with oak leaves budding out in the spring and full moons shining silently on the slopes and July storms pounding with wind and hail, and the place felt like somebody I knew. In growing determination, I began a search for its past.the history, if any, of one modest mountain sitting quietly off to the side of things.

The story was buried deeply in dusty archives. It emerged slowly, one puzzling detail at a time. All the characters of Western legend entered the tale: explorers; cowboys and ranchers and sheepherders; an anonymous prospector; rangers and saloon keepers; railroad men and loggers and a man who loved trees; a newspaperman; a deputy sheriff; a few spirited women; immigrants of many tongues and colors. There were deaths by sickness and gunshot, men and women who worked their way to wealth and respectability and others who didn't, children who grew up and heroes who grew old. There was love, or at least, people who married, and plenty of evidence of sadness in lives lived. And the sadness of silence afterward.

National politics reached out and touched the mountain. Its history was tangled with railroad land titles and water rights and grazing permits and logging regulations supervised by bureau chiefs in Washington. Entrepreneurs born somewhere else found in it the opportunities that western land offered. The story of old Flagstaff was visible from the top of Woody Mountain and beyond that, clear on the horizon like sandstone buttes, the story of the West.

Chapter One
The Mountain

5,860,000 B.C. to 1878 A.D.

A Devonian Sea was in the neighborhood of Flagstaff about 350 million years ago.
Museum of Northern Arizona

Creatures of the Mesozoic were in the vicinity of Woody Mountain
one hundred million years ago.
Museum of Northern Arizona

Woody Mountain was once an active volcano. Everything around Flagstaff was once volcanic, every bump on the horizon from the Verde Valley north. Even Mormon Mountain, so eroded it came to look like a beached whale, was a volcano.

But that was not the beginning. The beginning was below, in the hidden petrified silt of ancient seas. Think down. All the strata exposed in the Grand Canyon lie underfoot, layered in deposits of sand and mud from shallow waters that covered the land, as the continent drifted and water level rose and fell, and then slowly disappeared over the long geologic ages. The seas persisted a vast time, longer than mind can quite grasp, long enough to accumulate sediments several hundred feet deep. Remains of shells, ferns, reptiles, and cone-bearing plants drifted down through those waters and were preserved in the resulting stone.

Flagstaff's houses stand above land that was built in a time when most life on earth was in water. The great cliff of Redwall limestone in the Grand Canyon was deposited by an ocean 365 to 330 million years ago—three hundred and some million years of the planet's turning round the sun. Morning light in those days lay on a wide, quiet sea, part of the water that covered most of the globe.

After that there were several others, thanks to changes on a planetary scale. Under Woody Mountain, Redwall limestone is a dense band two hundred feet thick, 3400 feet below present pines. The formation above it, another ocean bottom, comes fifteen hundred feet closer to the light and a few million years closer to the present. Coconino sandstone, still a thousand feet down, silent now and dark, was once sand dunes in the open, breezy air. Deposited above all that was Kaibab limestone, the residue of a great body of salt water, warm and shallow, that covered the sediment of older seas 290 to 240 million years ago, give or take a few. It preserved in the grip of its silt the teeth of sharks.

And then there were dinosaurs. After all the deposits of the Grand Canyon had been laid down, *then* there were dinosaurs. During their time, the region was sometimes ocean, sometimes desert; often it was semi-tropical, depending on the position of the continent and the level of the oceans. It fossilized in stone what once had been swimming reptiles and flying reptiles and birds with teeth and giant sloths and forty pound dinosaurs and dinosaurs ninety feet long and dinosaurs that walked upright and the oldest mammals yet found in the Americas, mouse-sized creatures that fed on insects. The neighborhood teemed. Birds the size of biplanes wheeled overhead. Huge trees stood where one day there would be the Petrified Forest.

For one reason or another, or maybe several, all those various dinosaurs disappeared from northern Arizona in a long age of mass extinction. Rock layers formed by sedimentation during and after their time were eroded completely away around Flagstaff as aeons of local history washed slowly into old rivers. In the seventy million or so years that followed them, while the continents of Eurasia and North America were moving slowly apart, the area was above sea level several times. On grass savannahs, great tusked mammoths and camels and bison roamed across the land and then vanished like the sharks and dinosaurs and oceans. All of them, a record of billions of years, formed the foundation, solid beneath the surface, of Flagstaff and of Woody Mountain. Solid, but not permanent. Nothing has ever been permanent.

On a planet constantly in several kinds of motion, even a blanket of stone a mile thick could not be counted on to remain stable. Part of the continent bulged upward a long time ago until the land where Flagstaff would be was higher than any place in any state east of the Rockies. Then it was volcanos in every direction for millions of years, more than four hundred of them. The ground glowed red at night with slowly moving lava, and morning sky was dark with ash.

The mountain began to rise as searing magma from somewhere far beneath the surface 5,860,000 years ago, plus or minus half a million. There were no humans anywhere on earth then, on any continent. There were lizards and cave lions and the ancestors of dogs, but no humans anywhere.

Woody Mountain grew in slow symmetry during a long geologic stage spanning several million years. Bears and horses developed through the Cenozoic, while it was building. A river began to cut through rock layers to form the Grand Canyon. In Africa, *Australopithecines* stood erect and began to evolve toward *Homo sapiens*.

Probably there were at least two separate eruptions with a lapse of three million years between them; the base and flanks of the mountain were formed of dark basalt that was topped with lighter-colored basaltic andesite near the summit. Eruptions during those wordless aeons covered twenty-five square miles, south to what would be the Sedona Rim, west to Sycamore Canyon. At the base of the mountain, cinders and basaltic flow overlying the ancient sedimentary deposits averaged 453 feet thick. Oak Creek Canyon fifteen miles to the south had not yet been carved when the building of the mountain stopped one and a half million years ago.

Volcanic activity moved slowly to the north and east through the centuries, and Woody Mountain, left behind, stood silent in the rain, weathering. Half a million years in the past the massive volcano that had risen nearby became dormant. It was three thousand feet higher then, according to the guesswork of geologists.[1]

New mountains provided prime places for life to take hold. Spots of algae appeared on the margins of cooling lava and began to spread inward. Its cells wove

---

1 The Hopi named it Nuvatekiaovi (Snow on the high place/mountain). Spaniards called it after a thirteenth century Italian friar: Franciscan monks traveled into the country from Mexico with the early Spanish exploration and named the old volcano for St. Francis, "San Francisco" in their language. Never mind what you've been told. You can't see San Francisco Bay from the summit.

The San Francisco Peaks emerged ten miles from Woody Mountain.

Ponderosa pine, a specialist in hardship conditions and a prime colonist on shallow soil like that on weathering volcanos, concentrated most of its roots laterally withn two feet of the surface.

into the matrix of a froth of fungus that had blown in on the wind, and lichen developed. Proceeding slowly, as if it knew how much time it had, the tiny lichen produced acids which etched the rock, establishing shortly after the creation of Woody Mountain an opening for its destruction by erosion millions of years in the future.

After centuries, seeds of grasses found enough, just enough, foothold to provide a possibility. Eventually tree seedlings caught hold, soil built up slowly as the basalt softened, and a complex of roots worked away beneath the surface. Finally there were standing trees.

The orderly pattern of species succession had barely begun when the weather turned cold, and the northern hemisphere moved into fluctuations of freeze and thaw—the Ice Ages. Several times in the aeons after its forming, Woody Mountain stood white and cold, covered by unmelting snow. Forests grew and then died away to leave light from ancient stars glittering on the slopes as the pines retreated slowly in ragged lines to lower country, receding and advancing a few millennia later and receding again in a slow minuet, a dance of time and weather. Far to the north, humans crossed the Bering Strait and began to spread slowly south.

Around eight to ten thousand years B.C., by recent reckoning, air warmed a fourth time, snow melted in summer and the great ponderosa forest of the Colorado Plateau moved steadily north again from the Mogollon Rim. All the largest mammals—mammoths and mastodons, giant bison, camels, and saber-toothed tigers—disappeared from surrounding country. Pines began another climb up the slopes of Woody Mountain.

Finally afternoon shadows were long once again, and tree tops held sunset light while trunks were deep in dusk. Golden eagles and red-tailed hawks and ravens and turkey buzzards rode rising air currents. Great horned owls, jays, and woodpeckers flew among the trees. There were small, noisy birds: swallows, thrushes, chickadees, nuthatches, and swifts. At sunset, heavy wild turkeys flapped up into pine branches to roost for the night.

Antelope grazed the mountain's grass. Wolves and cougar and bear prowled the slopes, and now and then a grizzly lumbered past. For ten thousand years after the trees returned the fourth time, they had the mountain to themselves.

Humans were in the area by then, passing over; the lake to the west attracted game and neolithic hunters. Once, perhaps several times, one man or groups of men climbed to the top of the mountain and chipped off pieces of fine-grained, glassy, black basalt. In the afternoon sunshine on the flat ground of the worn crater, they sat down, working and talking perhaps, and roughed out hunting tools—spear points, hand axes, arrow heads—and dropped onto the ground debris which archaeologists, finding it uncounted years later, referred to as "lithic scatter." With their pieces of the mountain, they turned from the sound of wind on the summit and went away, down through the shadows of the trees on the western slope, to the lake. Near its shore, pausing to chip off more black flakes as they refined their weapons, the hunters marked their temporary presence by what they discarded and left behind.

But there was no evidence that anyone ever went near the mountain to stay, no indication of any permanent residence southwest of the Peaks—Hopi, Anasazi, Sinagua, anyone. Winters in the high country where the mountain stood were severe. Soil was too thin to support agriculture, and nearby meadows were boggy during the short growing season. Humans used the mountain for its rock as they needed it, but no one ever came to stay.

*T*he pines on Woody Mountain when humans arrived were left over from an earlier world. They had shared the earth with dinosaurs. Grasses and squirrels had had their beginning in a time when continents and oceans were in different places and the atmosphere through which the sun shone was of a different composition.

In the massive tectonic movement that had pushed up the Rockies and swelled the dome of the northern Arizona plateau and freed magma to become volcanos, life forms separated from others on the globe. Climate changes after the latest Ice Age accelerated the process, shrinking the range of ponderosa pine, isolating squirrels, until they were finally distinct from pines and squirrels anywhere else, unique to the West and old beyond imagining.

Chapter Two
Explorers
1851–1878

Samuel W. Woodhouse was a member of the 1851 Sitgreaves Expedition.
Museum of Northern Arizona

Richard Kern
Reproduced from the original by permission of the Huntington Library
San Marino, California

On an autumn morning in 1851, a grey-backed grizzly watching from the top of Woody Mountain would have noticed a haze of silent dust to the north. Antoine Leroux and fifty men under Captain Lorenzo Sitgreaves (Corps of Topographical Engineers) and Brevet Major H.L. Kendrick were leaving the spring ten miles away, where they had camped for a couple of days, and heading directly toward that bear.

They were the first official exploring party in an inexorable American migration into the ancient plateau country.[1] Two days earlier with 137 mules and some 40 sheep, they had come around north of a massive saw-topped volcano, which had been visible on the horizon for days, and into what later would be Fort Valley. Desperate for water, they were glad for the spring they found on a hillside among the pines.

The expedition's guide, Antoine Leroux, had been trapper, explorer and mountain man from the Yellowstone River to the Mexican border for thirty years. A tough, mature, sensible, experienced man who didn't get drunk in Indian country, Leroux was just the sort who was valuable to greenhorn surveyors and explorers coming out from the East. He was fifty years old in 1851 when he led the Sitgreaves party through northern Arizona. Grey-haired, the father of nine children, he was described as a dead shot, cool in the face of danger.

The expedition's draftsman, artist, and map-maker, Richard Kern, thirty-one that year, had been with Fremont on a trip into the San Juans three years earlier that resulted in the death of Bill Williams. In the diary in which he wrote daily, Kern recorded that while they were in volcano country in Arizona that autumn season, the temperature every morning at sunrise was below freezing.

A Philadelphia doctor with the group, thirty-year-old Samuel W. Woodhouse, was the first naturalist to visit northern Arizona Territory. A few weeks earlier he had been struck on the index finger of his left hand by a rattlesnake he thought he had killed. He described it as "a sad accident for me."

> Kern wished me to try the western remedy; that is to say, to get drunk. This remedy I had often heard of, and, determined to try its efficacy, I commenced drinking...half of pint of whiskey, one quart of 4th proof brandy, and ammonia ... Intoxication lasted 4 or 5 hours. During this state I vomited freely.

Swelling extended down his left side to the hip, his fingernail fell off, and his arm was paralyzed until the expedition reached California, whether due to the injury or the treatment he didn't say.

The party's camp cook, Moses Gibson, was a black man and an experienced explorer. The previous year he and Woodhouse had been part of an expedition into Oklahoma Territory.

It was Wednesday morning, October 15, when the Sitgreaves party packed to leave Leroux Spring. The men had been roused three times during the night by

---

1 To put that into a larger frame: on the east coast of the continent *Uncle Tom's Cabin* and *Moby Dick* both came out that year; the YMCA was organized; the *New York Times* began publication; I.M. Singer patented his sewing machine; and John James Audobon died a disappointed man, unable to sell his paintings.

their mules, which had been frightened, they suspected, by wolves or bears. They traveled south-southwest a little over ten miles that day, crossing the valley into hilly country "covered with small pieces of broken rock which was very hard on our mules."

A practical military man from Pennsylvania, Captain Sitgreaves was not impressed by the whole stretch of colored sedimentary bluffs, volcanos, and forests of towering pines from Albuquerque west to the Colorado River: he called it "barren and devoid of interest." Later the captain made a formal report to Congress in which he described the country the expedition crossed south of the Peaks.

> Our route lay across plains of gentle slope. Mingled with the pines were a few small post oaks; and in a green glade was found some white clover of a different variety from that common in the States. Flowers [most of them killed by frost] and birds were more numerous than upon the northern slopes...but no fragments of pottery or other signs of habitation were seen.[2]

Late on that Wednesday afternoon the 50 men, 137 mules and 40 sheep descended from a ridge into the dry bed of a seasonal lake a little over a mile west of Woody Mountain. Sitgreaves noted that they stopped "upon the dry bed of a lagoon a mile in extent, having some small pools of water hidden among the tall grass, from which our arrival put up a large flight of water fowl, crows and smaller birds." Sam Woodhouse listed sandhill cranes and so many ravens that he promptly dubbed the place "Raven Lake." The party was to stay there in the open at 7500 feet for five days, in freezing autumn weather, with a dying man.

Four days earlier Inemacio Valdez, one of the mule drivers hired in New Mexico, had been struck on the head by a rock during an argument with another man. On the morning of October 16 the group roused at four a.m. beside the dry lake and ate breakfast by the light of a fire, planning to make an early start. But one of the drivers asked Dr. Woodhouse to take a look at Valdez.

> I went to him and found him perfectly insensible. I immediately bled him and applied blisters to his temples and the back of his head and gave him a dose of Calomel and Opium. Having no means of carrying him we were forced to remain here. Towards evening he appeared to be more sensible.

It was unfamiliar terrain for Leroux. Delayed by the injured man, he went off with some of the mule drivers to scout for the next campsite. When they returned, they reported that they had seen blacktail deer and a large grizzly bear, which one of the drivers had wounded.

The next day Valdez was conscious enough to answer questions put to him and complain of his head but was still unable to travel. It was the doctor's opinion that he was suffering from compression of the brain caused by a blood clot. Woodhouse wasn't feeling well either, thanks to that rattlesnake.

---

2 The first naturalist on the scene, Woodhouse paid more attention to humble details. He named eleven animals which he recognized as distinct to northern Arizona, among them a pocket mouse, a kangaroo rat, and a grey, tassle-eared squirrel which had been geographically isolated in the dry ponderosa pine forests of the Southwest. He named it for Col. J.W. Abert, head of the U.S. Corps of Topographic Engineers—the Abert squirrel.

My finger this evening is very painfull, also the glands in my axilla. I took some blue mass and collocynth [a cathartic herb] and retired. This bids fare to be a cold night.

The injured muledriver was rolled in blankets and placed near a fire. Saturday morning, with the thermometer at sunrise barely above zero, he was sinking rapidly, and the young man who had thrown the rock at him was "very much worried." The doctor wrote in his diary, "I have been stimulating [Valdez] he does not look if he would live until morning."

Sitgreaves recorded that the daily variation in temperature at the lake was as much as fifty-five degrees and that the mercury climbed as high as sixty-five by afternoon. That Saturday was so pleasant at mid-day that Woodhouse, Kern, and twenty-three-year-old Lieutenant John Park decided to climb the volcanic cone to the east, "to fix the locality," and made the first written impression of Woody Mountain. Woodhouse said they had "a fine view of the surrounding country." Kern described the view from the summit as "immense."

> The big mountain loomed up in front...to the east a broad expanse of timber with isolated buttes jutting out [on what would years later be the Navajo Reservation] ... to the south could be seen the tortuous course of the San Francisco and its deep canyon [Oak Creek Canyon]...farther to the west were discernible the mesas and mountains through which it winds on its way to Salt River.[3]

They were not the first Anglos to see that view. There had been a prospector there before them, a solitary man perhaps, roaming in untenanted country. Near the summit were traces of the kind of old excavations a prospector would have made. In his report to Congress, Captain Sitgreaves speculated that they had been dug "apparently in search of the precious metals, but the surrounding formation gave no indications of their existence."

The group had been at the lake for four days by then, with provisions that were down to little more than three weeks rations. Half the sheep were in poor condition, and the bacon was shrinking in the dry air. Antelope and deer were abundant, bear tracks were seen, but the men had not managed to kill any game. Worried, they tried to make a litter for Valdez so that they could move on but could find only large pines and scrubby oaks.

On Sunday morning three of them went out hunting; Juan de Dios, chief packer, became separated from the others and did not come back for two days. Men in the party were sure he had been killed by either bear or Indians. Cold, hungry, and gloomy, they felt "a great deal of anxiety." Valdez, who was slowly sinking, groaned in the night, "driving sleep away."

Monday, October 20, shortly after noon, Inemacio Valdez died. They buried him at sunset there by Woody Mountain, in a grave five feet deep at the foot of a

3 Dr. Andrew Walalace, professor of history at Northern Arizona University, made transcriptions of the Woodhouse Zuni diary (4 Vols., Collection 387, Library of the Academy of Natural Sciences of Philadelphia), as well as the diaries of Kern and Lieutenant Park, and graciously made available the pages describing camps 17 and 18.

large pine tree, dressed and covered with his blanket and then with a layer of split logs. Dr. Woodhouse wrote, "The grave was filled in with well packed dirt and leveled off and a number of holes dug about it so as to account for the loose dirt and a large fire was made over it so as to deceive the Indians." In his diary Kern recorded that the men "cut a rude cross in the rough bark" of the tree that marked the grave. They renamed the lake, in the language of the man whom they had buried there, Laguna Inemacio.

On Tuesday morning the party struck camp at 8:25, left Valdez alone at the foot of the mountain, and headed off "a little south of west." After struggling for nearly two days in rough country along the rim of a deep ravine [Sycamore Canyon] and finding Juan de Dios along the way, they turned north again and on October 22 crossed the head of the canyon. A day or so later the Sitgreaves party disappeared from the sight of anyone or anything watching from Woody Mountain.

Their troubles did not end with their departure. Just over a week later Leroux received three arrow wounds from an encounter with "Cosninos" Indians.

> I was wounded by three arrows but luckily not so gravely as to prevent me from using my rifle. One arrow with a stone point struck me behind the ear, another in the forearm and the third inflicted a most painful wound on my wrist...My arrow wounds prevented me from aiming very well, so I broke off the shafts.

Other men in the party reported that he avoided further injury by swinging his big, stiff Mexican hat, which the Indians shot full of arrows. After the battle, despite his paralyzed left hand, Dr. Woodhouse treated Leroux.

> The head of one [arrow] near the wrist joint was embedded in the radius. My forceps slipped at each attempt to remove the arrowhead. I cut down to the stone and exposed it, using the forceps as a lever with my thumb as fulcrum, blistering my thumb and bending the forceps. I finally succeeded in removing the arrowhead with tooth forceps, using considerable force. The bone was not even splintered.

Leroux's wrist was useless during the remainder of the journey.

They moved on into the history of the West. Kern was with Lt. John Gunnison in Utah in 1853 at sunrise one cold morning when their scouting party was attacked by Indians in a little nook in a river bottom. Kern was one of the men killed. The body of the artist who had stood on Woody Mountain two years earlier lay where it fell and was gnawed by wolves. Leroux, who had been guide to the Gunnison expedition, had turned south to Santa Fe a few days earlier and so escaped the ambush.

In the time of the Sitgreaves expedition, three hundred years had passed since Coronado's venture up from Mexico. Santa Fe was 250 years old. But the country south of the San Francisco Peaks, with its five-month growing season and no rivers to ease transportation or carry commerce, was still not settled, and it remained that way until after Americans on the eastern third of the continent had suffered through their Civil War. Clouds piled white and high on summer afternoons in those years, and sunlight was hard as lacquer on trees, but there were few Anglo eyes to see it. Winter snow fell on trees, not rooftops.

In 1853 Stephen Foster published "My Old Kentucky Home, Goodnight." A chef at Saratoga Springs in New York invented potato chips. That year Congress authorized funds to finance a survey of a route for a transcontinental railroad, and the pace of exploration began to pick up. Under authorization by Secretary of War Jefferson Davis, four possibilities were examined. The 35th parallel across the Colorado Plateau was proposed as a central line, with the result that a parade of explorers began to move through the country around Woody Mountain.

Lt. A.W. Whipple (Corps of Topographical Engineers) led a surveying party past the Peaks at Christmas that year, crossing south of the huge dormant volcano, and reported sightings of wolves, squirrels, turkeys, bighorn sheep, and grizzlies in great numbers, but no Indians. The team included a botanist, a geologist, an astronomer, and—in those days before small hand-held cameras—an artist. John Sherburne, assistant to the scientists, wrote in his diary a disgruntled opinion of the country's campfire fuel:

> The timber is all heavy pine, giving out while burning a very black thick smoke.
> This smoke is settling on everything and everybody and renders the skin so black
> as to entirely change a person's appearance.

Four years later Lt. E.F. Beale surveyed a wagon road for emigrants to California and marveled at the green expanse of waving grasses, the deer and antelope. Accompanying him into volcano country were twenty-two camels as well as Greek and Turkish riders in their native dress. In his report to the Secretary of War, Beale described the area his colorful crew traveled.

> We pursued our course westward to San Francisco Mountain. The country at the
> foot of that mountain (a gradually ascending plain) although somewhat rocky, in
> places was covered with the finest grama grass, with timber sufficient for fuel,
> and water in abundance...[It is] well watered with springs, and is by far the most
> beautiful region I ever remember to have seen in any portion of the world. A vast
> forest of gigantic pine, intersected frequently by extensive open glades, sprinkled
> all over with mountain meadows and wide savannahs, filled with the richest
> grasses, was traveled by our party for many successive days.

Construction crews for Beale's wagon road arrived a year and a half later, in April of 1859, and began blazing trees and moving rocks. In 1863, twelve years after Leroux had guided the Kendrick–Sitgreaves party past the Peaks, gold was discovered near Prescott. Those two events marked the end of privacy for the neighborhood around Woody Mountain. Turning their backs to the Civil War, eager prospectors began to stream past on Beale's route and then turn south on the Overland Road toward the gold fields.

In 1863 the same old grizzly that had watched the Sitgreaves party could have seen a detachment of the California Volunteer Regiment camped at a nearby spring which the men named for themselves—Volunteer. Late that winter the newly appointed governor of Arizona Territory (an ex-Congressman from Maine named John Goodwin), several of his officials, and three companies of soldiers passed the spring on a slow trek to Prescott. The mountain looked a lot like other nameless lava cones close by, and their eyes moved across it without much interest. Like everyone at the time, they were men going someplace else.

In 1869 Major John Wesley Powell made his first exploring trip down the Colorado River. That winter General William Palmer surveyed a route past the Peaks with plans to extend a railway from Kansas to the Pacific. Palmer decided "for distinction" to change the name of the largest volcano in sight from San Francisco Mountain to Mt. Agassiz to honor Swiss-born Louis Agassiz, who had been a professor of natural history at Harvard for nearly twenty years by then.

The general was interested in a supply of timber for railroad crossties. He described the forest that stood on Woody Mountain and the land around its base.

> The trees are of immense proportions; some of them 200 feet high and ten feet in diameter...There is certainly no pinery in the interior portion of the continent superior to this.

When the party returned in March, traveling toward the east, Palmer noted:

> ...we have the finest country met with, perhaps, on our entire route...magnificently timbered, well watered, and covered with the most nutritous grama grass. Its soil, black and rich from the decomposition of the lava which has been ejected in immense quantities from the extinct crater of Mt. Agassiz, will provide, without irrigation, wheat, barley, oats and potatoes, in the heaviest crops. The summit and slopes of this range are dotted everywhere with beautiful little grassy parks, openings in the virgin forest of gigantic pines which cover the mountain. On all sides rise tall volcanic peaks, emulating the central figure of Mt. Agassiz.

They found more water that spring than they really wanted. Leroux Park [Fort Valley] was a lake three feet deep, Antelope Creek [Rio de Flag] was full of water, and "immense bodies of water [were] running down the sides of Mt. Agassiz."[4]

Prospectors and explorers moved about the Colorado Plateau in the 1860s and 1870s, and great herds of sheep and cattle were brought onto it for the grass. The first permanent settlers came to raise stock around 1875, half a dozen years before the railroad arrived. Charles T. Rogers, who had a ranch near Williams, or where Williams was going to be, ran cattle at summer pasture in the shallow basin

---

4 Palmer's repeated emphasis on the name did not persuade mapmakers. "Agassiz" remained to designate the second highest peak. The tallest, "Humphreys," memorialized a surveyor and Civil War general who was chief of the Army's Corps of Engineers; "Freemont" was called after an explorer of country to the north. "Doyle," at least, preserved the name of a pioneer and settler who lived near the mountain, which retained its dedication to Saint Francis. Toward the end of the twentieth century a movement began to title the eroded old volcano Kachina Peaks in honor of the spirits which, according to the Hopis, live there.

west of the mountain where the body of Valdez lay in its solitary grave, and Rogers Lake acquired its third name.

Wolves and grizzlies were gone not long after that, hunted off by stockmen. However, as it had been for one and a half million years, Woody Mountain was innocent of restless human plans. There were no deeds, claims, nor paper patents to verify its existence.

On July 4, 1876—the centennial of the signing of Mr. Jefferson's declaration—a group out from Boston to colonize camped near the Peaks and celebrated the day by flying their country's flag from a pine tree. The Boston party members found the area too empty for their taste, dispersed and moved on, but they left to the town that would grow on that site a name that celebrated American independence from the old idea of rule by royalty. In that year, when the Boston party decided the country around the big volcano was too desolate for human habitation, Colorado was accepted into the Union as a state.

John L. Harris, Deputy Surveyor for the U. S. Geological Survey, made the first systematic examination of land southwest of the Peaks in 1878. Harris didn't think much of it for farming. On every page he reported: "Land broken. Soil poor. Heavy pine timber." He cited the unnamed lava cone—"This line runs along the west base of a small mountain"—and mentioned a "scattering of aspen trees in NW 1/4 of Sect. 3."

Someone was there before him. He said of the mountain: "...on the north side...there is permanent water and water troughs, as I am informed, but not visible from any point on the line."

No one preserved the story of the man who built those water troughs at the spring before 1878. Such humble details about working people were left out of formal histories, which tended toward the significant. The carpenter might have been Rogers or someone like him. Or it could have been a young cowboy named John Woody.

When the first ranchers arrived, the ponderosa pine forest of northern Arizona was an unbroken band twenty-four to forty miles wide and three hundred miles long. Trees were widely spaced as in a landscaped park with no brushy undergrowth, the trunks receding in endless colonnade. Grasses which grew among the trees were, according to stockmen, belly-high to a tall horse in wet years. Grass grew everywhere in the forest, everywhere, in sun and shade. There seemed no end to it.

From ancient time grasses on the plateau had been a staple for rodents, antelope, browsing deer. Humans had used the seed for food. But immigrants from the east with their domestic stock did not realize that wild grasses in the southwest were not like the forage back home. Native grasses grew well on the thin soil, but they did not recover from heavy grazing.

The result was a significant change in vegetation. Within a dozen years after the introduction of domestic sheep and cattle, some varieties of native grasses had disappeared, here and there, and others had spread. Settlers introduced seeds from far away, from Africa, from Russia, and a ten-thousand-year-old ecology was altered.

Chapter Three
Pioneers

1875–1913

The earliest known photograph of Flagstaff was made in 1883.
Arizona Historical Society–Pioneer Museum

The lonely Ashurst cabin was photographed in 1919.
AHS–Pioneer Museum

The Doney cabin, built in 1882, was occupied until 1934 and, with funding by
Bob and Mary Riordan Chambers, was moved in the 1960s to the Pioneer Museum.
AHS–Pioneer Museum

The landscape around the Peaks was born in water and in fire. The map was a roll call of Anglo settlers, persistent homesteaders dwarfed by the Arizona sky. The Hochderffer family arrived early; so did John Elden and Ben Doney and Al Doyle, and their names remained on the land near where they lived or worked. Ancient hills and lava cones, parks and meadows, had no recorded labels until people of European descent moved in, and then, as a convenience, they were identified by ranches which the immigrants established. With them, after a million wordless years, Woody Mountain gained a human name.

In those days people nodded toward the lava cone southwest of town and said, "...out at Woody's place," and after a while it was Woody's Spring and then Woody Mountain and later Woody Ridge. If it hadn't been for that, he'd have disappeared into the past like the smoke from his own campfire. A lot of men did.

By birth he was a westerner. By work he became a cowboy, a small-scale rancher and, later, a lawman. He could arrest a murderer or drive a band of range horses to California, but he was no fancy hero. He held elective office briefly, but he was not a power in the community. A working man whose name was given casually to an old volcano, he did not have children or leave photographs or letters or anything to mark him as distinct from other men.

The past was built on such people, but they were not anybody spectacular. They went through life doing what they could, and when they were finished, there was hardly anything to show where they had been. By 1985 John Woody had been gone so long that only the older residents in Flagstaff, people in their seventies and eighties, remembered hearing their parents say that there had been such a man. For more than thirty years he lived in and around the town, but the sounds and movement of daily reality faded quickly, leaving only vague outlines in old documents. Most people a century later who had looked up to notice the mountain thought it was named Woody because there were trees on it.

He was a type, a man of the West, born in Oregon in 1856. The census for Oregon in 1860 listed three families named Woody in the entire territory, two of them down on the California border in Josephine County near the Jacksonville post office. Both men heading those families said they were farmers, both were from the Carolinas. The name James Woody was cited for a man who was sixty-five in 1860; A.J. Woody was forty. A.J.'s wife Anna, thirty-one that year, had come from Indiana. She had six children, all born in Oregon, and one of them was a four-year-old boy named Jonathan. There he was: a boy, a long time ago.

The year 1856, when he was born, was only fifty years after Lewis and Clark had reached the mouth of the Columbia. Twenty years earlier the first women, wives of Methodist missionaries, had made the overland journey. The Woodys were pioneers in Klamath/Pauite country, where life was hard for most people and amenities few. The age of their oldest Oregon-born child, a girl of twelve, indicated their arrival at least by 1848.

Later, sometime before Jonathan was thirteen, the family moved down into California, to Kingsburg south of Fresno in the great San Joaquin Valley: a younger brother was born in 1869 in California. Near the end of the century the younger brother and an older one and A.J. Woody were all listed in the 1892 Great Register of Voters for Fresno County. It described Jonathan's father: Andrew Jackson Woody, height 5'10", born in North Carolina, hazel-eyed. His hair was grey by then. Able to mark a ballot, write his name, and read the Constitution in English, he identified himself as a farmer.

Nothing was preserved to tell when—or why—Jonathan Woody moved to Arizona. The earliest evidence of him in the state was in the census of 1880, when he was twenty-three and Flagstaff was little more than a railroad camp. On the 11th of June he told a man taking a census on Goodman Street in the tough little town of Prescott that his name was John, that he was single, Oregon-born, of Southern parentage, and that his occupation was "herder." [That may not have referred to sheep: the term "cowboy" was just coming into wide use to denote a man who looked after cattle.]

Woody moved to Flagstaff in its first years and claimed land for himself. The spring at the base of the little mountain near the San Francisco Peaks was, according to early reports, a strong reliable source of water, but it was far off regular travel routes, not visible, the surveyor Harris said, from any point on his line, which ran a few hundred yards to the north. It was the kind of place a young cowboy, far from home and looking for a life to make his own, could run across while he was poking around on slopes no one else was using. John Woody, young and dusty, years of working outdoors already behind him, came up through the trees on a horse, dismounted, went down on one knee beside the water, decided on it for his own. It may not have been Woody, but *somebody* did that. Somebody built those water troughs.[1]

Not long afterward he built a cabin there made of logs he cut and trimmed himself. Or somebody did. One hundred years later, Joe Robinson, who worked half a lifetime at the ranch at Rogers Lake, said there was once a log cabin at the spring, by the elderberry bush.

The land was more appropriate to ranching than farming. The first man to use it, Woody perhaps, attempted only minor improvements—the cabin, a corral. Year-round residence was probably not even tried. Like most of the ranches at 7500 feet, it was deep in snow and inaccessible one-third of the year, never suitable for winter occupation.

If Woody was at the base of the mountain in the pioneering years before the railroad came through, he was not alone in the country. John Clark had arrived by

---

1 Yavapai County had no record that Woody or anyone else filed a claim on the spring in the nineteenth century, either for water or for land. Neither did the Bureau of Land Management nor the Arizona Department of Water Resources.

1876 with a herd of sheep, T.F. McMillan had settled in, and Frank Hart was at a spring in Fort Valley. A year later W.H. Ashurst built a cabin on Anderson Mesa.

In 1877 twenty-three-year-old Walter Hill drove a band of sheep through the pines to Volunteer Spring and built a homestead in the middle of what later became the Navajo Army Depot. He carried with him into the country of old volcanos something foreign to all its long history—a library. *The Arizona Champion* described Hill as "a man of education and taste" and praised him for his collection.

> It is supplied with many costly and some rare books, which would delight the heart of a scholar. Almost all of the English classics are represented and many works of rare typographical beauty. Mr. Hill has spent years in collecting his library; he has bought nothing cheap, but the best editions of everything, most of which are bound in solid calf. Men working on the range have all free access to the use of these books, and to many of them it is a great boon.

Hill's ranch house was only six miles northwest of Woody's cabin. Like his neighbor, he had a disposition appropriate to the West and necessary to survival in it. In 1966 settler William H. Switzer, who spent eighty-four years in Flagstaff, told his daughter a story about something that happened twenty years after Hill had homesteaded near Volunteer Spring.

> Due to the size of his cattle spread [Hill] owned many fine horses. During this time there had been a gang of horse thieves in the northern part of Arizona. They finally stole some of Mr. Hill's horses. He went to the sheriff about it and offered to accompany him to run the thieves down. They were able to track them down to a cabin owned by Colin Campbell, near the Grand Falls on the Colorado. Mr. Hill dismounted and crept up to the cabin. He looked through the window seeing the thieves, but they also saw him and shot him in the head. The sheriff rescued Mr. Hill and assisted him back toward town. They reached the edge of the cedars near Turkey Tanks and made a camp. Mr. Hill was unable to travel further and became apprehensive of his life. Feeling sure he was about to die, he asked the sheriff to go back to the cabin and bring back one of the thieves. He wanted to kill him before his time was up. The sheriff did just that and when he returned to the camp with his prisoner, Mr. Hill was so weak he could not get up from his camp bed. However, he did have the strength to hold his pistol and immediately shot the thief. Mr. Hill recovered from his wound, but the bullet left a deep hole in his forehead, the size of one's little finger in circumference and quite deep, said scar he carried to his grave.

After the War Between the States, because it seemed important to Americans to connect with California where there was money to be made, the continent was spanned by railroads along the 42nd Parallel route (Union Pacific and Central Pacific) and the 32nd Parallel (Southern Pacific). Track for a line between them across the vast, inhospitable plateau country, reached out from Missouri along Beale's wagon road. During route surveys, Sunset Crossing on the Little Colorado

River became a pivot of decision: go north up the river valley and westward north of the Peaks, or pass the line south of them? The decision was based on availability of water and timber and the number of canyons to bridge. After a final exploration by engineers Lewis Kingman and H.R. Holbrook, construction began west of Albuquerque in the summer of 1880, headed by the "End of the Track Gang." Back east, Mark Twain was working on *Huckleberry Finn* about then.

In mid-April, twenty men in an Atlantic and Pacific Railroad surveying crew arrived at the Peaks in light wagons and camped at a spring at the base of a lava flow seven miles southeast of Leroux Spring. Railroad construction crews and tie choppers followed, setting up tents around the spring to form a minuscule human island in the forest. People moved in fast in those expanding, westward-moving years, and by winter Flagstaff had two buildings, a log cabin that was a saloon and restaurant, and a tent-log combination for a general store. The population was heavy on bachelors: a census showed twenty-seven households with sixty-seven people, only three of them adult women.

A few months later the Prescott *Weekly Arizona Democrat* reported that the population of the settlement was two hundred on week days, double that on week-ends, and said that dance halls, saloons and gambling houses operated full blast from Saturday night until Monday morning. Gun fights were common, the *Democrat* said, and it was usually not safe to go out after dark.

In mid-summer of 1881 W.J. Murphy, grading on contract for the railroad, arrived with his wife, Laura, and three small children riding on a wagon loaded with sacks of rolled barley for feeding mules. They found eight log buildings, seven of which were saloons. Murphy rented the other, a warehouse, as a residence for his family and hired an armed guard to protect them from men who tried to enter, assuming that any real building in town was selling liquor. After a week in which seven men were shot in saloon fights, Murphy moved his family out to Fort Valley, which, Apache scare or no, seemed safer than Flagstaff.

Not long after that Henry Lockett, age twenty-five, pulled in from Kansas in a covered wagon drawn by a team of mules. He looked around awhile and homesteaded along the road to Fort Valley. William H. Anderson, a stonemason born in Scotland, drove into town in a buckboard, set about finding a home for his wife and children, and took a farm near Lockett, where for years he grew part of the town's potato supply—local people came to know him as "Spud." Soon Ben Doney arrived; born in New York thirty-two years earlier, Doney finally chose a place for himself twelve miles out to the northeast.

The southwest territories were almost the only places left in which opportunists could have free swing with no competition from older businesses. Another summer, and there were twenty frame buildings and twenty tents in Flagstaff holding a number of saloons and other such necessities of Western living. A post office was established in a tent selling general merchandise with Peter Brannen as acting postmaster, and that required a committee to choose a name for the town. It rejected Flag Pole.

Before railroad tracks had reached the Peaks, American-style civilization (education, business, and religion) was established. The first school was set up, with six children, in a twelve by fourteen foot log cabin with a brush covering for a roof. In March a Methodist minister preached a sermon there. When E.E. Ayer started a sawmill at the same time to provide ties for the railroad, the new town in Arizona Territory had one street, and a pipeline had been laid from O'Neil Spring seven miles to the south to bring water up to the line for steam locomotives.

The railroad was delayed for six months in 1882 while a bridge was completed to span Canyon Diablo. Tie-laying crews continued to work toward the west while the bridge was being built, and when steel rails were finally laid across the stone abutments, the tracks raced past the Peaks toward Needles and link-up with the Southern Pacific. The first through train left Albuquerque for San Francisco in mid-October of 1883 with a postal car, smoking car, passenger coach and Pullman sleeper.

John Woody was among the town's first settlers. Early in 1883, before that first train went through the insignificant little tent town under the Arizona sun, the local sawmill carried the name J. Woody on its books. Twice he was paid "by salary": in January $46.73 and later $16.63, although there was no description of what services he performed. Three times in January he was paid "to cash," a total of $26.75. Once a "balance" was entered for $19.98. Those were fair sums for a frontier town in 1883, whatever he did to earn them.

When the first beef cattle, sixty head, were shipped out on the railroad from Flagstaff, there were six hundred inhabitants and four general stores to supplement the establishments selling alcohol. At the Log Cabin Saloon that year, Jim Bailey cut in half his price for a shot of whiskey, which had been selling for twenty-five cents, and someone blew up the place with dynamite. Guesses pointed at competitors.

No one in Flagstaff in those years left a personal statement about John Woody's disposition or character. But the men whom he knew wrote letters and memoirs about the life of the town and about themselves. Photographs were made of what Woody saw and the people he talked with. He heard the sound of his boots on those wooden sidewalks and tied his horse to the hitching rails, and in rainy weather he smelled manure in the mud of those streets. Like all of them, his character would have been the resilient, tenacious, sometimes vulgar and always vital character of Flagstaff. To look at the town as it was in those years was to see the only clues that remained to the kind of man he was. Godfrey Sykes, born in England, wrote about the people who chose the hardship of building from scratch in northern Arizona. He called them "super-folk...predominantly of the more pronounced enterprising and adventurous type—both men and women—able and willing to stand upon their own feet and manage their own affairs under any and all circumstances."[2] Woody was one of them from the beginning. His story was inseparable from the story of Flagstaff.

Some of those settlers seized opportunity in business, and others worked for them in town, in the spreading forest, or on the range. Some of them were rowdy: it was a raw little town at first. In September of 1884 the *Champion* described "frequent forays of drunken cowhands, who love nothing better than to ride full tilt down Railroad Avenue, whooping and firing their six-shooters into the air as the terrified populace scamper for cover."

Shootings and killings were commonplace. In 1885 the *Champion* said:

> Flagstaff is at present inflicted with a number of cut-throats, some of whom are wanted for crimes elsewhere, ostensibly "tin-horn gamblers" by profession, who ought to be ordered out of town and not stand upon the order of their going.

But the settlers Woody knew weren't all outside the law. A local post of Union Army veterans—the Grand Army of the Republic, the G.A.R.—built "a commodious hall" about 1885. By 1886 "a German brewer of long experience" was in business making beer near the town spring. The weekly *Coconino Sun* described the enterprise in February of that year: "New Brewery Will Make You Flop Your Lip." About that time a local branch of the Women's Christian Temperance Union was organized.

A listing of accounts at Ayer's Lumber Company in the town's fourth year named a local cowboy just turned thirty—Woody. And again, Woody and Co. John and his partner or partners had bought ninety-three dollars worth of lumber. Not content to work for someone else as a cowboy, he had apparently gone into business, but what he was building, the account book didn't say.

The key to the growth of Flagstaff was the railroad. Without the transcontinental line, there might never have been much of a town, or a sawmill either, since the mill was started to cut ties for the tracks. It was the daily presence of the trains, rumbling through from far away, that made it all possible.

Trains became the river the country never had, carrying out shipments of cattle, sheep, and lumber, bringing in food and mail, books and bicycles; but more than that, trains were a daily connection with east and west. Visitors came and stayed a while. News flowed past from both coasts. The world came through Flagstaff on the trains, removing any sense the settlers might have had that they were isolated on the great barren Colorado Plateau.

The arrival of the coal-burning locomotive with its huge diamond-shaped stack was an event, an exciting treat for the children. Grown-ups went down to the depot on a daily pilgrimage "to meet the train," to listen for the sound and see it come around the bend. Then they adjourned to the post office to await the distribution of

---

2 *A Westerly Trend: Being a Veracious Chronicle of More Than Sixty Years of Joyous Wanderings Mainly in Search of SPACE AND SUNSHINE* by Godfrey Sykes, Fellow of the Royal Geographical Society, was described by Frank Lockwood as "the greatest autobiography that has come out the southwest."

mail and to look over Kansas City or Los Angeles papers bought from the news butcher on the train.

Locomotives departing toward California had difficulty getting up speed to make the grade to the west. Even with three engines pulling, west-bound trains went slowly out of the depot. Indeed, out of sight: a person walking at an ordinary gait could keep pace with them for a long way.

Flagstaff in its natal years of the 1880s was not entirely the culture that the railroad imported—from the beginning it had its own character. Bear were often seen on the outskirts of town then, and the Peaks were alive with mountain lions. Indians loomed in the town's background. In the Treaty of 1868, fifteen years before Flagstaff was founded, a large tract of land in northern Arizona Territory had been reserved for Navajos. The last climactic years of Geronimo's rebellion were 1885 and 1886; Flagstaff had its start during an Apache scare of ferocious proportions.

At first life in the toe-hold community was such bare subsistence that settlers carried water home in barrels from the few outlying springs. Work was constant for both men and women, and the way people lived and earned their keep could not be prettied-up nor hidden away. Years later Arizona Senator Henry Fountain Ashurst had this to say about the town's first married women:

> I have no pen dextrous enough, no tongue eloquent enough truly to describe the courage, capability, endurance, loyalty, and the sacrifices of the pioneer women. In hunger, in thirst, toil, privation and child-birth pain they walked their uncomplaining way and with an amazing gameness and faith they cheered their men onward.

It was gallant of Ashurst, but reality for women in a dusty Western settlement was not noble. Those were the years when a woman lived by the adage, "When you wake up, get up. When you get up, *do* something." Her cookstove and scrub board were constant companions. When she sat down finally late in the afternoon, it was to mend socks.

In summer of 1884 the fledgling town out in the middle of nowhere was burned out. The *Champion's* report was vivid:

> Early Tuesday morning a fire was discovered in old town by James Bailey [whose saloon had been dynamited the previous year], in the rear of Drake's dance hall. He immediately gave the alarm, and although he had a large building close by, before proceeding to move his goods personally, went from house to house to wake up the occupants. The fire had gained too much headway to be extinguished, and as it was sure to sweep the whole row west, the wind blowing from the east, the owners at once commenced moving out their goods, but the flames sprang from building to building with such rapidity, that in some instances the

owners had barely time to get out with the clothes they could get on. The fire went clear down the row, and aside from Beal's and McLaughlin's buildings, the old town is a thing of the past, as those who had enough left to build with are coming to new town.

New Town grew along a stream in the flat area between ancient lava flows a few hundred yards east of Old Town Spring, and it tried to be less disreputable than Old Town had been. In 1886, when a Methodist church formally incorporated, parishioners decided to build a thirty- by fifty-foot frame building with a twenty-foot steeple facing Aspen Avenue. Boasted of by its members as the first church on the A&P line in Arizona Territory, it seated three hundred people, which, given the size of the churchgoing population, was optimistic construction. A bell, purchased with contributions from the town, was rung eight times on Sundays and was often used as a fire alarm. The unfinished building was first used in 1887 for a funeral resulting from a shooting.

By 1887 there were two physicians and one drug store and such Catholics as the Babbitts and the Riordans. The first Mass said in Flagstaff was in that year, and it also was for a funeral, but for a woman of seemly reputation, the mother of P.J. Brannen. The Mass was recited in the Brannen home; the Catholic church with its ornate iron ceiling had not yet been completed.

On a freezing February night two years later, the night telegraph operator at the railroad depot went out on the platform about 4:00 a.m., saw flames in back of the post office, and ran up the street kicking doors as he went. Within twenty minutes the whole block was burning. Fire leaped a street and swept on, destroying everything. The roof of the Methodist church was singed; its steeple repeatedly caught fire. F.S. Clark and F.J. Hochderffer defended the church until their clothes caught fire, and the mustache of the fire chief was singed. J.J. ("Sandy") Donahue was reported to be "here and there and everywhere, fighting the fire like a demon."

The flames had originated in the roof of a Chinese restaurant. Sam Kee, owner of the restaurant, said that he had been awakened by the fire and had fled, but nineteenth century Westerners tended to feel strongly about Asians and react without much vigorous thought. Next day the Chinese were ordered to leave town within twenty-four hours. Most went that evening on the westbound train, came back two days later, and resumed work.

In those early years Flagstaff's weekly papers noted, in columns of local news, social items about people with English or German names and did so with tact. Names of people of other national origin were printed if they had caused trouble or been arrested but not when they married or had children or went off to other towns to visit. The impression that Flagstaff's population was exclusively of Anglo parentage, like Woody, was not true. There was never an even balance, but right from the beginning there was enough variety to excite people who were disturbed by difference.

A photograph of New Town was made from the top of the A&P's water tank,
which was painted black to delay freezing in winter.
AHS–Pioneer Museum

The Heiser and Randolph men posed for a photo with their wives one day
on the board sidewalk at the Heisers' house.
AHS–Pioneer Museum

Chinese were in Flagstaff from the first; in 1884 there was a laundry "managed by almond-eyed celestials," according to the *Champion*, "enjoying a liberal patronage." That same year ten acres of land east of town were leased for five years to a group of Chinese gardeners, who proposed "to supply Northern Arizona with all kinds of vegetables dirt cheap." Those Chinese residents were all men. It would be thirty years before the first women and children arrived, before there were Chinese families.

A third fire in a Chinese restaurant renewed expulsion agitation: coal oil had been poured on the roof. Local Anglo businessmen offered a five hundred dollar reward for information leading to the arrest of the arsonist and appointed a committee to decide what to do about "removing the Chinamen from Flagstaff." The Chinese—fewer than a dozen small, thrifty men—were accused of attracting fires, not of setting them, but that was enough. They were waited on by the committee and notified that they must settle their business affairs and leave within two weeks. They stayed away only long enough to be tactful (three days in Williams) and then came back and reopened their restaurants and laundries.

But it wasn't finished yet; an anonymous note was given to *The Champion* for publication a year later.

> You are hereby commanded to get the Chinamen who reside in your houses in new town out of same inside of ten days or suffer the consequences.
>
> Committee

The next week Emma Gonzales, formerly Emma Treat, a native of New York state who had recently married Brazilian-born rancher A.S. Gonzales, responded in print.

> In answer to the above anonymous letter received this a.m. written by a person or persons styling themselves "Committee" on the Chinese question, I have only this to say. That if another spasmodic eviction of Chinese is to convulse, *let it be so*, but don't think for a moment to bulldoze me by such letters, much less to make me your servant. Every man, woman or child our government welcomes to our ports, so far as I am concerned, shall know the meaning of <u>Three Cheers for the Red, White and Blue</u>.

The Statue of Liberty was unveiled in New York harbor that year. Ten years later John Phillips Sousa published "The Stars and Stripes Forever."

Flagstaff was a shanty town for years, with wide-open saloons and gambling houses and "soiled doves," whom it licensed at a fee of five dollars for three months. But there was no indication that Woody was more intemperate or quarrelsome than was usual or that he caused any remarkable trouble. Probably he drank as much as most of the men and smelled as strong, and he no doubt wore a gun and could use it on anything he had to, but his name never showed up on arrest records.

Neither was he licensed to operate a business, nor taxed as an owner of property in the center of town. John Woody, born in the West, was never much more than just an ordinary man, at least as far as wealth and power went.

Flagstaff's success stories one after another were of brothers who worked together. It was amazing how many sets of them emigrated to the little town on the railroad line in Arizona Territory. There were, among others, the Daggs brothers and the Riordans, the Locketts, the Switzers, the Hochderffers, the Abineaus, the Brannen brothers, Patrick and Dennis, and their nephew Peter. The first of the five Babbitts arrived in 1886.

Half a dozen of the ten Black brothers were in Flagstaff early. George, born in Virginia the year John Woody was born in Oregon, traveled up from Prescott with his brother Matthew about 1880, the two of them riding a mule and an old broken-down horse, moving at night and hiding during the day for fear of Apaches. The ninety mile trip took ten full days.

The Blacks homesteaded south of town at what came to be known as Black Spring and grew prosperous in cattle and real estate, gambling, saloons, livery stables. Brought up strict Methodists, they nevertheless liked a good card game and were willing to bet on anything. George maintained a liquor and gambling establishment—where the games were monte, craps, and roulette—and became respectable on the house cut. Until well into the twentieth century the family was prominent; the game of croquet was introduced to Flagstaff at a Black home.

They were quiet and slow-speaking men of dry wit, laconic, sometimes quick-tempered. In the 1890s, Matt was charged by a coroner's warrant with shooting a man named James Griffith who had gone about calling Black a "long-nosed son of a bitch" and accusing him of running Griffith calves up the canyon for meanness. Griffith had threatened a shooting; witnesses testified that Matt Black had been heard to say, at a dance at George's house, "If there has got to be a killing made, it might just as well come off now." When they met in the forest, Griffith went to his horse and reached for his rifle. Black said, "You pull that gun and I'll shoot the living piss out of you." He dropped Griffith with one shot and regretted it the rest of his life. The killing was ruled a case of self-defense.

In old newspapers and county records the names of John Woody and the Black brothers were linked several times. In December of 1892 the weekly *Coconino Sun* reported "John Woody has left for the San Juan River with Matt Black and M. McCarthy." The *Sun* did not say what they went looking for.[3] In 1894, George filed notice of intention to make final proof on a land claim and named John Woody, Perry Aston, and his brothers Sam and Marion Black as witnesses to his residence and cultivation. When Woody sold his place on the northwest side of Woody Mountain, it was to George and his brother-in-law.

Woody was neither as prosperous nor as prominent as George W. Black came to be. But the inference was that he may have been, like the Blacks, quiet and

---

3 It might have been coal. Five years later Al Doyle and several men took horses, buckboards, picks, shovels, drills, and powder to "the coal fields on the Little Colorado sixty miles northeast of Flagstaff."

F.J. Hochderffer was photographed with his sons in 1891. Frank was at the top left, George, one year older, at top right. The other boys were Fred, Will, Peter, and Cleve.
AHS–Pioneer Museum

Three of the Black brothers, Matthew, George, and Marion ("Bain"), were photographed in 1879. Bain was later captain of Flagstaff's baseball team.
AHS–Pioneer Museum

slow-speaking and sometimes quick-tempered, not opposed to a drink or a card game or a good joke, and like them, like the town itself, trying to be respectable.

In 1985 George's daughter, Mary Annetta, was ninety-three years old and living in California. Oh yes, she said, she remembered John Woody. He had had blue eyes and was sandy complexioned. She had thought him a handsome man.

Like the brawling town he lived in, he was probably a conflicting combination of old-fashioned and up-to-date, or what passed for it in those days. Sanitary arrangements were rudimentary, and the streets were boggy in wet weather, but the Atlantic and Pacific Railroad ran summer excursions on special rates to the Pacific Coast. The immigrants from more settled places imported civilization as fast as they could. Ads in the *Sun* included drawings of bicycles, that "new fad." The Bank Hotel described itself as "a leading hotel with dining room attached, where nothing but the best the market affords is served to guests."

But life was lived close to the quick. Years later Charles Stemmer, who was born in Flagstaff in 1883, remembered the town in its first unruly decade in his autobiography *A Brand From the Burning.*

> Cattle rustling was rampant and only conquered by stringing the culprits to a limb of a tree and riddling the bodies with bullets. Many were the shootings in the town, knifing and bludgeoning. Many a time from where we lived, we would hear shots and cries of those hit. They write about Tombstone and other early settlements, but Flagstaff was as bad as any of them. Many died those days with their boots on...

It was the town John Woody walked in and rode his horse through and got drunk in too, probably, and lived in most of his life. George Hochderffer wrote that it had "attained some of the popularity previously held by Dodge City, Kansas, caused perhaps by the emigration of some of the reputed bad men from that city." It tried hard to be genteel, but it was no place for men, or women either, who required convenience and soft living, no place for invalids, weaklings, those who gave up, or those who could be easily broken.

In 1889 Chinese were again on the pages of the *Champion.*

> Early August: On Sunday night our peace officers made a successful raid on a hop [opium] joint kept by some Chinamen in the washhouse known as Hop Sing's, capturing three Chinamen and one white man.

> September 28: NOTICE. All boys that have been in the habit of throwing stones and clubs at Chinamen, will take notice that hereafter they will be promptly arrested for any unnecessary assault upon Chinamen.

The boys had also been pulling the pigtails, the queues, of the Chinese men, who had names like Tom Dew Ah Wee and Jo Ah Jo. Locals laughed to tell the story about the Chinese cook who was so bedeviled by boys that once he took out after a few of them with a meat cleaver.

Boys didn't change much from century to century. In 1890 a letter was written to Thomas McMillan by T.A. Riordan, president of the logging company south of the tracks:

> The boys on our train have just informed me that three or four youngsters had been riding up and down our track on an A&P handcar. They were out three or four miles on the track today and I understand that the car got away from them on a high grade and jumped the track and injured your boy, who happened to be one of the party. My brother, M.J., informs me that he sent your son down with the buckboard and that he seemed to be pretty badly hurt, although he thought not seriously. I hope that...it will be a lesson to him to give up railroading for awhile. They are very fortunate to get off with their lives, as our train makes four or five trips out over the road for logs, daily, and would be liable to smash into them at any time.

Those boys were the sons of family men. After the first flush, most of Flagstaff's settlers were steady working folks looking for good and prosperous lives and always trying to "better" themselves. It showed in the societies they formed to study literature and music, in the concerts they organized, and in the Flagstaff Free Library Association, which opened the first town library in 1890 with four hundred donated books shelved in the Methodist church parsonage. (It offered in addition nineteen periodicals as well as chess, checkers, and dominoes.)

Civilized attitudes included getting used to the native people. In 1891, twenty Havasupai were in town briefly, handsome people of whom residents were a trifle apprehensive. Hopis began coming in with wagons to buy lumber, and Flagstaff residents traveled in groups, with pack outfits and Indian guides, up to the mesas to watch the Snake Dance.

Riordan Mercantile was buying wool of Navajo sheep by 1890 and shipping it to Boston on the train. The Flagstaff company sold flour to traders at Keams Canyon and Fort Defiance and advised that it had "a very large assortment of Pocket Cutlery selected for the Indian trade, ranging in prices from 6 to 20 cents." The Riordans bought calico from Philadelphia and Marshall Field in Chicago for sale to Navajos, specifying "something flashy...the brightest possible colors...very loud with big figures and flowers. (Don't send any more dull plaids.)"

Trade in art of the surrounding tribes began early. Riordan Mercantile notified Nathen Joseph & Co. in San Francisco:

> We have a very large and complete stock of Navajo blankets, the prices ranging as follows: 75 [cents], $1.00, $1.25, and so on up to $35, from which we will allow a discount of 20%...We can secure for you Pueblo and Zuni Pottery, Navajo Silver Bracelets and other ornaments and Moqui Plaques.

Within a decade of the town's founding it was possible for tourists in Flagstaff to buy blankets made by the Northern Ohio Blanket Mills from authentic Navajo patterns bought by the Riordans and mailed east.

Flagstaff's men admired the capitalist Riordan brothers but held their heroes closer to myths like seventy-three-year-old Jesse Jefferson Howard, who had been in the Flagstaff area since 1875 and looked it. From his homestead down on Oak Creek where it was joined by West Fork, long before there was a road through the canyon, he hunted bears all over the country and sold them first to railroad crews and then to local restaurants and butchers. Flagstaff men stood in awe of him: he was six foot eight, they said, and all his teeth were molars. Better yet, it took two cow hides to make him a pair of size 16 boots. He never combed his hair and did not really start to slow down until he was ninety. They called him Bear—Bear Howard. [see page 34]

There were many small ranchers like Woody in the area around the Peaks, and local sentiment was with them. In July of 1885 the *Coconino Sun* said:

> The authorities at Washington seem to think that the cowboy is a genius with horns, prowling about the country seeking whom he may devour. The cowboy of Arizona is a hard working man, pursuing a laborious and dangerous vocation for a livelihood, and is in no sense a criminal. The proportion of offenses committed by this class is small, and the eastern pictures of them are exaggerated and ridiculous.

The pages of the *Sun* were full of items directed toward the interest of local cattle growers. There was a regular column titled "Stock Notes," or sometimes in a burst of whimsy, "Hoof and Horn," which told the ranchers to which points most Arizona cattle were being shipped and what rates and prices they could expect. In 1885 local beef went to Kansas City with liberal rates by the A&P. Two years later shipment was to California, where cattle dealers offered two and a half cents a pound on the hoof in a depressed market.

When Yavapai County was divided early in the '90s and Coconino County was established across 18,000 square miles with Flagstaff as its seat, a total of 1418 men registered to vote. John Woody, age thirty-five, was on the list. So were nearly two hundred men, most of them born in New Mexico, with such Spanish/Mexican surnames as Montoya, Rodriquiz, Castillo, Ruiz, Chavez, Ortiz, and Garcia. There were no Chinese names.

The massive ledger that preserved county corporate filings in offices on the second floor of Babbitt's Opera House listed a partnership of John Woody and Perry Aston in 1892 for the purpose of stockraising. That was in time for the nation-wide Panic of 1893, which intensified a crisis in northern Arizona's livestock industry: ranges were overstocked, and two years of drought had contributed to a severe shortage of grass. As prices dropped all over the country, profits to stock raisers slid also, and in 1893 they lost fifty percent of their herds.

Until the middle of the decade Woody apparently owned more horses than cattle; early in 1894 he was on the delinquent tax list for four saddle horses and twenty stock horses and "imp. poss. rt."—improvements on possessory right: this

One day in 1890, two years after George Eastman began selling his Kodak camera,
Bear Howard rode into town was a couple of dead black bears and put them down
on the wooden sidewalk in front of the tailor shop on San Francisco Street.
A group of citizens gathered for a photograph to mark the occasion.

The town took great pleasure in nicknames: the man at the far right was called
Three Finger Hennessy. There were also Skinny Jones, Gooseneck Charley, a cowboy
named One Eyed Riley, a logger known as Frenchman Black, and Rubber Face Shorty,
who was renowned for juggling cuspidors. There was only one Woody in town;
if he had a nickname, it did not survive.
AHS–Pioneer Museum

was a reference to houses, fences, barns and that sort of thing. There was no identification of the "possessory right" (perhaps he was being taxed for the cabin and
corral at Woody Spring). He advertised several horses for sale in the *Sun*, and
apparently survived the Panic. The minutes of the county Board of Supervisors
indicated for July of 1895 that the tax assessment for a stock company of Woody
and Morrison had been raised from $300 to $1435.

John Woody was a stock man, but now and then he joined a popular Western
sport and dealt in property. In 1892, according to ledgers in the County Recorder's

Office, he purchased four lots on the Rio de Flag, just below the place where Flagstaff High School would someday stand, and sold them the same day. For a few months in 1900 he owned a lot south of the tracks in the block where the Downtowner Hotel would later be located.

Woody also filed a formal claim to 160 acres close to Lindberg Spring, southeast of the base of Woody Mountain. In 1895, he received from President Cleveland a patent grant to the land. It was recorded in February of 1898 and sold on the same date to Doctor Brannen for six hundred dollars in gold coin. Perry Aston and a couple of the Black brothers, cited as Woody's witnesses, claimed adjoining parcels. No evidence remained that any of them ever tried to live there: land meant money in the West. With trees already logged by the timber interest that was working the country and grazing regulation still in the future, Lindberg Spring was valuable to owners of livestock.

That 1875 Boston party had been right: it wasn't a hospitable country. Thirteen earthquakes were recorded among the old volcanos after Woody and his friends arrived. In 1892, the *Sun* reported with characteristic flippancy:

> At exactly 12:30 o'clock Monday night, those of our citizens who had retired for the night were suddenly awakened from their slumber by the swaying to and fro of buildings, creaking of doors and windows, and other unusual manifestations. The cause of all this disturbance was an earthquake, the vibrations being from north to south, and taking in a scope of country as far east as Winslow and west as far as Williams. The trembling was very distinct here, but was only of a few moments duration. Quite a number of people hastily got into their clothing and made for the street, not knowing but what the majestic peaks of the San Francisco mountains had given forth once more to volcanic eruptions. In fact, one citizen declares that he was on his way home when the earthquake took place, and that accompanying the rumbling noise, the entire surrounding country was brilliantly illuminated for a period of six or eight seconds, and he is sanguine in his opinion that the sudden flash of light came from one of the extinct craters. We give this statement for what it is worth, not being familiar with the brand of cigars our belated informant had been using that evening; we are in no position to criticize his remarks.

In the severe winters at Flagstaff's 7000 feet, residents of all ages and sexes wore long underwear and lived in hard-to-heat houses sometimes insulated with sawdust or cinders in the walls. Fires in their kitchen stoves were started with "waste" wood from the local box factory. They cut ice from spring-fed ponds and packed it in sawdust from the mill to preserve it into summer—in January of 1896 Al Doyle and "a force of ten men" cut two thousand tons one foot thick from ponds near Bellemont.

Charles Stemmer described the street scene.

> Snow began to fall about Thanksgiving, and all winter long there would be two or three feet of it on the ground up to about April first. Merchants delivered their

An earthquake on north San Francisco Street shook no high rise buildings.
AHS–Pioneer Museum

Transportation summer and winter was by horse.
AHS–Pioneer Museum

wares by horse-drawn bob-sleds and making their deliveries were always accompanied by the jingle of sleigh bells. When a gay young Lothario took his flame for a spin, he took her in a horse-drawn cutter and finer bells would announce their travels.

Housewives in the dusty frontier town had no easy time of their year-round household work. Water for washing and scrubbing had to be dipped out of barrels at the back door. They kept food cool in storage pantries they called "milk houses," square holes dug into the ground, roofed over with sod and wood, and lined with shelves on which they stored food preserved by long cooking at wood-burning kitchen stoves.

Flagstaff's proper married women were the social leaven of the town. It was at their initiative that the Presbyterians organized in 1890 and "socials," balls, concerts and plays were held to raise money for a library after the first one burned to the ground with all its books in September of 1893. The Methodist ladies on one occasion, in that time when plump was definitely preferable, held a fund-raising party with an admission price to men of one penny a pound for the weights of their wives or female friends.

The women were company to each other in the vast emptiness of northern Arizona. When there was illness or death or birth, they helped with the cooking and baking. They visited down the road and exchanged recipes. Ladies who had leisure for daytime society entertained in their parlors after the English-born wife of Godfrey Sykes introduced afternoon tea and weekly "at homes," a genteel counterpoint to the male-only saloons and the fraternal clubs which were taking the time of their men.

Childbirth was an ordeal which women faced often, usually at home. Babies were always acknowledged in the newspapers, if their parents were of the proper color and social position, with such announcements as: "Dr. D.J. Brannen reports the arrival of a boy of the usual weight at the residence of Mr. and Mrs. George Black," and "Monday the population of Flagstaff was increased by the appearance of a baby boy at the residence of Supervisor Jas. A. Vail. Mrs. Vail is caring for the boy, as the father is so overjoyed by the event that he is unfit for anything." Mrs. Vail was George Black's sister, Mary.

The women did not vote, but territorial democracy required participation by every man in town. In 1892, the *Sun* reported that Woody had served on a jury to hear a case in which Arizona Lumber and Timber Company was being sued by an employee for damages for the loss of an eye while running a saw. One end of a plank had caught and the other struck him in the eye, knocking it out. The case was "hotly contested." Jury returned for the plaintiff with five thousand dollars damages although he had asked twenty thousand.

A studio photograph of some of Flagstaff's prominent ladies included
two Riorden wives and a Babbitt, a Campbell, a Clark, and a Fulton.
AHS–Pioneer Museum

The men of those long-ago years all over the country had forms of business
and recreation that they liked to keep closed to most women, and they pursued
them with vigor and, usually, with alcohol. In Flagstaff on June 16, 1892, a fire in
Old Town destroyed the brewery and two houses adjoining it. A long bucket
brigade of every man who was available stretched from a wooden tank at the lumber mill to the burning buildings. The brewery was lost, but there was some con-
solation to local drinkers in the fact that one hundred kegs of beer were saved.
They were of the opinion that much would carry them over the 4th of July which,
as Flagstaff's namesake holiday, was always marked by enthusiastic celebration.

In 1894, after circulation of a petition signed by two-thirds of the taxpaying
men, Flagstaff was incorporated by the county board and began to keep official
records. The town business license register for that first year calmly listed liquor
dealers, saloons, gambling houses, and "bawdy houses." It also offered evidence

Women in front of the T.A. Riordan house in 1892 were (l to r) Mrs. Harry Hoskins holding Arthur, Alice Metz back at the gate, the Hoskins family maid, Caroline Riordan with Mary, Mrs. Sisson with Marjory, Mrs. Ellenwood and Cornelia. The men were John Wesley Powell, a guest of the Riordans, Timothy A. Riordan and Matt Riordan.
Courtesy of Riordan State Historical Park

that Chinese involvement in the community was growing. Included among licensees were:

Lame Sing—Bakery	Yee Lee—Laundry
Quang Hing—Restaurant	Quang Wa—Laundry
Sling Gee On—Restaurant	Hop Sing—Laundry
Hop Sing—Lunch Counter	Ah Lem—Vegetables

Flagstaff's first town ordinances enjoined the men from public intoxication and racing in the streets and forbade their horses, cattle, sheep, hogs, goats, and geese to run at large. "Immoderate riding" and obscene language also violated the published standards of the community; so did the sight of women loitering or drinking in saloons.

In 1895 Jem Foo and Sing Foo (not related) were added to the tax rolls for their bakeries. Ah Him started a restaurant. Yee Lee died of pneumonia on a Monday morning in mid-September of that year. The *Sun* described him as "intelligent and highly esteemed, a resident for the past eight years" and reported that his burial with Chinese ceremonies had been "attended by a large number of citizens."

In July there was a furor in the court of Judge Hawkins about enforcing the ordinance prohibiting women from frequenting saloons. When thirty-five-year-old Sandy Donahue, born in New York, hired a woman named Alice Nelson to play piano in his establishment on Railroad Avenue, both of them were charged and fined ten dollars. Donahue appealed, saying, "She does not loiter and drink and is supporting a family with her earnings. I don't want trouble, but she is going to stay there." The editor of the *Sun* wrote: "The question is clearly an issue between law and order on the one side and license and immorality on the other," but Donahue won his case. Flagstaff statutes were amended to provide that no woman could frequent a saloon—unless she was there to work as a musician. It was that year that Scott Joplin, seventeen years old, arrived in St. Louis and began playing ragtime.

Donahue, Vail, and Frankfurter each paid the town $10 a month for the privilege of employing female entertainers. Bicycle shops were licensed at only 65 cents, livery stables at $3.15, saloons at $6.50. At $10 a month it cost more to employ a woman to play the piano than it did to license the whole saloon. That put the women in a class with faro games at $15 a month, monte at $10, roulette at $10. They were also comparable with billiard and pool tables at $12 each.

In the 1890s the waltz "After the Ball" was wildly popular all over the country, the first song to sell over one million copies of sheet music. Other hits of the decade were "Ta-ra-ra-boom-de-re," "Two Little Girls in Blue," "When the Roll Is Called Up Yonder," "The Sidewalks of New York," "The Band Played On," and "America the Beautiful." Probably they were played on pianos in the saloons on Flagstaff's Railroad Avenue by those women musicians.

With relish, Godfrey Sykes described the attractions offered to working men in Sandy Donahue's establishment in saloon row.

> The proprietor was a husky two-fisted ex-logger known as Sandy, who ruled his place with a heavy but competent hand whenever an emergency arose. He maintained a full assortment of games running night and day, which were reported to be reasonably "straight," and an excellent lunch-counter in the rear which specialized in large, thick, and juicy steaks, garnished on top with a row of two, three or four fried eggs, cooked "sunny side up," as one's appetite and order might call for. Such a piece de resistance, flanked by a generous side-dish of "French-fries," another of hot sour-dough biscuits, topped by a quarter-section of pie and washed down by several cups of strong, hot coffee, made a very pleasant prelude to an evening at faro, keno, or roulette for cow-hand or logger after a long day in the saddle or woods. I sometimes called for a particular steak and egg combination of my own invention. It was known as a "double-header" and consisted of a specially-cut porterhouse steak some eighteen inches in length, served upon two platters held tandem-fashion by the waiter. It was garnished by a row of *six* eggs. Then, as I did not care for the coffee, I substituted a pitcher of water and a double serving of pie. I found that the combination was always conducive to an excellent night's sleep.

Some of the loggers and cowboys in from the forest for a spree at Donahue's left little more paper trace than had the native people who had lived on the land for hundreds of years. They moved through like cloud shadows and went on, and no one remembered their names. But those who stayed a while and those who made their homes among the old volcanos paid property taxes, and the records remained as official proof of lives lived. Tax assessment rolls for Coconino County for the 1890s listed what John Woody owned that was considered worth taxing.

for John Woody: Personal Property

1894

Brood mares $60
3 Stock horses 120
Saddle horse 20
3 Two years olds 30
Harness 15
Imp Poss Rt 200
          Tax $13.05

1895

Ledger not preserved

1896

5 Brood Mares $100
Stock Horse 40
1 Saddle horse 25
5 Yearlings 25
30 Stock Cattle 231
Saddle 10
          Tax $37.05

1897

100 Stock cattle $97
1 Saddle horse 25
Saddle and bridle 15
Ponies 50
1 Buggy 25
Poultry 3
Organ 50
Furniture 25
          Tax not listed

1898

30 Stock cattle $310
4 Stock horses 40
6 Saddle horses 150
2 Dairy cows 50
12 Poultry 3
Buggy 20
Harness, Saddle 15
Organ 50
Furniture 25
          Tax $47.74

1899

30 Stock cattle $310
10 Stock horses 5
3 Saddle horses 75
1 Yearling 10
2 Dairy cows 50
12 Poultry 3
Buggy 20
Harness 20
Musical Instrument 50
Furniture 50
Lots 19–24 150
          Tax $53.12

As contrast, Babbitt Brothers tax in 1897 was for 1 Stallion, 4 Work horses, 10 Brood mares, 20 Saddle horses, 300 Stock horses, 3000 Stock cattle, and 1 typewriter.

In the early years of the decade Woody looked on paper like a typical rancher, single and getting by despite a severe drought in surrounding country and the worst depression the nation had ever experienced. But by 1897—a bachelor might suddenly acquire cattle, two dairy cows, twelve chickens, two ponies and a buggy, but would he have an organ worth as much as two horses? In June of 1895, he opened an account with Babbitt Brothers for merchandise totaling $45.75. Somewhere in there, that man got married.

The register of marriage licenses in the office of the Clerk of the county Superior Court recorded that on August 16, 1895, Jonathan Woody, age thirty-eight, married Mrs. Ella Black, age thirty-four, D.R. Prime, Justice of the Peace, officiating. Their witnesses were Thomas B. Woody and Mrs. F.G. Hochderffer.

He used the old name Jonathan in that formal situation. Thomas Benton Woody was his brother, seven years older, who had come over from California on the train to be at his wedding. According to the Fresno County Great Register, John's brother was 5'11" tall, hazel-eyed, dark-haired, of light complexion.

W hat kind of woman was it who chose to marry that reticent, Western-born cowboy all those years ago? Apparently, an uncommonly independent person, self-reliant and resilient as the rest of them. John Woody's new wife had been born in Missouri as Mary Ella Burford and had grown up and attended a one-room school in Arizona, down in the Verde Valley. At the age of seventeen, in the home of her parents, she had married Luther Ben Barney, who lived near Camp Verde. A year later she had borne her first baby, a boy named Oswald, and after that there was a second child, a daughter, Pearl. They had moved to Flagstaff in 1885, while it was still half tents and open to violence and opportunity, but the marriage had ended in divorce, and Luther Barney had left town.

The *Sun* reported on January 1, 1887, that a woman referred to as Mrs. Barney was, in partnership with a Mrs. Bradshaw, operating the G.A.R. Restaurant on Railway Avenue, "serving excellent homelike meals with every delicacy the market will supply, and meals can be obtained at all hours of the day." The G.A.R. was one of only four restaurants in Flagstaff in 1887. Ella was twenty-six that year, a hard-working divorcee with two children, in business for herself in a frontier town.

In 1886 she attended the Christmas Eve Ball. In 1887 she was at the Thanksgiving Ball. In 1888 the *Sun* listed a Mrs. Barney as attending the 4th of July Grand Ball. A proper upper crust was important to the Eastern-born people, barely keeping barbarism at bay as they were; Ella's presence at their fancy balls implied careful social respectability despite her divorce. As the town's ladies termed it, she was "accepted."

Probably she was at that 4th of July Ball in the company of Calvin Crittington Black, a distant cousin of George and his brothers. Six weeks later, at the age of twenty-seven, she married him, the Methodist minister N.L. Guthrie officiating.

In 1896 the Ladies' Aid Society of the Methodist Episcopal Church published the *Flagstaff Cook Book* with recipes contributed by the ladies of the town—not the women, the *ladies*—no matter their affiliation. To be represented in the cook book meant that one was acceptable in the best company that Flagstaff afforded. Ella was there, cited as Mrs. Ella Black. Her recipe originated in the days before the discovery of cholesterol.

COFFEE CAKE

One cup each of butter, sugar, molasses, and strong coffee, one-half cup sweet milk, 1 teaspoon each of soda, cream tartar, cinnamon, and allspice, one-half of a nut meg, 3 eggs, flour to stiffen.

She didn't state baking time or temperature, which would have been meaningless for a woodburning cook stove, nor did she specify type of pan or frosting or how much flour was "flour to stiffen."

Ella's marriage with Crit Black did not last either. Seven years after she married Black, she divorced him, charging that for the previous four years he had "failed to provide for the plaintiff the common necessaries of life because of his idleness, profligacy and dissipation." She had ceased to live with him four years earlier "because he failed to provide a living for me and my children." In addition to the two children from her first marriage, there was a boy named Earl Black, who had been less than a year old when his father left.

Under questioning by her attorney at the hearing, Ella said:

> He has not provided but six dollars cash in four years past...He was in Andaconda [Colorado] last I knew of him...running a gambling hall...I have earned a living for myself and children for the last four years.

Her witness, Frank Hochderffer's wife Lizzie, testified that she was an "intimate friend" who had lived within one hundred yards of Ella for more than two years and knew that C.C. Black had not contributed support to his wife and baby son. Asked whether Ella had any bad habits, Lizzie answered, "None that I know of. She seems to be a very industrious lady."

Between 1890 and 1899 sixty-six actions for dissolution of marriage were brought in Coconino County, seven in the year of Ella's suit, on grounds deemed just by territorial statute. Most of the divorce pleas were by women claiming desertion and non-support, which Arizona law specified as adequate reason. The few men who sued did so charging that their wives had been lazy housekeepers: "You never saw such a mess." Most of the actions were uncontested, and most were granted.

After Ella's divorce was initiated in January of 1895, C.C. Black was served in Colorado with a summons to which he did not respond. The decree granting dissolution of the marriage was granted by default in May. Three months later, Ella Black married John Woody. She had been in Flagstaff nearly as long as he had, so he had known her for at least ten years.

One month after Ella had initiated the divorce action against Crit Black, she had filed with the county an oath that she was a "married woman with separate property," which implied that she had held land in her own name even before she married Black, acquiring them when she was Mrs. Barney. The tax record was specific. In 1896 county books recorded a six dollar tax on Mrs. Ella Woody, not her husband John, for improvements on Flagstaff lots 19 to 24, Block 3G, one fourth of a town block on the west side of Mogollon Street between Birch and Cherry.

Fire inspection maps dating from 1901 depicted the neighborhood as sparsely settled. There were few houses near, nothing at all to the north. In the early 1890s it was on the edge of town. The big old map showed that Ella's lots, held as a unit like a small farm, had one frame residence facing Cherry, with a metal carriage house in the back. For at least five years, maybe more, she had lived several blocks from the center of town and had harnessed a horse to her buggy to drive in to buy supplies and attend to her business affairs, whatever they were.

John Woody's income through the 1880s and 1890s was apparently from livestock. He maintained a cabin as ranch headquarters out at Woody Spring, a good part of a day's ride from town on a horse. Probably the little log cabin was in use

Lizzie, Frank, and Willard Hockderffer were neighbors to Ella.
AHS–Pioneer Museum

Ella's daughter, Pearl, wearing a dress with fashionable sleeves, sat with her
10th grade class for a photograph in 1896, in the second row, center,
her elbow on the knee of the girl to her left.
AHS–Pioneer Museum

from May until the cattle drive in the fall, one room where a man slept and ate and brewed his coffee and sat on the doorstep to drink it.

Winter was a different matter. The spring was on the north side of the mountain and waist deep in snow through the cold months, impassable to a wagon hauling groceries, difficult for a horse. Like most other ranchers, Woody spent winters in the Verde Valley or in town. Perhaps, before he married Ella, he lived in one of the boarding houses, where furnished rooms were rented for as much as five dollars a month and table board was available for up to six dollars. As her husband, he moved into her house in a domestic neighborhood. It was only one of the arrangements that she changed for him.

In September of 1885, the *Sun* had printed a warning that the legislature had passed a law requiring all stock brands to be recorded and cautioned:

> "If you do not have your brand recorded any man can duplicate it...and then
> claim all the cattle marked in the recorded brand. This is important, gentlemen,
> and should not be neglected."

It was a full twelve years later, at 10:00 a.m. on the third of June, 1897, that John Woody finally registered his brand in both his name and that of his wife. It appeared on page 109 of *Recorded Marks and Brands of Live Stock* for Arizona, a design from his initials.

		C—Left ribs. H—Left thigh.
Ⅎᒣ	⊘⊘	John and Ella Woody,
		6016 Flagstaff, Arizona

A second brand, again registered in both names, might indicate that an industrious lady's interests had expanded beyond restaurant keeping: Woody's tax assessment had just recently included stock cattle.

Ear marks were identical for both brands. On June 4 of the following year a brand was filed in the names of two of Ella's children, Pearl Barney and Earl Black, with the same ear mark.

E-L	⊘⊘	C—Right hip to ribs to shoulder. Mrs. L. Hopen, 7737 Linden, Arizona
ELA	⊘⊘	C—Left ribs. John and Ella Woody, 1982 Flagstaff, Arizona
⊔L⊔	⊘⊘	C—Left ribs. H—Left jaw to shoulder. Lee Solomon, 8437 Aravaipa, Arizona
ELI	⊘⊘	C—Left ribs. H—Left thigh. Eli Bates, 6490 Wagoner, Arizona

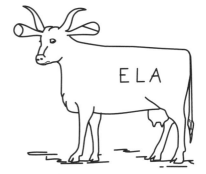

In the mid-1890s Flagstaff was little more than a clearing in the surrounding forest.
The Woody house was just out of the frame at lower left.
Courtesy of Lowell Observatory

About the time John and Ella Woody were married, Flagstaff was growing up and moving toward the twentieth century. Still part of Arizona Territory, it was the seat of the new Coconino County and had a court house, funded by the national Congress, to dignify its position. In its big new building, Emerson School was doing its best to teach the town's children, and a large stone structure south of the tracks looked as if it might, with a little political maneuvering, become a Normal School for training teachers and providing secondary education. Lowell Observatory was in place up on the hill.

George Black's daughter, Mary Annetta, was four years old the year Ella and John Woody were married. Some eighty years later she prepared as a personal record several manuscripts titled "I Remember When: Memories of Early Flagstaff."

> For many years our street lights were like kerosene lanterns. A man would come
> every evening about dark and clean the chimneys and put more oil in the bowl. It
> would burn all night. The light was not very bright but better than nothing.

But the Riordan brothers organized the Flagstaff Electric Light Company, only three years after Edison's pioneering company was merged to form General Electric, and built a light plant south of the railroad tracks near the hoped-for Normal School on the site formerly occupied by the old public school. In early November of 1895 the company installed a dynamo, got up steam, and turned on the lights. There was no current during daylight—power was not available until dusk.

Customers were charged for each "sixteen or thirty-two candle power burner" and specified whether they wanted power until eleven o'clock or one o'clock. It was "not permitted to the residential consumer to use all of the lights in his house continuously for illumination purposes" unless he agreed to pay the same rates as business houses. In 1898 the *Arizona Republican* printed: "Flagstaff has more electric wires, it is said, than any other town in the West. There are electric lights in nearly every house in town."

Flagstaff was pleased with its progress during the last decade of the nineteenth century. The *Gem* boasted that the town could claim "more miles of plank sidewalks than any town of her size in the U.S.," and reported the organization of the Flagstaff Literary Society (non-sectarian and non-partisan). There were fifty-eight telephones in town by then in such places as Lowell Observatory and the offices of the *Coconino Sun*, the homes of the Abineau, Babbitt, and Riordan brothers, and the saloons of Sandy Donahue and James Vail on Railroad Avenue.

Progress was appropriate to the town's status as a travel junction. Tourists from all over the nation came through in summer to see the nearby marvel that was the Grand Canyon. After a night at the Bank Hotel across from the train tracks, they transferred to the hard seats of a stagecoach for a 12-hour ride, fare $15, with stations along the route for changing horses.

George Black sat for a photograph with his wife and son and Mary Annetta in 1895,
the year his friend, Woody, married Ella Black.
AHS–Pioneer Museum

Afterter 1895, a married man with responsibilities and a noticeable increase in taxable personal property, John Woody began to appear more often in public records. The minutes of the county Board of Supervisors for April 6 of 1897, listed payment to three dozen men for what was described as "Indian trip." Woody's name was on the list of men paid for "Act. Services," and so were Matthew Black, Ben Doney, A.J. LeBarron, John Marshall, Henry Lockett, and William Friedlein. Hay was furnished by Bowers Brothers.[5]

There were several fraternal clubs for men in town by then. Ella Woody's new husband was accepted into the Independent Order of Foresters, which met on Tuesday evenings and enrolled, among other settled men, three of the

5 The minutes did not state the purpose of the trip, and there was no mention of it in the pages of the *Sun*. One month earlier Congress had forbidden the sale of liquor to Indians, but that may have had nothing to do with it. The group could have been a posse: three weeks later murderer Jim Parker was tracked by a posse across the Navajo reservation. Flagstaff's ranchers were much upset about that time by the discovery that Navajo animals had been grazing off the reservation near the Little Colorado. Maybe that was the reason.

After 1895 there was a power pole in front of the Bank Hotel,
which offered an electric light in each and every room.
AHS–Pioneer Museum

Hochderffers, a few of the Blacks, two Hennessys, Harry Hoxworth, John Clark, D.J. Brannen, and "Spud" Anderson. On January 5, 1897, Woody was installed as an officer in the lodge as one of its officials. Ella's daughter, Pearl, delivered a "recitation" for the program following the ceremony, and then they all adjourned to the banquet room for "a most elegant and inviting spread which continued to a late hour."

In those years Flagstaff's citizens were fond of fancy dress balls, masquerade and costume parties, and parades of all kinds. In January of 1898 the Foresters held a masquerade ball at Babbitt's Opera Hall. John Woody attended costumed as a "Lord," which showed that marriage could work wonders even with a cowboy. Bain Black went as a clown, Sam Black as a gentleman, Chester Black as a Spanish Cavalier, and the irrepressible George Hochderffer as "the New Woman," which probably meant he was wearing Bloomers. Fifty-one people were listed in attendance. But the guest list printed in the *Sun* was mostly male; as was deemed seemly, names of none of the married women were published. Pearl Barney was there that Friday night, dressed as "Blue Bell," and Creola Black, who was in her class at school, was a "Japanese Princess."

The *Gem* described the party.

Music was fine and dancing was continuous from 9 till 11 o'clock at which time the dancers unmasked. At 12 o'clock an excellent lunch was served after which the dancing was resumed and kept up until 4 o'clock a.m., when the large assemblage dispersed and went to their respective homes.

Flagstaff newspapers gave prominent coverage to national and international events, especially if they were disastrous, but showed personal interest in all details of life closer to home. Frank Hochderffer painted his barn red, and the papers cheerfully reported it. The *Gem* urged, "Flagstaff has a number of baseball players and a team should be organized for next season."

Early in February of 1898 the *Gem* lectured its readers:

> Candidates for city offices are beginning to "pip." From the music in the air we presume we will have the pleasure of announcing the names of several aspirants for city offices next week. The "moss-back" idea of the office seeking the man is played out. If a man wants an office he must ask for and rustle for it; if he don't, the presumption is he don't want it and hasn't the energy to discharge the duties of the office if elected.

The battleship *Maine* was blown up in Havana harbor two weeks later, much exciting an assistant Secretary of the Navy named Theodore Roosevelt. Until war with Spain was declared, the city election shared Flagstaff newspaper space with shrill cries of patriotic outrage, much of it copied from Hearst's and Pulitzer's New York papers. On March 10, along with war news, the *Gem* announced that John Woody was one of eight candidates for city marshall.

The *Gem* found virtue in all aspirants to for all offices and endorsed none.

> If a candidate had just been pardoned out of the penitentiary (for horse stealing) to restored citizenship, we would speak of him as a first-class citizen. If he had robbed a train and was behind with subscription to this paper and would pay up, we would say his honesty was unquestioned.

Fifty years later Godfrey Sykes's son, Glenton, recalled election customs.

> I was holding tightly to my Father's hand, as we approached some sort of a demonstration going on down at the main street corner. There was quite a crowd of men standing around and there were others sitting on horse back, and there was a team of horses hitched to a big lumber wagon. Standing up in the wagon was a man; he wore a bowler (hard boiled) hat, a black coat, maybe tails, and he seemed to me to be shouting in a loud voice. I thought there was a fight and I asked my Father what was the matter. He told me the man was a candidate for office and that he was making a political speech.
>
> There was another feature connected with the affair that might be worth mentioning. On the wagon seat stood a keg of whiskey from which the candidate would from time to time hand out refreshments to select members of the audience. I saw him pass a tin cup to a man sitting on a horse. Of course I didn't know at the time that the keg held whiskey, at least I don't think I did, but I do remember the string of tin cups hanging around the rim. I have since been informed by old-timers that this was quite a customary procedure..."No sense having a thirsty audience when you were trying to impress folks."

With a poll tax in effect, election day of 1898 was in April. There were 258 voters eligible and, according to the *Sun*, participating with some energy.

> At an early hour Monday morning the candidates without exception were tackling the voters on every corner for their support. Hacks and carriages were soon in the streets to assist the voters to the polls, and the excitement ran high. The free distribution of cards and circulars were also in evidence to a marked degree. If there were any partiality shown in this matter we failed to detect it. The balloting had grown fierce and strong by twelve o'clock and the election board moved on adjournment so that the candidates could take a much-needed rest.
> After dinner, the temperatures still being high, the backers of the respective candidates began to place the cigars on their favorites. The bluffing business was kept up till the polls were closed and the votes counted. It was then ascertained that all the bets were lost, and it was decided the bettors would have to set up the cigars for the crowd.

John Woody, with forty-five votes, won the contest for city marshall and "entered upon the discharge of his duties as such" next day, replacing the previous marshall, George Hochderffer. The *Sun* announced that the new town marshall had donned his star to begin transacting the business of his office and advised that he could "earn the praise of a good many of the citizens of Flagstaff by commencing a war of extermination upon the collarless dogs that take possession of the streets and sidewalks."

The town paid a bounty of ten cents for each unlicensed dog brought to the pound and allowed the marshall five cents a day for feeding them. Before long the *Gem* reported that the marshall "has declared war on unlicensed dogs in the city, and after next Monday he will commence the slaughter and will not quit so long as there is a dog left to tell the tale."

The marshall's hours of duty were ten a.m. to twelve p.m., minus time to go home for meals. Two weeks after the election the *Gem* was approving of the way the new man was doing his job, saying, "City marshall John Woody has caused some cleaning up to be done this week, which improved the looks of the streets a great deal. Let the good work go on."

The *Sun* reported one story with apparent glee.

> A hobo came up to a gentleman on Front Street Monday morning and tapping him on the shoulder said, "Mister, would you please give me some money to get something to eat?" "Come along with me," said the gentleman, "I'll give you something to eat; I'm running a boarding house up here." The gentleman the hobo had struck was City Marshall Woody.

The marshall had no uniform to distinguish him from unofficial citizens, but he did have a shield badge. And he wore a large moustache. Years later Senator Ashurst wrote:

> In Flagstaff's early days...full beards or, at least, piratical moustaches—sometimes reeking with Macassar oil—seemed essential to success for professional men.

It was generally believed that inability to raise whiskers indicated inability to raise a family.

The town marshall had responsibility everywhere he looked. In addition to discouraging public intoxication and racing in the streets, he was expected to enforce all of Ordinance #10. A document that revealed Flagstaff's intentions as well as its problems, it prohibited:

> ...maintaining slaughter houses, soap factories or any other business offensive to the senses;
>
> ...allowing cellars, privies, vaults, pools, sewers, or private drains to become nauseous, foul, or offensive to the senses or prejudicial to the public health;
>
> ...appearing in public places in dress not belonging to one's own sex or in an indecent or lewd dress;
>
> ...making any indecent exposure or performing an immoral play;
>
> ...maintaining, visiting, patronizing, or in any manner contributing to the support of any place where opium was smoked;
>
> ...making noise, disorder, or tumult to the disturbance of the public peace or uttering in the presence of two or more witnesses bawdy, lewd, profane or obscene epithets;
>
> ...making a breach of the peace by challenging any person to fight or by fighting or by threatening to fight;
>
> ...throwing upon any public street or alley any broken glass, ware, or filth;
>
> ...loitering around saloons, out houses, houses of ill repute, parks, wagons, or boxes by able bodied persons having no visible means of support;
>
> ...going from house to house or upon streets begging or soliciting alms.

The council was emphatic about the volatile combination of alcohol with what it referred to as "lewd women," whom it identified as prostitutes and courtesans. It forbade them to "loiter in or frequent or drink in any saloon, club house or gambling room" and warned any "keeper, or proprietor or employee" not to permit them to do so, provided, of course, that nothing should be construed "to prevent any female from playing upon musical instruments or singing in any saloon wherein there may have been paid a license tax for such occupation."

The minutes of the Council stated that in June the town attorney was instructed to "act together with the Town Marshall to enforce Ordinance Number Ten." Then the Council enacted others "to suppress practices tending to annoy persons and frighten horses passing upon the streets or sidewalks," specifically "the discharge of torpedoes, fire crackers or fireworks of any kind" and to prevent street loitering after certain hours and declared that no persons under the age of seventeen were to be on the street after 10:00 p.m. unless accompanied by a parent or guardian. It was the duty of John Woody as marshall "to arrest upon view or the oral complaint of any reputable citizen any person violating the provisions."

Since ordinances were usually enacted to take care of situations that had already developed, or that looked as if they might, all those regulations revealed a good deal about Flagstaff in the 1890s. So did the Council's decision to request the marshall to appoint at $2.50 per day a special night watchman to serve July 2 through 5.

Few of the marshall's duties were life-threatening. George Hochderffer had served a term as town marshall previous to Woody's election. In March he had drawn up a report of arrests for the first quarter and presented it to the mayor and common council.

Total number of arrests, 80, divided as follows:

Assault with intent to murder 1
Assault and Beat 8
Burglary 2
Carrying concealed weapons 1
Drunkenness 35
Drinking in a saloon by a female 1
Delivered to other officers 4
Fast riding 2
Frequenting a saloon by a female 1
Indecent exposure 1
Resisting an officer 1
Selling drink to a female 1
Using profane language 1
Vagrancy 20

Godfrey Sykes agreed that the town's lawlessness was usually harmless.

Our lives...were very similar to those of the members of rural communities in other parts of the country, and we seldom devoted ourselves with any intensity of purpose to the perpetration of manslaughter. Of course...occasional moods of peevishness and belligerency, which were possibly due to an unfavourable aspect of the moon or planets, although more probably to the importation of an explosive brand of liquor, would become manifest, and a season of fights would occur, but on the whole Flagstaff was a peaceable town and the bickerings seldom got beyond the "knock-down-and-drag-out" stage...Gambling was prevalent, certainly, but there were some rather decent men engaged in the business professionally in the local establishments and I fancy that most of the games they ran were reasonably straight. This, at all events, seemed to be the general impression.

A month after he was elected, Woody was ordered by the town council to serve Ed Wilcox notice that his barn, woodshed, and woodpile had been declared a nuisance and "that after ten days same must be torn down." Wilcox petitioned the council to keep his barn and shed temporarily. That was tabled, and a petition by Sandy Donahue "to reduce the license on women musicians in saloons" was refused. However, the council did grant Donahue permission "to dig a cesspool hole in the alley back of his place of business," and heard J.W. Weatherford's request for permission to erect a hotel of brick or stone on the corner of Leroux and Aspen and a sidewalk on the sides of the new building. As a deterrent to fire, frame construction covered with iron or tin was prohibited within town fire limits, as well as "frame or wooden buildings of any kind."

The town marshall was responsible for endless housekeeping details. He oversaw all elections and collected all city taxes and license fees, including dues from business places, gambling houses, bawdy houses, and saloons. George Hochderffer had done the same:

> This was a common procedure: whenever I called at a saloon to collect a license tax, the bartender would call or motion to all the loungers. Some of them would get up from the sawdust and greet me with "Hello George," "Hello Marshall," "Good morning George," "Glad to see you George," "You are looking fine George." Well you know it is natural to take kindly to those fellows and we all like flattery, so George would set them up. At the end of the year George was obliged to get a loan from E.S. Gosney to pay up his bills.

Responsible for purchasing and maintaining fire equipment as well as running the jail, Woody was appointed to a committee to "make estimates on the extra pipe needed" for a new water works, and the council wanted him to investigate the cost of a new flag and pole. It granted a franchise for a town telephone system; specified that all telephone, telegraph, and electric poles be regulated at eighteen feet; prohibited ads on the poles; and then ordered the marshall to see that the requirements were met.

Woody was instructed "to use every effort together with the night watchman to prevent the spread of smallpox in the town and to prevent any suspects of the disease entering the town both day and night." He and his deputies even had time to arrest "five Chinamen for running or frequenting or being intimate with a hop joint."

Only one civil suit was ever brought against John Woody in Coconino County. In 1898 M.F. Taylor charged that on July 24, Woody...

> acting within the scope of his authority as town marshall did...wrongfully, unlawfully, and violently make an assault in and upon the person of the plaintiff...in and upon the head and face...and did bruise and seriously injure said plaintiff to the damage of $10,000.

The complaint did not state why the town marshall punched Mr. Taylor. Defendants with Woody were George Babbitt, J.F. Hawks, George Black, and John Hennessy, although the role of those gentlemen was not defined. They denied "each and every, all and singular" allegations and demurred on the grounds that facts sufficient to constitute a cause of action were not stated. The complaint was dismissed.

During the summer of 1898 local papers were full of news about the Spanish-American War. Seventeen men from Coconino County enlisted when two troops of volunteer cavalry of Arizona cowboys passed through town and were cheered by Flagstaff's Company I with its band, perhaps with "There'll Be a Hot Time in the Old Town Tonight," the most popular song of the war.

But the center of interest was always close to home. There were bicycle races. Flagstaff had a Fat Man's Club with four members. In April the *Gem* reported:

> A game of baseball was played on the Flagstaff ground last Saturday and for a try-out proved that this town has a bevy of players, who, from the game they put up will make any outside team play ball if they have a ghost of a show for the championship this season. A game will be played next Saturday afternoon and the local team will be prepared to meet any team in Flagstaff or vicinity.

Teams played for $150 a side. In July the *Gem* printed:

> A violent threat has been made by some of the lovers of baseball to improve the ball grounds south of the railroad tracks. The plan is to level the diamond and cover it with red sand and roll it until it becomes smooth and hard.

In autumn men who had enlisted from Flagstaff to fight the Spanish-American War, which had lasted only 112 days, were coming home, the Great Wallace Circus was in town with a parade and a tent show, and the *Gem* editorialized: "What's the matter with organizing a football team in Flagstaff?...Get together boys and get to practicing."

Fire remained a constant danger. The City Council offered a reward of $3.50 in the day and $5 in the night to "the first party with a team who hitches to the fire engine and takes same to and from any fire that may start in the town."

Horses were everywhere. Marshall Woody rode one or drove a buggy to work from that house on Cherry in the West End. There were no automobiles in Flagstaff at the time, although news of them had appeared in the *Sun*. Henry Ford had driven his first car only two years earlier.

Like every man, woman or child in town, Godfrey Sykes knew all the problems that went with horses.

> Nobody walked more than a block or two without experiencing great fatigue, except when out horse-hunting in the early morning in order to catch a horse for the day. A few miles counted for little then, for the cunning old rascals would quit grazing about daybreak, so that their bells would not jingle any more, and would stand grouped together and absolutely motionless until one, knowing approximately whereabouts they would be hiding under different conditions of weather and feed, discovered their hiding places and caught and unhobbled them...I think that as a fair guess we horse-folk spent at least one quarter of our waking day while in town, hunting our horses or in passing out information to our neighbors as to the probable location of theirs.

Bicycles were another story; riding "the wheel" was a national craze during the 1890s. According to George Hochderffer, during the years when he was marshall twenty-five prominent citizens[6] were fined $2.50 each for riding bicycles on

---

6 Among them were J.W. Francis, Ben Coffin, E.S. Gosney, Dr. Robinson, Robert Hennessy, E.S. Clark, M.G. Layton, Fred Sisson, Robert Lewis, John Weatherford, Harry Cullman, Jeff Moyer, Dr. Miller, A.B. Crofford, John Verkamp, Charles Carroll, Sandy Donahue, and G.C. Hochderffer.

the sidewalks in town, but the two-wheelers were unwieldy any place else. Streets and surrounding roads were still dirt (or mud) and unsuitable for recreation, and they would be too rough even for automobiles for at least another decade.

On October 15, 1898, six months into his job, the *Sun* described Woody's involvement in a...

Shooting Affair

About 1:30 a.m. Friday last, marshalls Woody, Black and Drummond approached the Chinese dwelling in the rear of Coffin's grocery store and demanded admittance, which was refused. A general firing of pistol shots ensued, and after a hot battle, the door was opened and the officers entered. One Chinaman was found shot through the left arm, the bone being broken. A couple of opium-smoking layouts, one pistol and five Chinamen were taken into custody. On being arraigned before Judge Milligan, bail was given and the trial postponed. The officers say that the Chinamen commenced firing when the demand for admission was made.

While he was beset with the duties expected of city marshall, Woody continued to graze as many head of cattle and horses as he could on the land around Woody Spring and found that he couldn't juggle both jobs. He had held his busy office for two months when the *Gem* reported:

Sylvester Woody, brother to our city marshall, John Woody, came in Sunday from Fresno, California, and will make this his future home. He will assume charge of his brother's cattle and farming interests.

Sylvester was 29 that year, blue-eyed, blonde, six feet tall. Apparently it didn't work out: there was no subsequent reference in any records to Sylvester Woody. Too bad. A brother in town might have made all the difference. It left Woody with the problem of finding a responsible man, preferably family, whom he could trust to manage his cattle while he was busy enforcing Ordinance #10.

A few years earlier a man named James Barney, an uncle of Ella's first husband, had examined the way the steep rise of Woody Ridge on the east, the sheer Oak Creek cliffs on the south and the drop-off into Sycamore Canyon on the west isolated what amounted to a wide peninsula of fairly level land. He had seized the situation, built a fence about four miles long across the north side, and created a range to confine his horses. "Barney Pasture," elevation 7500 feet, became a part of the Coconino map.

When his mother married John Woody, Ollie Barney, sixteen years old and ready to act as a man should, went to live with his forty-two-year-old bachelor uncle at Barney Pasture. On the third of December, 1898, a lease formally registered with the county recorder gave into the keeping of Ollie Barney all the cattle branded ELA, ⅃⌣, and A> then ranging in Coconino and Yavapai Counties, Arizona Territory, if O. Barney would "for a period of three years from the first of January 1899 take possession and run and manage at his own expense all of said brands of cattle in a manner according to the usage and custom of cattle." Ollie was to mark half of the increase in calves with his own brand. The document was witnessed by Pearl Barney and James R. Barney and signed by John and Ella Woody.

In late October, when low afternoon sun softened the land around Flagstaff, all three men probably worked the autumn round-up and the annual noise and confusion of the slow drive in a cloud of dust to the rail line. Mary Annetta Black remembered the yearly event:

> When the beef cattle were driven in to the Stock yards for the cattle buyers to make their selections, a group of boys and girls would ride out to meet the herd. I don't know how large the herds were but there were a lot of cattle all milling around and bawling and the cowboys calling to them to keep them quiet and avoid a stampede. The dust and noise was terrible, but we did not mind that as it was so exciting. We would all stay and have supper with the cowboys around the campfire, my father and brothers among them. The next night there would be a big dance to celebrate the end of the drive. The cattle buyers, cowboys and town people all attended.

Cattle loading pens were on the railroad line east of town. Ranchers like the Hochderffers and the Michelbachs, who were north and west, often drove their herds through the dusty streets of.Flagstaff. On windy autumn days that caused no end of vexation to housewives.

So Woody had a stepson to manage his cattle while he tended to affairs in town. But even the marshall's job produced no written record of the kind of man he was. Page after page of the city ledgers recorded in the ornate script of clerks the responsibilities of his job. On the back of each warrant was Woody's endorsement, as clumsy and ill-formed as that of a ten-year-old, its ungainly capitals and repeated acute angles a product of that long-gone Oregon schooling.

As marshall, Woody published a notice in the weekly *Gem*: "On and after April 1st, I will strictly enforce the ordinance prohibiting stock of all kinds from running at large within the corporate limits of Flagstaff." He impounded such at-large animals in a yard with an eight foot fence back of the city hall, causing no end of noise and noxious smells. The place looked like a stockyard, in the opinion of the editor.

It was probably the kind of job that drew protests no matter what, and he had to parole the animals. The *Sun* complained: "The town cow is the biggest nuisance that crawls on four legs. There are a number of these assistants to the devil running at large."

In the same month Woody published another notice that he would impound and dispose of any dog found in Flagstaff without collar tags indicating that its owner had paid the dog tax, which as marshall he collected and turned over to the treasury. South of the tracks in Mill Town, T.A. Riordan, President of Arizona Lumber and Timber Company, had similar problems with wandering animals and wrote about them.

TO WHOM IT MAY CONCERN

The past two nights dogs have been howling around nearly all night long.... This is simply to call the attention of any one owning a dog up here to the above facts and to request them to tie their dogs up in some way at night until the moon goes down, or some other condition arises that will prevent their moonlight concerts.

Dear Madame:

Pigs are pigs the world over, no matter which way their tails curl, and the ordinary pig is very frequently an extraordinary hog. A tribe of pigs with the appetite of a rhinoceros has been parading about, and this tribe of pigs is reputed to be your property. Their appetites are equal to any diet from new potatoes to railroad iron, and nothing escapes them unless it is hung on a tree or piled on the roof. These being the facts, the Vigilance Committee of this village has entered condemnation proceedings against the said tribe of pigs, reputed to be your property, and I am informed that proper execution will take place on the first occasion of depredation by said pigs after this date. I write you this note to acquaint you with the facts so that you may take proper steps to prevent a bristle of the swiney tribe being injured.

Dear Sir:

I notice that...sheep of yours in our yard...the last few days knocking the stuffing out of the trees and plants. As I write this letter he is chewing up an imported bush that cost a great deal of money, and yesterday I saw him chewing the life out of a small pine tree right in front of my office window. If this fellow keeps up his present gait we will have to get a hatchet brigade and attack him.

As the only employer and property-owner in Mill Town, Riordan could adopt a tone not allowed to Woody.

The lives of those Flagstaff settlers were hard and often brief. Rose Lockett, twenty-eight years old, wife of Hank Lockett, died in June of 1898 after being "very sick" for six weeks with cerebral spinal meningitis. The baby daughter of George Hochderffer died in September of that year. In the winter of 1899, Woody's second year as marshall, there were illness and grieving families. News came in from west of the Peaks of Frank Hart's death. Children were dying of the suffocation of croup, which killed James and Mary Vail's baby.

Through the years there was hardly a month without the death of a baby or a child, sometimes by illness and sometimes pitiful accident, and the papers told that with appropriate tenderness. In one week in 1898 Matt and Belle Black lost two children, aged five years and eighteen months, to meningitis. Frank and Lizzie Hochderffer's baby died of what the town called "cholera infantum."

Newspapers carried advertisements for patent medicines good for La Grippe (influenza). Chamberlain's Cough Remedy was said to cure all symptoms. And there was this:

> Good whiskey is both doctor and tonic. Better looking than many doctors, better tasting than all medicines. For general family use, nothing equals whiskey, and Harper Whiskey is preeminently the family whiskey.
>
> Sold by J.J. Donahue

In March of 1899 the *Sun* reported: "Mrs. John Woody, who has been quite sick for the past three weeks or more, is still but little improved." On May 7, in the evening, she was gone.

The *Sun* gave details in a prominent obituary.

A GOOD WOMAN PASSES AWAY

Died at her home in Flagstaff, Arizona, on May 7, 1899, Mrs. John Woody. She had been sick for about two months, but hopes of recovery were indulged in by her husband and friends. She was perfectly conscious until her death and talked with her husband and children until a few minutes before she died. She was born in Missouri, and was about 37 years old. She had lived in this country for many years. For the past several years she had become converted and lived a Christian life but had not joined any church, although she was of the Presbyterian faith. She leaves a father and mother and two brothers in Oregon, one sister who lives on the Verde in Yavapai County, Arizona, a husband and three children, two boys and a girl. The deceased was universally loved by all who knew her. Kind in disposition, tender in feeling, she won the esteem of all. In her death three children lose the care and devotion of a loving mother, a husband the love and affection of a good and tender wife, the community a good neighbor and a Christian lady. The funeral took place Tuesday afternoon at 2 o'clock from the Presbyterian church, Rev. George Logie conducting the funeral services. The funeral was attended by a very large concourse of people.

Only two monuments in the cemetery were taller than the one John Woody, listed as "easement holder" in the record book at the office, placed on the grave of his wife. Mounted on a cement slab, it was decorated with a sheaf of wheat, drapery, flowers, an anchor, a cross, sheep, and a praying angel, all the symbols which sentiment offered to loss. The date on the headstone differed by one year from the date of publication of her death in the *Sun*. Probably he bought the marker later, after he had forgotten exactly when she had died.

Woody's entire Forester Lodge was there in a body to carry her coffin out of the little wooden Presbyterian Church on San Francisco and Cherry. She was buried in Citizens Cemetery in plot 77. That night was clear and cold.

She lay alone, beside the cemetery road, the nearest graves those in the Hochderffer family plot. At her head her husband placed a large cast metal monument bearing the legend "Over in the Summer Land." Within sight, off in the distance, was Woody Mountain.

The marshall had been a married man for less than four years. The following week he caused to be published in the newspaper a statement thanking the people of Flagstaff for their kindness and signed it "John Woody and children." It was a standard courtesy from bereaved families.

Woody was administrator of Ella's estate. George and Matt Black as court-appointed appraisers estimated it to be worth $1200 in cattle and horses on the range in Coconino and Yavapai Counties, in Lots 19-24 Block 3G, in household goods and a buggy, in a half interest in the quarter section of land in Township 20 North, Range 6 East, Section 3, the north side of Woody Mountain. It was the earliest legal reference to Woody's claim to property on the mountain that bore his name.

John Woody was appointed guardian of the persons and estate of the minor children of Ella Woody, deceased. Earl Black was eight years old when his mother died, Pearl Barney about eighteen; Ollie and Jim Barney had sold out down at Barney Pasture and moved to southeast Arizona a year earlier. One week after the funeral the *Gem*, in smooth, social-column style, stated: "Miss Pearl Barney, accompanied by her little brother and stepfather, John Woody, left for Cottonwood, Yavapai County, yesterday to spend a couple of months visiting with friends." That probably meant he was giving them into the keeping of Ella's sister down on the Verde. And then he was a bachelor again.

Woody had made a good many changes, apparently to please his wife. He still had the town job to which he was elected after he married her. A month after she died, the newspaper referred to him by title: "Marshall John Woody was thrown from a horse yesterday and received a few slight injuries which causes him to have to use a cane in walking." He was forty-three by then, strong and active and experienced. But he was a man past youth, his sandy hair turning grey, his body probably thickening a little. His hands, calloused by more than a quarter century of hard work, had freckles and prominent veins on the backs—the signs that passing time leaves on hands.

There was a Presidental election in 1900. Although men in Arizona Territory could not vote in national contests, William Jennings Bryan stopped off in Flagstaff in his second presidential campaign. His arrival was made known by the blowing of whistles and the firing of dynamite near the depot, but it had no long-range benefit: McKinley and Roosevelt were the victors.

The national election shared headlines in the *Sun* with a prolonged discussion about a principal at the local grade school who had struck a ten-year-old girl and knocked her down. It seemed she giggled constantly, and the poor man heard one giggle too many and lost control. He resigned.

Also, the automobile was coming. Headlines read, "Horseless Carriages to be Tried on Our Mountain Roads." The news was that the Santa Fe Railroad had contracted for nine steam-powered cars, capacity of fifteen each, speed forty-two miles per hour, to be used for sight-seeing between Flagstaff and the Grand Canyon. The automobiles were reported to be able to make the ninety mile trip in less than four hours.

John Woody, widower, was up for re-election that year. But the *Sun* was searching for someone who would take care of those ambling town cows. Woody tied for third, behind George Hochderffer and W.C. Bayless, who had been marshall in 1894. The tally, as preserved in city records, was:

The census for Flagstaff for 1900, with a population of only 1271, listed such Japanese names as Wakasaka but, except for a family living out on the Navajo Reservation, no one named Woody in Coconino County other than the former marshall. His household included a partner, W.D. Black, and an employee, Alva Smoots, both close to his age.

Personal tax entries showed that he still had the organ and that the number of cattle he was raising had increased, along with taxes for them, but the chickens and cows were gone.

1900

Woody		Woody and Black	
50 Stock cattle	$517	200 Stock cattle	$2070
3 Saddle horses	.75	3 Saddle horses	.75
Saddle	1	1 Wagon	.10
Organ	.50	1 Saddle	.10
Lots 19–24	.150	Imp Poss Right	.100
Tax	$49.50	Tax	$87.50

The possessory right was for Lockett Tank on a ranch forty-five miles north of Flagstaff, which George McDowell had sold in 1899 to John Woody and William Black, including a frame house and the entire stock, with marks and brands of cattle.

When his wife died and he lost his bid for re-election, Woody had been a steady presence in the Flagstaff area for twenty winters. It was time for a change.

Forest Reserves, with their federal restrictions on commercial use of public land, were three years old; the Forest Service was only four years in the future; there were regulations on cattlemen that had never existed before—Frank Hochderffer lost his ranch to those regulations. The old free-wheeling days were gone. Around Flagstaff, they had lasted only a little more than thirty years.

In February the *Sun* reported in its "Local Brevities" column: "John Woody left this morning for Fresno, California, to visit his father." He didn't stay long. Two months later the *Sun* printed: "J.A. Vail returned today from his red rock ranch where he turned over a band of range horses to John Woody and others, who will drive them to California, where they expect to sell them." Six weeks later there was this line: "John Woody returned yesterday from Fresno, California."

Beginning to settle his affairs in northern Arizona, he sold all his cattle to James Vail and George Black for $1100; all horses and his brand went for $150 to Joseph Fisher. In May, after filing a verified claim on the property, he sold the lots on Mogollon and Cherry and turned the frame house over to the Arizona Central Bank. On June 6, 1901, he deeded the northwest side of Woody Mountain to Black and Vail for the sum of $300. And on June 16 the Sun informed its readers: "John Woody has disposed of his cattle and ranch interests here to Vail and Black and has gone to Fresno, California, to live."

From that date Woody disappeared from the city tax rolls. He seemed to have intended a complete break. He was back in town within four years.

Flagstaff was not quiet while he was gone. By 1901 there was a long-distance toll-line telephone at Timmerhoff's drug store. And there was cultural progress: a new bowling alley and billiard room were constructed, and a golf club was organized including women, both married and single. The town established a free circulating library, with fifty books and a librarian, to replace the one that had burned seven years before. At the opera house a traveling moving picture show requiring seven trunks to carry necessary machinery was guaranteed "to be first class in every particular."

Los Angeles artist Oliver Lippincott shipped in by train a new automobile. It had "ten horsepower high-speed machine engines, copied after the US torpedo-boat style, fitted with water coil and flash boilers...storage capacity for 30 gallons of oil and 57 gallons of water." Lippincott's car made forty-two miles an hour under 175 pounds of steam. The *Sun* reported that in "a severe test" he drove it up the hill to Lowell Observatory and said solemnly that "mud, snow or ice cannot seriously impede its progress."

Accompanied by the Sunday editor of the Los Angeles *Herald*, Lippincott took his car on the first automobile tour from Flagstaff to the Grand Canyon, expecting to make the trip in three and a half hours. Al Doyle went along as guide.[7] The people of Flagstaff were out *en masse* to see them off, but they were barely out

7 Allen Doyle, for whom the smallest of the Peaks was named, was in the Flagstaff area by 1878. A Western archetype, he was used as a model by Zane Grey in his novels and by Hollywood as a basis for the typical cowboy/frontier hero.

of sight of town before mechanical trouble began. To their dismay, it was three days before they completed the trip.

As always, there was political interest. President Theodore Roosevelt came through on the railroad on his way to the Grand Canyon, causing a social flutter for weeks ahead of time. Welcoming committees were formed, and everyone was very excited. But the train sped past at 4:30 a.m. and did not stop. The committees rode over to the Canyon "in hot pursuit" and were graciously received by the President that afternoon. Mary Annetta Black was among those invited to shake the presidential hand.

It was still a boisterous town. Navajos "percolated," according to Glenton Sykes, "through the brush-cleared, rocky swaths that constituted the road pattern...right across lots, through private property, across the so-called street and into the next place and always past the wood pile where they hesitated long enough to pick up the family axe. This and a shovel if found lying loose were considered fair game."

The *Sun* reported a typical entertainment for Anglo men:

A crowd assembled in front of Timerhoff's drug store to witness a blood-curdling tragedy Tuesday. A mouse was placed in the same cage with a Gila monster, while the crowd waited in breathless expectancy for the reptile to devour the little rodent. But his mouseship was not built that way. In fact he knew a thing or two about Gila monsters and their peculiarities. His first movement after being placed in the cage was to climb on top of the monster and scratch his head. This pleased the monster so much that he kissed the mouse and offered to divide an egg he was eating. An effort is being made to starve the monster into eating his little companion, but up to the time of this writing the mouse was still rubbing the back of the monster and the latter continued to like it.

After a fire in frame buildings along the railroad, news traveled up and down the tracks to other towns that Flagstaff had burned completely down with winter snows not far away. Glenton Sykes remembered that people from as far east as Albuquerque collected "a lot of stuff for the relief and comfort of the homeless and sent it to Flagstaff by railroad."

It seems that the saloon keepers in the various towns also got into the spirit. They argued that if Flagstaff was without shelter and warmth they were going to need a fortifying beverage to help them through the winter. Accordingly, these gentlemen dispatched to Flagstaff a dozen kegs of whiskey. The local distribution committee was a bit stumped as to just how best to handle this situation. The initial suggestion was to sell the whiskey to the local saloon keepers. But others said, no this would not do at all, the stuff was given to the people of the town, it would not be right to sell it and besides the local saloon men would reap a profit on the deal. No, this would not do. The final solution arrived at, so as to be fair to all and maintain the spirit of the free gift was as follows. They decided to place a keg at each corner (if there be enough corners), break in the head and allow folks to serve themselves. It is said that this scheme worked very well and was quite popular with a lot of people.

Flagstaff was picturesque at the century's turn if you weren't close enough to see alleys
and back yards. Six years after its construction, there was no clock
on the courthouse tower.
AHS–Pioneer Museum

Fashionably-dressed men met trains at the passenger depot in 1902.
AHS–Pioneer Museum

On January 25, 1906, an earthquake caused chimneys to fall, and the *Sun* took its usual sly view of the affair. It reported a severe shock in the afternoon, lasting less than a minute, with a second at 7:30 the same evening and said it was "long enough to satisfy everybody." People were described as rushing from buildings in panic.

A.E. Douglass was in the county courthouse at the time and recorded that he "heard no sound except the motion of the building, but it was followed a few moments after by shooting at the oil tanks over south east of town." T.A. Riordan wrote to a friend, "The earthquake shook us up a few but did no particular harm aside from the scare. It broke some loose rocks in the mountains, which cleaned out a couple of sections of pipe line." Two and a half months later the famous quake hit San Francisco.

Probably John Woody was back in town by then: he registered to vote in May of 1906 and listed himself as a Flagstaff resident. Probably he had stepped off a train on Railroad Avenue—which was also called Front Street until residents decided Santa Fe was a more elegant name—and nodded to the men there, who said, "Why, hello, John," and walked across the street to George Black's saloon, open day and night.

Local news columns had not reported his arrival. He was not listed on city tax or water rolls. However, in April, implying a return from California and another trip west, the *Sun* stated that he had come back from Fresno "where he has been for several weeks on account of the illness of his father." Andrew Jackson Woody was eighty-seven by then, an old pioneer coming to the end of his story.

Woody may have returned as early as April of 1905, when old-timers organized the Pioneers Society of Northern Arizona "to perpetuate the memory of the early times and early incidents of the pioneer days." Membership was restricted to persons who were bona fide residents of Arizona on or before Valentine's Day of February, 1886. In the minutes of the first meeting, John Woody was enrolled as member #119, an addition in a hand different from that of the secretary who had made the initial list, as if he had not been in attendance at the meeting.

No clue remained as to what he was doing or where he was living. But a hint of things to come appeared in 1906 in the minutes of the Board of Supervisors when it listed John Woody as among the men elected to represent Flagstaff precinct at the county Democratic convention to be held at McMillan Hall. The convention endorsed the policies of William Jennings Bryan and nominated John Francis as candidate for county sheriff.

The *Sun* professed itself a Republican paper and advocated the election of Republican candidates, but when Flagstaff voted at city hall in November, Democrats took eleven of the sixteen offices, and John Francis was elected 530 to 516. Both deputies of the defeated sheriff resigned and joined, the *Sun* said, "the force of forest rangers." In January when Francis took office, he appointed John

Woody his undersheriff, his second in command, and Woody was back to enforcing laws.

In 1907 the county Board directed the sheriff to refuse to issue to any woman a license to sell liquor in Coconino County. Mary Annetta Black remembered the district where most of the saloons were located. Women didn't go around on that side of the block, but daring girls did, sometimes. [see page 69]

> Sandy Donahue had in his saloon (so they said) a beautiful back bar of mirror which cost a lot of money as mirrors in those days were scarce. We girls were never allowed to go on that street but sometimes in the early evening we would ride our horses down there, stand up in our saddles and try to look in. We could hear the music and get glimpses of the entertainers. It was so exciting. Our parents never knew we did this or we probably would not have been allowed to ride.

The first report in the *Sun* of Deputy Sheriff Woody proved its efforts to provide interest for readers. In March he left for Humboldt with a warrant for the arrest of a man named Hildebrand on an alleged charge of larceny. The man had left Flagstaff suddenly with a trunk containing all the clothes of a woman of his acquaintance to whom he was not married.

In October the *Sun* informed its readers:

> A man giving his name as Thomas Brown was taken into custody by Deputy Sheriff Woody on Thursday afternoon. Brown was evidently insane and an examination was had before Probate Judge Kidd and he was committed to the insane asylum at Phoenix. He was a stranger here and was traveling over the country afoot and was affected with a religious mania. Among his effects carried in gunny sacks and weighing about 175 pounds were a choice assortment of old tin cans, stones and trash and each article possessed according to Brown some especial virtue. Brown was taken to the asylum by Deputy Woody.

After that Woody went off to "his home in California to visit friends and relatives" for Christmas. In January he went to the Verde "on business connected with the sheriff's office." Then the *Sun* was silent about him until April, 1908, when he and two other deputies left for Yuma's territorial prison with six prisoners after the regular court session.

On Friday, May 8, 1908, the *Sun* carried this item on its front page:

> ### UNDERSHERIFF WOODY MARRIED
>
> The many friends of undersheriff John Woody were surprised to learn that without any previous notice of his intentions, he was married Tuesday evening to Mrs. Myrtle Binkley of this city by Probate Judge Kidd.
>
> His many friends regret that he was careless in not advising them of his intentions as they would have assisted in making the vicinity in which he happened to be located merry with splendid robust noises of a large variety.
>
> Mr. Woody is to be congratulated upon securing a most estimable lady as his helpmate.

The license and certificate had been issued a full week earlier. E.S. Carlos, janitor at the Court House, and Maggie S. Carlos were witnesses. It was a deliberately private ceremony, probably designed to avoid splendid, robust noises.

The affidavit of marriage identified Myrtle Binkley as being "of legal age" and said nothing else about her. County records showed that in 1900 a woman named Myrtle Landers, age fourteen, married John W. Binkley, thirty years old. In 1907 the Board of Supervisors paid Myrtle Binkley thirty-five dollars for nursing services at the hospital. And then in April of 1908 she divorced John Binkley. Her formal suit stated that she had been a resident of Flagstaff for ten years and cited the customary charges: "...the defendant has, willfully and without cause or provocation on her part, deserted and abandoned this plaintiff for a period of more than one year...and now does desert and abandon her, without her consent and against her will, and until said desertion, as aforesaid, this plaintiff had during all the times of their said marriage been a good, loyal and dutiful wife to defendant." Binkley was served with a summons but did not contest, and the divorce was granted by default. One month later Myrtle married John Woody.

The census of 1910 offered further information. According to that document, she was born in New Mexico of parents who were both born in Missouri, and she was twenty-nine years younger than Woody. He was fifty-one in 1908; she was twenty-two. She was the mother of four children, three of whom were still living, aged seven, five and four at the time of her second marriage. The census indicated that Woody had fathered no children of his own.

A month after the wedding a general roustabout at Williams was found dead at Joe Dixon's cabin north of Maine at six o'clock on a Sunday evening with his head badly beaten and a bullet wound in his back. Blood stains were found on the floor and in the yard. Sheriff Francis was notified and Deputy Sheriff Woody was sent to the scene. He arrested Joe Dixon, better known as Limpy Joe, and took him to Williams with the body of the dead man.

It hadn't been so very long since Inemacio Valdez, killed because of an argument, had died without benefit of a county sheriff. The Kendrick–Sitgreaves expedition had passed through untenanted forest at the base of the Peaks only sixty years earlier and had left no trace. Nearly thirty years had gone since the first settlers had arrived to found Flagstaff. The seasons had circled across the slopes of Woody Mountain during those years and made no change in its silhouette, but the settlers themselves had grown older, and many of them had already moved on into the past.

There was another election in November of that year and local men climbed the steps of the county courthouse to vote. (Arizona women could not vote until 1912, eight years before the suffrage amendment was ratified for national elections.) Taft

Sandy Donahue's bar was known later in the century as The Monsoons.
AHS–Pioneer Museum

An illustration of women's fashion was in this 1909 wedding photograph of
Hedwig H. Leissling and Eli Giclas, superintendent of Flagstaff's water department.
Attendants were the bride's sister Johanna Leissling and the groom's sister
Aurora Gicquelais. The minister was Mr. Clark.
Photograph courtesy of Henry Giclas

was elected President of the United States, and Francis was returned to office as county sheriff by 142 votes. He retained John Woody as deputy at one hundred dollars a month.

In 1909 Flagstaff had a moving picture house, four Chinese laundries and four Chinese restaurants. John Woody was back on the personal tax rolls of the county with a cow, some chickens, and a piano valued at one hundred dollars.

In May the *Sun* reported that he and Marshall Wheeler "swooped down on Jim Guiterrez's place of business and broke up a monte game and toted all eight of the men involved up before Judge Harrington." In September Woody went to Globe "in quest of witnesses in the case against several Mexicans for breaking windows in George Black's saloon with rocks last spring."

Founded almost two decades after the War Between the States, Flagstaff never had to overcome the shame of a history of human slavery. Black residents of the town were few in proportion during the early years and seldom saw their names in local papers, but they were there. In the 1890s, "colored gentlemen" John Prince and T.A. Anderson worked in the sawmill. Marshall Ford, colored, was a porter at the Panier Saloon. Three black men stood for a photograph on the Slattery Plumbing wagon decorated for the parade that celebrated the dedication of the town's first cement sidewalk.

Civic development had been uneven, almost schizophrenic: there were twenty automobiles and no paved street in town in 1910, but Halley's comet was photographed up at Lowell Observatory that year. Ghirardelli chocolates from San Francisco were for sale at Riordan Mercantile. Despite hopeful literary and musical societies, citizens took primitive inconveniences for granted. T.A. Riordan wrote to the Santa Fe agent in Flagstaff:

> Several times I have been going to call your attention to the wagon crossing at your tracks in town west of the depot at the Beeson wood yard [on Beaver Street]. This as you know is the principal crossing in town, I suppose fully 95% of the wagon traffic crosses there, and at the point over your tracks there is not room for two teams or motors to pass and this should be widened to enable at least two vehicles to pass or there is likely to be an accident. I have already noticed a few close shaves. It is a very dangerous place and by filling in between the rails to enable two rigs going in opposite directions to pass it would reduce the risk considerably. The coal shed on one side and the wood yard on the other makes it hard to see trains at times when there is switching going on and two or more trains at work in opposite directions and when vehicles are sometimes waiting for a chance to cross and the trains are at work they start to rush across and meeting a vehicle going in the opposite direction on the track where there is not sufficient room to pass.

In the thirty years since that first A&P railroad survey, Flagstaff's frontier status had nearly disappeared. Without his knowing it, John Woody's time too was almost finished. He had only four more turns around the sun, but he went on with Flagstaff plans and arrangements as he had for years.

The first cement sidewalk in Flagstaff was dedicated in 1910.
AHS–Pioneer Museum

The Slattery Plumbing wagon pulled on east of the court house.
AHS–Pioneer Museum

One of the Fourth of July parades during the first decade of the 1900s featured
Deputy Sheriff John Woody, ribbons across his chest and tied to the reins,
riding a refined little mare with English bridle and a cavalry saddle.
AHS–Pioneer Museum

A parade paused at the corner of San Francisco Street and Railroad Avenue.
Was that John Woody on the horse at the far right?
AHS–Pioneer Museum

City ledgers for water assessments billed him from 1909 on a homestead out on the Lake Mary Road, and a citation for $108 in the city treasurer's records stated: "John Woody to Water rents and taps, a/c pipe line and ditch built by Woody to be paid for in water rent." Listed as a stockgrower, he was the original entryman on the land, with ninety-five acres, seventy-five of which were in unfenced range. In the release of the land to him, it was described as "cut over, no water."[8]

In 1911 he bought from Tom Pulliam for fifty dollars a brown cow and a black two-year-old heifer with a white face, as well as the brands on both. That year Pulliam, another Democrat, was elected county sheriff and retained John Woody as jailer and undersheriff. Minutes of the Board of Supervisors showed that he resigned effective May 1, 1912, for reasons of ill health. He was fifty-seven years old.

The next year on September 12, 1913, on the front page, the *Sun* printed his obituary:

> John Woody died last Saturday morning at his old home at Kingsburg, California. Mr. Woody was a pioneer resident of Flagstaff having held the offices of city marshal and deputy sheriff for a good many years, serving last but for a short time under Sheriff Pulliam. After resigning Mr. Woody took up a homestead near Flagstaff but during the last year his health necessitated his going to California. He gradually grew worse until death released him of his suffering. ...Mr. Woody leaves a wife and several step children to mourn the loss of a good father and husband. He was buried at his old home at Kingsburg, California.

Documents relative to the settlement of his estate filed in the county Superior Court stated that he died September 5, 1913, in Dinuba, near Kingsburg, still a legal resident of Coconino County. Myrtle Woody, heir, waived her right as administrator and chose George Black to settle his affairs.

The estate was appraised for the court at $1484.

Improvement on possessory right: house, barn, fencing, etc $300		
4 work horses 350	6 head yearling cattle 150	1 old buggy 5
? head 2 year olds 125	9 head small hogs 45	1 calf 10
3 colts 50	farming implements 20	1 wagon 30
13 head cattle 390	1 harness 10	

Most of the equipment, horses and cattle were sold to Frank Lauder for $1065.

There were several claims against the estate. Half interest in all hay, grain and potatoes on the property was sold as part payment on a promissory note of $994 to George Black. In addition Woody owed:

Fred Hensing $66.99
Wm. Beeson for hay 313.00
	15.75
A. L. & T. for lumber 28.90
Manning, M.D 10.00
	40.00
Dickinson 100.00

8 It looked much that way seventy-five years after John Woody established his homestead, but by then it was occupied by the Hitching Post Stables.

and to Abineau Brothers for

onions	ham	blueing	turnips
apples	milk	bucket	bacon
beans	baking powder	soap	tomatoes
spuds	vinegar	axe	pork
lettuce	butter	pole	syrup
oats	malt	rope	prunes
radish	flour	knife	catsup
peas	lard	starch	beef
garlic	salt	fish hooks	cheese
corn	candy	pipe	corn meal
	sugar	file	chili

Total $104.59

The total debt was $1669.72. He left to Myrtle, when everything was paid, only the land out on the Lake Mary road.[9] The homestead was granted to her as "widow of original entryman" by Woodrow Wilson in 1914; within the month, she sold it for $1200 and married a third time.

John Woody lived between 1856 and 1913, taking for granted a way of life and a kind of skill that were already fading. The legend of the far west was opening when he was born and closing as he died. He might have learned to use a telephone, probably he had ridden on a train, but he may never have driven an automobile. The Sixteenth Amendment instituting a personal income tax was passed into law in 1913. The previous year Arizona had become a state, restricted gambling in saloons, and voted to prohibit the sale of liquor within three years. In 1914 World War I began and changed everything.

Apparently a self-possessed man of the old West, accustomed to living in open country, John Woody must have schemed and laughed and gone to bed tired, as they all did, but no record survived of important things: what made him angry or how he treated his wives, his stepchildren, and his horse or what condition his boots were in or what he liked to eat or whether he was at ease in company or what other men thought of him. When he died, he disappeared as completely as the years he had lived in, and nothing was left but a name on a mountain, a few slips of paper in dusty boxes, entries in county records, and an occasional reference in local newspapers.

So he was gone, the little boy with blue eyes, the young cowboy, the deputy sheriff, gone in a long-ago September. He had made his way almost alone in a

---

9 In 1990 Joe Mehan of the Pioneer Museum found in a box of old documents a paper stating that in December of the year Woody died, she applied to the county for $6.45 to pay for flour, bacon, sugar, baking power, lard, coffee, rice, milk, and rolled oats.

rugged country and a vigorous community, and if he didn't achieve the wealth and power of some of the men in town, at least he finished even with the game.

There was no shame in his record. He seemed to have acquitted himself, as far as character went, as well as most of them, and he did respectable work that needed to be done. Gone just short of his sixtieth birthday, he never learned the truths of being old.

Most of the highest of the volcanos near Flagstaff were named for men who were never in Arizona or on the scene only briefly—Kendrick, Sitgreaves, O'Leary, Humphreys, Agassiz, and Fremont, not to mention St. Francis of Assisi. Woody Mountain stood as a monument to an ordinary, hard-working cowboy who belonged to the country. Nothing could have been more suitable.

*W*ild turkeys were extinct in Arizona a dozen years before
Woody died, thanks to hunting and habitat destruction.
Grizzly bears, jaguars and wolves were nearly gone by
then, pulled up by the root to make room for sheep and
cattle and horses.

On Woody Mountain chipmunks and golden-mantled
ground squirrels still rushed about in summer sunshine
seeking food and retreated to their burrows for winter
sleep. The Abert squirrels named by Dr. Woodhouse
did not hibernate; all year, with back feet that rotated
180 degrees and front feet that they used as hands, they
ran up and down pines, flicking their huge white tails
like plumes.

Tassel-eared Abert squirrels had grown over centuries to
be inseparable from Ponderosa pine. They lived and
nested in the trees, feeding on buds and seeds and the
inner bark of twigs. Where there were no pines growing
close enough together to provide a canopy for traveling,
there were no Abert squirrels.

They built snug nests for themselves fifty feet above the
ground, large balls of interwoven branches that sheltered
hollowed centers lined with grass. The squirrels were
solitary creatures. They slept in those nests alone,
swaying with the wind, the sound of it in their ears all
night.

Chapter Four
Loggers
1904

In spring Rogers Lake was a square mile of shimmering water.

By June the lake was a square mile of grassy Meadow.

In a basin shallow as a soup bowl and rimmed by lava flows and volcanic cones, Rogers Lake two miles west of Woody Mountain collected run-off from surrounding hills. If winter had been wet, in May the lake was deep enough for sailboats, but no creeks or springs fed it. The water began to disappear after snow had melted, draining down the fault that cut east–west across the basalt just north of Woody Mountain, and into the fault that formed Oak Creek Canyon, a few miles to the south. By June the lake was a meadow, boggy in the middle. That was how the Sitgreaves party had found it in autumn.

When Flagstaff was still building New Town, residents rode out to the lake now and then for sport. Local news columns mentioned such recreation in 1885: a few men "went out to Rogers Lake this afternoon on a duck hunt. They will camp there tonight and return tomorrow."

The locality was full of wildlife, some of it unfriendly. In June of 1886 the *Sun* reported a man "severely bitten on the lips and face by a skunk Thursday near Rogers Lake." Readers were informed that the bite of a skunk was said to be poisonous.

Hunters persisted, although their reputation was not one of good sense. The *Sun* reported:

> E.R. Jones from Rogers Lake says deer hunters are so thick in that vicinity that it is unsafe for people to be outdoors. There is little danger of deer being killed, but other stock is in danger from stray shots from unsteady marksmen.

The fates of the lake and of Woody Mountain were tied together by geography. Both had been quiet for thousands of generations of elk and grizzly bears. When immigrants finally appeared from the east, it was in small numbers at first as explorers, then as ranchers. Suddenly they arrived in crowds to take away the trees. The lake and the mountain were not the same after that, caught up as they were in human affairs. Loggers made a more violent change in them than any force since the Ice Ages, with the assistance of American politics and a powerful nineteenth century economic influence—railroads.

Shortly after the Civil War ended, the Thirty-ninth Congress, returning to business interrupted by the conflict, had designed an act to help finance a cross-country railroad and granted to the Atlantic and Pacific a right-of-way two hundred feet wide along the entire length of its track and the odd-numbered sections on each side in a strip that stretched away twenty miles. The broad cross-country belt totaled 155 million acres to be used as the railroads saw fit to offset costs of construction. As the transcontinental tracks approached the Peaks from New Mexico in 1881, sawmills went into operation to cut the ancient virgin forest to provide ties, bridge timbers, and supports. They operated on oral agreement with the A&P railroad, which owned timber on its sections on either side of the line, thanks to that congressional grant, and wanted to use the trees to its profit.

Michael J., Helen (Nell), D. Matthew, and Timothy A. Riordan were the
children of an immigrant Irish carpenter.
Museum of Northern Arizona

In 1883 Edward E. Ayer, a lumberman from Chicago, signed a contract to buy and cut the trees on seventy-seven of the railroad's land-grant sections near the Peaks, with eighty-five percent of his saw timber sold to the A&P and Mexican Central railroads, fifteen percent to the general public. A year later Ayer hired Matthew Riordan to manage his mill, already the largest west of the Mississippi, and Matt sent for his younger brothers, Tim and Mike, to come out from Chicago.

Tim and Mike Riordan married the Metz sisters, cousins of the Babbitts and the Verkamps, and settled into Flagstaff. Genial and high-spirited, involved with everything and everybody, Tim became in no time at all one of Flagstaff's favorite characters. People loved the big man. If they liked him at all, they loved him.[1]

In 1887 the railroad negotiated a logging agreement with the Riordans covering 853 sections, making the Flagstaff lumber company the most important commercial enterprise along the whole A&P line. That year Matt Riordan and his brothers bought the operation and opened a branch at Rogers Lake. In August the *Sun* reported:

> There are about fifty men employed at the sawmill at Rogers Lake, which is turning out an average 15,000 feet of lumber a day...The mills are running at their full capacity day and night. The lumber from these mills is hauled to the Spur, on the railroad, five miles west of here.

Company correspondence mentioned orders to the lake mill for telegraph poles, and lumber cut to 1 x 12, 2 x 4 and 4 x 4 inches.

Soon there was a name change to Arizona Lumber Company, and Rogers Lake had men enough in residence to be considered a county precinct and send delegates to county political conventions. Twenty-eight-year-old Tim (T.A.) Riordan, superintendent in full charge of the mill at the lake, was the Democratic delegate. When fire gutted the Flagstaff sawmill in July, Matt Riordan was in Chicago, and T.A. moved the smaller mill in from Rogers Lake—engines, boilers and everything—and restored production in less than two weeks. A letter from T.A. to his older brother referred to the event.

> I have everything down from the Lake now and will have the frame and floor up tonight—expect to saw a week from to day. I have not heard a word from the insurance man yet. Celine [Matt's wife] left for Prescott last night—everything else well.

In 1887 the company built a telephone line from the lake to its office in town and a pipeline to a tank near the depot. But plain workaday history tended to get lost along the way; the people who lived it took it for granted. No clear evidence was left to indicate just where the telephone and pipeline and the logging road were located, no geological survey maps, no Forest Service topographical maps, no diagrams in the big map case in the Riordan house.

---

1 They didn't all like him. During the 1893–1897 Panic, his company did all it could "toward shaping a wind-up" for the Greenlaw brothers' company, which was a competitor. He referred ruefully in a letter written in the 1930s to people who accused him of running his business in the style of the Nazis.

Tim Riordan married Caroline Metz. Riordan had no descriptive nickname.
The town spoke of him by his initials, T.A.
AHS–Pioneer Museum

Loggers did not leave many trees standing south of town;
ox wagons pulled away everything that could be cut or sold.
AHS–Pioneer Museum

There was evidence for the location of the early road, and the phone and pipe lines that may have taken the same route, in Riordan's letters, which described the Rogers Lake road as a county road "8 or 9 miles in length from the point...where it branches off from the Williams road."

> I was talking with Hooky Fisher this morning...He said the present road from Flagstaff to [Rogers] Lake around the base of Woody Mountain was impassable in winter and spring as the heavy snows fall on the divide and it is shaded from the sun...

Riordan described the road as "considerably traveled and...impossible to get over anyway but horseback as the hill on the Divide is in fierce condition and other parts of the road are practically impassable."[2]

Roads were a fraction of his vexation. Logging in the ponderosa pine forest around the Peaks was rife with the unexpected, as indicated by figures for the three years before the Riordan purchase.

1884—44,344,440 feet	. . . .	Value $178,913.77
1885—8,379,531 feet	. . . .	Value $152,351.02
1886—7,647,227 feet	. . . .	Value $156,471.21

There were recurring contract changes as the railroad charged improper lumbering methods. But the brothers worked through to notable success. Before they were finished, they owned major interests in Arizona Lumber and Timber Company, Central Arizona Railway Company, Greenlaw Lumber Company, Flagstaff Electric Light Company, Spangler Sheep Company, Howard Sheep Company, and Johnson Cattle Company, and were participants in several other concerns. They controlled more land and water than any of the stockmen.

With the depletion of white pine in the old lumber states around the Great Lakes, the market for Riordan lumber products expanded until it extended throughout Arizona, New Mexico, Old Mexico, Southern California, up into Colorado and Nebraska, east to Ohio, Illinois, Missouri and Kansas, even as far as Chicago and New York. Products covered everything that could be made from pine timber: building materials, railroad ties, bridge timbers, moldings, piles, timbers for

2 The Riordans formed the practice early on of preserving copies of all out-going correspondence. On tissue-thin paper, they were bound in volumes of one thousand each and stored on the top floor of the stone office building on what would later be West Highway 66. A fire in the roof in 1921, started by sparks from a logging locomotive, resulted in water damage to the old letter books, and they were moved to an upper room in T.A.'s house. A malfunctioning furnace there in 1960 left smoke and ash on the volumes. They were finally moved to the archival Special Collections Library on the NAU campus. And there they stayed, neatly labeled and filed eight to a cardboard carton, still holding unread secrets, until 1986. Pages were stuck together, requiring a careful touch to separate them, or sometimes fused into a lump or blurred and darkened with ash. However, enough of them were legible to reward the effort. As the twentieth century neared its close, they were the only source that remained to explain what had happened in the beginning.

mines, fruit and vegetable boxes, and varieties of woodwork. That included plank-ing for sidewalks all over the A&P district.

The initial force of workmen for the mill and the forests was imported by the A&P, sometimes at no charge. The railroad needed ties and had an interest in providing men to cut them. Sometimes fares were paid by the logging company. As a solution to a labor problem, it wasn't entirely satisfactory. In 1887 Matt, writ-ing to the A&P Superintendent in Albuquerque, reported:

> ...in addition to the men that you passed in here free we paid fares on about two hundred ourselves, and I believe that out of the whole number there are not fifty men now at work for us...they do not and will not stand by the work...Many of the men have gone to the Mineral Belt [Railroad], some have gone to sheep herding on the ranges, etc., some have gone to work on the sections on the A&P, but many have kept right on and gone to California.

Wages for common labor in 1886 were $1.60 a day without board, which wasn't bad for the time, but there were men who preferred lower wages and easier work.

In January of 1887 loggers out near Woody Mountain joined an impromptu strike that put pressure on the profit margin. Matt Riordan appealed to the railroad for help.

> Trouble comes and more threatening on the tie business...Just this moment (8:30 p.m.) word is phoned to me that all the tie-choppers up near Prentice Spur had quit and were coming down in a body. Don't know why.
>
> Tonight some chaps came in to talk ties and demanded 25 cents apiece for chopping alone. This price would not permit of ties being hauled and delivered for the price I get. They were told such a price could not be paid, and went out saying we'd just have it to pay, that the price was paid when the A&P was built and it would have to be paid now. That means ruin if we cannot get your aid. If we pay fare for all the men we want to bring in here it puts such a heavy tax on us we simply cannot bear it, but if you could manage in any way to pass such men as we need in this emergency we would put in four or 500 as fast as we could get them. The Santa Fe should be willing to assist us in this crisis...As the material is for the railroads, I trust they will not look upon this request as unreasonable.

Men who worked in logging camps were not always regarded by those folks in town who were trying to make a genteel show as the better sort. The *Sun* took its customary impudent tone in 1888: "At present little lumber is being hauled, and the jovial bull-whackers are making merry in Flagstaff," probably in the saloons on Railroad Avenue. When they did work, their mood was equally jovial. In 1889 T.A. wrote to the man in charge of the mill at Rogers Lake:

> ...I wanted to say that after leaving the mill yesterday afternoon I drove up to section one and just about ¼ of a mile this side of the section on the road I came upon three logging teams loaded and all of the drivers lying down under a tree, I suppose for the reason of passing a couple of hours away, being afraid of getting in too early. It was just 10 minutes past two o'clock when I met them and it was

Old logging photographs of High Wheels also showed horses and working men.
AHS–Pioneer Museum

Work crews unloaded logging trains at the AL&T yard, at the base of Mars Hill,
as early as 1887.
AHS–Pioneer Museum

just 20 minutes past 12 when they started out after their load as I was going out
to the mill. If there is any reason in this world why these teams could not have
made three loads yesterday in at least eight hours, then I do not know what it is.

Movement of timber out of the forest was hard work. In the beginning,
when there were plenty of trees close to town, logs were moved to the mill on
four-wheeled wagons pulled by three yokes of oxen under the management of
"bull drivers." [see page 82] As operations moved farther and farther out, they
were replaced by the longer reach of trains. Within its first decade the Riordan
company began to use High Wheels [see page 85] for skidding logs to the rail line.
Ten feet in diameter on an axle more than seven feet wide, logging wheels could
carry as much as four thousand board feet at once. The *Sun* reported that the company had received a shipment of "18 big draft horses from Iowa to pull them." And
mules were useful; one pair was named Gallagher and Kicking Bill.

Soon the trees near town were gone. All timber south and west—from Mt.
Elden down to the Mogollon Rim—had been cut except for the rough country in
"the Oak Creek Breaks." (Later, in 1894, Riordan proposed to the Land
Commissioner of the A&P that he "clean up that particular township.")

The nineteenth century was gone before trains reached the neighborhood of
Rogers Lake. In a letter to the Secretary of the Interior dated September 1903, two
years after John Woody had sold his ranch, Mike Riordan requested a permit to
"erect and occupy a logging railroad" out near Woody Mountain, stating: "The
topography of the country surrounding applicant's tract is such to make it impera-
tive for a right of way for a logging railway."

The application was accompanied by a detailed report on the route for the
proposed line, again dated September, 1903. It stated that the right of way crossed
the northeast slope of Woody Mountain in a section of rocky, broken land and that
in the same half mile "Rogers Lake County road" crossed the line.

The Secretary of the Interior prescribed regulations to which the Riordans
agreed on September 12, 1903, promising while they were at it to "furnish free of
charge such assistance in men and material for fighting fires as may be spared without serious injury to applicant's business."

The paperwork was formal and proper. However, the *Sun* printed item after
item that indicated some tracks were laid down and logging had begun in 1902, a
year before the application was mailed to the Department of the Interior. In
October of 1902 the paper reported that the company was building a branch railroad to Rogers Lake and planned to "begin logging in that section."[3]

A year later there was confusion about the need to be legal with short spurs
from that line across sections that were not owned by the A&P. A letter from T.A.:

> You will remember that after we secured our right of way the question of
> extending branch spurs out from the main line for timber was still unsettled. In
> talking over this matter yesterday with Fred, he was very positive that we should

---

3 The application apparently was a belated attempt to make legal something that was already done. The Riordans
  had been in the lumber business for twenty years. The government had been increasingly involved in
  regulation for almost ten, but there was a lag before rules caught up with custom.

The Walter Beeson homestead was on the south side of Rogers Lake
at the turn of the century.
Courtesy of Miller Brothers

The logging roadbed ran across the east side of Rogers Lake.
In summer it held the trains above muddy meadow.

not undertake to build any of these spurs without first receiving permission from the Government and doing whatever is necessary and that otherwise we will surely get into trouble. I was going ahead on the program of building these spurs as we come to them without saying anything. In fact we are just finishing one now where we run a spur entirely across a University section and onto the middle of the adjoining railroad section.

The new logging railroad ran from the sawmill in Mill Town—which in those years was everything south of the transcontinental tracks—to a junction where Fort Tuthill would later be established and then west in a meandering line to the divide north of Woody Mountain. Clearing the rising slopes, it ran on a straight line down the east side of Rogers Lake.

Beds for the logging tracks were usually built of material close at hand, often by a machine standing on newly laid rails and scooping up dirt or gravel from either side or by wooden blades pulled by horses to shape and relocate materials. Bases of the track beds were usually constructed of malapais rock moved by wagon and placed by hand, or in some instances logs laid side by side. Rails were laid on "green" ponderosa pine railroad ties, which often twisted as a result of frost heaving and tore the tracks out of the ground.

Some of the men who hired out to place the rock on that roadbed came from the Great Lakes states, some from the South. Many of them were men up from Mexico or their sons and grandsons. The payroll for 1895 listed Canera, Guiterrez, Chavez, Montoya, Montano, two Rodriguezes and four Garcias.

As the line approached the Rogers Lake basin, the bed was mounded earth. Across the lake itself it was founded on a four-foot-high causeway of piled rocks. In spring when the lake was flooded, the embankment was barely above water.

Usually there were ten to twelve miles of sidings and spurs, the length of track depending on how much had been taken up behind advancing logging crews. Two were run up the drainage on the west side of Woody Mountain, between the mountain and the lake. [See frontispiece map.] The main line through Rogers Lake, into which those temporary spurs fed, was narrow gauge. Ties were untreated pine.

Daily log trains, running out empty, kept camp supplied, and men rode them back and forth. A water train ran out on the track to camp every morning, returning empty in the afternoon. Dirt wagon roads were often impassable, especially early in the season; the railroad was the only connection loggers had with town.

The line hummed with activity for twenty-five years. Hunters, ranchers, politicians, representatives of other firms—all used logging trains in preference to the primitive roads. Ranch supplies were delivered and unloaded at designated places. Families from town rode out for a day to visit relatives working in the camps. Company policy was that "any neighbor or traveler...was to have any hospitality we could extend to them"; neighbors and travelers took advantage.

Now and then livestock were struck and killed or injured by the logging trains, although T.A. advised the operators to try to avoid it, if only because of the danger of a wreck. He was scrupulous about compensating ranchers for losses.

> I am dropping you a line to say that the boys reported sometime ago killing two of your cows and another young animal and I thought that this was rubbing it in on you pretty heavy and wanted to say to you that we want to pay for these animals and sometime when you are around call in and we will settle up.

The Riordans had troubles in every direction, and they dealt with them doggedly. In 1887 the Atlantic and Pacific had complained that the Flagstaff company operated with too casual an attitude toward its timber contract. Loggers went wherever they wanted to, the railroad charged, cutting the choice trees and reporting they had taken everything of value, but leaving trees that could have been marketed, some of them rotting on the ground. In the early 1890s the railroad canceled the previous agreement and negotiated a third one, and the trees continued to come down until, inevitably, the Riordans got around to logging on Woody Mountain and ran into a morass of controversy.

National politics, often heated, were entangled in the story. The Riordans had bought timber rights on all those sections that Congress had given to the A&P, as well as rights to cut trees from land controlled by several large Eastern-owned cattle operations. Their company finally owned all available timber on the railroad line between Kansas City and Los Angeles, with a monopoly on the Colorado Plateau. That gave the sons of an Irish immigrant sizeable wealth and influence.

The Flagstaff mill had barely begun to saw when a new-born conservation movement entered the picture and inflamed tempers all around. As early as the 1870s, about the time the American Forestry Association was organized, Arizonans had appealed for some kind of federal regulation of lumbering. Carl Shurz, Secretary of the Interior, termed historical logging practice "wanton, barbarous, disgraceful vandalism"—strong words about a prosperous business. In 1881 a Division of Forestry had been established in the Department of Agriculture under vague mandate and small budget, but by 1882 when the Flagstaff sawmill was established, slopes around Prescott had been cut over, and the *Prescott Courier* warned that timber famine was no longer a remote contingency.

There had been houses to build and cookstoves to fuel; national per capita consumption of timber products was approaching 155 cubic feet. The growing citrus industry in California needed crates for shipping oranges. United Verde had used thousands of timbers down in its mines at Jerome, approximately ten million board feet of timber in one two-year period. Those were all legitimate uses, but the effect on forests had been staggering.

Matt Riordan had spoken in favor of regulation of Arizona's forests, in order, he said, to "perpetuate our forest conditions for the benefit of future generations in the territory," and he made a plea for government protection. [He held timber rights on the railroad's sections; his company stood to benefit from government withdrawal of the others from use by competition.] But the words "perpetuate our forest conditions" signaled a basic difference of outlook between the Riordan brothers and the new Sierra Club.

John Muir, one of the founders of the club in 1892, was making effective use of his own rhetoric.

> Much is said on questions of this kind about "the greatest good for the greatest number"...but the greatest number is too often found to be number one. It is never the greatest number in the common meaning of the term that make the greatest noise and stir on questions mixed with money...Let right, commendable industry be fostered...but as to these Goths and Vandals of the wilderness, who are spreading black death in the fairest woods God ever made, let the government up and at 'em.

In 1891 Congress passed legislation that gave the President power to establish forest reserves and withdraw them from public entry. Permits were authorized for cutting trees on public domain; the Interior Department was given power to monitor, manage and conserve. That was language aimed directly at the pockets of everyone involved with logging, as far as they were concerned.

As part of the effort to protect natural resources, President McKinley moved to set aside in north central Arizona the San Francisco Mountain Forest Reserve, containing more than three million acres of the even-numbered sections, which the railroad did not own, removing them from unrestricted exploitation by private concerns. The mayor of Flagstaff called it a "fiendish piece of business." The *Williams News* said it was "an evil deed." The *Gem* headlined: "Our Citizens Are Red Hot—An Outrage That Affects the Homes and Property of the Farmers and Stockmen of Northern Arizona." Using terms like "injustice"..."wicked"... "diabolical scheme," it indulged in flaming protest:

> Little did our people believe that the government would take away their prospects for an honest living to make a few petty offices or places for unworthy men.

There was federal reserve land anyway, and it was on even-numbered mile-square sections. Except for homestead and school grants, odd-numbered sections remained the property of the Atlantic and Pacific. On an odd-numbered section, Woody Mountain was still owned, as much as a mountain more than a million years old could be, by a railroad, which soon changed its name to the Santa Fe and Pacific. [The Atlantic and Pacific became a subsidiary of the Santa Fe in 1880 and went into receivership during the 1890s depression; it became a part of the Atchison, Topeka and Santa Fe in 1902.]

Everyone concerned with the nation's forests agreed that public domain was running out. Muir and his preservers wanted to save the remaining trees; conservers with an eye toward future harvests wanted to use them more wisely; businessmen wanted to cut all of them that were worth sawing. No one could escape

Flagstaff men worked in the mill yard for AL&T, which was responsible for more
workmen in Flagstaff's growing population than any other employer.
AHS–Pioneer Museum

From Cherry Hill, hikers could look across town to smoke from the sawmill
and Woody Mountain in the distance.
AHS–Pioneer Museum

the close of the pioneer epoch. The old, unregulated society was changing, and Flagstaff, in the middle of Arizona Territory, was about due for attention from some idealists in Washington.

The Forest Service was still in the future. The Secretary of the Interior had delegated authority for administering forests to the Commissioner of the General Land Office, leaving Bernard Fernow, Chief of Forestry over at the Department of Agriculture, unable to accomplish much beyond education of the public. He resigned, and Gifford Pinchot was appointed Chief Forester. Determined to "get forestry from the books into the woods," he hadn't much power either. With a staff of only two foresters and a tree scientist, he joked that to take on the supervision of the nation's forests was a lot like embarking on a new Children's Crusade. To make things even more tense, there was talk of removing forest protection from politics by giving the job to the Army.

The odd–even nature of the San Francisco Mountains Reserve had been a serious problem for everybody. Lumber companies could not log efficiently by cutting to the borders of one railroad section and then jumping across federal land to the next one. The United States was unable to administer the forest by scientific principles because the hopscotch patches were managed differently. Ranchers could not graze sheep or cattle on alternate sections unless they built fences, which would have cost more than they could have justified in a region where it required more than one hundred acres to graze one cow for a year—not to mention the question of resulting effective enclosure of public property.

Nobody was happy with the arrangement. Even the railroad was willing to talk about relinquishing its odd-numbered sections in exchange for land elsewhere. And that was a possible solution. That act which had created National Forest Reserves had authorized the railroads to reconvey their lands within the National Forests to the federal government.

Therefore, when the T.R. Roosevelt administration decided to consolidate most of the sections around Flagstaff into one reserve, it gathered back into its arms land formerly granted to the railroads. T.A. discussed it on paper with officials of the Santa Fe.

> ...we have naturally recognized that the consolidation of the forest reserve will work an injury to Flagstaff and Coconino County, and consequently to us; that the development of the town and county will be retarded thereby; that our taxes and expenses will be increased and our local business decreased...In this part of the country...we are all opposed to it.

National political opinion was against them, and the consolidation was completed. The Santa Fe contested some reconveyance parcels, but it left no paperwork indicating that it minded giving up Woody Mountain. That section was relinquished without protest, and the mountain—except for the quarter section that Black and Vail had bought from John Woody—was returned to federal ownership, where it remained.

❦

Matt Riordan resigned from the logging company late in the 1890s, and his younger brothers bought his stock. There was a second name change to Arizona Lumber and Timber Company, shortened locally to a breezy AL&T. T.A. Riordan, who had already come into Woody Mountain's story when he was in charge of operations at Rogers Lake, became company president.

In the reconveyance of railroad land to the United States, saw-timber on them was not included in the deal. Around Flagstaff that meant the Riordans, who had a long-standing purchase agreement with the old A&P, could go on "harvesting." From the time of the act, all the land AL&T logged was subject to federal regulation, but the Riordan brothers had paid for rights to cut the trees.

Confrontation was bound to occur. It pitted T.A. Riordan, president of a large company and grantee of the Santa Fe Railroad, against the Department of the Interior in the person of Fred Breen, Supervisor of the San Francisco Mountain Forest Reserve.

Breen had been a newspaperman in Illinois from the age of eighteen. He applied for a position in the new government agency, and in August of 1898, when he was twenty-nine years old, he received a letter from the commissioner of the General Land Office in Washington telling him that he had been assigned to duty in the Prescott Forest Reserve.

Several years later Breen described his introduction to Flagstaff for the *Sun*.

> I didn't get to Prescott—not on that trip. At Lamy Junction, N.M., Supt. John D. Benedict met me and waved me and my collar box back onto the train saying: "Hell and another forest reserve has been created at Flagstaff."
>
> It was the famous San Francisco Mountains Forest Reserve, created August 19, 1898. It was a vast affair covering over three million acres, but a checkerboard with every odd-numbered section belonging to the Santa Fe railway company. It was also spotted with homesteads, pre-emption claims, university and school sections.
>
> On a fine sunshiny morning—Sept. 5, 1898, to be exact—we stepped off at the old dee-pot and got the first glimpse of old Railroad Avenue in all its old pioneer glory, hitch-racks, cow-punchers and all. It was a fine day and there was a committee of sheep-men to meet us, not the committee that we had been given to believe might be present for a sort of an executive session....
>
> The *Williams News*, in a very objectionable article [had said that the] best methods to adopt in retaliation against the government was "to hang these U. S. tree agents to the trees they had come to save."

Flagstaff residents, John Woody among them, came to know Breen as "a humorous sort of man." His charm and wit eased him through the initial tension, and he got down to work. Before long he was complaining, after his own fashion, about any number of things.

The Land Office Commissioner had assigned rangers to the reserves and tried to develop a forest management program. As usual, chaos was a fact of life.

Fred Breen was ten years younger and a good deal shorter than T.A. Riordan
AHS–Pioneer Museum

There were few forestry professionals, and many of the new rangers in the field were political appointees; many had tuberculosis and wanted to move west and get well. They were described by disgruntled supervisors as

> ...cowboys, prospectors, bar keepers, professional gamblers, farmers, lumbermen, sheepherders, gunmen, ex-soldiers and what not, leavened with a sprinkling of university graduates, clerks, clergymen, carpenters, and "lungers."

Breen protested that four of his rangers had been sent west for their health and had no experience in the forest or riding a horse and were "delicate in appearance...incapacitated for the work by lung trouble." He wanted to establish a practical plan of management, but he was continually frustrated by colossal responsibilities and lack of authority to make decisions.

He stated his feelings in a letter to the Commissioner:

> Since I have been compelled to be a land lawyer and special agent for the Department, I am wondering what kind of a job I'll be jobbed with next...I am slightly fatigued from jumping from a timber expert job to law, and from law to an expert stockman, then into experting mineral lands. If I could only have a couple Indian Reservations, a railroad, the itch, and a Waterbury watch to take care of, I really think I would be properly supplied with a few small matters to interest me now and then.

Money was a constant problem. Out of their salary his men were expected to maintain two to six horses and pack animals.

> The U.S. land office division felt they should be liberal with me and allowed five rangers at $50 per month to cover the 3,000,000 acres of a rather interrupted country where the boys claimed "ya hadda climb fer water 'n' dig for wood."...Each ranger had to "eat and sleep himself" and his horse or horses on $50 per month...How they lived on the salary and made good I don't know yet. But they did dissipate all advance sentiment against all such government agents in this section of the country at that time.

Most of the forestry professionals were in the East, and Western businessmen were often inclined to keep on doing things in a way they were accustomed to. They tended to be scornful of "these $50 rangers." (T.A. Riordan's monthly salary in 1904 was more than ten times that amount.) It was a volatile situation of new ideals and old habits with high feelings on both sides. Arguments about AL&T's prior contract rights came into it within two years, just in time for logging on Woody Mountain. The resulting struggle—political, financial, and environmental—touched the fate of a mountain that everybody suddenly cared a lot about after centuries of quiet obscurity.

The story of that harvest unfolded slowly through thousands of pages of AL&T correspondence, preserved in cheerful disorder among personal notes and orders and friendly contacts which T.A. dictated after he walked into the office in the morning. Letters to government officials were followed by price lists sent to prospective customers, and then there he was ordering new razors or writing off to Marshall Field in Chicago for stockings for his daughters and wallpaper for his house or placing orders to a book company for five novels by Joseph Conrad and a copy of Thoreau's *Walden*.

Among his letters were clues to controversy he was embroiled in during the removal of trees from Woody Mountain. Years later, when all the principals were long since gone, those letters were the only record of what had been at the time a heated issue. AL&T even preserved a few messages from Fred Breen and enough of one side to suggest the other. Both men felt much imposed upon by circumstances. Neither enjoyed it much.

From the beginning of logging in eighteenth century Maine, American lumberjacks had resented government restrictions, sometimes with violent results. But the Riordans were, according to people who knew them, agreeable men not given to angry behavior, and they seemed to have tried to avoid trouble. Early on a note had gone out of the office:

> Every person employed by this company is strictly forbidden to cut any timber
> on Government land under any circumstances whatever. Immediate dismissal
> from the service of the Company will follow any known violation of this order
> and the person or persons so transgressing shall be held liable for all the
> consequences of their own acts.

In March of 1901, T.A. wrote to Breen to request "the number of each...section belonging to the government." Breen furnished the information and repeated it in 1903. Among seventy-nine others west of town, he listed the legal description of Woody Mountain and warned, "All cutting on [former] railroad sections must be done under government rules...operations on any of said sections without compliance with government rules makes you liable under the provisions of your contract."

By 1903, Breen and the Riordans were engaged in a frequent exchange of letters. Breen was a Republican, Riordan a Democrat. Flagstaff took politics seriously enough for that to be an important difference. But in the small paired communities of Flagstaff and Mill Town separated only by the railroad tracks they saw each other often, ran into each other on the street, and apparently enjoyed jokes and teasing.

> Dear Sir:
>
> The description of lands upon which the AL&T Co., are to cut timber under
> rules provided by the Government was received by me as per your agreement,
> but being near sighted I can read it.
>
> If you will kindly take your feet off the radiator and did it up, all right, if
> not, you won't need a radiator when I see you again.
>
> Very Respectfully,
> F.S. Breen
> Forest Supervisor

But there were also formal exchanges. In October of 1903, Breen warned the Riordans about carelessness: "...tops have been fallen across the line onto these government sections and left where fallen. This is a direct violation of reserve law and constitutes a trespass." T.A. responded courteously and then sent a memo to Ed McGonigle, his superintendent of logging:

> We have just received word from Forest Supervisor Breen, stating that the Department has complained about our trespassing on their lands and felling trees over the lines between us onto their lands, and they say that we must remove these tree tops at once. We will arrange to do this ... Please nail this letter up in your office for reference.

The year of the consolidation of railroad lands into the Reserve and the resulting regulation was the year the logging company began to extend its tracks around Woody Mountain and down through Rogers Lake. Two years later, after new contracts had been signed between all parties, it cut the trees on the mountain.[4]

In a letter dated April 21, 1904, to James Vail, who, with George Black, had purchased the quarter section on the northwest side from John Woody three years earlier, T.A. requested passage across their land. Access on the northeast would have been made difficult by the deepening fault, and sections two and four on either side were not part of the railroad contract. It would also seem that while he was at it, Riordan offered to buy timber on Vail's parcel.

> I wrote you about a month ago regarding removal of your fence and sale of timber on section 3, township 20, range 6, but haven't had any reply. I saw Hicklin yesterday and he has just moved to this section and expects to begin cutting on it soon and we are now cutting some piling. It will be necessary to remove most of the fence and it ought to be done now very soon. Please let me know how soon you can conveniently arrange to do this and if you have reached any decision about the timber.

The lumberjack of the 1880s had had few restrictions on the trees he cut. He had operated on a clear-cut basis, toppling everything that looked as if it might have commercial purpose, and he hadn't bothered about avoiding young trees in the process. Sometimes a whole tree had been felled, a log taken out, and the rest abandoned. Trees in the way had been cut and left to decay. There was no thought for regeneration of the forest or for leaving trees to provide the seed for it.

The *Sun*, reporting the consolidation of local forest land into a Reserve, said, "The government will formulate rules for cutting timber." Early in 1902 a conference had been arranged between (a) William Dermont, of Saginaw–Manistee in Williams, and T.A. Riordan—who were both afraid that strict rules would threaten their clearcut operations and invalidate their contracts for timber on former railroad sections; (b) the Santa Fe—which was interested in realizing the full value of

---

4 People farther east were meeting at St. Louis at the fair that year, where the hamburger and the ice cream cone were introduced to an enthusiastic public.

the trees on land which it had relinquished; (c) the Reserve men—who were supposed to save the forest.

Riordan was apprehensive about federal regulation of logging. In a letter in December of 1903 he wrote to William Dermont:

> I have just learned that of late you have been operating cutting your timber under government supervision, and as we are contemplating the same thing we would like to have your opinion of how the thing works. Do the Government fellows harass you in any way in cutting your timber, and do they make you leave any timber of value for seed trees, etc., or delay you waiting to have the trees marked? Any information on this subject that you can consistently give us will be greatly appreciated and considered confidential, if you prefer it.

There was an urgency in Riordan's letterbook for that year. He wanted to get contract changes arranged with the railroad before he had to sign with the Interior Department, and time was running out. Several times he wrote to the Land Commissioner of the Santa Fe trying to keep matters clear.

> I enclose for your information copy of letter just received from Forest Supervisor Breen...I presume that the Government's action is based on the idea that the proposed change in the timber contract between your company and ours has been consummated ...Please hurry the matter and let us know at once how soon you expect to close it. One of us perhaps could go east if necessary to hurry the matter.

The agreement finally arranged between AL&T and the Santa Fe Railroad was entered with the Coconino County Recorder in 1903 and filed in the county courthouse. There were twelve provisions.

1. All trees to be cut were to be marked first by the government. No unmarked tree was to be cut.
2. Marked trees could be left standing if lumbermen decided to leave them.
3. Young trees less than eleven inches when measured eighteen inches above the ground were to be left in the forest.
4. Loggers were to leave on each acre two seed trees above 14 inches to serve for the regeneration of the forest.
5. A few small trees could be cut for such logging purposes as skid poles.
6. Waste was to be avoided.
7. Trimmed tops were to be moved far enough away from standing timber to prevent injury to them when the tops were burned.
8. Loggers were to take precautions against fire and to work with the government to extinguish any fires which started.
9. The government was to have access to former railroad sections for administrative purposes.
10. The government was not to be held liable for injury to timber by fire.
11. Logging was to be under the supervision of a forest officer.
12. Appeal from decisions of forest officers was to be referred to a committee of three disinterested persons.

T.A. Riordan was forty-five years old in 1904.
Riordan State Historical Park

His loggers felled the big pines with cross-cut saws.
AHS–Pioneer Museum

When late in December of 1903, the company agreed with the local Reserve on a set of regulations for logging on former railroad lands, the rules were identical to those the company had signed with the Santa Fe.[5] AL&T was required to apply for a permit to log the timber it had purchased earlier from the railroad. A ranger was then to select and mark trees to be cut. Although the agreement with the Reserve had not yet been signed, T.A. promptly informed his logging bosses that they were to proceed to work under it immediately. He cautioned them:

> These rules have to be obeyed to the letter and from the start in good faith. We want to cooperate in every way with the Government in this work, and you will have all men under you instructed as it is important to strictly obey these rules and work in harmony with the forest reserve policy.

In January of 1904 the agreement with the government was signed and Riordan wrote again to the Land Commissioner of the Santa Fe:

> ...the only difference between our cutting before the rules and since is that now in felling the trees we aim to keep the tops away from the young trees and now we leave seed trees. There are really I think enough seed trees left on the ground under our old cutting.

As things worked out, disposal of tops was to be an issue for years, and the question of adequate seed trees was to generate reams of paperwork concerning proper interpretation of paragraph 4 of the agreement:

> The right to retain two seed trees on each acre above fourteen inches in diameter shall be reserved to the government, when necessary for the good of the forest. Such trees shall be chosen from individuals unsound or otherwise undesirable for lumber.

Woody Mountain was logged during that summer, after the agreement was signed. It would have required 960 large pines to be left for seed on the part not privately owned. When logging moved away from the mountain, only sixty-four seed trees remained on the federal quarters, approximately one for each seven and one half acres. The whole top was stripped bare; the south side was shaved as if it had been cut with a razor.

Why? The contract seemed clear enough to everybody, and T.A. stated repeatedly that he did not want to violate it. But misunderstanding lurked in the simplest language, legal or otherwise, especially when the rules were new. The neighborhood of Woody Mountain became a focus of the whole regulation issue as the combatants thrashed it out and came to an arrangement that worked. It was as if they had put their fingers on the map and said, "We'll begin the fight here."

Signatures on the 1904 papers were barely dry before disagreements about seed trees developed between Riordan and Breen, with the Santa Fe a collateral party.

---

5 Eighty years later a surviving copy of those rules was found in a carton of miscellaneous and forgotten papers in the Riordan house.

T.A. felt that he was the victim of surprise government action. He interpreted the contract with the Santa Fe he had signed the previous winter and paragraph four in the agreement with the government as allowing him to take all trees that were sound and usable for lumber, whether that provided seed trees or not. It was right there in writing. His correspondence left no doubt that he understood that the rule applied on Woody Mountain. In several exchanges with Breen he was specific about "excepting only the NW 1/4 of Section 3"; both applications and reports listed the section as included within government jurisdiction. He proceeded with logging under his understanding that he was entitled, by the contract he had signed, to take all trees that were fit for sawing, but the government didn't see it that way. The first thing he knew, rangers were claiming some of the trees he had bought from the railroad and refusing him permission to cut them.

Only a few days after the papers had been signed, T.A. wrote to the First Vice President of the railroad about the financial damage:

> In view of the fact that the Government employees are in some instances marking [for seed stock] trees which are valuable for lumber, we felt that there should be a clause in the agreement which should protect us in the stumpage value of such trees.

He protested to Breen what he considered violation of paragraph four in the written contract, and Breen answered that the Interior Department understood the rule to mean that where it was impossible to find unmerchantable trees to leave for seed, sound ones had to be left. In growing agitation, Riordan wrote to the Commissioner of the General Land Office in Washington, setting out his position:

> We have begun work under these rules in good faith and our policy is to work in harmony with the Department and do all in our power to conserve the timber of this forest, and believe that the interests of the Department and our own are nearly identical. For this reason we agreed with the Santa Fe RR Co. to work under these rules and without remuneration. We relinquished our ownership in all timber 11" in diameter and under, and have agreed where it is necessary for the good of the forest to leave two seed trees to the acre sized 14" in diameter, such trees to be chosen from individuals unsound and otherwise undesirable for lumber...However, the question has just come up, between the forest supervisor and ourselves about interpreting paragraph 4 where the Department might want to mark some seed trees 14" and over in diameter and where unmerchantable trees could not be found for this purpose. In such a case the forest supervisor contends that he would of necessity be compelled to leave sound seed trees...We are paying the stumpage value of all trees above 11 inches in diameter desireable for lumber on the lands included in our contract to the AT&SF R'y Co., and would not knowingly have agreed to pay for anything that we could not cut...We have written assurance that "we were not to be expected to reserve trees for seed purposes that would be desireable for lumber," and that the rule in question would not be interpreted otherwise. Upon this written assurance we executed the contract. We will now therefore take the matter up with the Santa Fe and ask it to protect us against loss.

Breen also consulted with the General Land Office. In a stiff letter signed by the Land Office Commissioner, he was advised to tell Riordan he was under contract and would abide by it.

> ...you are instructed to call upon them and call their attention to the provisions of the rules and inform them that compliance with those provisions will be required, and that it must not be delayed beyond a reasonable time.
>
> It appears from your statement that they have all acted to a considerable extent in disregard of the rules they were instrumental in making, and they should be required to make answer without delay as to what course they now expect to take. Prompt report relative to this feature of these matters will be expected.

And there Breen was, caught between the Washington office and his friend in town.

T.A., struggling with the issue, often felt caught between bureaucrats in Washington and his own men in the forest. Not a deliberate scofflaw, he made frequent trips into the field (sometimes on horseback, sometimes in a buggy with a matched team, driving over "logs and rocks and anything that happens to be in the way") to check on men in actual charge on the ground. They were contractors, not employees, and it was in their interest to cut as much timber in any section as they could. The rangers charged that they were ignoring the new regulation whenever it was convenient to do so. Riordan's memos to them were sharp.

> I enclose copy of letter to Mr. Breen, which will explain itself. You see how embarrassing it is to us to have to take up these matters constantly with the Department, and we don't want to have this happen any more, so that you will please watch the matter close and see that of your own knowledge every man working for you understands all points in connection with what he may or may not cut. Don't let it be go-as-you-please. Be sure that they understand and stop getting us into such trouble.

Riordan assured Breen that if a contractor persisted in ignoring regulations, "we surely will not arrange with him for any more of this work." And he warned the offending men.

> Be sure to pay more strict attention to the Forest Rules, or I fear they may exercise the power which they undoubtedly have, and insist on our not permitting you to do any more work for us, as I learn they have done in many places where repeated failures to obey their rules have been practiced, whether through mistake or otherwise.

But the contractors, burdened with their own paperwork and all the details of camp, were often not present when actual logging was going on. As usual, unsupervised workmen did the job their own way. T.A. protested when he heard about it: "The fact of your men cutting a seed tree the other day within two hours after it was marked, and then claiming that they had no knowledge of this, looks bad, no matter what the cause was."

Riordan's letters to Breen were courteous and conciliatory.

> I regret to state that we have just discovered that some of the tie and stull makers
> have cut a few trees over the line on reserve land. The men that made this
> mistake are Americans and there seems to be no excuse for their blunder...We are
> very sorry that the thing occurred and will renew our efforts to prevent any
> further mistakes of the kind.

"The men who made this mistake are Americans," he said. AL&T logging crews included Swedes, Macedonians, Austrians and Mexicans, who did not speak English and could not understand their orders without translation. T.A. emphasized to his logging bosses that everyone should be made aware of the regulations:

> I should think the best way to have them all understand would be to have all the
> men at each camp assembled and then explain these rules to them, using an
> interpreter where necessary.

Nor was Riordan an office man who cared nothing about the area. He was destroying scenery for miles around, to the distress of some of the local people, but that didn't seem to him incompatible with an old-fashioned sense of civic responsibility. Deeply involved with his community and concerned that its development be what he thought intelligent, he wanted "to see the right thing happen." A good part of the property which became Northern Arizona University was his quiet and personal gift, and he proposed to the Santa Fe an agreement that would provide public recreation for his neighbors.

> I was considering purchasing [land] to turn over to the Town of Flagstaff, for a
> race track, ball grounds, fair grounds, etc. I will say that if your company would
> turn over this land to me that I would make improvements such as a good fence,
> fixing up the track, and other necessary work to put it in fair shape, expending for
> this about $2000 and then when the Town Council would close the few streets
> that run through the land and give assurance that they would care for the place
> and keep it permanently for the use of the people, I would in turn deed it over to
> the town for this purpose.

An exuberant outdoorsman who liked "to be outside in the air," hunting, fishing, picnicking, just plain riding around the country, he loved northern Arizona. He wrote to his delegate in Congress to inquire about stocking Lake Mary with Black Bass, to the Bureau of Biological Survey about getting rid of the prairie dogs which made hazards for horsemen in Mill Town. He imported cottontail rabbits for his yard and a Jersey cow for his barn and squirrels for the forest.

> to Lannom at Camp One: I am sending out to you by the morning train a pair of
> red squirrels that I just received from a Los Angeles dealer. I wish you would
> turn them loose at the camp but first warn all the boys not to shoot them as we
> would like to see if they will mix with the native breed.

He was not an absentee exploiter but a resident who spent all of his adult life in Arizona. It would have not been in his nature to allow any detail of the life, much less the work, around him to go unnoticed: his correspondence attested that little went on in either Mill Town or Flagstaff that he didn't care about. Therefore, although some of the fault in the virtual clear-cutting of Woody Mountain may have belonged to the loggers themselves and to their supervisors, Riordan too was responsible for the number of trees that were taken. He thought he had every right—he had paid for them.

He seemed prepared to cooperate with the policies of the Reserve, but he insisted that he was entitled to what he had bought from the railroad. It was a shame, he said, to leave large, straight, useful trees in the forest instead of snow-bent or fire-scarred or lightning-struck pines that would do just as well for regeneration. In addition, he was convinced that he was leaving plenty of seed trees, that ponderosa pine would regenerate easily without much interval.

Again and again he returned to that provision "unsound or otherwise undesirable for lumber," and the longer the controversy went on, the more he was sure he was being treated unfairly. In December he wrote to Dermont of the Saginaw & Manistee in Williams:

> ...I enclose all the correspondence we have had with the department on the
> subject...You will see from the secretary's letter of April 18th what a raw and
> unfair interpretation he has put on paragraph 4. I remember I was very wrathy
> when I read this letter and we determined we would not stand it, but would
> resort to our rights as given in the arbitration clause, and when I came to read
> this over I was still more worked up, when I found that the arbitration clause did
> not really mean anything.

Indignant, he appealed to a law firm in Washington, D.C., and was advised that the government actions were "something altogether different from what is required of you by the rules..." The attorney said:

> I also note your statement that you do not wish to have any conflict with the
> government officials, but you must have conflicts with them whenever they seek
> to impose upon you some rule that you have not agreed to accept.

Riordan wrote to the Commissioner of the General Land Office and received a formal letter from the Secretary of the Interior with the ruling that seed trees sound or unsound were to be retained when necessary for the good of the forest. In response he reminded the government that when the rules had been in negotiation, the fourth paragraph had read, "Such trees shall be chosen from individuals unsound or otherwise undesirable for lumber *where practicable*," that he had objected to the phrase, and that the last two words had been dropped from the contract which he had signed.

Nearly a year later, he was convinced that things were getting worse and that the government men had thought up a new outrage; they were charging him for open parks and meadows where no trees were growing. He reported to Dermont:

I have just returned from a couple of days in the woods, after investigating the new method of marking seed trees adopted by the Forestry Department in our work several weeks ago, and I find that they are measuring each acre on the section and reserving two trees for every acre, and for every acre that has no trees, they take two extra trees where they find them, to make up for it.

He had seen for himself what he considered outright violations.

I went with the government men doing the work for quite a while...I find that in a bunch of trees, where they could easily select one that was crooked or had a burnt butt, or with some other defect that would make it undesirable for lumber, but still was alive and growing and would bear seed, they would not mark such a tree, but would take one right by it, that probably contained from two to six times as much lumber and was in every way perfect. They did this right along ...There is no doubt that such trees belong to us and that they have no right to take them, in accordance with the Rule...It does seem that we should be able to stop them from taking lumber that does not belong to them.

Finally, in October of 1905, while Breen was out of town, Riordan took the issue to Gifford Pinchot, Chief Forester in the Department of Agriculture in Washington.

...We wish to call your attention to the matter in the hope that you will take such steps as will stop further violations of this Rule and compensate us for the large amount of our timber taken in this way...

I have no doubt that there are many places where trees in accordance with the Rules cannot be had, where they are needed for seed trees; but we cannot afford to furnish such trees free. Our contribution to the Forestry Reserve policy we think was sufficiently liberal in the single item of relinquishing, without compensation, all the timber under 11" in diameter...

We are glad the Forest Reserve is here, and we want to help in every way to conform to its Rules and to help out in the work; but we cannot afford to furnish any of our own timber for seed trees. Therefore, we respectfully ask that you take such steps as will immediately stop any further infringement of this Rule.

Riordan soon received "prompt and fair consideration" from Pinchot, who agreed with his position, saying:

Forest Supervisor Breen has received instructions that two seed trees—non-merchantable if possible—are to be left on every acre logged; that is, on every timbered acre, and not 1280 trees to the section regardless of parks or open country. Where it is absolutely essential for the good of the forest that merchantable seed trees be left, I will see that these are estimated and the loss made good to you from merchantable timber of forest reserve land—thousand for thousand feet—in such a locality as to enable you to log it during your present operation.

Riordan assumed that nothing further needed to be done except for Pinchot to notify the local office. One month later he was back to protesting to Breen that rangers were marking all immature pines above eleven inches. "This is contrary to the Rule," he wrote, "and we cannot agree to it."

Finally they all worked out a compromise which provided that seed trees were to be marked by rangers "assisted by an agent of the company," who were to meet each morning at Camp One before they started work, and it was agreed that after the exact count of seed trees was made, the company was to be reimbursed by the government for all merchantable timber over fourteen inches left in the field. As late as 1910 T.A. was still trading missives with the government about seed trees, but the issue settled into an Exchange Account, balanced on the basis of board feet, that both sides seemed to find workable if everybody paid attention constantly. The compromise came far too late to save the old forest on Woody Mountain.

The implication of it all was that most of the large trees on the mountain in the spring of 1904 were straight and true, excellent commercial timber, and that, while the officials were arguing, loggers took them. The sixty-four that remained after the crews had finished were usually crooked or forked at the top: most of the old pines on the mountain eighty years later, except for those on the north side, had one defect or another.

Then there was the question of size. Government regulations specified that no trees under eleven inches in diameter were to be taken, but logging crews apparently left few black-jack (immature, black-barked) trees; eighty years later they would have been huge and yellow-barked, obvious in the forest. Given first-growth conditions of that time, there may have been few trees under eleven inches on the mountain.

The permissible size of trees had been part of the contract that Riordan had signed, and he intended to stand by it. He apologized to Breen for infringement.

> The cutting was done by a new crew...each man and crew has been personally instructed by McKiernan, and all that possibly can be done was said to this crew, to avoid possible mistakes of the kind in the future. We have got after the matter as hard as possible and hope that we will be able to succeed in stopping these mistakes altogether.

But the loggers had been accustomed to cutting all the small trees they wanted, to use for such purposes as loading or skidding poles, and they kept right on doing it, despite the anger of men in offices in town.

> ...I have seen Supervisor Breen, and he was pretty mad about this cutting. I told him I could not understand it...If it is a fact that you have placed us in this position again, after all the cautioning and repeated assurances we made to the forest officials that it would not happen again, it shows that you are not attending to the work and are unfitted to handle this job...we simply won't stand it any longer.

Riordan notified men in the forest that anyone cutting timber under size would pay five dollars for each tree cut and lose his job. He also tried, right from the beginning but without much success, to train loggers to avoid dropping large trees on small ones. He allowed no excuses for slope or wind.

Loggers left on the mountain only pines that were unfit for timber,
like these snow-bent trees.

...I also noticed that the log cutters were falling most of the trees up hill and in many instances the tops landed among small unmarked trees, whereas in most cases there was an open space if the trees had been fallen in the opposite direction. The sawyers claimed that on account of the strong wind today it was difficult to control them, but I think that, while this is true to some extent, with a little extra labor and caution they could have avoided a good deal of it...

Constant haggling finally became so annoying that Riordan appointed his Supervisor, William A. Lannom, "in charge of looking after the observation of the rules of the Forestry Department." By then Woody Mountain had been cut.

Work on the mountain started in May and was finished in October. However, in August T.A. made a formal request to the Interior Department that seed trees on Section 3 be marked; in October Breen informed him that such notice must be given through the Santa Fe; in December T.A. requested the railroad to notify the department that he desired the section to be marked for cutting. Action out-ran paperwork more than once in those years [and in years thereafter]. Riordan was probably trying, as he had with the logging railroad through Rogers Lake, to keep paperwork even with regulations.

AL&T records did not specify the number of trees taken from Woody Mountain, but they did leave clues. In logging practice of the time, there were somewhere around four hundred board feet in a large tree. Before government regulation, lumbering men "high-graded"—took only thirty-two foot logs from the bottoms of trees where there were no branches and left the upper third on the ground.

Camp One out by Rogers Lake cut 16,086,535 board feet of lumber in 1904, 285,280 feet of it left banked in the woods at the end of the season. The conjecture: in 1904 the men in Camp One cut upwards of forty thousand trees using six-foot cross-cut saws.

There had been "some hard logging" on Woody Mountain, T.A. wrote, "...all fairly short haul and down hill." The Footage Record book for 1904 listed logs and board feet taken from the mountain.

	Logs	Board feet
May	937	159,492
June	5650	846,690
July	442	37,206
August	1623	258,130
September	1246	152,805
October	21	2,027

Those numbers meant that somewhere between three thousand and four thousand trees were cut down and hauled away, most of them 100 feet tall and several hundred years old.

AL&T papers confirmed Forest Service records that the hard-working sawyers left only sixty-four large trees for seed instead of the 960 that had been agreed upon. There was an average of only 138 board feet in each of them; probably the seed trees were no more than twelve to sixteen inches in diameter, just above the size limit.

Logging was difficult, dirty, dangerous and poorly paid, and it required tough, skilled people to do it right. Noise and sweat were part of the mountain that year, noise and confusion and men hardened by hard work. Wages for sawyers, limbers, skidding teamsters, truck teamsters, and truck loaders were two dollars a day including board, double the pay for loggers in the South, but about the same of that in the Pacific Northwest.

Good sawyers could drop a tree where they wanted it, uphill if possible to lessen the chance of breakage, and do it with an ax and two-handled saw, precisely, so that the trunk would not splinter or block other trees. The new rangers respected their skill. "Those loggers knew their stuff," they remembered in later years. "Some of them, middle-aged even, could almost keep up with a modern chain saw. It was hard work, but it was a profession. No matter whatcha got, it's always hard work."

It was up to skidding teams to get the logs off the mountain. With hooks and chains they snaked trimmed sections down the slope to the nearest skid road, shouting, swearing at the straining horses. It was widely believed in those years that strong men used strong language.

Other men and horses took the logs to the rail line on wooden runners, skids, on which they were piled as high as the horses could handle. During those years the company owned as many as 125 head of logging horses and mules, large and healthy animals, "weighing not less than fourteen hundred pounds, not under three nor over seven years in age, well built, perfect, sound and true and well broken."

When they were not in use, the horses were held in the company pasture, on a site where, three-fourths of a century later, University Plaza shopping center would be built. In winter when operations in the forest closed, many were sent down into the Verde Valley to rest and graze. The company bought from three to five hundred tons of hay to feed those that were kept on near the mill. During the season, hay bought from local farmers was a major logging expense.

Hard-muscled horses strained to get the trees, as much of them as the mill wanted, off the mountain that summer and skidded them to the rail spur. After that, machines took over the job of moving them into town, where machines cut them into lumber.

Slash—tops and branches and such material—left by loggers in the states around the Great Lakes had helped to spread nineteenth century fires that had killed

After the initial crash, loggers cut off limbs and bucked the fallen pine
into whatever length was most needed at the mill.
AHS–Pioneer Museum

In 1906 the company bought a steam-powered machine, a "Clyde Skidder," which could
pull logs in from half a mile away from a 7/8-inch rope, but trees from Woody Mountain
were moved by horses.
Special Collections and Archives Department, Cline Library, Northern Arizona University

At the rail line logs were lifted onto flat cars by a steam powered A-frame loader fitted
with center tongs, swivel pulleys, and $5/8$-inch cable.
AHS–Pioneer Museum

The same method was used for Camp One, which was a temporary location. The cabins
had cables attached to each corner so that log loaders could pick them up, load them
on flat cars, and take them to a new location when logging moved on.
AHS–Pioneer Museum

hundreds of people. With the advantage of hindsight, the new rules which the Forest Reserves had negotiated with Arizona logging companies required removal of discarded tops. Riordan was not convinced that it would do much to retard fires, but he reminded his contractors to abide by the regulations, although it meant an extra expense.

He arranged with a local man named Gandee to follow logging crews with his team and clear slash for seventy-five dollars per section, which proved to be an underestimate.

> ...we have just cleared one (section) that cost us $259, and there is still one or two days' work to be done on it. To-day I have just closed a contract with one of our own men to whom we furnish horses free, to clear seven of our old sections, which will clean up all our own back work, paying him for the seven sections $1585.

It was one more headache. Logging slash remained on Woody Mountain for at least a year after the trees were gone, causing so much trouble that T.A. decided, "We now think it will be better for all concerned to clear the tops immediately after the loggers."

Dealing with people who were telling him what to do was maddening in the midst of serious problems concerning safety of the men. Accidents—fatal, mutilating or just plain disabling—were frequent in the forest. In the years prior to 1930, logging was more dangerous than war: more men in proportion to the numbers involved were killed nationally cutting trees for market than exchanging bullets.

Dropping a solid giant several hundred years old was spectacular, but it did not produce the real injuries. Limbers and buckers with their two-man saws were in constant danger from logs, parted from the trunk, which rolled suddenly on the down-hill man. From the beginning the pages of the *Sun* were full of matter-of-fact reports of accidents near Flagstaff. In July of 1885 a man named Burpee Brown, knocking bunk blocks from under a load on a wagon, unsettled the stack. Before he could get out of the way, a log rolled off onto logs on the ground, catching the top of his head between them, crushing his skull.

Skulls were fractured, fingers were severed, chests were crushed under logging wheels or between railroad cars. In 1901 the *Sun* had described an accident which, because it involved no death, was considered fortunately minor: a man named Frank Taylor had been skidding and was caught between two rolling logs. His left knee and calf were badly bruised.

The work was dangerous even when moving logs was not involved. Riordan sent a letter to Illinois in October of 1905:

> About nine o'clock this morning word was received in our office here from our Logging Camp in the timber that when the boys were starting to work at the Camp this morning, Alfred Milan got on one of the work horses to ride to the woods and that the horse in some way got scared, jumping around and throwing

Milan and, it is believed, killing him instantly, as he struck on the back of his head. In some way his leg got caught in one of the traces and the horse ran away through the woods for about a mile, dragging the young man ... . We understand that the face and other parts of the body were badly disfigured by the unfortunate accident, but we will have all that is possible done to have it prepared in proper shape and give him a decent burial.

All the boys in the Camp were very greatly distressed by the accident, as a great number of them witnessed it, but it happened so quickly that none of them could give any help, as they tried to catch the horse, but failed. It appears that the young man only came to work in the camp, a stranger, a couple of weeks ago, and no one knew anything about him, but a memorandum book found in his pocket gave your address, and we suppose you are probably the boy's father. We hope to hear from you by telegram to-night and, if not, the funeral will probably take place, as above stated. Assuring you of our deep sympathy in this unfortunate matter ...

For years it was assumed that logging was dangerous, that was all, and they couldn't get around it. The steep slopes of Woody Mountain would have been unusually perilous for moving enormous logs: any object out of control could have rolled quite a distance before stopping. However, if there were accidents on the mountain, there were no reports of them in the *Sun*, which probably meant that there was nothing serious, since the *Sun*, in the time-honored journalistic manner of providing reader interest, seemed to be ready with any news that was gruesome.

AL&T maintained on Riordan Road its own Mercy Hospital for injured employees, a large home converted to an operating room, two private rooms, and an eight bed ward. A man injured on Woody Mountain would have been taken into town on the logging train and treated at the hospital. From 1889 AL&T had collected a medical fee of a dollar a month from each employee and paid it into a hospital fund for "the Physician in charge, for medicine furnished to, and medical treatment of, sick and injured employees."

If employees needed more than hospital treatment, it was arranged; the Riordans tried to care for their own. That sort of thing later came to be criticized as "paternalism" which robbed workers of independence in lieu of the dignity of a living wage. At the time it was seen as proper responsibility of an honorable employer for his people. T.A.'s wife, Caroline, of the same opinion, regularly visited and cared for sick employees and trained her granddaughters to that sense of responsibility. "We weren't asked whether we wanted to," they said. "There wasn't any question about it. We were expected to go with her."

T.A.'s correspondence was full of letters in regard to the welfare of the men who worked for him. A memo was sent out to Camp One about August Hill ...

... the Finlander who came in sick from camp a few days ago [and] has been having hemorrhages and had a severe one last night, and if this continues it is likely to kill him. He is pretty weak today and I was talking with him a while ago and he asked me to see if there were any Finlanders here and if so he wanted one to see him, and to write a letter for him in Finnish to his brother. I have not yet found one here but Hill says that Charley Hayman in the grading Camp is a Finlander and a friend, and if he is there now please send him in at once so he can attend to the matter.

In 1895 T.A. wrote several times to Thomas Devine in Kansas City about an injury to his son, also Thomas (the father of a local boy who later became film actor Andy Devine.) The younger Thomas Devine had been braking on a logging train which ran into a small burnt culvert. In the pile up "Tom's foot in some way got caught and broke his left leg just above the ankle, and the bones in the ankle were badly crushed."

AL&T doctors waited a week and decided they could not save the foot, which they amputated eight inches below the knee. Every day or so T.A. wrote to Tom's father, offering reassurance about the attention of a priest, and Tom's friends (who brought beer to him when he asked for it), and the doctors, who were confident "it would take a miracle to kill him now." Within a few weeks, Tom Devine was put aboard an eastbound train for Kansas to be fitted for an artificial leg at company expense. When he returned to Flagstaff, he was given a job firing on the logging trains.

Despite the danger, logging went on. Snow made it a seasonal job for most of the men. Crews went into the forests in May, as soon as the ground was dry, and usually wrapped up work at the end of November. Then many working people moved south to lower, warmer country for the winter, especially men who had lived as bachelors in isolated logging camps all summer and had no home in town.

Now and then the company gave a man permission to take his wife out to live in camp.

> ... under the circumstances I think it might be all right to let Harry Carter when he is married take his wife to Camp One. We want to be fair about such matters and if we can keep the families down to the present number with this one added there won't be much trouble but we will have to try and confine it to not exceed three or four families at the most.

One-room cabins were provided by AL&T and rented to the men for fifty cents a month, occupancy of two to a cabin. They were little more than shacks to keep weather off, but they were referred to as "homes out in the woods." Windows in the cabins were small, but men at the camp spent few daylight hours in them. A working day in the forest lasted twelve hours; the eight-hour day and the five-day week had not yet even been talked of, and vacation with pay was forty years in the future.

The ladies of Flagstaff's Presbyterian Church, concerned about what seemed lives of unrelieved monotony (and lack of beneficent influence), offered to furnish books to the men at Camp One, but Riordan answered:

Camp One served logging south of Rogers Lake.
AHS–Pioneer Museum

Sanitation was rudimentary. Pigs were sent out on the train
to roam at large around the cabins and eat the garbage.
AHS–Pioneer Museum

I have found that they really read very little. After the day's work they generally go to bed about eight o'clock and are up and at work again early in the morning. Under these circumstances I hardly think that it would be worth while.

I appreciate the offer just the same and wish to thank the ladies of your Society and yourself for your kindly offer.

Food in camp was prepared under difficult conditions, and the men grumbled about it, but the Riordans were proud of it. Cooks Charley Nelson and Shorty Flynn were paid $2.50, 50 cents a day more than the loggers to whom they served food. The company tried to provide ample board, ordering beef from Babbitt's hundreds of pounds at a time and from local suppliers such produce as

potatoes	.............4 tons	beets	...........300 pounds
cabbage	.........1500 pounds	onions	...........500 pounds
carrots	..........500 pounds	parsnips	.........300 pounds

T.A. thought it was good business to feed the men well.

We are paying very high wages in our logging camps, much higher than any place that I know of, and our grub is the best that can be had, and is much better than that at any other camps that I have seen. We are glad to be able to feed and pay the men well, and, in return, hope to get the very best possible results.

In November, with Thanksgiving coming up, Camp One ordered turkeys by the hundreds of pounds and "enough cranberries to furnish sauce for this quantity." In 1911 that was 126 pounds of turkey and 50 quarts of cranberries, although Riordan observed: "This looks like a lot of cranberries...but I suppose they boil down a good deal, and whatever is about the right amount, we will want it."

T.A. strictly forbade the sale of alcohol in Mill Town. However, in May of 1904 he wrote to Secundo Guasti, Los Angeles:

Please ship me by freight the following order of good quality:

1 5-gal. keg sherry wine
1 5-gal. keg angelica
1 5-gal. keg claret

I want this as an experiment with a lot of Macedonian and Austrian tie makers that work for one of our tie contractors in the timber. They seem to require something to drink and have been buying a very poor article of whiskey, and I thought if they would substitute good wine it would be far cheaper and more wholesome, so I want to experiment with this. I thought the sherry might be best but by getting a variety they could decide themselves which was the best. Send bill to me direct.

There was no shortage of applicants for jobs. Company correspondence was full of letters in response to inquiries about work from all over the country.

to California—

We are full-handed in all departments and in fact there is a number of surplus men in this vicinity. We have few clerical positions and while we can nearly always find room for one more in our regular crew of laboring men, still at the present time we have perhaps a dozen clerks working at common labor in the hope of something better turning up and with very slim prospects.

to Minnesota—

There is nothing that we could offer you at the present time except common labor around our lumber yard or mills at from $1.75 up per day, according to ability.

to Michigan—

We have plenty of men, but a good workman can always find something to do here. We can make no promises. You will have to take your chances, as we have letters like yours almost daily.

When Woody Mountain was cut, the crews had a wet time of it. In March of 1903, men from the logging camps had been in Flagstaff on holiday because of mud in the forests. In April a *Sun* headline was: "River de Flag Slops All Over." In August the *Sun* described heavy rain that produced "a torrent eight feet high and several hundred feet wide through Fort Valley." The flood was audible for half an hour before it rushed into the Rio de Flag above town at 7:30 in the evening. A horseman pounded in at a run to warn of approaching disaster, but residents had heard the sound and scrambled to high ground. The crest arrived at ten o'clock that night.

In October of 1903, Riordan had written several letters citing wet weather as the reason for slow deliveries.

We had a very bad winter, but we then thought that the spring would be mild. Then we had a very bad spring and we thought that the summer could give us good operating conditions. But we have had the worst summer that we have had in years. It is still raining...with the result that the ground is so soft that our logging operations have ceased and we will have to shut down sawing until the ground is dry, and meanwhile we will put our force to work changing our logging track, in the hope of reaching drier ground.

The next year was worse. Weather bureau records listed 1904 as the wettest year between 1898 and 1911 by 18.36 inches. Through the winter a drought made dry range and empty water holes, and in March the *Sun* said, "Rain storms are reported on the coast with heavy winds. It is hoped that this vicinity gets its share of the rain—we have all the wind needed." The drought was broken by storms later in the month.

By the first of April, rain was so heavy that the Rio de Flag broke over its banks again and flooded the area between Leroux and Sitgreaves in the depression north of the tracks to a depth in the lowest places of fifteen feet. Water was reported more than a foot deep in the basement of the Weatherford Hotel. South of the tracks was solid mud. The *Sun* reminded its readers that in 1888 water where the Weatherford stood had been deep enough to swim a horse.

There were three inches of rain in July and floods again in early August. There was rain every day in August, 9.77 inches for the month. The *Sun* termed it "excessive" and reported that streets in Flagstaff were in "bad condition." In the forests and logging camps, mud slowed work enough to cause a layoff of the night force at the mill. The roadbed through Rogers Lake was often under water. Despite the rain, Woody Mountain was denuded by early October, with only slash and stumps left tangled on the muddy slopes and, here and there, a few small trees and sixty-four crooked big ones.

Riordan loggers, like an invading army, had needed only six months to turn a peaceful mountain into wreckage. It would have been automatic from the environmental point of view eighty years later to label them all, in the office or in the field, as classic destroyers of natural resources in the pursuit of money. Within a few decades they wrought such a change in the forest around the Peaks that five hundred years would not restore it to what it had been when Antione Leroux first came exploring. Eighty years later that seemed immoral.

But a concept of natural ethics was new in the time of the Riordan brothers. Fairness would require that they be judged by their own values, and that of their community, and the Riordans thought of themselves and were considered by Flagstaff as responsible citizens who made significant and beneficial contributions.

AL&T correspondence was full of letters that proved T.A.'s efforts to treat people well, even better than the standards of his time.

October 31, 1894, [only fourteen years after George and Matt Black had traveled to Flagstaff by night for fear of Apaches]—To Whom It May Concern: The bearer of this letter, B'goo-et-tin, a Navajo Indian, is going on a trip to hunt some stray horses, together with a number of other Navajos, and asks me for a letter stating this fact which he can present to any of our citizens that they may aid him in finding his lost property. I have known this Indian for a long time and believe him to be a very worthy person, and from all the information I can gather, he is a very reliable and honest man, and I believe that any courtesy extended to him or information given him will be appreciated by him as it will also be by, Yours Very Truly, T.A. Riordan

October 29, 1903—My dear Mr. Wells: I have your letter of the 26th in regard to lumber for children's hospital. As we have no institution of this character here to permit us to assist it, and as we consider it an obligation to be of help in any such worthy cause, we wish you would say to Mrs. Wells that it will give us great pleasure to furnish the institution with which she is connected lumber to the extent of a full carload without cost.

December 23, 1903—J.E. Sargent, Camp #1: Replying to your letter of the 22nd in which you say you have four or five hundred dollars saved by economy and perseverance, and which you wish to loan to this company: will say that we can allow you 7% on this money, giving note for one year. We pay only 6% to those outside of our employees, but have decided on giving 7% to our own

T.A. posed with a snowball on his bowler, Caroline standing at—
that is, *below* his shoulder.
Riordan State Historical Park

In 1905 Mike's son, Arthur, was photographed with some of the longest legs in town,
those of his uncle and Ambrosio Armijo and Bear Howard,
who was eighty-eight years old by then.
Riordan State Historical Park

workmen as a special inducement to have them save their earnings instead of wasting the same in dissipation or otherwise, until such time as they can invest it in something worthwhile...so that in time they may be able to get into some business for themselves or own their own homes. Wishing you a Merry Christmas.

People in trouble appealed to him constantly for assistance, and they got it. In 1899, saying that the matter had not been mentioned to anyone, he applied to the general manager of the Santa Fe for its cooperation in the case of the wife of one of his employees, "a colored man, M.F. Taylor." Mrs. Taylor had "been in miserable health for the past year...her chances for recovery or even for living very long very slim." T.A. had promised to pay for her medical treatment in a hospital in San Diego, and he requested that the railroad give him reduced rates, perhaps half fare, for her transportation and that of her husband and a nurse to accompany them.

In 1905 Mrs. Gus Backman, wife of a house painter in town, asked for help to take her crippled eleven-year-old boy to a hospital in Los Angeles for treatment of a spinal ailment which he had suffered since he was two. T.A. made arrangements for the hospital, paid railroad fare and notified a company representative in Los Angeles:

> Kindly request them to have an ambulance meet #1 on Friday on [the Backmans'] arrival—Any expense for ambulance, braces, or other special treatment that may be needed in the case, I will be glad to take care of.

When pioneers Ambrosio Armijo and his father wanted to lease grazing land from the Santa Fe, Riordan wrote to the Land Commissioner in Kansas requesting that a section be made available to them for ten years, describing them as "among the very best citizens we have in this Territory...of limited means...good and deserving people."

T.A. stood almost a head taller than most other men in town. His wife, Caroline, was a diminutive lady who held her own against the over-sized employer of hundreds of men. Millard Kuhn, driver of T.A.'s car in early years of the twentieth century, liked to tell a story about her.

> ...on this trip we went down to Phoenix...and come back...by Roosevelt Dam. We got up around the Payson area and Mr. T.A. was quite a collector of rocks...so we stopped in a crick bottom down there in a wash and we pick up some rocks and ...he puts 'em in between the seats...He says, "Millard, Mrs. Riordan's going to give us hell when we get home with these rocks." And she sure enough did! She was about half his size, just a very small woman...I remember her comin' out and seein' those rocks...and she says, "Millard! What did you let him do that for? You knew better than that!"

T.A. and his brother organized a Society for the Study of John Milton's Poems and decided to give their community a higher tone by changing the name of the street that connected it to Flagstaff from "Mill Town" to "Milton Road" in honor of the author of *Paradise Lost*, defending the name when the Flagstaff City Council wanted to change it to Prescott Avenue.

While the Riordans were at it, they changed the name of the whole town to Milton. It was not legally a part of Flagstaff.

> Of course we are practically in Flagstaff as Milton, as we call our little settlement, is closer to the Town hall than a good part of the rest of the town of Flagstaff. The town has always wanted us to come within the corporation of Flagstaff, but we have objected for private reasons, that we wanted to miss the possibility of annoyance by city ordinances regarding our operations, especially maintaining saw dust piles, and the way we handle our material. Aside from this though we are practically the same as if within the town limits, having the city water service right to our plant and a better fire organization than the town itself has, and of course the town and ourselves help each other whenever there is any fire...Milton of course is not an incorporated municipality and all the property in it is owned by this company.

Flagstaff thought well of T.A. In 1988 old-timers agreed that he had been among Flagstaff's leading citizens in both influence and the esteem of his neighbors. Lillian Hall, Coconino County Treasurer in later years, was as a child occasionally a guest of the Riordan grandchildren in T.A.'s home. She said he spoke with a heavy Irish accent when she was there, looking up at him.

> He'd tell us stories in a rollicking accent...I don't know how it was when he was with adults, but when he was with children, he really r-r-r-rolled it. And then he did a little jig.

He was a big man. His orders to Marshall Field in Chicago indicated that he wore "Indianapolis" collars, size $16^3/4$. But he danced Irish jigs for admiring children, and that brogue was for their benefit: he was born in Chicago.

His letter books contained correspondence with Flagstaff children.

> My dear Clarence: Some of the boys have just told me that you were the boy that flagged our train the other day when the bridge burned out in the Rock Cut on Section 6 and I want to thank you for your thoughtfulness and your courtesy in performing this neighborly act and to assure you that your action is very greatly appreciated by the officers of this Company and all the boys connected with it especially the train boys. It is a fine thing to see nowadays that anybody has some thought for the life or property of a neighbor and it is especially good to see it in a young boy ... You did the right thing and left nothing to chance. As a little token of our appreciation Mr. Dutton has selected a watch and chain for you this day which he will give you at the first opportunity.

> My Dear Friend Caroline: I was very glad to receive your nice letter, and to know that you are so happy in your little home with your rabbits, goats and birds...I think we can fix you out with the lumber to fix up the place for the rabbits...

T.A.'s granddaughters—Rita, Mary, and Helen—called him Timmie or, when they were very young, "Yaya," because he would come into the house and announce himself with a loud "Ya!" His daughter, Mary, and her three children spent their summers in Flagstaff at his home, while his son-in-law went back and forth to Los Angeles by train to attend to business. "Oh, we used to have fun," his granddaughter Mary reminisced near the end of the twentieth century. "I wish my children could have known him. They would have had so much fun."

He took them dove hunting and let them caddie when he played golf on the course he maintained. Now and then he'd say, "Let's go out to the logging camp for mutton stew." But he often warned them that camp food would taste better if they didn't look at the cook. Helen said later, "It was true. I looked at the cook once and I couldn't eat the food."

There were trips, two or three families together, to Second Mesa to the Hopi Snake Dance when the journey by buggy took two days and hay was carried for the horses. There was "a lot of going out around the mountain" and stopping to visit people along the way. He always took Ry-Krisp on those outings and picnics because someone had told him it was good for him, but he never ate any of it himself.

They drove down to Oak Creek Canyon in later years, when the road was so primitive that you needed to back up and ease around the curves. "You'd get in the car," Mary remembered, and he'd "boom out," such songs as "Louisa" and "The Man on the Flying Trapeze" surrounded by children in the back seat.

For most of his life, T.A. used horses, preferring one "with a good walking gait and one with a good loping gait, and of course gentle enough to get on him without having to be an acrobat." He didn't learn to operate an automobile himself until he was eighty, taught to do so by his driver, Ernie Yost, although all of the girls could drive before they were twelve. Mary rode with him often:

"Timmie, you're still in second."

"Oh, by George, so I am."

She considered herself lucky to have had such a grandfather. "He was a dear...a kindly, charitable soul..thoughtful...a good Christian gentleman...unimpressed with money or wealth in famous people."

> He loved life, and Northern Arizona was certainly heaven to him. You could put him down almost anywhere in that area and the first thing he would tell you was where there was water. He had ridden all over by either horse back or buckboard and knew that water was of first importance.

He "loved people around the country," talked and joked with them, asked sheepmen about the feed.

He was no more a bad man than anyone else: logging on Woody Mountain was a story with no villains. T.A. Riordan turned out a useful product. The lumberjacks needed jobs. Forest Reserve officials in Washington were people fighting an unfamiliar crusade, struggling to form new policy with no precedent as guide. Fred Breen was a cheerful fellow who wanted an interesting career, caught between two strong forces and trying to follow orders, receiving more trouble than money.

In 1908 he decided to resign and wrote to federal headquarters a letter of explanation.

> You see, since my salary is less now than it was about ten years ago, after two "promotions" in the Forest Service, I rather felt that some one was afflicted with the ingrowing salary habit, and it wouldn't be long before my creditors would notice my financial lassitude.
>
> I had received a number of letters approving my work, or at least I took it that way, and I understand my inspectors give me a fairly good recommend, and recommend for promotion, so I do not fully understand just where my promotion caught loco-motor ataxia.
>
> I guess I must have misunderstood, but I thought there was a good possibility of an increase up to $28 a year if one could deliver the goods—folks in the Service intimated that I could. I thought I had a bright future before me, but the durned bright future has certainly side-stepped me along the route somewhere, and must be loafing behind.
>
> I was not promoted in 1905, when the transfer was made from the Land Office. I didn't think much about it at the time one way or the other, but when I did get promoted in 1906, I was glad I wasn't "promoted" in 1905. I was getting $2371 until my promotion came along in 1906 which gave me $2200. I know it was a promotion, for my commission from the Secretary of the Interior said so right square in the middle of it.
>
> In 1907 I was raised to $2300; so I am still shy of some of the good old salary that I started with away back in September 1898, with only the San Francisco Mts. National Forest to handle. The fellows on the Black Mesa and Grand Canyon forests were getting the same amount that I got but when they fell by the wayside I fell heir to their territory and their troubles, but none of the pesos they were getting.
>
> I fully acknowledge your right to assay the intellects of us wood chucks, and raise, drop or fire; and it is up to me to raise, fall or git, as the case may be. As I didn't get the first (raise), but the second (fall), I thought I had better take the third myself.
>
> One can get a heap more money out of a little old band of sheep, or something of that kind, even if his intellect does not average over 30%, with a whole lot less trouble, and retain some friends; but with this job, the general public just naturally gets cross if you try to enforce the rules, and if you don't enforce the rules then you get cross; so the Supervisor gets the double cross whatever happens, and has no pension at the end of the game, to sorter ease down his old age when the pace is too fast.
>
> While I think a good deal of forestry, I realize that a man can't live in this country and lay up anything, unless he gets a good salary; consequently believe I should go out and make money while I can.

Fred Breen's office at the newspaper was in front, looking out on the street.
AHS–Pioneer Museum

He married a pretty school teacher, Carolyn Austin.
AHS–Pioneer Museum

I feel slightly relieved at the prospect of seeing some other feller being accused of prejudice, ignorance, partiality, graft, ulterior motives, laziness, salary grabbing and other such innocent pastimes.

Ten years is a long time to wrangle over the same ground and troubles, then to look ahead to a heap more of it in larger varieties and quantities, which will assay a heap stronger strain both mentally and financially, and it certainly aggrivates one's desire to sorter seggrigate.

I am glad there will be a bright young man here March 15, to separate me and my troubles and let me wander away to new fields, where neither the bleat of the sheep, the height of a stump, the brand of a cow, nor even a special privilege, can hop up and fill me with fright or woe.

Breen did not leave Flagstaff. He purchased the *Sun* and the *Gem* and merged them in 1911. George Hochderffer called him "...the man that makes the *Sun* shine."

For ten years he was a lieutenant colonel in Flagstaff's Company I of the Arizona National Guard, which earned him the nickname of "Colonel" in local circles. And he was elected to both the Arizona Territorial and State legislatures.

For 30 years Billie Yost—daughter-in-law of Riordan's yard foreman, wife of his driver—was on the staff of the *Coconino Sun*. She remembered the Breen residence:

> ...the Colonel Breen home [was] on W. Birch (a beautiful two story house) that was torn down a few years ago to make room for Wheeler Park [in front of the city library]. Thanks to someone's foresight they left the beautiful trees that Col. Breen had planted all around his home.

A small, "curious, talkative" girl named Mary Moormann knew Breen when she was a teen-ager. Later, when she was Mary Sweitzer and he had been gone for fifty-five years, her face lit with a quick smile when his name was mentioned. She had liked him. He was a nice man, she said, neat and short and rotund as he grew older. He had no children of his own, but he could take time to stop and talk with her. In her smile of memory, over half a century later, was an enviable measure of the man.

Well, loggers came and went, and the trees were gone, into town to the sawmill. After that their destination could have been in several directions. Sandy Donahue bought 22,600 lath in August for use in his Commercial Hotel. The Santa Fe ordered pilings and five thousand railroad ties eight feet long to be delivered each week until further notice. United Verde Copper Company wanted thirty cars of stulls for use down in the mines in Jerome. The trees from Woody Mountain may have gone for mouldings for the Albuquerque hospital; that order came in April. In Spring and Summer of 1904 AL&T had orders for cantaloupe, asparagus and apple crates from California Pine Box and Lumber Company.

The Riordan brothers' double house was joined by a room for recreation.
Riordan State Historical Park

T.A. did not want to command the head of the table,
so he had his men build one that made such seating impossible.
Riordan State Historical Park

Tim and Mike were building their fine new house at the end of Riordan Road in 1904, and it was a possibility that some of the trees from Woody Mountain went into it. Or maybe the distinctive dining room table in T.A.'s side of the house, fashioned of native pine by men at the mill, was Woody Mountain trees that didn't travel far.

Perhaps they served all those purposes: there were enough trees taken to make a good many things. Like the scarred old mountain, the silent pines had been caught up in human need and turned to human purpose. Eighty years later, some-where—in things that were built in 1904—parts of them, no doubt, could still be seen by people who knew where to look.

Change for one kind was change for all. Loggers erased from Woody Mountain the Abert squirrels that had been there for thousands of years. Their nests were gone with the trees, and so was the staple of their food. Without a canopy of pine branches they were exposed to predators. Chattering in protest, they fled the commotion down the slopes into uncut state-owned sections, range of other squirrels, and died there the next winter, probably, of exposure and starvation. Half a century would go past until there were new pines large enough to allow the return of a few.

It was different for Gambel oak, which was also a species of Western high country and companion of ponderosa pine. The Sitgreaves expedition had measured the oak and judged it to be at home in the forest around the Peaks where, unlike its brushy relatives in Colorado, it grew as tall as sixty feet.

With pine gone, the few oaks on the mountain had sunlight and moisture and room to spread. Shortly after the first pines dropped, new oaks sprouted in torn ground from the damaged roots of older trees. They grew rapidly, taking advantage of the sudden space. Fifty years later when a new forest of pines had overshadowed them and slowed their growth, acorns were plentiful enough to be a major food source for the returning squirrels.

Density of the ancient grasses, so important to stockmen, also increased on the disturbed slopes after the trees were gone, especially blue grama, which loved the sun. Those like native brome, which preferred shade, diminished. Evaporation of what little moisture Arizona provided was greater on the sunny ground after the trees were gone, and grass on Woody Mountain didn't grow as tall again as it once had, before the loggers came.

Chapter Five
Men of Business

1901–1980

Duane Miller, Coconino Cattle Company
Courtesy of Miller Brothers

The meadow at Woody Spring.

Water was always scarce in the West. From 1810 maps labeled everything west of the Missouri as "The Great American Desert," but the huge basin between the Divide and the Sierra was arid beyond Eastern imagination. People who settled Arizona joked about how dry the place was: some years, they said, you couldn't even spit.

Water determined human lives. There were no homes, no towns, no businesses without it. It meant life and wealth and power in the deserts, on the Colorado Plateau, everywhere in Arizona Territory. Location of the railroad line was determined by it—Flagstaff existed only because of springs draining the Peaks. On Woody Mountain competition for water was a complex web of laws and regulations and an ever-shifting line of people. Their part of the biography of the mountain was the story of the West touched at one illuminating point.

The land around the Peaks received twenty or so inches of precipitation in an average year, ample by Southwest standards, but most of it evaporated, was taken up by trees, or percolated into underground aquifers. Like the rest of the plateau, the area had streams that flowed only occasionally, after rainfall or snow melt. The two side-by-side vents that made Woody Spring—producing as much as five gallons of cold water a minute in a year of average rainfall—were not just valuable; they were essential to loggers and to cattle and sheep ranchers. Title to land around the spring passed quickly from one entrepreneur to another.

Or more precisely, title passed through a series of what was known in the press as "buccaneers of finance," opportunists with a gift for capitalist success in raw country. They were a colorful cast of characters, those owners of Woody Spring, and like many successful men in town, they had brothers or brothers-in-law. Some never lived anywhere near Flagstaff. Once they disagreed about who was to have control of the water, and twice they piped it somewhere else.

They had, in addition to brothers, another thing in common: they were businessmen, not cowboys. It was one more matter in which Woody Mountain was an example of the American West. Land around the Peaks quickly passed out of the hands of homesteaders and small owners like John Woody and into the possession of men who knew how to hold it, especially if it had water.

Laws about water in the states to the east from which most of the settlers came had been adopted from the English riparian system and were based on land ownership. They were decidedly inappropriate to the arid West, and people who could see beyond their own habits recognized that. For at least a decade before Flagstaff was founded, John Wesley Powell warned Eastern policy makers about the consequences of trying to impose on a dry country the customs formed in a wet one.

The Western system which finally evolved was based on use—prior use, beneficial use, *use.* The West was less concerned with who owned the land on which water was found or through which it flowed than with who had first used it and used it to good purpose. Water became public property; it was too precious to everybody for any of it to be wasted. A real Arizonan was made uncomfortable by the sight of water "runnin' loose."

A formal state code was developed, with provisions for outright appropriation of idle water, to insure that such a scarce resource would not be entirely under the control of a land owner who would not turn it to some need. The owner of a right to streams and lakes and springs and even canals had to use them in as many ways as possible or lose the right to them. Within five years unused water became public property, "up for grabs," the first person to appropriate it considered to have the better right.

There was a good deal more land than water, and it was easier to acquire. To people in the crowds of the East and to disappointed farmers in the Midwest, it looked as if northern Arizona was empty and unused, if they ignored a dozen tribes that were already there. After the Civil War they headed out like flocks of crows to claim it or buy it from someone who already had. John Woody's friend George Black and Black's brother-in-law, James Vail, were as aggressive as anyone else. With Vail often acting as lawyer for the partnership, they bought within the first decade land that would later form parts of Kachina Village and Mountainaire, land south of Lindberg Spring, land near what would be the Lake Mary store, land beyond Oak Creek Canyon.

In 1895 they purchased the DK Ranch out near Woody Mountain. The D stood for Dorsey, the K for Kelsey, both pioneer ranchers. C.W. Kelsey sold to Black and Vail "improvements, houses, corrals, water rights...on unsurveyed railroad land." The price was one dollar, which implied an unspecified swap of some kind. The DK brand, sold to George Black by the Kelsey Brothers that year, was similar to several other brands owned by Black and Vail.

There was no mention in county records of any land transfer in the sale by the Kelsey brothers. However, Black and Vail promptly began buying property all over the country southwest of town to give substance to the ranch. In 1901, with the logging railroad planned, they paid John Woody three hundred dollars for his spring and the north side of an old volcano, although the steep slope was of little use for grazing. That same year Ollie Barney sold to Black and Vail all cattle and horses marked and branded OLA; James Barney sold them all his cattle and horses. In 1903 George Black and his brother-in-law acquired from a homesteader the land on the north side of Rogers Lake for use as headquarters.[1]

The holdings of isolated bits and pieces that formed the DK covered an enormous stretch of forested land. George Black and James Vail, who had migrated to Flagstaff as young men with nothing much except ambition, had become prominent citizens within a couple of decades.

---

1 In autumn they drove their cattle to winter range in the Sycamore Basin down what came to be known as "Black and Vail Trail." The Taylor Brothers, Ben and John, also used it. One year, after the drive into the canyon, the Taylors returned to Flagstaff up the trail and reported they could see no cattle tracks because bears were so numerous in the wilderness that they had obliterated all other sign.

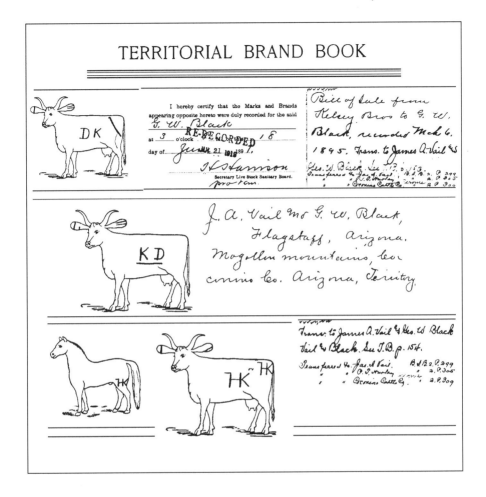

James Vail had arrived in Flagstaff at twenty-two, about the age at which Woody arrived and in the same year. He married George Black's sister, Mary, got involved in cattle, real estate, retail businesses, liquor, and "Gents' Furnishings" in the corner store of John Weatherford's hotel.

In Flagstaff tax records for 1897 Vail was listed as having real estate to the value of $9950 and personal property worth $2936, twice the amount listed for John Woody. For 1898, in addition to the usual horses, cattle, dairy cows, poultry, saddles and buggies, he was taxed for "stock goods, bar fixtures, a library, two musical instruments, a watch, jewelry, furniture, a safe and a bicycle."

He was a delegate to the Territorial Assembly, a member of the county Board of Supervisors and the Flagstaff city council, a stockholder in Citizens Bank,

Within the first five years James Vail had a saloon on the northwest corner of
Railroad Avenue and San Francisco.
AHS–Pioneer Museum

treasurer of the Coconino County Cattleman's Association. He was Somebody,
altogether a successful man who lived in what the *Sun* described as a "large splendid nine-room home with all the modern improvements [a bathroom] on an emi-
nence on north Leroux Street." It was his horses that Woody later drove to
California.

In a letter written to Flagstaff historian Platt Cline half a century later, his
niece, Mary Annetta Black, insisted that Vail was never called Jimmie.

> It was always Mr. Vail, Jim Vail, or James A. Vail. He was definitely not a
> "Jimmie" as he was over six feet tall and quite heavy.

He was a big man and a successful one, but he should have been more careful about Woody Spring. Although he and his brother-in-law had paid for it, they
didn't have title. The railroad did.

In the older volumes that recorded land transfers during Flagstaff's first
years, railroads occurred again and again—in evidence of the Congressional land
grant after the Civil War—so often that a stamp was used to record railroad transactions on page after page. For a while there was a flurry of activity in the columns

Vail sat on a boulder at far right in an 1890s photograph
made at a Temperance Society picnic.
AHS–Pioneer Museum

that listed Woody Mountain: legal ownership of the section shifted among the
Atlantic and Pacific, the Santa Fe Development Company and the Santa Fe
Railroad in a corporate reorganization accompanied by a change of name. Paper
title to Section 3, T 20 North, R 6 East, Gila and Salt River Meridian, was held by
railroads, courtesy of the United States Congress.

In 1904 Black and Vail bought the quarter section on the north side of the
mountain a second time, from the Santa Fe, for five hundred dollars—two hundred dollars more than they had paid to John Woody three years before. It was a
fair price: market value of land around Flagstaff that year was two to four dollars an
acre, according to the *Sun*. But they bought the land twice, and the reason was lost
through the years.

The Bureau of Land Management preserved no record of activity in Woody's
name for the section. There was no evidence in county legal records of a court suit
to establish clear title. Back in 1897 T.A. Riordan had specifically excepted the
quarter section in a contract he signed with the Santa Fe to log on railroad land,
indicating he recognized it was owned privately, but the Santa Fe preserved no
relative documents. Woody had filed properly on the quarter section south of
Lindberg Spring, but the Coconino County ledger recorded no claim by him in
Section 3. Yavapai County indices back to 1864 contained no reference to him for
property action of any kind for the valuable water and the land on Woody
Mountain.

Maybe he just didn't get around to it—it took him twelve years to register his brand. Perhaps he had been associated for so long and so openly with the mountain that he thought he didn't need to file a claim on it. In early territorial years many settlers did not file on the common law assumption that "possession was nine-tenths of the law."

Conflicting rules and customs surrounded Western land. The Homestead Act of 1862 was designed for farmers who would cultivate it. That principle was repeated in the Forest Homestead Act, which had as its stated purpose "to put the available farming land into the hands of farmers who will farm it and not to provide merely a stock headquarters for a cowman or sheepman." As a cattle grower, Woody would have been ineligible under that act: the slope of the mountain was far too precipitous for agriculture. Patent to land around Rogers Lake was applied for by ranchers who made an attempt to raise hay and potatoes, at least enough to satisfy homestead requirements, but Woody couldn't have managed even that on the rocky forested slopes of the mountain. Maybe he tried to file a homestead claim and was refused.

Or the omission could have been due to legal fog and confusion relating to the railroad. By mid-June of 1903 railroads had received from Congress somewhere around eight million acres, depending on who was doing the figuring, of public land in Arizona, extending in odd-numbered sections both north and south from the tracks—that is, from Flagstaff. More than half of the land had never even been surveyed (taxes were not levied on unsurveyed land), and nobody knew just where the boundaries were. Woody may not have known he was on land to which the railroad had title; it was possible no one in town knew at the time he sold it.

Chaos was an element of Western real estate, especially if it had any connection with railroads. Legal status of the railroad sections remained in question for years. Over a million acres of the railroad land grant had been pre-empted ahead of time by farmers, ranchers, and timber operators, and unclear titles were common. C.T. Rogers, for whom Rogers Lake was named, had lost his ranch near Williams in 1892 in a claim dispute with the railroad.

As if that weren't enough, the creation of forest reserves produced a series of claims, court action, appeals, repeals, and government judgments which impressed even the West. In the middle of it all, in 1901, Woody sold a quarter section on the mountain to his friends as if he thought he had a right to it. The sale was properly entered on county books, but Black and Vail had clear title to the land only after they had purchased it twice.

A few months later James Vail bought both the Woody Spring and the Rogers Lake parcels from his brother-in-law for one dollar. In a letter to Los Angeles, T.A. Riordan reported local gossip about the transaction:

> [George W. Black] has recently acquired the Parlor Saloon in Flagstaff, having succeeded James A. Vail in this business and we believe he has made considerable money. We understand that Mr. Vail paid Black some cash in addition to giving

deed and bill of sale to his saloon for the latter's interest in their joint cattle business. This is simply current talk and we are, therefore unable to state it as a fact.

Local talk was accurate: Mary Annetta Black confirmed it years later in a letter to Platt Cline.

> When my father and Mr. Vail, who had been in the cattle business together, dissolved partnership, my father accepted the saloon property as part payment for his share of the cattle. Mr. Vail took the cattle and my father the saloon.

By the time Vail took charge of the DK Ranch, cattle and sheep men had grazed their stock on the grasses of the future Coconino Forest for thirty years with no restrictions except what their own power could create. They had free, unregulated use of it for summer range, just as they did of all public domain. Most of them saw no reason to own land and allowed their animals to roam at large.

Water, always scarce in relation to land and resources, was a critical factor, of course; lack of access to water curtailed that "free use" to people who controlled the springs and water holes and therefore large tracts of adjacent land. But no outside agency placed a limit on the number of animals a stockman could drive onto the range, and most brought in as many as they could acquire. Ranching was a business, not an adventure.

By 1891 some Arizona stockmen were voicing fears that, if numbers of sheep and cattle continued to increase, the range would become overgrazed. Despite what some owners seemed to think, mistreated grasses could not recover year after year indefinitely: some species no longer grew in the state. Within the decade both the growing conservation movement and the National Livestock Association began agitating for some effective control of grazing practice on the public domain.

The resulting law startled the West by prohibiting grazing and all other commercial uses of the forests. It was largely ignored. Ranching, logging, and mining were woven into every aspect of western economy, and ranchers, loggers and miners continued to take what they wanted. With no specific provision for regulating or policing, livestock ranged as freely as before.

A second regulatory action in 1894 prohibited "the driving, feeding, grazing, pasturing or herding of cattle, sheep or other livestock" within any of the reserves. Western ranchers and their representatives reacted by bringing pressure to bear in appropriate places. In the words of Gifford Pinchot, at that time head of forestry in the Interior Department, "they raised the West in arms." In 1897 the Secretary of the Interior issued a ruling that pasturing livestock on public lands in forest reserves would not be interfered with so long as injury was not done to forest growth. And that was how things stood when James Vail took control of the DK Ranch, which included Woody Spring on the northwest side of Woody Mountain.

He was not sole owner for long. In issue after issue of the *Sun*, the story unfolded. In 1904 he was reported as having suffered a crushed ankle in a wagon accident.

George Black, wearing a dark jacket, stood behind the bar in the saloon he had acquired
from Vail. When Black retired and moved to California, he sold his Flagstaff interests for
more than a million dollars
AHS–Pioneer Museum

In January of 1906 there was an ominous entry: "James A. Vail is confined to his
home this week on account of pieces of bone working out of his leg which was broken several months ago and not yet healed." In February he was in Los Angeles to
"submit to another operation on his leg, which was broken last year."

And then, on April 7, 1906, the headline on the first page was:

TRAGIC DEATH

James A. Vail, Prominent Citizen and Pioneer of Flagstaff
Commits Suicide by Shooting Himself Through the Head

The death of James A. Vail, by suicide on Friday was a shock to his many
friends in Flagstaff, as well as elsewhere in the territory. For he had friends
wherever he was known.

The tragedy took place in the carriage house in the rear of his residence, a few
minutes before 12 o'clock in the morning. About 10 o'clock in the morning he
went to the hardware department of Babbitt Brothers, where he purchased a Colt
.45 caliber revolver, and a box of cartridges, and with that gun he committed the
act. The bullet entered just above the left temple and came out on the right side of
the head a little lower and near the ear, and death must have been instantaneous.
The shot was heard by a number of persons who rushed to the scene.

An inquest was held in the afternoon by Coroner Harrington...The jury
returned the following verdict: "We find the deceased to have [come to his death]
by a pistol shot in the left temple administered by his own hand during a temporary

James Vail was buried in Flagstaff's cemetery near the graves of two of his children.

attack of mental derangement brought on by worry over the injury to his leg about nine months ago, and that his death was the result of said pistol shot wound."

In June last Mr. Vail was thrown from a wagon, the team which he was driving running away, and his right leg was broken and crushed above the ankle. The injury did not heal rapidly and caused him considerable pain and worry for fear an amputation would be necessary. In January he went to Los Angeles for treatment and returned last week, having received but little benefit from the treatment received in the city and the fear that he would always be a cripple drove him to take his life.

Mr. Vail came to Flagstaff in 1882 and engaged in business in which he continued until about a year ago, when he disposed of it, giving his attention to the cattle business.at the time of his death he was one of the largest cattle owners in northern Arizona, owning, it is said, about 6000 head and numerous ranches. He was 45 years of age.

The *Sun* reported business houses closed during the funeral, which "was attended by a long concourse of sorrowing friends."

To acquire ranch holdings consisting at the time of his death of twelve thousand acres south and west of Flagstaff, Vail had gone into debt to a total of $111,783.51, an amount that would have seemed over-whelming to a crippled man in 1906.[2] Vail had died intestate, all his property in community status with his wife, Mary, age thirty-nine. Left with six children, the youngest only three, she looked with all that debt to be in an unenviable position.

However, she held property that was suddenly more scarce and valuable every day: land, leases, and water rights in a National Forest that was only one year old. New rules restricting grazing privileges on the summer forage among the pines surrounding Flagstaff made Mary Vail's ranch a highly desirable prospect for potential buyers. And it was for sale.

M rs. Vail's situation had been much improved by politics in Washington. Just after the turn of the century, Gifford Pinchot had convinced President Roosevelt that the forest reserve system should be transferred to the Bureau of Forestry, a division of the Department of Agriculture. His argument was that it was irrational that the government's trained foresters should be in Agriculture while public lands remained in the politically oriented Department of the Interior.

Logging regulation had been basically settled by the time the reserves were transferred from Interior to Agriculture, but grazing remained, Pinchot said, "far and away the bitterest issue of the time." It was regarded as the number-one problem facing the new agency. Pinchot, who had fought for the creation of the Forest Service, summarized the situation.

> Before the Forest Reserves came into our hands, all we could say to whoever controlled a forest, public or private, was "Please." That we said it to some effect was proved by the number of applications from timberland owners for forest working plans for millions of acres of their private lands...Before the transfer, we were limited to peaceful penetration. While many still regarded Forestry as pernicious nonsense, comparatively few people were sore at us because nobody was compelled to do as we said.
>
> After the transfer the situation was radically changed. While we could still say nothing but "Please" to private forest owners, on the national Forest Reserves we could say, and we did say, "Do this," and "Don't do that." We had the power, as we had the duty, to protect the Reserves for the use of the people, and that meant stepping on the toes of the biggest interests in the West. From that time on it was fight, fight, fight.

There were only 115 foresters with degrees from American colleges in the United States in 1905. Their average age was under thirty years. Attracted to Pinchot's "Children's Crusade" by the lure of "brave young dreams," and what

2 George Black alone held notes in the amount of $14,621 at interest of 12% and $7000 at 8%.

seemed a worthwhile adventure, they served under President Theodore Roosevelt, who believed the Executive to be the custodian of public welfare. New and untried in politics, they began the task of creating for the national forests a system of controlled grazing that would work.

It would all have been much easier if they had started with virgin range rather than land that had been stocked for decades and in places badly depleted of its grass. There were people who believed the solution was nothing short of an absolute ban on grazing. But Pinchot was a life-long politician: he joined in publicly denouncing big stockmen and at the same time sought and obtained their support, and the support of Roosevelt, for regulations that would control rather than prohibit. In a clever move, he brought in an Arizona stockman, Albert F. Potter of Holbrook, to be chief architect of Forest Service grazing policy.

A powerful weapon in that new policy of control was the establishment of permits which required fees. Pinchot expected to sell timber and considered the government was also in the business of selling grass. Loggers could not get public trees for the asking, he argued; neither should stockmen get grass. In 1905, he requested an opinion from the attorney general and was advised: "...you are authorized to make a reasonable charge in connection with the use and occupation of these forest reserves..." Western legislators reacted furiously to the idea and called on President Roosevelt to reverse the decision. Roosevelt, enthusiastic about grazing fees, refused to intervene.

Permits were issued for one year for a restricted number of stock on unit areas termed "allotments," the boundaries of which were based on physical features and quantity of forage. To prevent overgrazing after unusual weather, the total could be changed from one season to the next. Permits showed brands, maps of intended grazing areas, and the period owners were allowed to keep stock on the range, as well as the dates when cattle were to be moved and routes of travel across the reserve. Construction of fences and corrals of not more than one acre was allowed. The permittee was required to repair damage to roads and trails caused by stock and to fence springs and build water troughs.

That much alone spelled the end of the old free range for nomadic herders. Even more critical was a system of preference which tied the grazing privilege to base property, that is, to land ownership. It was an important distinction. The prime Class A permits went to small landowners within the forest, Class B to larger near-by owners, with an initial determination of "prior users" who were on the range at the time it was included in a national forest. Possession of watering tanks and springs was recognized, on the theory that ownership of large tracts of land meant nothing if water was not within easy traveling distance for herds. There wasn't much left over for newcomers.

Forest policy had been designed partly as an influence in favor of the small resident rancher who made his home on the forest. The "little man," they called him. For years homestead laws had opened public land in 160 acre parcels to his settlement. The new base property preference to small local stockmen was in keeping with the tradition of making land available to people of limited means. However, homesteads had a way of becoming part of empires, and grazing permits were tied to land. It was recognized immediately that the way to purchase grazing privileges on a national forest was to purchase the base property of an existing permit.

James Vail had been a prior user who had held leases on the reserve; Mary Vail was a property owner of land and of water sources within the forest. In the new situation ordered by Pinchot and his foresters, the debt-ridden widow had assets that attracted sharp attention from cattlemen who lived across the Verde Valley in the mining town of Jerome and in the burgeoning settlement of Phoenix down on the Salt River. Within a few weeks of Vail's funeral, they were actively bidding for the DK Ranch.

Vail died in early April. In May, Bill Cox and Walter Miller of Jerome and Pat Hurley of Phoenix were making sudden trips about the north country "in search of cattle." Cox, long-time rancher in the Verde Valley and trustee of the Jerome school board, drove a new team of mules from Jerome to Flagstaff on "a business trip." Hurley was in Jerome in June, "looking after his business interests."

Just four years earlier Patrick Hurley, prominent Phoenix cattleman and meat packer, had purchased a spring, pens, and slaughter house on the Bitter Creek mining claim near Jerome as well as the meat business of Ed Tovrea, former Jerome mayor.[3] The meat company was incorporated in September of 1902 to engage in "wholesale and retail meat, meat packing, slaughtering, buying, selling, and dealing...and acquiring property necessary for the carrying on of such business." William Cox was manager of the operation.

In June of 1906 the principals, with their meat company as a separate stockholder, suddenly incorporated as the Coconino Cattle Company, Pat Hurley president, for "raising, buying and selling of livestock and acquiring necessary property." Less than one week later the *Jerome News* reported that the Jerome Meat Company had paid $113,250 for the "ranches, cattle, etc. of Vail and Black of Flagstaff."

> Monday last the Jerome Meat Company, of this city, consisting of Walter C. Miller and W.H. Cox of Jerome and P.T. Hurley of Phoenix, purchased at auction in Flagstaff, the ranch holdings, forest reserve leases, range cattle, saddle horses, camp and range equipment and all paraphernalia used in connection therewith, belonging to the estate of Vail and Black [sic], paying therefor the sum of $113,250. The property consists of ranch holdings located between the Verde River and a point ten miles south of Flagstaff, consisting of 12,000 acres of patented land and certain possessory rights.

The purchase of "Vail cattle ranches, water rights, etc." was the first act of the new corporation. The DK brand passed to it with that sale, as did the north side of Woody Mountain. (After all claims against the estate were settled, Mary

3 Son of an immigrant Irish farmer, Hurley had arrived in Phoenix in 1881 at the age of twenty with three brothers and four dollars. Within two decades he had acquired a large ranch near Tempe and a meat packing business that pioneered cold-storage in Arizona and shipped to various places on the Southern Pacific line. The Jerome Meat Company, which he organized with Cox and Miller from Ed Tovrea's company, was a matter of expanding his operation.

Vail and her six children were left with a balance of $24,031 and fifteen lots in Flagstaff. Mrs. Vail died forty-one years later, at the age of eighty, in California.)

Pat Hurley and his brother John owned a majority of the shares issued by the new corporation. The Jerome Meat Company held a few and so did William Cox, designated as manager and authorized to "enter into any agreements with the Supervisor of the San Francisco Mountain Forest Reserve which he deemed in the best interest of the company." Miller and his brother and his brother-in-law had most of the rest of the shares. Miller was resident agent in Jerome.

Hurley was 47 years old that year; Cox was 44. Walter Miller was 34, younger than Cox and Hurley and holding less stock, but he had connections to balance Hurley's influence: he was nephew of what journalists described as the richest man in the United States and owner of the last private railway car in the country, Senator (thanks to a great deal of money spent in the right places) William Clark of Montana, owner and sole operator of the United Verde Copper Company. Walter Miller's father, T.F., was married to Clark's sister. As they used to say, "Walter's kinfolks helped him."

Walter Miller was to direct the fortunes of the DK Ranch and the use of Woody Spring for nearly thirty years. A frequent dealer in Jerome real estate, he was mayor in 1902, a member of the Miller Hose Company of the volunteer fire department, and half owner of a Franklin, Jerome's first automobile.

But he was junior in both age and experience to Pat Hurley, who was deeply involved in Arizona water controversy. One of the organizers of the Salt River Valley Water Users' Association, Hurley had filed a suit in 1905 on behalf of farmers and ranchers in the valley to determine their rights to Salt River water. He won the case with a decision affirming Arizona's legal principle of beneficial use of water, which was declared to be public property. For almost three decades Hurley controlled the company that owned the Woody Spring quarter section. He was in a position to know that, as public property, the water had to be used to be held.

After the purchase of the Vail estate, the Coconino Cattle Company promptly bought up more land, including 136 acres at Fry Lake and cattle interests owned by Little George Black. By 1921 it was a major landowner on winter range between Clarkdale and Sedona and on summer range among the pines southwest of Flagstaff. And that was home ground to Camp One of the Arizona Lumber and Timber Company. In no time at all the cattle company began to show up in T.A.'s correspondence.

> This letter is to again request you to call to the attention of your cowboys to be on the lookout for that milk cow of ours on your range. I would like to get her sometime this summer if they should locate her. I have had the hardest kind of luck to get hold of a good milk cow for the past two or three years. We had a couple of cows that seemed all right but something happened to them and half the time we are without milk...There seems to be a sort of hoodoo working on us in this line and I thought perhaps this cow we had on the range whose mother was a very fine satisfactory milk cow might turn out likewise if we can get hold of her.

Dealing with cattle was never easy, and the next year he wrote again to the DK manager at Rogers Lake.

> I wish if you could without too much trouble have some of the cowboys try and find that milk cow that you brought in for us last fall. You know she got away again a few weeks after we brought her in and we have not seen her since and no doubt she went back on your range and is now with your cattle.

The DK cowboys had similar problems: according to grazing permits, twenty percent of their cattle drifted off the forest that year and into Sycamore Canyon. Some could not be found; they roamed wild in the canyon, getting harder to catch every year.

For a long time Riordan hospitality on logging trains down to Barney Pasture had been strained. Finally in 1910 T.A. wrote to the conductor on the logging line:

> I notice a good many men go down to the Y here in Milton and get on the train and go to the camp where they bum their meals and get a free ride. This has been complained about at the logging camp a good deal on account of the expense of feeding these men...Therefore you will please instruct all train men to stop taking out men to the camp excepting where you are sure that they need men, and that the men wanting to go can fill the bill.
>
> Also stop men getting on the trains at the Y at Milton, and take no men on the train except at the office.
>
> Also do not have your trains stop anywhere between here and the camp excepting on company business. Do not have the trains used for the purpose of carrying goods free or passengers to sheep camps, and be starting and stopping trains and adding to the expense. Any business of this sort must be arranged for with the proper officials.

Apparently the Coconino Cattle Company made such arrangements. T.A's letter books were full of bills for merchandise from Riordan Mercantile or from the Camp One boarding house, delivered by logging train and "unloaded at the cut this side of Rogers Lake." The list offered a view into the life of a cowboy about 1912, the year the country first heard Irving Berlin's "Alexander's Ragtime Band." There were such items as 30 sacks of barley, 27 sacks of oats, 1990 pounds of hay and some blocks of salt. That was for the animals.

Groceries for the men included:

19 pounds of bacon	canned fruit
14 pounds of sugar	lard
5 pounds of baking powder	syrup
5 pounds of evaporated apples	canned tomatoes
20 pounds of potatoes	catsup
10 pounds of butter	sauerkraut
3 pounds of salt	2 pounds of pepperbeans
15 pounds of onions	soda
100 pounds of flour	cornflakes
175 pounds of beef	eggs

one case of jam

3 gallons of molasses

10 pounds of coffee

a keg of pickles

rice

canned chilis

milk

15 pounds of cabbage

Work supplies brought out on the train:

matches

sledge handle

Vaseline

overalls

tobacco

candles

soap

caps & coil fuse

cigarette paper

an axe handle

a wash board

a wash tub

gun

socks

underwear

a bottle of caustic balsam

one steel

shoes

a pocket knife

an alarm clock

2 pair garters

2 boxes 32-20 cartridges

1 box 32-Colt's cartridges

28 pounds of iron

3 sets of hinges

coal oil

gloves

a skinning knife

The new cattle company prospered and retired the purchase price of the DK ranch within one year. In 1909 it paid $13,050 in dividends to its eight stockholders, who included a new man, Elbert Harvey (Jack) Crabb, a twenty-five-year-old who had been raising range cattle with his brother near Show Low and who had bought 130 shares. After some training by the Forest Service in Washington, he became a familiar presence around Woody Mountain.

When Pinchot and his men were getting organized and working to form policy for grazing in the national forests of the West, Crabb seemed a likely fellow to add to the staff. His wife, Abbie, described the situation.

> ... the officials were on the lookout for promising young men. Jack attended a
> number of their meetings with other range men, and his intelligence, popularity,
> and fair-minded attitude, together with his knowledge of range requirements,
> attracted their attention.

Early in 1908, at the age of twenty-seven, Crabb joined the Service in its grazing division and was assigned to the Washington office to learn the operation at the top from Gifford Pinchot and fellow Arizonan Albert Potter. He returned to Arizona as Range Examiner and in 1911 was offered the position of supervisor of the Sitgreaves Forest. With Fred Breen's experience close in view, he declined the job. Hurley, Cox, and Miller apparently thought his experience with Pinchot's Washington grazing division made him a valuable man, and they offered him instead the position of manager of the DK Ranch at $150 a month. He accepted the offer.

In 1914 a big cowboy named Joe Hancock took up a ranch near the DK winter range. The road to his place went through his neighbor's land, and he ran into Crabb now and then. Seventy-four years later, at the age of ninety-four, Hancock remembered him as "an educated cowboy...pretty fair size. He seemed to be a serious guy...didn't do much drinkin'."

Joe Hancock remembered that there were quite a few DK cowboys, most of them "single guys...a lotta them named Tex." Because there was a good deal of hand work on a ranch in those days, he said, Crabb kept most of his cowboys on year round.

Jack and Abbie Crabb spent winters on the DK's Windmill property west of Sedona and summers at the ranch at Rogers Lake, which had its own blacksmith shop and salt house. Four decades afterward, Abbie remembered details of the life.[4]

> As far as transportation, for pleasure I took the buggy; for supplies we sent the wagon into town, a twenty-mile round trip. It was not a time just to be traveling around; when we stocked up on groceries (twice a month), it was in bulk quantities—one hundred pounds of potatoes, for instance.
>
> In 1914 we bought a Hupmobile car—the ranchers liked the Hupmobile because it was built high and could clear the uneven ground better. Of course, when we had a car and were called from Flagstaff to Phoenix on business, it would take two days and a night traveling at 20 to 25 miles an hour. There was no pavement and we didn't dare go any faster.
>
> On the ranch we killed our own beef. We'd hang a quarter of beef in a tree overnight, then in the morning cover it with canvas and take it to the cool, rock storeroom for keeping. Beef was the staple of our diet, usually served at breakfast and dinner. I cooked on a wood range which had no temperature control, you just had to know either by putting your head in the oven or learning how much wood (juniper and oak) to put in. No broiling, of course, that was impossible; frying was done in suet and bacon grease. We always had hot biscuits. I baked all our bread, including sourdough.
>
> Milk products came from several milk cows on the ranch; the butter I churned myself. We could buy canned vegetables at the store, and the fruit was mostly dried.
>
> I washed on washboards and ironed with three flat irons I kept hot on top of the range; when one was in use, two were heating. With these modern appliances I performed such miracles as ironing twelve starched petticoats.
>
> It never seemed as if we worked all the time. There always was free time for knitting, reading, making jellies and jams. In the winter when we moved down to lower ground, I remember leaving beef kidneys in the trees for the birds to eat while we were gone; they loved the fat. We got up early in the morning and went to bed early at night. You know, you don't mind anything if you don't know any better.

In 1911 a son was born to Abbie Crabb. He died at the age of two. A daughter was born in 1913 and died two years later. In 1915 Jack's brother's wife died of

---

4 Abbie Crabb Keith's reminiscence was published in 1984, after she died, in the *Arizona Cattle Grower's Association* magazine *Outlook.*

E.H. "Jack" Crabb ran the DK for ten years.
Arizona Cattle Grower's Association

Cattle operations on the Coconino in 1914 used the new automobile.
Special Collections and Archives Department, Cline Library, Northern Arizona University

childbirth during a flu epidemic, and the Crabbs adopted and took to the ranch her two little girls, aged one day and five and a half years, and children lived where the Sitgreaves expedition had camped sixty years before.

To move its cattle to Rogers Lake in the spring, the Coconino Cattle Company used the Mooney Trail, which climbed up the sheer walls of the Sedona rim out of the Verde Valley. It had been in use since the early 1880s, when the five sons of widowed stockraiser Jane Newman had moved the family's cattle to Rogers Lake, where they hollowed out logs to make watering troughs for livestock. Bear Howard, who bred and raced horses in preference to herding steers, drove his horses up the trail and into Barney Pasture where he lived part of the summer in a cabin with Jim Barney.[5]

In 1912 the DK proposed to improve the trail from its Verde Valley range up through that rough country between Sycamore and Loy Canyons, onto the Rim, and into Barney Pasture. The Forest Service notified T.A. Riordan and requested his views on the matter. He responded that he wished any action to be "fair and square to all concerned."

DK cattle were driven along the Mooney Trail twice a year for more than fifty years. But the Crabbs went by an easier route. More than half a century later Earl Van Deren, life-long rancher in the Verde Valley, remembered one of the manager's annual two-day moves by the Oak Creek route from winter to summer range at Rogers Lake.

> When we lived at Clay Park, south of Flagstaff, the DK chuck-wagon stayed all night at our place—1911 or 1912—and used our corral to keep their horses and mules in. When Mr. and Mrs. Crabb arrived in a fancy buggy with fringe on top and side curtains, a tent was erected for them to sleep in, and the chuck-wagon cook prepared their meals.

From the Black and Vail purchase of the quarter section on the northwest side of Woody Mountain, through the sale to the Coconino Cattle Company, to Crabb's management, and through all the succeeding years, ownership of the land was clear. But right to use the water in Woody Spring was for half a century as likely to be tangled as a discarded fishing line. Four interests were there at once—the cattle

---

5 After a shooting in a range dispute in California, J.J. Howard had fled to northern Arizona, where for a while he used the name Charlie Smith, causing confusion for later historians. There was no end to the stories about him. People said that once in a saloon he accepted a wager that he could kill a bear with nothing but a hunting knife. The next day, after local gambling men made sure he had no firearms with him, he left Flagstaff. Three days later he was back with "a good-sized bear carcass" on a pack horse. But he did not kill a man a day, and his family did not know him as the dangerous character that tales made him out to be. Even his in-laws said, "There never was a kinder, better man." His great-granddaughter, Laura McBride, defended his reputation: "I know Grandpa Howard probably didn't comb his hair much when he lived by his self, but knowing my Grandmother well, I am sure he was more neat when he was around her."

company by title to the land, AL&T logging locomotives by lease agreement, sheep herders by right of prior use, and the Forest Service, which used the top of the mountain as a lookout site. It was the only reliable water for three or four miles in any direction, and people stepped on each others' toes to claim a share of it.

Sheepherders may well have built the first water trough at the spring: there were sheep in volcano country before there were cattle. In 1875, Ashurst brought in a large flock; by 1877, John Clark had three thousand head; and in 1882 the three Daggs brothers imported sixty-six purebred Merino rams, which sometimes yielded forty-pound fleeces from a twelve-month growth. In 1886, when a profit of fifty percent was common, the Arizona Sheep Breeders and Woolgrowers Association was organized in Flagstaff.

A sheep was called "the animal with the golden hoof" because, owners said, "prosperity followed in its footsteps." They joked that "a cowboy was a sheep-herder with his brains knocked out": a good shepherd earned twice the wage a cowboy was paid.

Sheep shared the range with cattle as big business. It did not make a friendly neighborhood. In 1887 and 1888, Pleasant Valley, ninety miles southeast of Woody Mountain, had rung with a feud between the cattle-owning Grahams and the Tewksburys—who had bought sheep on shares from Flagstaff's Daggs brothers— that had left tempers high and somewhere around forty people dead.

In the last years of the nineteenth century Fred Breen and the Forest Reserves had struggled with the issue. Sheepmen attacked Breen as arbitrary and unfair. Cattle growers claimed that sheep were not in the public interest in the arid southwest. The Interior Department went along and asserted that sheep grazing destroyed forests. Sheepmen contended they did nothing of the kind, that in fact they were useful in trampling pine needles into the earth and thus preserving the forest from fire, that their droppings were more valuable for fertilizer than any-thing cows produced, that they were smaller, lighter, and more easily moved than cattle. Politicians supported the sheepmen. The Arizona Sheep Breeders and Wool Growers appealed to Pinchot, chief of forestry and confidant of Theodore Roosevelt.

In May of 1900 he made a trip to Arizona to see the effect of sheep grazing around Flagstaff and recommended to President Roosevelt that the order prohibit-ing them be canceled.

> From some forest regions sheep should be kept out. But northern Arizona is not
> one of them...The answer to the grazing difficulties in Arizona [is] to control
> sheep grazing on the Mogollon Mesa, and not to shut it out.

In 1902 "cowboy" Roosevelt ordered that sheepmen should not be excluded from the San Francisco Mountains Reserve, although he pounded on the arm of his chair with his clenched fist and stormed, "Gentlemen, sheep are dee-structive."

In northern Arizona sheep owners were often people with political power. Before the nineteenth century had played itself out, both the Babbitt and the Riordan brothers had begun to diversify into flocks of their own. When talk began of a consolidation of Reserve lands into a national forest, the Riordans bought up

Sheep grazed around Woody Moutain early in the 20th century.
AHS–Pioneer Museum

land with tanks and water holes that could be used for their sheep, although T.A. worried:

> I suppose you have read about the consolidation of the forest reserve here, whereby the government gets all of the odd-numbered sections, and thus will be able to make a solid reserve, and probably keep the live stock off of same. If this is done, of course we will probably all have to get out of the sheep business in the long run.

Grazing permits on National Forest land were less exclusive than he feared they would be. Allotments were not restricted to one kind of stock—sheep and cattle often shared the grass on "dual purpose" pastures. Both were at Woody Spring: it was not reserved for the use of either. Boundaries were not marked by fences anyway, and animals tended to cross over, especially cattle, which were not usually under the control of herders. It was the kind of confusion that left room for both opportunity and hard feelings all around.

The first sheepman of record who grazed his flocks on Woody Mountain was Hannibal B. Kelly, who held a Forest Service allotment, based on prior use of unspecified date, from 1910 to 1914. One of his range employees was a new kind of man in the kaleidoscopic story of Woody Spring—Jose Antonio Manterola, a Basque who had been born into the sheep business in Navarra, Spain.

In the old world, Basque country was barely one hundred miles across in any direction. Navarra was in the mountains, its people (and those of the Pyrenees on the French side of the border) recognized as different not only from Spaniards but also from Basques who lived along the seacoast. In America they kept themselves

Jose Antonio Manterola was a sheep owner at the age of 23.
Courtesy of his daughter, Sylvia Manterola

separate by kinship and regional distinction. It was the mountain sheepherders, the Navarrese and French, who moved into northern Arizona after drought and population pressure pinched off available grazing land in California. Some historians maintained that the first man killed in the Pleasant Valley War was a Basque sheepherder employed by Flagstaff's Daggs Brothers. Valley cattlemen cut off his head and drove his sheep off a cliff. He was variously termed by others a Mexican or an Indian. No one remembered his name.

Sheep owners praised the Basques as reliable and efficient. Hank Lockett hired them to watch his flocks. They became camp tenders in charge of several bands and later, as Anglos found it more and more difficult to earn a profit, the herders began to take over flocks on shares.

Jose Antonio Manterola had left the Spanish mountains and sailed to America in 1907, when he was sixteen. He worked in Texas for a while, then moved on to Arizona where he had cousins living. In 1910 Kelly hired him for eighteen dollars a month to herd sheep.

Harry Embach, punching cattle with a partner, met Tony early that spring in Canyon Diablo. It was cold and windy one day when they chanced upon the Basque herders of the Kelly Sheep Company, and the cowboys' lips were chapped.

> Manterola and his friends took us in so we could get warm, and in their
> hospitable way offered us bowls of hot chili to warm our innards. But it did more
> than warm our insides. That hot chili was murder when it slopped over our
> chapped, cracked lips. We were in agony—and I mean agony.

In June of 1914 Kelly sold to Tony Manterola for one dollar "and other valuable consideration" 2221 head of sheep carrying fourteen different ear marks, 81 head of burros, one mule, 21 horses, one saddle, one buckboard "and all harness, tools, utensils and ranch equipment of every sort and nature...used in connection with the running of the above mentioned sheep." He also sold the permit for the Woody Mountain allotment, which the Forest Service transferred to Manterola.

For another year he was a neighbor of Jack and Abbie Crabb and, by right of prior use for the permit, shared with them the water in Woody Spring. Then he sold the sheep, horses, mules, burros, wagons, buckboards, etc., to Bernardo Bidegain, another Basque, and went off to join with three other men from the old country to form the Ohaco Sheep Company. Thirty years and a lot of story later, Tony Manterola returned to Woody Mountain and bought the allotment a second time.

To complicate a situation already crowded with sheep and DK cattle brought up the Mooney Trail, for several years livestock shared the water at Woody Spring with logging locomotives. That entry onto the scene was described in T.A.'s letters, in illustration of the way use of land was manipulated as homesteaders were replaced by men who used it for business.

Earlier AL&T had acquired the Tappan Ranch north of Rogers Lake. On fairly level land, it was a good spot for cattle ranchers. In November of 1910, T.A. wrote to Little George Black:

> [Bill] Cox was just in to see me about a trade for his timber on the Cox quarter
> and on the Woody and Jones quarters, and in the discussion he stated he was
> considering a trade for the Woody place which you know has a couple of small
> springs on the hill...Possibly we might use the water to advantage by piping it
> down to our track for the locomotives...Maybe we could trade them some other
> land, maybe the Tappan place north of Rogers Lake...which would give them
> their range rights.

He liked the idea: Woody Spring was only a few hundred yards uphill from logging tracks for locomotives that were powered by steam.

The cattle company was negotiating some sort of trade with the Forest Service for the quarter section around Woody Spring, but T.A. was ready in April with a suggestion in case that deal fell through.

... I thought if our water and land at the Tappan place would be of any use to you and you could control it and keep from being crowded on the north of the Lake, that we might make an exchange on a leasing basis, we letting you have the use of the Tappan place for a term of years and you letting us have for any of our purposes what water we might need from the Woody Spring...We might be warranted in putting in a pipe line from the spring down to our track and putting in a good sized tank to use what water we might need at any time for our locomotives...You know that ordinarily we have had plenty of water at Rogers Lake but it is more or less of a nuisance pumping with the windmill and the water for camp use we have to take from Flagstaff...so it might be of some advantage to us to have water from your spring especially as it would flow by gravity.

The deal was off and on again all year. In July T.A. wrote to the C.C.C. principles in Jerome, requesting permission to put in a two-inch pipe line from Woody Spring down the slope to the logging tracks. He wanted to erect a storage tank there where trains could stop to take on water for Camp One. In return, he offered "the use of the Tappan place for such a period of time as we use the water from the Woody Spring."

He protested that he didn't want to sell any land that had water on it, but he was prepared to do so if he had to "by putting a price on the Tappan ranch and taking a lease or sale of the surplus water in the Woody Spring for a long term of years." Other ranchers had been asking about Tappan spring, he warned, and "I was up at [Woody] spring in passing several days ago and find it flowing such a small quantity that we are in doubt whether or not it would be worth our while to do anything with it." Nevertheless, he wanted it.

In October T.A. sent to Cox a draft of a warranty deed which would give the cattle company title to the Tappan Ranch in exchange for the remaining timber on Woody Mountain and a long-term lease for water in the spring giving it "the right to enter upon said lands and premises for the purpose of developing water upon all or any part...[with] an easement and right of way for the construction of pipe lines."

The Coconino Cattle Company did not sell the land. It retained possession and reserved right to the use of as much water as it needed for livestock at two troughs which it agreed to maintain, leasing "surplus water" to AL&T. Later a line was built to convey water down to pasture on lower land.

Another sheepman, Dr. R.O. Raymond,[6] had come into the picture by then. A native of Illinois and a graduate of Washington School of Medicine, Raymond

---

6 Later several elderly ladies said, "His name back East was something else. He changed it when he came out here—some scandal, I think, a murder or something. I'm not sure." Microfilm in the office of the Clerk of the Superior Court of Coconino County preserved the original name and the cause of the change. The man was born Raymond Oliver Outhouse. In 1901, after finishing all his schooling and tired, no doubt, of the jokes, he discarded the patronym in favor of a repetition of his given name. Two of his brothers chose the name Owens for themselves.

moved to Arizona in 1904 at the age of twenty-eight for the reason so many people did—tuberculosis. For four years he first lived in a sheep camp and then worked as a licensed physician in Williams, and when his health improved (he lived another fifty-one years), he transferred to Flagstaff and took over supervision of the AL&T hospital, the only one in town, at a salary of three hundred dollars a month. In addition to injured loggers, he "doctored" people in the community.

Jose Montoya, who was running a band of sheep on the south side of Rogers Lake, was a patient of Dr. Raymond. One day in 1910 he mentioned that his allotment was good for more sheep than he had on it but that he did not have money enough for more than the one band. The doctor offered to finance more sheep. Montoya accepted.

Sheep ranching seemed more profitable (and perhaps more interesting) to Raymond than doctoring, and in 1913 he bought out Montoya and gradually eased away from his medical practice. As a base for sheep permits he acquired old homesteads around the country every time he found one available and added to the original place south of Rogers Lake. Within a few years his interests were as far-flung as Howard Lake south of the Grand Canyon, a ranch at the head of Sycamore Canyon, and the Bloody Basin area below the Rim, with permits on the Coconino for 2065 sheep.

By 1926 Raymond owned the Mooney and Woody Mountain grazing allotments. While AL&T held the lease on Woody Spring, there was no problem about his stock sharing water troughs with cattle and the logging company. But that triple use was to cause heated argument twelve years later.

Control of Woody Spring, always a counter in somebody's money plans, had see-sawed from John Woody, who used it, to the Santa Fe, which didn't; from Black and Vail, building a ranch, to Hurley, Cox and Miller, who needed a property base in a national forest; then to T.A. Riordan for a while. Sheepherders were a presence all through those years. Another businessman owner was in the future, but in 1913 T.A. was busy building pipe lines.[7]

That brought Eli Giclas into Woody Mountain's story. Giclas, born in Missouri, had come to Arizona in 1902 as an engineer for the Santa Fe to develop water sources for main line locomotives. He decided to stay on as water superintendent for the city, which was in perennial crisis about its water supply.

But the job included more political strife than Giclas wanted. In 1908, when he was forty-six, he moved to Milton and a position as chief engineer in charge of all water problems for AL&T, married Hedwig Leissling from Washington, D.C., [see page 69] and brought her to live at the base of the Peaks. After two years T.A. ordered a promotion for Giclas—to boilers, engines and sprinkler systems—and a

---

7 In 1913, when the first pipe was installed at Woody Spring, there were other innovations around the country: Henry Ford opened his first assembly line, and Charlie Chaplin made his movie debut with Mack Sennett's Keystone Cops.

Henry Giclas was photographed at about age five with his father Eli.
Courtesy of Henry Giclas

Water tanks for AL&T steam locomotives were built with railroad ties.
Special Collections and Archives Department, Cline Library, Northern Arizona University

raise in pay to $125 per month. Working with Eli Giclas, AL&T developed Woody Spring and installed valves and a one-inch pipe that carried water downhill to the logging rail line. There was a wooden water tank on stilts at that point, and engines stopped beside it to take on water.

Several times each season Eli Giclas rode on the logging train to Woody Spring to check on the pump and clean the intake valve and sometimes took his son Henry, much to the boy's delight.

> We normally rode on the tender. The only other person on the train besides the engineer and fireman was the switchman, brakeman, car-coupler—all one person, named Ray Simington, who also rode on the tender in good weather. The log cars were just heavy open frames with rails running the length of the car for the loader to run on, so they were very unsafe and uncomfortable to ride on...Since the locomotive was fired with crude oil in order to prevent forest fires from the engine, Ray Simington had a box to sit on in the engine when the weather was cold or bad for the ride out to the logging camp. There was a caboose available at the car yard, but normally it was not used unless there were several people going to the logging camp at one time.

The road from the rail line to the spring was only a two-wheel track through the woods. Once Henry and his father buried an old overturned water tank to hide their round-ended digging shovel so they wouldn't have to carry it back and forth from town. The boy saw no sign of a trail to the top of the mountain, and he and his father never tried to climb, but Eli Giclas did tell his son about John Woody, who had died a few years earlier.

While Giclas tended valves at the spring, Riordan moved to cut the trees he had bought from the cattle company in the 1912 agreement. In May of 1916 he placed in his files a memorandum of a talk he had had in Jerome with Jack Crabb and Walter Miller.

> Mr. Crabb asked if they could arrange so that we would not cut the few trees close to the spring on Woody Mountain around the cabin or corral. I told him that this had been our intention and we would gladly do it.
> Also that we would do the same about the trees close to the house and in the yard at their camp headquarters [at Rogers Lake], and I suggested to Crabb that if they would have these trees blazed which they wanted to reserve...we would be glad to leave these trees forever.

He warned in the memo that he "...might not cut the timber on either of these places for several years longer."

The steep north side of Woody Mountain, burnt over several times in the nineteenth century and covered in most places by aspen, was worked by the loggers only on the lower slopes. Level land at the base of the mountain was cut sometime in the 1920s, one of the last parcels "harvested" before the Depression ended logging by AL&T. Despite Crabb's request and T.A.'s assurance, most of the

A photograph made in 1914 at Rogers Lake showed that the top of Woody Mountain was bare, that there were still trees on the northwest side, and that the land between the mountain and the lake, which was a state land-grant section, still had its pines.
Special Collections and Archives Department, Cline Library, Northern Arizona University

Gambel oak had no commercial value to AL&T.
Loggers left a veteran four feet in diameter.

trees were taken from around the spring. An occasional ponderosa seed tree was left on the slope above it, and an aspen or two, and a few Gambel oak trees which were not suitable for lumber.

Jack Crabb, who had become chairman of the Arizona Livestock Commission and president of the Arizona Cattle Growers Association, was probably not around to select which trees fell. One day in July of 1921, out on the ranch on a horse, he could no longer ignore the pain in his side and went back to the house with a ruptured appendix. Cowboys carried his bed out to the railroad line and loaded it onto an empty flat car behind the engine, which pulled him into town under the sky, but emergency surgery was too late. He died at the age of forty. Cattle company minutes spoke of it as "sudden and untimely."

After his death, cattle continued to share water from Woody Spring with Riordan locomotives and Raymond's sheepherders: T.A. Riordan and Dr. R.O. Raymond were friends on that ground and on many others. In 1910, when Raymond was in St. Louis, T.A. wrote to him.

> I was glad to have your letter of the 30th, and to know that you have gotten into the hands of good friends in St. Louis, who will insist on having you remain there with them for a while. I hope they will fix your nose up so that it will operate all right, and while they are at it improve the shape of it.
>
> There does not appear to be any present need for you to hurry back so I think you can stay long enough to take the full treatment and become thoroughly cured before your return, that is if you have any bad habits that should be treated and cured before your return to work.
>
> About the Russian wolf hounds, I think they would be lots of fun when we would be using them if we ever got around to it, but I would hardly know what to do with them meanwhile, and fear they might be considerable trouble to keep.
>
> I am glad to know that you have gained some in weight, and have been going to the shows. I believe this should do you good.

As he grew up, Henry Giclas considered Dr. Raymond a family friend.

> My earliest recollections were of Dr. Raymond...and my father making field trips to Oak Creek Canyon to gather Dogwood bushes for transplanting in our yard or on Dr. Raymond's places; or to the inner basin of the Peaks to collect other specimens that my father was conversant with. Dr. Raymond was a natural conservationist. He would carry a pocket full of seeds most places he went (alfalfa, gramma grass, chamisa, etc.) and scatter them where he thought they might grow. In particular I remember how proud he was of his lily pond in Sycamore Canyon north of Poison Spring.

The doctor occasionally gave grass seeds to children like Tony Manterola's daughter, Sylvia, and advised them it would be a good thing to toss handfuls out the car window on the way home.

For himself Dr. Raymond chose Corgis, and he was devoted to them. On the kitchen
door he posted diet schedules for his housekeeper. She grumbled that
"the dogs ate better than the doctor."
Platt Cline photograph—AHS–Pioneer Museum

T.A. Riordan had been in the lumber business for nearly fifty years
when the Great Depression struck.
Riordan State Historical Park

Over the years Raymond earned impressive profits from his sheep business and investments. A life-long bachelor, he became a primary benefactor and philanthropist in Flagstaff. As Henry told it:

> Dr. Raymond was a friend of everyone. The rich, the poor, the down and out; anyone who needed help. I know at least a half-dozen young people he helped financially to get a university education during his lifetime. Most paid him back, some never did—it was never a consideration with him. He was always called upon by some of his less erudite friends for bail money when they were held in jail for some offense ...

The doctor was on good terms with most people. Henry remembered that one rancher ...

> ... never paid much attention to his health, believing that if he had enough alcohol in his system, nothing would ever harm him. In fact he had frozen his feet so often riding his horse in the cold of winter that he could hardly walk. Dr. Raymond was concerned, and admonished him not to drink so much that he could not tell when his feet were cold. [He] said, "That's good advice Doc—but I ain't a gonna take it."

T.A. Riordan and R.O. Raymond, with almost a twenty year difference in their ages, were frequent companions in hunting and fishing jaunts around the country. In 1929 T.A. wrote to a friend:

> It's astonishing how many sheep and cattle deals the Doctor is mixed up in. He seems to understand the game pretty well and to have a lot of friends everywhere, and I guess an occasional enemy who breaks in on his grass and water, but I think it's a fine thing for him to be able to get out in the open and away from inside work. I have a lot of fun with him.

Stockraisers who worked with Raymond were likely, of course, to be less complimentary. One called him "a hard man to understand...quite an old guy...set in his ways." Another exploded sixty years later: "As many people woulda shot him as gone to his wedding." All agreed that nobody could tell him what to do.

Henry Giclas would hear no criticism, and he had reason. Three years after Jack Crabb died, when Henry was fourteen and the country was roaring through the 1920s, Eli Giclas also died.

> In February 1924 my father's health was declining and Dr. Raymond seemed to be unable to help him; so he proposed to take him personally, on the train, to the Mayo Clinic in Minnesota. It was diagnosed there as cancer of the stomach and too late for surgery. They returned to Flagstaff and Dr. Raymond arranged for a last ditch exploratory operation at the Seventh Day Adventist Hospital in Glendale, California, with radiological treatments at the Soiland Radiological Laboratory—a new and innovative treatment technique at the time. He passed away there on May 23 of that year. It was Dr. Raymond who was waiting out in front of the Orpheum Theatre on the night of May 23rd to tell me my father had passed away. The next day he put me on the train for California. I remember he bought the train ticket. Whether he was ever repaid, I do not know—I certainly

did not have that kind of money in my pocket, and my mother had been with my father for months there.

Eli Giclas missed seeing the pipes at Woody Spring, which he had tended for a decade, dismantled and carried away, leaving the water to run free for a while into wooden watering troughs for the use of sheep and a few C.C.C. cattle. The logging railroad the spring had served was also taken apart, and locomotives disappeared into a silent past. When those changes were complete, T.A. Riordan was no longer a part of Arizona Lumber and Timber Company.

The process began in 1929, although no one seemed to recognize it at the time. Until autumn of that year, business at the logging company went on as usual. There was a new manager, I.B. Koch, who took some of the workload from the Riordan brothers. T.A., who had recently turned seventy, wrote to a friend, "My health has not been of the best for the past few years and I am only able to do about half a days' work, but hope to improve from month to month."

Orders were filled and shipped out. Logging camps and railroad lines and mill saws continued to run as they had for half a century, employing several hundred local men. In May of 1929, T.A. wrote in a letter: "We are plugging along just the same as we have been for many years and it seems to be getting a little more difficult all the time to make both ends meet." Business was slowing, but he was not alarmed. In the first week of October, he wrote: "We are piling up lumber as orders are a little below production, but this is not a serious condition, that is going into winter."

He seemed more concerned about his diet—"I am now 197 pounds"—and the condition of northern Arizona's roads—"I really won't get into a motor at all if I can avoid it around these parts." He and Carrie played rummy in the evenings. He still went hunting and fishing with his friends, and he was delighted when his doctor advised him to play golf for the exercise.

Then in October of 1929, in the first year of Herbert Hoover's presidency, the stock market crashed. On November 6, T.A. wrote to a friend in Brooklyn:

> I suppose you have all been up on your toes for the past week or two in New
> York because of the big business on Wall Street...To a man in the woods it
> appears to be a most amazing condition...I am wondering whether the worst has
> come to pass yet or whether it is ahead of us.

AL&T shipped Christmas trees on its regular orders in mid-December, but T.A. was speculating: "There is a possibility that the sawmill and lumber yard will be closed down during the first part of January."

It was what was called "whistling in the wind." The sawmill and logging camps had already ceased operations, and negotiations were under way to sell the horses. Orders to specification were refused, as the company tried to sell off 22 million board feet of lumber stacked in the yard.

Toward the end of 1929, AL&T correspondence began to feature terms like "reductions recently published...new reduced rates...readjustment of rates." Riordan subsidiary companies were also in trouble, as were companies in which T.A. held stock. Other lumbermen wrote, offering to sell their equipment.

In the early 1930s, business letters began to mention "changing times...slump...general gloom...badly shattered market...the old order of things disturbed" and to talk about "trimming ship." In its report to the Bureau of Labor Statistics in 1930, the company listed two hundred to three hundred people employed seasonally in the mill (without mentioning contract labor in the logging camps) but said that there had been a cut in wages. Men were working for fifteen cents an hour on a ten-hour shift and were glad to get it. Banks in Flagstaff were closed; the company shipped money in from California by Railway Express to meet its shrunken payroll.

In a sad series of replies to inquiries about employment from all over the country, the company repeated, over and over: "We have nothing to offer you at this time." Logging contractors were cut off, "for sixty to ninety days, as conditions develop": "The cancellation of heavy contracts for lumber and timber by the mines, etc., has compelled us to curtail our output, and of course, we have to begin at the woods end."

T.A. tried to sound his old cheerful self in his letters—"We will forget all about it in a year or two when the good times come"—but he was an aging man, and he wasn't well. "I am not yet able to fill the position of full back on a foot ball team and hardly able to bat the ball as far as first base on a ball field."

In 1926, his only grandson had died, a little boy three years old. A year later his younger daughter Anna, her father's chum, and Mike's son Arthur had died of poliomyelitis on the same day, after members of both households had exhausted themselves in frantic efforts at proxy breathing. Then in the fall of 1930 his brother died. And in December, on the day after a subdued Christmas, the commissary and all its contents were destroyed by fire.

He didn't feel at home in the twentieth century:

> We have been so speeded up that we do not in these days seem ever to have time
> for anything like the old delightful days when we could have a highball and a log
> fire and a smoke and some real genuine human heart-to-heart talks and songs
> and even a jig. This era of useless activity and seeming efficiency is so different.

Although the AL&T Annual Report continued to list expenses for maintaining the logging railroad and operating trains, it filed the line in 1931 with the Arizona Corporation Commission as inactive and let the charter for what once had been an ambitious venture expire in 1935. And that was the end of it. Annual reports began to list "cost of track removal."

Not all the rails were taken up and carried into town. Local ranchers and cowboys pried loose sections that were left and used them to fashion cattle guards, which they installed across the roads that took up the function of the logging trains.

In 1933 T.A. Riordan, aged seventy-six, saw his brother's share of the stock in AL&T sold to someone outside the family, and he resigned the presidency of the company. He continued to hold an interest, and occasional letters above his signature went out on company stationery, but he was no longer in charge.

His friend R.O. Raymond managed to survive the hard times, even to help several Basques who had been his partners or employees in the sheep business. One of them was a Basque-born man named Frank Auza, who had arrived in Arizona in 1915 at the age of ten and had begun to work as a sheepherder when he was thirteen. Auza started a long relationship with Raymond, as employee and partner, in 1933.

Through the 1930s Auza regularly moved Dr. Raymond's sheep to Woody Spring, "the only water we had" on the northeast side of the Woody Mountain allotment. It was "a good big spring," a six-log spring. In those days water troughs were often made of split and hollowed logs so arranged on a slope that they drained into each other in series; a spring was measured by how many logs it could keep full. In most places on the Coconino an eight-log spring was about as big as you could find. There were two troughs at Woody Spring, twenty-four inches wide, always full to overflowing, but it was designated in local parlance at "six logs." It was a water source worth protecting.

Forest resource managers decided early that if sheep were to be kept from over-grazing an area, they must be kept moving. To supplement the spring with water across his allotment, Dr. Raymond built Auza tank, a mile south of Woody Mountain, and a pond at Aspen Spring, two miles to the southwest, on land which he owned. During summer months while the sheep were in high-country pasture, Frank Auza and his wife Elsie lived in the house and raised their children among the meadows at Aspen Spring, surrounded by corrals and outbuildings.

With those new water sources, Woody Spring was less vital to the sheep business than it had been. Locomotives no longer needed it. And the depression had hit Coconino Cattle Company hard; its herds were down to nearly nothing.

From at least 1878, when the government surveyor mentioned water troughs, the spring had been in constant use for three of the big economic forces of Arizona. Not more than two acres in size, the meadow had felt the boots of loggers and stockmen who may have noticed its charm but who cared more for profit than for place. The lower slope was stripped of trees; grass had been trampled by hooves; water was piped out and down; the old cabin was used and abused until the roof fell in.

The appearance of the place was finally restored by an aggressive new owner, a man of paradoxical qualities who, in the name of organized efficiency, returned it to peace and beauty and finally excluded cattle, sheep, woodcutters, and vandals out for a frolic. Named Miller, he was not related to the organizer of the Coconino Cattle Company, Walter Miller in Jerome.

Auza's opinion was the Dr. Raymond "never knew his livestock.
Some people like that are hard to work for, but he never told me a word."
Courtesy of Ann Auza

The herder's house at Aspen Spring was finally abandoned because annual damage
by roistering city folks was too expensive to repair.

Cecil Miller, born the youngest of seven in Texas, was poor enough when he was a boy to have no shoes. His mother died when he was four years old, and the family moved to New Mexico, to Phoenix, to Buckeye and Peoria and Glendale. But he had two assets: brothers and a mind attuned to finance. He was only nine when the family reached Arizona, but his sisters noticed he already knew the price of every farm commodity.

His father acquired a place west of Phoenix and helped the older boys, Carl and Simon, to incorporate as Miller Brothers in a farming and cattle operation. Cecil worked for the family business until at sixteen he graduated from high school. And then his father, who had managed to save four hundred dollars, sent his bright youngest son off to college in Iowa. On the roundabout way, he went through Oregon and liked it so much that he stayed and enrolled at Oregon State.

Three years later he graduated with a degree in agriculture, but his college years weren't all farming courses. He pitched for the school baseball team with the game strikeout record of seventeen men, played professional ball for Portland, and boxed under an assumed name. He was a short and vigorous man who believed in himself and usually got what he wanted.

While Cecil was playing baseball, his older brothers had organized in Buckeye the Miller Cattle Company—with a twenty-five percent investment by the Flagstaff Babbitt Brothers—and had bought a sheep operation in Coconino County. They wired Cecil to forget about baseball and come home to manage the animals. He obeyed the summons but as a sideline hired on to play small-town baseball in Flagstaff for a $350 a month salary from local merchants. He was known around town as "Lefty" Miller.

In 1921, when Cecil returned to Arizona, the Babbitt Brothers had ten family-owned retail and automobile stores, as well as nine trading posts, and controlled by loans, financing and partnerships thirty-eight cattle and sheep operations—the A-1, the Hashknife brand of Aztec Land and Cattle, the Apache Maid ranch, Aso Sheep Company, and on and on and on. They collected partners with the business shrewdness of the Miller brothers the way Dr. Raymond acquired water holes and homesteads. When Cecil was only twenty-one, he and his brother Simon formed, with the Babbitts as a co-partnership, the Glendale Stock Farm "to buy, breed, grow, raise, feed, and sell all kinds of livestock." The initial stock inventory was:

10 cows	1 bull	200 chickens
6 horses	11 calves	72 hogs
17 mules	126 steers	5 turkeys
8 dairy cows	300 ewes and lambs	

For a poor boy from Texas, young Cecil Miller was doing well. He was vice-president, assistant secretary-treasurer, general manager, and agent with power of attorney of a company capitalized at $250,000 as part of the Babbitt empire. When crisis hit Babbitt businesses with serious money troubles in 1922 and 1923, Miller

Cecil Miller posed with his father about 1915.
Courtesy of Miller Brothers

The DK ranch buildings at Rogers Lake were modest in 1928.
Courtesy of Miller Brothers

was a participant in meetings with bankers and saw firsthand what could happen, even to a giant, without hard-handed control. It made him careful, at the age of twenty-eight, when he and a partner started Hampshire Farms on two thousand acres near Tolleson, where they raised, among other things, four thousand Hampshire ewes.

Going into the Depression in 1930, stockholders had sold the Coconino Cattle Company, the DK Ranch, and the north side of Woody Mountain. Old-timers remembered years later that it had been "down to nothin' for a long time...they didn't have no cattle...in the drought of 1918 a lot had died on short feed." A group of investors bought "land, ranges, range rights and privileges, brands and permits" for $65,000, half the purchase price paid to Mary Vail twenty-four years earlier.

But business credit everywhere was strained, and banks were "takin' outfits right and left." The new owners, "unable to fulfill the terms of their contract, failed to make payment," and the sale was forfeited, with a return of most of the stock to original stockholders Walter Miller and Pat Hurley. Hurley was nearly seventy-five by then, an elderly man with a hand that trembled when he signed his name. Walter Miller had long since moved to California. Neither was interested in raising cattle in Arizona in a depression, and in 1933 they proposed to sell the Coconino Cattle Company and the DK ranch, bought for $113,000 in 1906, for $40,000.

Cecil Miller was a farmer/bookkeeper not a rancher, but he knew trading, buying, and selling, and he had been learning about the livestock business for a dozen years. Suddenly he had twenty-four hours to put together ten thousand dollars to buy an option for three-fourths of the Coconino Cattle Company, and he managed it on equal shares with a partner from Phoenix Title and Trust—who pledged First National Bank stock—and two men named Mickle and Cowden, who were involved with him in Hampshire Farms. A year later, Cowden sold his shares to Miller, which gave the thirty-four-year-old who had started with nothing control of the run-down DK ranch and its grazing permits.

Miller's childhood showed in the way he ran the DK. A farmer's son with a degree in agriculture, he was careful about his garden, which was important to him. Poor as a child, he was thrifty, refusing to buy either new clothes or new cars unless he absolutely had to. But he was the first owner since the early homesteaders who actually lived at the lake part of the year. He maintained the ranch buildings and remodeled them as he went along. The place looked nice, according to Forest Service patrolmen. A year after he and his partners bought the DK, the ranch had a permit for 267 head of cattle on national forest range. To serve fifteen cowboys, there were fifty to sixty horses and two wagons, with a camp cook on the trail.

Cecil and his wife Phyllis had two sons—Cecil, Jr., and Duane—who grew up on the ranch. It was theirs from their first memories. Like most ranchers who owned property in high country, the family did not live at the lake in winter. But summers when the boys weren't in school down south in Glendale, they explored. On the east shore they found an overturned rowboat tied to a tree; until it rotted away, they went out there regularly to see what kind of creatures they could find under it. They did not find the eighty-year-old grave of Inemacio Valdez. No one ever did.

Awed, the Miller brothers looked at a dark spot on the floor in the doorway of one of the rooms in the bunkhouse and listened to the story of how two cowboys had quarreled and one grabbed a shotgun and the other a pistol, and how one had fallen there in the doorway and bled and died. When the boys got in the way in the barn, ranch hands put them into gunny sacks and hung them on the wall where they couldn't do anything but watch. All the summers of their growing up they woke now and then to find Rogers Lake shrouded in mist after rains.

DK affairs and facilities and books were in poor condition when Cecil Miller became owner, and he promptly set about putting things in order. The old cabin at Woody Spring was a ruin—the tin roof caved in, logs from the walls scattered on the ground—so he set his men to tearing it down and carrying away the pieces. He began organizing water: drilling wells and digging more than one hundred stock tanks. In August of 1935, he wrote to Walter Miller, who was living in Los Angeles by then, requesting information about water rights.

The reply was friendly and rambling, a view into ranching practices before modern managers took over.[8]

> This Rogers Lake country is surely "God's Country"—especially from June 1 to Dec 1, and I would like to be able to be right with you good people right now—if I ever come to your vicinity, I shall be pleased to "grab a plate and have some beans."
>
> On all the water holes that we developed on registered or leased lands, or on University sections are recorded in that way. If you keep the leases paid up, they will be yours, just the same as when you owned the lands, and not nearly as much expensive as owning them.

He told Cecil Miller what he remembered about actions taken concerning several tanks and springs on the DK range and offered his advice, based on old custom and understanding of the law.

> Water belongs to the people who <u>uses it</u>, I think that I would file a locat on <u>every University</u> section as well then if for some unknown reason some thing slips up and you loose a lease, your filing will hold as you are using the water.
>
> The "Pump House" ranch was very valuable for both its water and grazing, but now the fences have driven us away from the range, and you have no use for the land. I would see that you protect yourselves about the water...We always had an idea that the "Pump House" ranch would be valuable for rasing lettuice, celery, turnips, etc etc—you might investigate and sell the property for something.

8 Walter Miller apparently did his own typing: the letter was full of strike-outs, type-overs, write-ins, etc., in addition to his individual syntax.

Cecil Miller, jr., spent his summers at the ranch.
Courtesy of Miller Brothers

Cecil, sr., and his younger son, Duane, saddled up at the old barn on the DK ranch.
Courtesy of Miller Brothers

We always held onto that little piece of 40 (?) acre tract of land on "Spring Creek", as that is the "key" to any out standing cattle out the "fence". I would see that nobody ever tried to farm or fence it, as you can always say that you have some cattle running there and need the water right.

If I can be of any assistance at any time, command me, I remain,

Very sincerely yours,
Walter Miller

P.S. We had a contract about the water at "Woody Butte"—the AL&T had to keep two troughs from the two springs and they (AL&T) for the surplus, and they had a pipeline running to the "pass" where the railroad went through.

One day, about 1927 (?) they tore up the pipe line—now I understand that they will have to replace the pipe line when they want to cut the timber in the "Crater" country.

I would see if you can get them to put the pipe line there now (possibly it has already been done) and then arrange for the surplus to be conveyed into your side of the fence. Some day those sheep men may claim a title, and you may loose a valuable piece of property.

C ecil Miller moved immediately to establish his right to Woody Spring. Within two weeks he wrote to Joseph C. Dolan, the new president of Arizona Lumber and Timber.

I have recently taken over the management of the Coconino Cattle Company with headquarters located at Rogers Lake. In going through the records, I find we have a lease with the Arizona Timber and Lumber Company, covering water located on [Woody Mountain] wherein it provides that you are to have the use of the water from a certain spring located in the above described property, and are to maintain troughs suitable for watering the cattle of the Coconino Cattle Company. Upon investigation, I find that the pipeline from this property leading down to our pasture has been taken up, and I further find that sheep troughs have been installed adjacent to the spring itself, and that apparently sheep have been watering there. As far as I can determine from the lease, and from talking with Mr. Hurley, who has been a part owner of the company for many years, it is my opinion that your right unto the waters are only as your company would use them in connection with your timber operations.

We would like to know whose sheep are watering from this spring, and by what authority they are permitted to water there.

A week later the AL&T manager answered:

If you happen to be up this way again, will be glad to talk the matter over with you.

As to any sheep which are being watered at this spring, this is being done without our permission. Of course, you have the first right to the water.

The sheep were Dr. Raymond's. And Miller knew that long use—more than 25 years—gave sheep every right to be there; the letter from Los Angeles had advised him of that in reference to other springs. But he was, according to people who knew him, an ethical and dynamic man, but a ruthless one, who "pushed any legal fact in his favor" without actually bringing issues to lawsuit. They called him "a diplomat...a pretty good mixin' and drinkin' man...who would pat you on the back with one hand and stab you in the back with the other," and "the kind of man who built mountains and moved lands," but "a tough guy who played for keeps...difficult...aggressive...exacting"..."a man who loved competition. He didn't play golf for the social exercise," they said. "He played to *win*."

Miller was a complex, paradoxical person with the talents necessary for success in America's strained economy. He was not the kind of man anyone wanted to engage in conflict. Gruff with other people and strict with his sons, he was a strong man—as his granddaughter, Susie, later described him—"with nothing flimsy about him."

He owned the land at Woody Spring, and he wanted control of the water. The next year he applied to the Forest Service for permission to build a pipeline to carry it from the spring a couple of miles west to the ranch houses at Rogers Lake. To protect the line from vandals, he wanted to put a locked gate in the fence around the quarter section, which he owned. That would have effectively excluded Dr. Raymond, and the doctor was a tough man himself. He would not relinquish his rights.

In May of 1938 Raymond sold to the cattle company land in Fry Park and Mill Park and on the south side of Rogers Lake, all within DK range, and Miller sold to Dr. Raymond land around Lindberg Spring and Pumphouse Wash (in what was later Kachina Village) to add to property which Raymond held in that area. Both sales were for one dollar. Miller wanted sheep excluded from Woody Spring as part of the swap, and he finally made a scene with the fifty-two-year-old doctor.

One summer day they met in the meadow. Cecil's two boys, aged nine and eleven, were with him. They were impressed to see grown-ups in a heated argument—at least, their father was angry, and voices were raised. Frank Auza, twenty-two, was with Dr. Raymond. As he remembered it, "We never had no trouble until Miller got there. He was not a very good neighbor. Him and the doctor didn't get along."

The Flagstaff District Ranger, Oscar McClure, was also present.[9] Miller had developed a good relationship with Forest Service personnel in town. Joe Hancock said, "They were close as black-eyed peas...Miller was always in the office...and you couldn't hardly get in when he was there...They were all standing around tellin' jokes." But Raymond had Arizona water law for support. He claimed prior beneficial use, and McClure disallowed Miller's intention to close off the spring. The owner of the land, Miller finally got exclusive control of the water, but it took him fifteen years, and he had to wait until Raymond was out of the picture.

9 Born in Missouri, McClure had moved to Arizona in 1910 and gone to school in Glendale with Cecil Miller. He was a big man with one good eye, the other covered with a smoked glass, and he like to recall that he had meet Gifford Pinchot one day at Rogers Lake.

Water level below Rogers Lake had stood high enough all summer at the beginning of the twentieth century for a well and windmill to provide water to the ranch. But as the years went on, the well failed. Woody Spring was finally essential to any life at all at the ranch.

Miller and his cowboys dug out the spring, which after more than a quarter century of heavy use was in poor condition, and built boxes of redwood to protect it. Leaving troughs for sheep, they constructed above ground a line of steel boiler pipe, bought from the Jerome mines, to convey water by gravity flow down to the ranch. The new pipeline ran night and day and supplied water for three houses and four to five hundred head of stock.

But with an unlocked gate, town campers, hunters, and wood cutters had access to the land. They misused the system, breached it or simply broke it to pieces. Spring boxes were opened to cool milk and beer, and garbage was left in them, much to the distress, the Miller boys said, of the womenfolks.

Arizona's water code specifically listed as guilty of a class 2 misdemeanor anyone who "knowingly and without authority opens, closes, changes or interferes with a...water box...[or] uses water to which another is entitled...[or] wastes water to the detriment of another." City users of the forest, ignorant of water law or outdoor courtesy, disregarded private claim completely.

The DK water system needed constant attention. Cecil, Jr., complained, "That sucker'd freeze every winter." Anonymous vandals out from town pulled the pipe apart, letting it slide ten to twelve feet downhill. Sometimes it was necessary to hire a tractor to pull the pipe back into place and a welder to re-attach it. Major repair was necessary at the beginning of every season, when the family spent a week cleaning the pipe, repairing it, and hooking it up. It was the boys' job through their high school years; they remembered it as "a real chore." Finally in 1945, the Millers brought in a grader, dug a trench all the way to Rogers Lake, and buried the line.

Cecil Miller raised a few horses for a while, but he didn't have what ranchers called "much of a cow and calf operation." Initially, before hoof and mouth disease forced a border closing, he stocked the DK with 3500 steers brought up from Mexico. From "a fella beyond Prescott" he bought yearlings and put them on his winter range west of Sedona.

Every year in June, DK cowboys, starting before daylight, drove six to seven hundred head single-file in one day from Black Tank on the Windmill property past Loy Butte and up the Mooney Trail to the pass at Buck Ridge. Seven to thirteen cowboys were needed for the job; two of them were Miller's sons. He trained his boys to the business, incorporated the second generation of Miller Brothers for

DK cattle near the top of the Mooney Trail were high above the Verde Valley.
Courtesy of Miller Brothers

Until 1955, the year of the last trail ride, the Miller brothers, Cecil (l) and Duane (r)
were part of the annual move. Both were on the board of Hampshire Farms when they
were barely out of college. Cecil, the older, held 183 shares of stock, Duane 182.
Cecil, sr. and his sons ran the sheep farm as a family corporation until it was
liquidated and dissolved in 1969.
Courtesy of Miller Brothers

them before they were out of high school. For several years they "cowboyed" as soon as school was out—the drive was held until they could get there.

In autumn the steers were driven into Flagstaff and shipped out on the Santa Fe. Only the horses were taken back down the Mooney Trail to winter range and another beginning of the cycle.[10]

Steers brought up to the northeast side of the DK range were watered by Woody Spring through those years, and so were sheep on the Woody Mountain allotment. But in 1945, Dr. Raymond, turning seventy and losing his sight, began to sell off his sheep interests. The base property at the head of Sycamore Canyon and the Woody Mountain grazing allotment were bought by Tony Manterola, who had sold them years before.

He had done well in the meantime. In partnership in Ohaco Sheep Company, he had been quarter owner of the sheep he herded. Through two decades of dry and wet years, good times and bad, Manterola had found grass ample on the Coconino summer range. Through later years he never had forage trouble on the Woody Mountain range..."always good feed up there," he said.

When Dr. Raymond began to withdraw from active business, Manterola sold his interest in Ohaco and bought some of the doctor's allotments and land holdings, and that included access to Woody Spring. The old metal-lined log troughs had deteriorated by then until they were almost unusable. Herders moved their animals across the northern base of the mountain but used the spring mainly for their own clean, cold drinking water.

The year Tony Manterola moved back to Woody Mountain, Cecil Miller, tired of the annual repair of boxes and pipe at Woody Spring, buried the spring itself. Manterola continued to use the water, but his access was slowly closing. Frank Auza, who had stayed on with the sheep after Dr. Raymond sold them, as Manterola foreman, said of the outcome that Tony "didn't know the rules." Other people put it differently: "Tony was a good guy." "He was not a fighter." It wasn't enough to know animals: a stock grower in the West needed to be half lawyer.

Manterola split his sheep operation between winter pasture around Casa Grande and summer allotments on the Coconino, trailing them across the Verde River suspension Sheep Bridge and up established driveways. With his French–Basque wife Marianne, his son Joe, and three daughters, he changed residence

10 Mooney was a name given to the canyon and trail below the Rim and to a mountain west of Woody. Its origin is unclear. A prospector, James Mooney, died in Havasupai Canyon in 1880. As the story was told, Mooney, on an expedition with several other men, made a rope ladder with cottonwood limbs for rungs to descend the cliff beside the lower falls. One rung broke, Mooney slipped and held on, and one of the ropes stuck in a crack. He hung suspended for two days while the other men tried to reach him by tunneling through the sedimentary rock beside the falls. On the third day he fell to his death on the rocks below. His body remained there for four years, preserved by minerals in the spray, before the tunnel was completed and the body retrieved and buried at the top of the falls. He may not have been the Mooney for whom the DK trail was named but, as Mark Twain said, a good story will do just as well as the facts.

with the seasons, like other ranchers in the neighborhood. The operation was prosperous under Manterola's management: by 1950, he was one of the directors of the Wool Growers Association.

Tony Manterola died in 1956, at the age of sixty-five, and Frank Auza stayed with the family corporation another three years, continuing to use Woody Spring. In the words of Manterola herder Jose Celestina Aguerrebere (also Basque), it was always reliable, "muy bien agua." He never saw it dry.

During that time Cecil Miller filed in the name of Coconino Cattle Company with the Arizona Department of Water Resources Public Water Rights Registry an action to claim the Woody Mountain spring. Uses were listed as Domestic (662,400 GPA) and Stock (200 cows/horses—529,920 GPA). The application stated that the water was "in use." That filing was retroactive to 1906, a common legal statement under Arizona law to safeguard water rights.

In 1959, Dr. Raymond died in his eighty-third year, not of the tuberculosis of his youth but of arteriosclerosis. At his death he owned real estate in town and outlying areas to a value of $921,374 and stocks in investments at $503,641. His bank accounts held $69,199. Thirty-four people in town owed him a total of $105,119. It was a sizeable estate.

Anticipating his death several years earlier, he had taken Frank Auza and newspaperman Platt Cline out to his ranch south of town, the one which included the old railroad pumphouse, and showed them where he wanted to be buried. In a pine box, he specified, cushioned with pine boughs. He wanted no ritual. When the time came, it was a simple burial; Dr. Fronske spoke a few words, but there was no pageantry for the man who had been a prominent Flagstaff citizen for fifty years. [see page 176]

Raymond, with no children, provided a bequest to Frank Auza and to a few other people. A good part of his estate went to the foundation he had established to provide grants and scholarships to Arizona students. That was in addition to land he had made available to the community hospital, to an antelope and buffalo refuge, and to the Boy Scouts for a summer camp. He had given to the state the Lindberg Springs rest area south of Flagstaff and land for Flagstaff's first National Guard Armory.

Everybody in town in following years felt the influence of Dr. Raymond's philanthropy. After 1959 the Raymond Foundation became a major supporter of the Flagstaff Symphony, the local historical society, and the scholarship program at Northern Arizona University—to the amount of over a quarter of a million dollars annually.

Cecil Miller, who had stood at Woody Spring that day in 1938 and argued with Dr. Raymond, survived him by twenty years. He was a gardener and a vigorous

Dr. Raymond's grave was protected from cattle by a low stone wall. When the ranch became Kachina Village, the site was part of a five-acre state park.

cook in that time: when there were guests at the ranch, he insisted on preparing all the meals. It was hard, his family said, to get him out of the kitchen.

As the twentieth century wore on, Miller and his boys were much entertained by a story of contraband in Rogers Lake. There were lots of versions, depending on who had heard it and from what source. It was a Flagstaff bank robbery of silver coin and a high speed pursuit in Model Ts on the dirt road out from town and a man in a hurry standing on the end of a dock on the north side and dumping money into the water. No, it was a stagecoach robbery of gold bars from the mine at Crown King and desperadoes on horseback who buried them at the south end of the lake in autumn when water was low, and next spring the level was up and they couldn't find the spot. No, they cut a hole in the ice in winter and threw in gold bars that were three feet long. Anyway, Dave Joy, who was fire lookout up on Woody Mountain, once found some old coins on the west side. That proved it was so.

The story was fabricated some time around 1965 by a prolific local writer named Gladwell Richardson, who was not above telling a stretcher now and then if it improved "true fiction."[11] He sold his Rogers Lake story under the pseudonym of Maurice Kildare to *True Treasure Publications*, which printed it in 1967 and again in 1973 under the title "Rogers Lake Loot."

In Richardson's version, in 1881 two outlaws stole from a mining company on the Agua Fria River eight bars of gold three feet long and four inches square (weight: better than seventy pounds each) and loaded them onto two big Missouri mules that just happened to be handy. In snowy autumn weather the outlaws drove those laden mules across the Verde Valley, up the Mooney Trail, and through twelve miles of forest to Rogers Lake, where they stopped because they found a deserted cabin as another snow storm "hurled down." Later they robbed a stagecoach of two ten-gallon oak kegs filled with twenty-five thousand dollars in gold and silver coins. As Richardson told it:

> The kegs were too heavy to carry far on saddles. Turning into a canyon, the outlaw pair busted in one keg with a rock. It contained $10 and $20 gold pieces...When the second one busted open it proved to be filled with silver dollars.

In the story, the outlaws attracted too much attention spending money freely in tent saloons in Flagstaff that spring and fled their Rogers Lake cabin one jump ahead of a posse, but first:

> They decided to put all of the loot into the lake for safe keeping. Walking out on the ice of the nearest point, they chopped a hole. Through this into deep water went the gold bars and the retopped kegs.

11 Titles of some of his three hundred novels, most of them published abroad, were *No Name Ridge, Sorry Cow Town, Spurtin' Lead, Stagecoach Round the Bend, Lobo Country, Dry Gulcher's Creek, Cattle Army, Greasewood Sink, Ride the Last Mile*. Richardson was published in, at last count, ninety-five periodicals under twenty pseudonyms and translated into German and Dutch—*Een Zware Opdract*, for example, which was an unusual name for a Western.

Richardson did not mention that the lake was usually almost dry in winter, as the Sitgreaves party had reported, and that it never had "deep water" in any season. Nevertheless, his story rushed on. Later one outlaw was killed in a bar brawl in Holbrook. The other became involved in the Graham–Tewksbury feud in Pleasant Valley, was arrested trying to steal silver bullion out of Globe, and spent twenty-four years in Yuma Territorial Prison. When he finally got back to Rogers Lake, he searched unsuccessfully for that lost gold and silver until he was "too aged to work and crippled with gunshot wounds."

Richardson filled his tale with references to C.T. Rogers, John Marshall, Dave Joy, and George Hochderffer, and he mentioned Woody Mountain. It all sounded plausible, even his mention of "a dam three-quarters of a mile long," which was obviously the AL&T logging railroad bed. He concluded with a paragraph on subsequent searches for the treasure and said:

> It is surprising how many stock bells, horseshoes, tin cans and other castaway metal objects have been dug up. But so far no one has hit the jackpot. The gold is still there for the finding.

It wasn't true, of course, but when the story got back to Flagstaff, as a powerful rumor, it made quite a stir. The Millers watched in fascination as people hurried to the lake "by the swarm" to dig. One expansive fellow brought a backhoe and tore up the south shore. Others came with metal detectors. There was never a summer for thirty years without someone on a treasure hunt, once from as far away as Illinois with sophisticated diving equipment for investigating the lake bed. That one caused a good deal of laughter. They all did. After solemnly requesting half of any gold recovered, the Millers sat on the porch of the ranch house on Sundays and watched the frenzied digging in their pasture.

Growing up as Arizona ranchers, the Miller brothers were as good as anybody at Western humor and high-country parties. For twenty-five years they sold cattle from the DK ranch to Manning Beef Packing in California. It was their custom each year on the first of September to meet Mr. Manning at Rogers Lake and then go up to Woody Spring for a picnic to settle the price of the cattle. More than a custom, a picnic at the spring was a kind of special privilege they offered to selected people. For real parties, by invitation, they brought in portable privies and garbage trailers and treated the meadow with the courtesy due to any living organism.

Both Miller boys married in their mid-twenties, Cecil to the daughter of a Colorado rancher, Duane to the granddaughter of Hank Lockett. There were eventually children and grandchildren (the great-grandchildren of Flagstaff pioneers) to gather at the spring for family picnics to play ball and horseshoes there in the meadow. For years there was a huge oak at the spring, a venerable thing more than two hundred years old, that overhung the fire ring. Someone, an anonymous town camper, who did not know or care about the importance of bark to the life of an oak tree started a fire against the trunk and burnt it to the core, killing it. It fell in a winter storm, to the regret of the whole family.

Katherine Lockett Miller and her son Claiborne were at Woody Spring in 1975.
Courtesy of Miller Brothers

Hoping to protect their land against hunters and woodcutters and town campers, the Millers enclosed the entire quarter section on the north side of Woody Mountain with a fence in 1972. Six years later, after operating for twenty years as sole and legal claimant of Woody Spring, they filed with the state a formal application to appropriate the water. Finally, their patience frayed, they felt that they could no longer tolerate the behavior of thoughtless ("Well, they don't think; they just don't *think*") trespassers.

In 1980 the Millers notified the Forest Service that the road which crossed the DK quarter section to the fire lookout on top of the mountain would be legally closed to public traffic and the gate locked. That effectively excluded all other users past, present, and future—lookout personnel, Manterola sheep, Coconino Cattle Company stock, and the general public—from the meadow at the spring, leaving it to its slow, quiet return to the way it looked before John Woody arrived seeking opportunity.

May and June were the annual drought, with an average rainfall, both months together, of little over an inch. Then came July and August when moist air from the Gulf of Mexico was pushed westward by high pressure to meet currents from the Pacific and updrafts of hot air from sun-heated land to rise and condense above the mountains. Those were the wettest months.

Summer mornings began with a white cloud no bigger than a marble above the Peaks, but cumulus developed out of nothing visible. By mid-day the sky was mottled in every direction by clouds with flat grey bottoms. They seemed to grow from within, surging upward, thickening until they became a dark mass, dropping black curtains that hid the shapes of volcanos.

One-fourth of the moisture that fell on the mountain came in July and August in wind-driven rain and pounding hail and sometimes in fine mists. Not until then did grasses like grama, mountain muhly, and dropseed, which had been hardly noticeable through the hot dry months, suddenly turn green and thrust up seed stalks.

Grass and tree roots took most of the water and held some back long enough for it to sink out of sight and filter away to the spring. But there were places, especially after the loggers had left, where it ran downhill, carrying particles of dirt, wearing small paths that grew as the years went on into gullies and ravines filled after every storm with plunging brown water. The mountain wore away slowly, a little more each summer.

Chapter Six
Scientists

1894–1950

A.E. Douglass
Courtesy of Tom Hardin
Laboratory of Tree Ring Research
University of Arizona

Godfrey Sykes and his brother Stanley ("Shorty") worked on that new fad, the bicycle, in their Flagstaff shop in the 1890s.
Lowell Observatory

By the last decade of the nineteenth century, science on America's eastern sea-coast had outgrown its adolescence. A full fifty years earlier the Coast Survey, the Smithsonian Institution, and the Association for the Advancement of Science had appeared on the scene. Harvard College had opened its observatory and was doing astronomical photography. After the War Between the States both the National Academy of Science and Massachusetts Institute of Technology were organized, and Louis Agassiz had his Museum of Comparative Zoology on the Harvard campus. In 1871 M.I.T. admitted its first woman.

Science had expanded from the East into the nineteenth century West; it was inseparable from the development of the country between the Rockies and the Sierra. All those Army expeditions had traveled about mapping, with geologists, anthropologists, and paleontologists integral to the parties. Samuel Woodhouse had accompanied Sitgreaves as naturalist, as well as physician, and made daily observations. One of the men killed with Gunnison and Kern on that fateful morning in 1853 in Utah was the group's botanist. When John Wesley Powell, a young professor of natural science, made his first trip west in 1867, he had with him a botanist, a herpetologist, a mineralogist, entomologists, zoologists, and ornithologists, or at least people who carried those labels. His heroic 1869 Colorado River adventure was officially titled a Scientific Exploring Expedition.

By 1882, when Flagstaff was born, there were in the country 144 astronomical observatories maintained by schools, private individuals, and the national government. All of that, however, was in the three-hundred-year-old communities in the East. On the frontier the story was quite different.

In 1894 the University of Arizona in Tucson, only three years old, had fifty-seven students and a total of nine "hopeful" faculty members. Equipment for science classes, which focused on mining and agriculture, amounted to not much more than a handful of garden tools. The state museum established a year earlier by the Territorial Legislature was contained in a few display cases.

Flagstaff was only a dozen years old then, and Coconino County was brand new. There was no Emerson School, no available secondary education, no Normal School south of the railroad tracks for "higher" learning. With a population of eight hundred, the town had fewer residents than late-twentieth century city high schools would have students. Arizona Territory was a long way from Harvard.

But Flagstaff, with its daily trains delivering newspapers and magazines, was neither benighted nor ignorant of progress, and it was getting practical matters under control. In April of 1894 the *Sun* reported that a sidewalk was being built on the south side of Railroad Avenue to extend to the town's only schoolhouse, which was across the tracks. There was agitation for a municipal water system so that people could drink from faucets instead of dippers at the family buckets. The Riordan brothers had begun to talk of organizing an electric company, and telephones were becoming available.

Eager eastern scientists were all over the country. Godfrey ("Red") Sykes, somewhat to his amusement, found himself involved.

> Scientific bodies in Washington and other reputed centers of culture and scientific research were, at that period, just beginning to become "Arizona conscious," and earnest young scientists, representing almost all branches of research, from astronomy to zoology, were being shipped West in platoons to look the country over and make examinations and reports. Flagstaff, from its position on the map, was judged to be a convenient centre to radiate from, so many disembarked there...They came upon us in hired conveyances, upon hastily acquired or borrowed horses, and even on foot. We welcomed them, found most of them to be mere human beings like ourselves, and helped them in their several investigations as well as we could. They found new plants, new birds, undescribed rocks and minerals, and myriads of new reptiles and bugs upon every side of us and appeared to be well pleased with the country and what it contained.

The Sykes brothers, "Fixers and Menders of Everything," never treated scientists, even the abstract kinds, as eccentrics. The result was that scientists began to congregate in the Sykes brothers' bicycle shop, where they sat around watching the mechanical parts the brothers could turn out on the forge, the foot pedal lathe, the hand-operated drill press.

In 1894 a young astronomer arrived in Flagstaff from Boston and established the first real scientific facility in Arizona Territory. Its staff settled in to live and in doing so began an immigration of scientists that made the little logging and ranching town on the railroad unlike any other place for hundreds of miles.[1] Flagstaff's story was always inseparable from that of Woody Mountain; inevitably some of the outdoor work of those scientists touched the lava cone in the forest southwest of town.

The harbinger of the intellectual flood was Andrew Ellicott Douglass, who had begun his study of astronomy, as a boy in grammar school, with his great-grandfather's telescope. As an assistant at Harvard College Observatory in 1894, Douglass was introduced to Percival Lowell, twelve years older, a wealthy son of Boston

---

1 In 1988 the Coconino National Forest employed twenty wildlife biologists, silviculturists, archaeologists, hydrologists and soil scientists. Lowell Observatory had a staff of thirty, twelve of them Ph.D.s in astronomy. The Museum of Northern Arizona, with a roster of fifty, employed approximately fifteen scientists, interns and summer assistants. Rocky Mountain Forest and Range Experiment Station's staff of thirteen to twenty (depending on projects) included five scientists and four technicians. There were eighty-seven professors in the classic sciences (biology, physics, chemistry, geology, etc.) on the faculty of Northern Arizona University, with other professors in such disciplines as forestry, psychology and anthropology, and an uncounted number of teaching, research, dispensary, and laboratory assistants, as well as graduate students and a knowledgable group of secretaries for each department. Add to that ten full-time astronomers and four technicians employed at the U.S. Naval Observatory, eight botanists at the Arboretum west of town, and two hundred geologists and other professionals at the U.S. Geological Survey facility, plus scientists on the payrolls of the city, county, and state. The total, in a town of 42,000 inhabitants, gave to Flagstaff a ratio of scientists to non-scientists rivaled in the southwest only by Los Alamos.

With the agreement to take a leave of absence and work with Lowell,
Douglass changed his life more than he could have anticipated;
he spent the next sixty-eight years in Arizona.
Special Collections, University of Arizona Library

families and an amateur astronomer who was fascinated, like a lot of people at the time, by the possibility of intelligent *engineering* life on Mars. The red planet was due to approach close to earth that summer, close enough perhaps for a good look at those "canals" which Schiaparelli claimed to have seen in 1877, and Lowell was eager to examine them. He decided to finance with his "portly pocketbook" an observatory in the West, perhaps in Arizona where population was sparse and air was clear, and he accepted Douglass as his assistant on the advice of Harvard's W. H. Pickering.

A.E. Douglass was twenty-seven when he arrived in Benson in March of 1894, carrying Lowell's six-inch refracting telescope and instructions for a hurried selection of a site. Lowell wanted a place at least two hundred feet above the surrounding land, removed from mountain ranges and in the middle of a large level platform. He specified "the best procurable air." Douglass was to look not so much for clear skies as for steady air with a minimum of atmospheric currents. Pickering back at Harvard had devised a new "scale of seeing" for rating star images from zero to ten, depending on air stability, and Douglass began his survey confident that he had a scientific basis for judgment.

Everywhere he went, everybody wanted an observatory. Representatives of the Southern Pacific railroad recommended Picacho Peak, which was on the S.P. line. The Mayor of Nogales, the District Attorney of Yuma County, the Tempe Board of Trade all wrote suggesting their areas and promising to build any necessary roads. Benson, Tombstone, Tucson, Tempe and Prescott were prepared to cooperate in any way they could, and Douglass took sightings on stars in each location. On his scale, he could rate none higher than six or seven. After a month of observing nearly every night, Douglass hadn't found a site in southern Arizona which he could approve.

Matt Riordan, who was still in charge at AL&T in 1894, had been busy using his influence on behalf of Flagstaff: he had written directly to "the authorities at Harvard." The little town on the central railroad line would at least be a convenient place. Mars was approaching closer with each day, favorable opposition was due in mid-October, and time was short. Lowell, who had stayed in the East, telegraphed to Douglass to investigate Flagstaff.

The young man from Boston stepped off the train on Railroad Avenue after sunset on April 3, 1894. For the next twelve years he would be a popular resident; for the next two weeks he was a much-catered-to guest. Flagstaff people wanted an observatory as much as anybody else did, and they offered all the help they could think of.

The search was reported in the *Sun* on Thursday, April 12, under the title "The Most Favorable Point."

> Prof. A. E. Douglass is making observations with his six-inch telescope from various points in the vicinity. On Saturday his instrument was moved to the mountain south of Fort Valley, but the weather was unfavorable for observation until Monday and Tuesday nights. The result of the observation has been that

the professor has found almost perfect conditions of atmosphere...Prof. Douglass is so well pleased that he will remain some time yet and take observations from the peaks of the San Francisco mountains, and from some of the lower points east of the mountain.

The Riordans put teams and men at his disposal and pledged help for the project on behalf of the A&P railroad. Douglass made observations on every clear night, carrying the telescope to at least eleven different places around Flagstaff. He tried A-1 Mountain and probably Wing Mountain and Mt. Elden. Lowell cabled "Try highest available spot in neighborhood," so he might have climbed up the Peaks and perhaps onto O'Leary, one of the "lower points east of the mountain." Possibly he tried other places farther from town—Mormon Mountain and Sheep Hill and the Turkey Hills near Elden, all of them old volcanos.[2]

Did he climb up Woody Mountain to take sightings? Probably he did. It was close to town and very visible. The road to Rogers Lake skirted its base close to Woody's spring, a good source of water, and the Riordans would have done all they could to help him investigate there. The branch mill had been established at Rogers Lake for seven years by then with a telephone line into town. T.A. would have thought it "a lot of fun" to have an observatory in the neighborhood. But Douglass's notes on his Flagstaff survey disappeared and with them the answer.

Another observatory site search fifty-six years later provided an inkling to what Douglass's opinion might have been. In 1950 John S. Hall, director of the U.S. Naval Observatory in Washington, proposed to evaluate Woody Mountain as a possible "dark sky" site for a Naval Observatory to specialize in measurement of star positions and provide data for accurate navigation. He wrote to V.M. Slipher, Director of Lowell.

> Our Council met on June 14 and passed a resolution to the effect that our 40-inch reflector should be moved to the vicinity of Flagstaff, Arizona...We are anxious to choose a specific site for this instrument at a reasonably early date. It appears that we should locate at least five miles from the town. Also, due to the direction of clear-weather winds, we should look northward, west or southwest of the town for the clearest atmosphere. Areas which look promising (on a survey map) are: A 1 Mtn., Mt. Wing, Woody Mtn., and a knoll at 7700 feet a mile north of Rogers Lake.

On a cold night in November of 1950, Mr. Hall climbed Woody Mountain to determine whether there was room enough for a transit circle division: a level terrain in the north-south direction over a distance of three hundred yards. He eliminated the mountain from consideration because the top just wasn't broad enough and thought that Douglass probably had come to the same conclusions.

2 The *Sun* informed Flagstaff that Douglass had reported a comet as being visible in the southeastern sky, best seen at four in the morning. Front page news, however, was of a petition being circulated in town which would require that hogs be fenced and kept from wandering freely through streets and back alleys.

We measured the elevation at three points, made a rough sketch of the top and paced off some distances. The top was flat enough for a transit circle but not extensive enough for the north and south markers used in circle work.

Mr. Hall and the Navy astronomers chose a knoll northeast of Rogers Lake and two miles north of Woody Mountain for their observatory. It became one of the few institutions in the world and the only one in the United States to specialize in astrometry, that branch of astronomy in which the positions and motions of the sun, moon, planets, and selected stars are precisely determined and their future positions computed.

John Hall became director of Lowell Observatory in 1958. He never examined the notes made by Douglass in his 1894 site search; they were missing from the archives in the basement of the observatory's library. Diary pages of readings from southern Arizona sites were there with the wires and letters which Douglass exchanged with Lowell, but there was a crucial gap in the collection for several days of April, when he was in Flagstaff. With the exception of A-1 ("the mountain south of Fort Valley") and the site which was finally chosen, and Lowell's reference to "the Spring Valley Station," which could not be identified on later maps, the exact locations which had been evaluated could not be determined.[3]

There was some uneasiness about the location which was chosen for Lowell's observatory. "Steady air" was a major issue in the site search. There were rumors that Douglass preferred building the observatory on an elevation farther from the turbulence created by the Peaks: "...these mountains project up into the great stream of air moving overhead and cause eddies of various kinds." But Lowell at long distance overruled him. It was Lowell's money. By 1900 both men conceded that air currents were a handicap to viewing; astronomers in later years continued to complain of them.

Whatever the reasons, Percival Lowell decided from Boston that the eleventh of the sites Douglass had investigated near town would do for his observatory—it had rated an eight on Pickering's "scale of seeing"—and telegraphed, "Flagstaff it is...Push on the work there as fast as possible." Residents promptly dubbed the place, the end of the long A-1 lava flow, Mars Hill. Douglass broke ground on April 23. It was a convenient site, on land that had already been surveyed, close enough to Flagstaff restaurants and boarding houses to make the staff comfortable without immediate domestic construction.

Eighty-four citizens—including all three Riordan brothers, four of the Babbitts and two of the Hochderffers—signed a commitment on behalf of the community to see that title to the land, to the extent of ten or fifteen acres, would be deeded to the observatory "for the sum of One Dollar." They further pledged

---

3 Gossip among old-timers was that after a quarrel in 1901, Lowell, a man of stormy moods, systematically removed from his archives as many references as he could to Douglass, going so far as to cut pages out of books with a razor blaade. One theory was that he disposed of the missing notes in that general exorcism.

"that a good wagon road shall be constructed and maintained from the Railroad Station at Flagstaff to the Observatory Site."

On April 19, 1894, the *Sun* reported that Al Doyle was recovering from bilious fever and that the ladies of the Presbyterian Church were arranging a musical evening of lullabies and serenades of all nations, to be given at Babbitt Hall. On the 26th it noted that the sisters of A.E. Douglass had stopped off in town for a few days and confirmed the good news that Flagstaff had won the state-wide competition.

> It has been definitely decided to locate the observatory on the mesa just west of town, and just outside of the town limits. Work was commenced Monday on the foundation, and the work will be pushed until the building is finished. A road has been surveyed to the site of the observatory, which is about 400 feet higher than the town. Work will be commenced on the road next week, and it will be an extension of Aspen Avenue to the top of the mesa.

By May 3, the road was "passable for a light conveyance" and local workmen had finished the foundation for a dome. Matt Riordan put his influence with the railroad to good use in getting "four or five tons altogether" of telescope, cast iron foundation, and some woodwork shipped quickly from Tucson. Douglass simply gave Riordan his Bills of Lading for the equipment, which had been sent to southern Arizona in anticipation of a site there, and Riordan took care of the whole matter for him.

Flagstaff had the coveted observatory and a resident scientist. On a salary of eight hundred dollars a year, Douglass bought meal tickets at local restaurants and carried them until all their numbers were punched out.[4] He was a congenial fellow, a healthy young bachelor with a strong jaw and a big sandy moustache, and he was much in demand for Flagstaff card parties and fancy balls with the ladies, whom Lowell called "the picnic half of the world."

The group of men who gathered around the Sykes brothers' bicycle shop also liked him and cheerfully took him into membership. "Red" Sykes welcomed them all.

> With the establishment of the Lowell Observatory the town was becoming more and more popular as a port of call for Scientific Cruisers in every line. In addition to Astronomers and Physicists we caught Geologists, Ethnologists and Anthropologists, Botanists, Ornithologists, and, in local parlance, "plain Bugologists a'plenty." This was very nice! We listened to them discussing solar systems, planets, satellites, molecules and atoms...Thus our modest engineering establishment became a sort of clearing house for advanced theories, nebulous hypotheses, and personal information concerning worms, bugs, and wild-life generally. Then a few of the resident members of the scientific coterie organized

---

4 Some of them remained among his miscellaneous papers in the Special Collections Library at the University of Arizona in Tucson.

An 18-inch refractor from the University of Pennsylbania was freighted into Flagstaff
and carted up Mars Hill.
Lowell Observatory

Andrew Douglass (left) joined Balzar Hock and George Babbitt
in watching Godfrey Sykes at work.
Lowell Observatory

themselves into a sort of informal club, under the name of "The Busy Bees." The daily meeting place was our workshop, the ostensible purpose of the gatherings was social intercourse and the exchange of current scientific gossip, but actually the members of the organization merely appeared to sit around on workbenches and other inconvenient perches and look on contemplatively while we hammered away upon wood or metal in the prosecution of our making and mending operations. They were very pleasant and soothing gatherings, nevertheless.

When the Sykes brothers had caught up on their making and mending, they participated with "The Busy Bees" in such intellectual activities as pitching pennies. Henry Giclas heard stories about their horseplay and wrote them down years later for preservation in *The Journal of Arizona History*.

Stanley and his brother looked very much alike; they would get up a two-bit or fifty-cent bet with a newcomer that they could beat him around the main block on a bicycle. The racers would start off together, but then the brother would purposely fall behind. The challenger was sure he had it won. The other brother in the meantime would proceed up through the alley and as the newcomer rode by would pop out with a burst of fresh speed and win the race. In the meantime, the first brother had returned to the shop and would compliment the winner on his great ability to overtake such a fast-pedaling opponent!

There was no end to the ingenuity of the Sykes' academic coterie.

In those days the wooden sidewalk in front of the shop was about two feet above the ground. A favorite prank was to drop a half dollar or more through the cracks in the boards and then tell one of the "Bees" of losing the money in under the sidewalk. Invariably one of them would crawl under the walk to retrieve the money, at which instant one of the brothers found it necessary to empty a pail of water on the sidewalk in front of the door.

Under the influence of "The Busy Bees," Douglass invented what he described as a "permanent bicycle lock" and a new kind of tennis racquet, but he had time for astronomy as well. For seven years he worked at Lowell's facility up on Mars Hill, supervising the construction of a dome and processing data. For the first four years illness kept Lowell in the East, and Douglass served as acting director. Most of his professional work during those years was on the solar planets, particularly investigation to support Lowell's theories about Mars.

Winter clouds often interfered with the use of the telescope, which came as no surprise to people who had been in town from the beginning. Winter snow often made it hard to get up the hill. Douglass punned that his "chief astronomical work was in studying the ski," and he learned how to use his snowshoes as a toboggan to slide down Mars Hill to his boarding house.

During the first winter Godfrey Sykes noticed that the astronomers were quick to use the excuse of "poor seeing" to spend a stormy night warm in bed, and Stanley Sykes devised a new scale of seeing for the observatory.

10 is when you can see the moon.
 5 is when you can see the telescope.
 1 is when you can only feel the telescope but not see it.

The Sykes brothers, "Makers and Menders of Everything," tackled mechanical problems brought down to them from the observatory,

> ...and their solution was generally a comfort and a joy, because apparently the mental processes of Astronomers differ markedly from those of ordinary mortals, and the difficulties which confront them when their thoughts are presumably innumerable "light-years" away are not at all those experienced in everyday life.

The brothers received an urgent request from Lowell to design and build a forty-foot dome. Godfrey, who came to be regarded as the observatory's man-of-all-work, relished telling the story in later years.

> I asked him for more explicit instructions as to details because, as I explained, the building of astronomical domes had not hitherto been one of my more common forms of activity. He replied that as we claimed to be competent makers of anything, that of course covered the case and settled the matter. He deemed it to have been a concession upon his part to have mentioned the diameter of the structure which he wished for and further discussion concerning details was clearly unnecessary.
>
> Alvan Clark, the most famous maker of great lenses at that time, had ground, polished, figured, and mounted the twenty-four inch lens for the refractor which the new dome was to house, and he spent the Summer of 1896 in Flagstaff as the guest of Mr. Lowell. He remarked one day, in my hearing, anent some of the difficulties incidental to the construction of this very successful telescope, and the pressure for greater speed to which he had been subjected, "Percival Lowell is a very fine and brilliant man and he has a keen mathematical mind, but his only idea for overcoming a mechanical difficulty is to write a cheque."

In so small a town, camaraderie between settlers and the new scientists was inevitable. From the beginning, the staff at the observatory scheduled viewing evenings that opened the facility to anyone who was interested. Mars and the moon were the most popular subjects, but other planets, stars, and nebulae were also shown. Hospitality was reciprocal: the astronomers were an immediate addition to dances, fancy balls, and card parties in town.

While the Sykes brothers were inventing a dome, Flagstaff accepted its sudden respectability by building a new grammar school. It replaced the Hochderffer's brick factory on the west bank of the Rio de Flag with two stories and a basement providing five classrooms, a storeroom, an auditorium, and a wide, twenty-two step stairway on either side. A couple of the older boys were hired at twenty-five dollars a month to carry coal and kindling from the basement to boxes in all the rooms. The bell at Emerson School could be heard all over town. In the morning children lined up outside by grades, the youngest first. To the beat of a triangle, they sang as they marched to their classes.

Three years later the *Gem* editorialized:

> Flagstaff needs a college. The demand for such an institution is growing rapidly. This is the best location for a college in the west on account of being so healthy, and the morals of the town are not surpassed in the territory.

Moral or not, Flagstaff already had a large stone building south of the tracks on land that had been deeded by the railroad. Established in March of 1899, it was first designed as a reform school, but citizens demurred. A mental hospital was proposed for the building, but they didn't want that either. There was suspicion that the initial suggestions had been steps in political maneuvering, but at any rate the town finally got what it wanted: a Normal School that would serve as both high school and teacher training college.

Over the years, while Flagstaff was building schools, A.E. Douglass up at the observatory began to be skeptical of Percival Lowell's enthusiasm for proving that intelligent life existed on Mars and his belief that insight was superior to eyesight, which Douglass considered unscientific. Indeed, he felt that the older man was in the tradition of the Victorian amateur, motivated more by the spirit of literature than the spirit of science.

The first photographs of the "canals" on Mars were made at Lowell's observatory, causing much international excitement. Then in 1900 there was a worldwide flap about a "message" flashed from the red planet, a story which the press attributed to Flagstaff's astronomers, much to Douglass's disgust. He wrote to Lowell's brother-in-law that the observatory should divorce its research from its patron's speculation: "I fear it will not be possible to turn him into a scientific man." The letter was eventually shown to Lowell, who reacted with predictable anger, and suddenly, at the age of thirty-four, Andrew Douglass was out of a job, with time to pursue new ideas. The long-term result was that his career once again touched Woody Mountain.

Douglass was a specialist with seventeen years work in astronomy, but there were no positions open at the observatories to which he applied, and he was at a loss for occupation for a while. After eight years in Flagstaff, he had friends. As the *Sun* put it:

> ...there isn't a cow puncher or lumberman in the whole section with whom he is ashamed to rub shoulders...all hands, from logging camp to the sheep and cattle camps are his staunch friends. They can't help it when they know him.

The obvious course for a man with friends and no job was local politics. About the time John Woody was selling his ranch interests and moving to

Fred Breen photographed Douglass and Al Doyle on a trip the three took out of town.
Special Collections, Univeristy of Arizona Library

Like Fred Breen, who was struggling during those years
as supervisor of the Forest Reserve, Douglass married a teacher,
Ida Wittington, music instructor and assistant principal at Emerson School
Special Collections, University of Arizona Library

California, Douglass became the Republican candidate for county probate judge. While on a campaigning trip to Williams, he stopped near Bellemont to eat his lunch on the stump of a large pine tree and sat observing the rings in the old stump as he ate. After lunch he traveled on, campaigning, and was elected to county office. He was re-elected two years later.

For a year Douglass was a teacher at the new Normal School. When the Territorial Attorney General advised that he couldn't find any law against it, Douglass combined his position as judge with a job as instructor of Spanish, history and miscellaneous subjects. Then, after twelve years in Flagstaff, he and his wife moved to Tucson, where he took a place on the faculty of the University of Arizona. He carried with him research data that formed the basis of work that would make him famous: an improbable link between astronomy and northern Arizona pines. It had all started that day of the lunch stop near Bellemont.

In the beginning of 1904, the year in which AL&T crews took the trees away from Woody Mountain, Douglass measured the width of growth rings in a log at the yard in Milton. In the months after Lowell had fired him, Douglass, with time to spare, made a practice of traveling out to logging camps near Flagstaff to examine ring patterns in freshly cut stumps, looking for evidence that the eleven-year cycle of sunspots had been recorded in the trees. He had a theory that the growth of ponderosa pines responded chiefly to precipitation, that their clear growth rings showed a difference in width between wet and dry years, and that if he could find some climate pattern corresponding to sun spots, it could be used to predict weather and to measure solar variation. T.A. Riordan, who thought almost everything was interesting, found the idea fascinating and gave Douglass freedom to investigate logs and stumps in the yard, the camps, the logging sites.

Over the next two years, Douglass took sections from forty-nine more trees cut by logging crews in various places around Flagstaff and noticed that tree rings showed the same pattern from one area to another, one camp to another, throughout northern Arizona. Around Flagstaff he found major dry periods occurring at 150 year intervals and minor drought every forty to fifty years, all clustering, he was sure, around the sunspot cycle.

For fifteen years Douglass measured 175,000 rings on 230 different specimens from all over the world, including California Sequoias. By cross-dating all those samples—establishing identical dates in different trees—he took his time sequence back three thousand years. Gathering momentum, he used logs in Indian ruins all over the Southwest, bored *in situ*, to reinforce his theories and in the process aided archaeological dating. Until his death at the age of ninety-five, he was constantly refining the field which he had created—dendrochronology, the study of the time sequence of tree rings to establish past environmental conditions.

Later it was not possible to ascertain that any of Douglass's original tree samples came from Woody Mountain: they were identified by number rather than site. He began his work during 1904, the year in which the mountain was logged. Dendrochronology may have been one of the purposes to which the Woody pines were put, but that could not be proved. More important was the insight which his work made possible into life on the mountain. The tree study, which had its origin so close at hand, was as revealing about the story of Woody Mountain as it was of archaeological sites.

In 1986—over three quarters of a century after Douglass began his work— the lookout was climbing around on the slopes taking, as Douglass had done, core samples from trees to count growth rings and establish the age of trees. The same year Steve Sackett and Jack Dietrich, both from the Forest Experiment Station on the N.A.U. campus, went onto the mountain to use Douglass's cross-dating meth ods to determine fire history on the north side, where some pre-logging trees still stood. Because of his work, they were able to look back nearly five hundred years to a different kind of forest.

Before Anglo settlement, the pines around the Peaks were so widely spaced that a horseman could go through them at a gallop. They were big, but they stood far apart, and they took up less actual ground than the grasses which grew among them. That abundant grass, especially when it was dry, spread fires from frequent lightning strikes during early summer storms across considerable acreage. On level ground those grass fires didn't usually get hot enough to cause much damage to the isolated trees. Flames flashed past, close-growing seedlings were burned and thinned, but mature pines were left scarred and alive.

It was on steeply rising slopes that fires left a record for later reading. In the days before logging altered the nature of the forest, when pines were far apart and natural burns were often confined to the forest floor, debris burned hot enough on the uphill sides of tree trunks, close to the ground, to char them and leave tell-tale evidence, triangular-shaped scars where bark had been repeatedly burned away.

Research foresters Sackett and Dietrich flaked away charred wood from those scars with their pocket knives and interpreted what they could see. In their opinion, fire had swept across the northwest side of Woody Mountain at least fifteen times in the lives of the older trees, but probably not seriously since the establishment of organized Forest Service fire crews early in the twentieth century.

In the gullies between ridges on the north and east there were dense stands of aspen, old enough for the groves to be decadent and the ground covered like jackstraws with white-barked trees that had died and fallen. It was Sackett's opinion that such rising gullies had made convection chimneys that had carried fire right to the top, burning hot, reducing to black ash everything that grew. Afterward aspen, always quick to take advantage of newly opened, sunny ground, had been the first trees to take hold, propagating chiefly by sprouts from their roots. But all that had been a long time earlier, a hundred years at least. It would have taken that long for aspen to grow to maturity and for new pines to begin to rise among them.

On an afternoon in October, with the Millers' permission, Sackett and two of his students went onto the slope again with a chain saw to slice sections from

An un-cut Ponderosa stand that had had centuries to develop had the aspect
of a park of tawny, widely-spaced giants with few young trees in their shade
and little undergrowth—an "open" forest.
United States Forest Service

On slopes like the steep flanks of Woody Mountain, debris—pine needles,
fallen oak leaves—accumulated on the uphill sides of trees
and made a pocket for burning at intense heat.

Fire scars were visible at the base of old trees high on the slopes.

fire scars on two of the huge pines which had survived the repeated burning, cutting through one-fifth of the circumference to the core of the trees.

Polished sections of the slabs cut from the Woody Mountain trees were taken to Douglass's Laboratory of Tree Ring Research at the University of Arizona in Tucson, where tree ring data had been filed in a computer. The pines had produced clear growth rings, with wet seasons distinct from dry ones, summer from winter. The number of fires that had occurred could be determined by counting annual rings and the dark lines that represented burning of the bark. Matching samples, comparing rings that variation in weather had produced, Swetnam and Bailey in Tucson supplied precise dating on those two trees and the fires that had swept past them. The record was as precise as if it had been written and less open to error.

Cross section #1, was from a pine sixty inches in circumference which had germinated in 1678, one hundred years before the American Revolution against England. It had been injured by burning seventeen times between 1694 and 1845, an average of once every nine years, the first time when it was only sixteen years old. Most of those fires had been in the dry months of May or June.

Tree #2 was even older: the innermost ring on its cross section showed that it had had its beginning in 1531, nine years before Coronado's first European expedition into the Southwest. With a circumference of ninety-three inches, it was 454 years old. [see page 200]

Its oldest fire scar was for the fall of 1736 or early in the spring of 1737—some time during cool weather while the tree was dormant—but Jack Dietrich did not doubt that the big pine had been singed often during its first two hundred years, with evidence burned off by subsequent blazes. In spring of 1747 red flames had swept up the ridge again, burned the uphill wood, and left a heavy black line on that year's growth ring. Between 1737 and 1863 the tree was injured by burning on an average of once every ten years, usually early in its growing season. Each time the pine had survived the damage, and lived quietly on, and worked slowly to heal itself.

According to the record in the tree, in early summer storms, century after century, there was a sound of wind coming up the slope of Woody Mountain toward the trees on the summit. As the wind came, pines began to sway, oak leaves turned pale side up, and air temperatures fell. Cloud shadow moved over the mountain.

With a sudden cracking explosion, a white-hot bolt of lightning, the first of the season, stabbed into a pine on the northwest ridge, blasting off the top in a fireball, splitting loose slivers ten feet long and hurling them in all directions. Spiraling down the trunk, it burrowed into the ground and left a mound that stretched away for three or four yards.

A line of orange flared along the wound made on the pine. Burning branches fell into grass withered after the drought of May and June. It crackled into flames that raced uphill and caught in the dry remains of a tree that had fallen fifty years earlier and lay stretched along the ground.

Growth of cambium had curled around to hide from casual view all scars dating after 1805.

Twice more powerful strikes hit the mountain before rain began to hiss down through the trees and send squirrels leaping for shelter. Fire in the grass subsided, but when the storm passed on half an hour later, logs and stumps and standing trees were still burning. Next morning as sun warmed the air, pale yellow blades of grass caught again and passed fire along the ground to scorch bark at the base of any tree in its path. Sometimes over the centuries for days at a time smoke from smoldering logs rose from the mountain.

Fire history on the north side of Woody Mountain had been complex. Those two pines sampled by research foresters were only a few hundred feet apart on the side of a ridge, yet the same fires had scarred them both only seven times. Aspen that covered the north slope, golden and clearly visible from town in October, had had their origin not after one large fire about seventy years earlier, as local wisdom guessed, but as a result of repeated burning from lightning strikes over more than a century, the last at least a century earlier. The stand was transient: within another hundred years, that side of the mountain would no longer be noticeable to people in town.

Untouched by T.A.'s loggers, the upper part of the north slope presented a glimpse into the past, a record not just of wet summers and dry ones, but also an image of smell and sound and blowing smoke and scurrying squirrels that stretched back nearly five hundred years. There were no ranchers or rangers around then to notice what happened, and they were not entirely necessary. Andrew Douglass had provided a key to the private history of trees; thus hundreds of seasons on Woody Mountain became clear for the reading.

Who would have guessed that such records were hidden in the pines? Their appearance did not seem to change from one season to another. There was a lot about them that nobody knew when loggers cut the other trees from Woody Mountain and hauled them away.

Not long after Douglass left Flagstaff in 1906, another man able to understand and explain pines came into the mountain's story. Logging slash had just been cleared to the satisfaction of Forest Service rangers by then. Grass grew up amid silence and wreckage, wood chips, gouges in the earth. And raw stumps. There were those ancient pines on the northwest ridge and aspen of varying ages across the north slope. On the east side a pine that had germinated the year John Woody was born held on near one that had begun before the Revolutionary War. Except for that, the mountain was bare to the sun.

A survey of forest conditions in 1904 by the Geological Survey had established that, before logging, the average age of pines in the Woody Mountain township had been 190 years, the average diameter twenty inches. Pines had made up ninety-six percent of the trees, oak four percent. The Survey's summary of the township was dismal.

Low reproductive ratio during the past 20 to 25 years. The pine forest is a forest long since past its prime and now in a state of decadence. The pine is slowly diminishing in reproductive vigor, and the ultimate result will be extinction of the species in these areas. This decline has probably been going on for centuries.

Excessively close logging, which is a common practice on private holdings in the reserve, does not provide for a sufficiency of seed trees to restock the denuded areas.

Closely logged lands will not again bear a forest equal to the one cut off during the next 220 to 250 years.

Loggers had heedlessly clear-cut around Flagstaff for twenty-five years at the time of the survey. T.A. Riordan told his granddaughter, Mary, that he had left enough trees to replenish the forest: "Ponderosa pine is the only tree that will re-seed itself naturally," he told her. However, the forest on the Coconino showed no signs of coming back.

A government circular admitted: "Reproduction has not been satisfactory, either in the virgin forest or after lumbering operations, and large areas once covered with good stands...are now practically bare." On whole sections of railroad land there wasn't a tree in sight; vegetation between Milton and the head of Oak Creek Canyon was mostly grass.

Fear began to grow that logging regulation had come too late, that unless something were done to help nature along, the forest around Flagstaff was rapidly on its way to extinction. Government, new to responsibility for such matters, decided it was time to supplement politics and idealism with a little science, and thus, in 1908, a group of research men laid before Gifford Pinchot a plan for establishing Forest Experiment Stations.

Eventually there would be twelve of those stations—one for each of the major timber regions of the United States—to provide a permanent organization for carrying on over a long span of years work that would provide a scientific basis for forest management. Ponderosa pine had a greater commercial importance than any other tree in the Southwest; it constituted most of the lumber cut in Arizona. Bare hills on the Coconino Forest made the area a prime candidate for those research men.

On a trip to Arizona Territory in the summer of 1908, Raphael Zon—transplanted Russian, immigrant forester, colleague of Pinchot's—arrived in Flagstaff, rented a horse from a livery stable, and began to look around for a location for the first forest station in the United States. One afternoon in August, accompanied by a young botanist named Gustaf Adolph Pearson, he went out to examine a site near Fort Valley. Later Pearson wrote about that afternoon.

Two miles short of our destination a thunderstorm crashed down upon us in true Arizona style. The downpour was more violent than usual, so we took shelter in a large barn of the old A-1 Cattle Company. When we emerged an hour later, the normally dry Rio de Flag was running a hundred yards wide with a fluid whose color and consistency told plainly that the country was going to the dogs even in that early day. After crossing the "river," it was only half a mile to the area we had come to see—a beautiful stand of Ponderosa pine. "Here," said Zon, "we shall plant the tree of research!"

The site they chose for that first experiment station was nine miles due north of Woody Mountain. The principal forest around it was a simple one—ponderosa pine—but as land rose toward the Peaks, it changed to fir and spruce, corkbark fir, even a few of the rare bristlecone pine, the five distinct life zones that C. Hart Merriam had identified in the layered forest on the steeply rising slopes of the Peaks, all of which made it a fine place to study forest ecology. G.A. Pearson was appointed the station's first director.

Tree research was an assignment to Pearson's taste. He had grown up near the old Oregon Trail in Nebraska, one of three sons of Anders Peter Pearson and Anna Christina Arvidson. His parents were Swedish immigrants who had taken up a homestead a year before his birth, in a colony of Swedes near Anders Pearson's brother, on the upland prairie south of the Platte River. It had been buffalo country with grass to the horizon in every direction. Therefore, and it was to be important, their son held from childhood ideas that he would defend the rest of his life.

From the beginning, settlers in that open prairie where young Gustaf grew up had a soul-fever for trees. They carried bare-root stock with them in their wagons when they traveled west, planted shade trees, osage orange for hedges, apple and pear orchards, and watered them all by hand. Every sod house had carefully tended seedlings in the yard.

Providing trees was a passion in Nebraska shared even by lawmakers. There were tax exemptions on real estate for settlers who would plant trees on their land, and "tree claims" were allowed to give immediate title to settlers who set out cuttings from river bottoms. A man could be fined, even imprisoned, for harming a tree growing on another man's land. The powerful Union Pacific Railroad could not escape Nebraska's legal preoccupation: it hired a Superintendent of Tree Culture to establish growth along the tracks.

For Gus Pearson, concern for trees was very nearly congenital. Eight years before he was born, Nebraska proclaimed the nation's first Arbor Day with a prize to the resident who planted the most trees. Three million were put into the prairie soil on the first day, and Arbor Day became a legal state holiday. When Gus was fifteen, the legislature chose as Nebraska's informal name "The Tree Planter's State."

Anders Pearson, an ardent planter like the rest of them, instilled in his sons John, Albert, and Gustaf the settlers' love for trees. It was given direction for Gus, when the young man went off to the state university, by his faculty adviser, Dr. Charles E. Bessey, an influential botanist of international reputation who had established the study of plants as a science based on observation. A course with

On February 20, 1907, the Botanical Seminar, a formal and professional organization, the most prestigious on campus, posed for a group photograph. Gustaf Pearson stood in the back row to the left of the door, Dr. Bessey, bearded, right of center in the front row. *Special Collections, University of Nebraska Library*

him was inspiration for a boy born on Nebraska's treeless prairie. Roscoe Pound, later Dean of the Harvard Law School, had studied with him and considered it "a profound experience."

> I remember when I used to work in botany, that the strength of Dr. Bessey's work with advanced students lay in his habit of drifting around quietly and sitting on the edge of a table where a student was at work and suggesting this thing or that, cross-examining him with an appearance of casually aroused interest, until before he knew it the student found himself engaged in long and difficult lines of investigation.

Just at the time Gus Pearson began to study with him, Bessey was involved in an attempt to plant a whole forest in the state, a forest of ponderosa pine, up in what was known as the Sandhills wastelands. With the cooperation of Professor Bessey and students like Pearson, government men planted it by hand, one seedling at a time in lines plowed with horses, and struggled to keep it alive. They said a forest would give the Sandhills some commercial value. Besides, they all liked trees. The pine seedlings which they set out were grown by the millions in a nursery which Bessey had established.[5]

Gustaf Adolph Pearson received the degrees of Bachelor of Arts and Bachelor of Science in 1905. Two years later he graduated from Bessey's instruction with a master's degree in Botany and Forestry. The effect of that Nebraska education was to reach all the way to Woody Mountain and the cut-over country around Flagstaff.

Fresh out of the university, Pearson went to work for the Forest Service, which was only two years old. His first assignment, at one thousand dollars a year, was to study revegetation in the range country of eastern Oregon. Foreshadowing a battle that would consume the last thirty years of his life, he wrote several pages to Dr. Bessey from Wallowa:

> I am working on the grazing problem. A large portion of the sheep range here...has been severely overgrazed, so severely that on many areas, several hundred acres in extent, nine tenths of the ground is absolutely bare of grass, and bears but little other vegetation...I am of the opinion that very few seedlings will survive where they are exposed to the tramping of the sheep, because the soil here is extremely soft, and, after a band of sheep has passed over, the surface soil is ground into a fine dust to the depth of from one to two inches...I feel very thankful in having had your courses in the study of grasses.

But he longed to work with trees. The scenery in Oregon was "splendid," the climate "delightful." He had "a fine time camping in the mountains." Nevertheless,

---

5 Bessey's was the first federal forest tree nursery. Between 1902 and 1964, thirty thousand acres of conifer seedlings from it were planted in straight rows across the Sandhills. It was the largest man-made forest in the United States.

he was pleased to be transferred to the Division of Silvics, which specialized in trees, and sent to Arizona in 1908. After he had been in Flagstaff for a month, he sent good news to Bessey.

> The problem first assigned to me here was the study of the reproduction of yellow pine, but recently the Forest Service has decided to establish an experiment station at this place, and I am to be in charge...I am to begin my experiments at once...This will include studies on different methods of cutting and disposal of brush, the influence of grazing, and the influence of the forest upon soil and atmospheric conditions...I feel that I am very fortunate in securing this station. Of course we shall start out modestly, but there are unlimited opportunities for development in the future. I realize that my training is insufficient to fill this position properly, but men with the necessary breadth of training are few in the Service, and possibly I am as well prepared as most of the younger men...Remember me to any of my acquaintances who chance to be at the University...I often think of the Forest Club and the Sem. Bot. [Botanical Seminar] and the lively times we used to have there.

Bessey answered: "We often speak of you and especially when the Sem. Bot. people are in evidence your name is spoken again and again."

Pearson was twenty-nine years old when he took up the work on pine trees at Fort Valley. Young and excited, he started research before he had station buildings.

> A two-room guard cabin solved the housing problem for the first year. In fact, no one thought much about buildings. The only construction undertaken the first fall was the establishment of three meteorological stations.
>
> After four busy months in the field I hauled a load of supplies to Fort Valley and settled down to figure out what it was all about. That winter was one of those in which the depth of snow was measured in feet. Between attending to my three meteorological stations and holding body and soul together I found some time for compilation and writing.

Finally he spared time from experimental work for construction of buildings and roads and fences, for installation of equipment.

> The building problem had its interesting, not to say amusing, aspects. Fort Valley boasted the first Forest Service bathroom in Region 3. To be accurate, it was a bath "house." Since the dwelling in which this luxury was to be installed had already cost all the law allowed, the situation looked hopeless. But the Fiscal Agent and the Assistant to the Solicitor were resourceful and cooperative...They decided that if the bathroom was not physically connected (nailed) to the main building it was legally a separate house. To keep well within this interpretation, the bath house was placed a full half inch away, and not a nail was allowed to violate the letter of the law.

The station established a troublesome single-wire telephone line to Flagstaff, a light plant, and its own water system, with a tank house and a pump at a well.

Lumber for houses at the station was ordered in September from AL&T, which responded:

> We have your letter of the 14th. We would like to have two or three days notice before your teams begin to haul so that we can have the material you request all ready for you. The windows we will have to order and it may be several days before they will reach here.

Pearson said later, "It was a young man's life, and I selected young men as my aides." He issued research tools to them: ax, shovel, grub hoe for fires, calipers, and a nickel-plated diameter tape. Emanuel Fritz lived at the station through 1916 and 1917 and never forgot the experience.

> We lived in very nice little cottages. They were pretty thin-walled and not too windtight, but they were heated by hot water from the greenhouse. As a place for living and concentrating on forest studies it was almost ideal for a city-bred bachelor who was more interested in the outdoors and the drama of forest development than in the bright lights of the cities. We bachelors *really* batched and...learned for the first time of Montgomery Ward's famous encyclopedia.

Like Breen and Douglass, Pearson found a local schoolteacher, a tall, quiet girl named May Perkins, and married her in 1910. May and, eventually, two children lived at the station, nine miles of dirt road away from town. The young bachelors decided that May Pearson was a wonderful cook and judged her "*awful* nice...a very pleasant, easy-going personality."

Winter residents out on the edge of Fort Valley were the Pearson family, the maintenance ranger and his wife, and two to four unmarried assistants. Fritz remembered it as a tight little community.

> "We had newspapers and mail infrequently in winter; we were snowed in for a month at one time...In winter we could go to Flagstaff only between the heavy snowfalls."

Sometimes on Sunday mornings Pearson invited the bachelors in for his Swedish pancakes, of which he was proud, but Fritz praised Mrs. Pearson for creating a pleasant, human atmosphere, "although she had many trials because of our isolation."

Pearson gave the station's mules, Pat and Mike, credit for "much of what is worthwhile in Fort Valley history...They transported men, supplies, and equipment." Fritz felt less warm about them.

> We had a wagon and two small light brown mules not much larger than donkeys. They were known as the Fort Valley insects and their top speed was about 5 miles an hour. Later we substituted two large crazy horses.

Pearson's boys usually managed to get into Flagstaff on Saturday evenings. In those early days, when they were all young, they were quick to find places in the social life of a small town. Winters they spent in the office working up field data, summarizing columns of illuminating figures. At sunset somebody had to go out

In 1917 Emanual Fritz drove Pat and Mike, whom he described as
"small, mean and self-determined."
Courtesy of Barbara Fritz

Ed Cummings, mules Emma and Carrie, Jim Winslett, an unidentified horse,
Hansen, and Bill, "a real dog." returned from an expedition to a weather station
on the Peaks in 1917.
Courtesy of Barbara Fritz

to build a fire in the tankhouse and turn off the water tanks to keep them from freezing overnight. In emergencies somebody skied into Flagstaff. For ordinary injuries like frozen toes they used aspirin and made a call to Dr. Fronske.

When spring came, temporary employees were added for major upkeep and repairs. The bachelors, still doing their own housekeeping and cooking, put in full days in the office and field, busy with data collection on reforestation studies. Fritz said: "We didn't even watch the clock. We worked as long as we could keep our eyes open sometimes to get the job done."

The first summer, with the approval of the Chief Forester in Washington, station personnel organized the Fort Valley Ranger School, two sessions of one month each, for training rangers from Arizona, New Mexico, Oklahoma, and Arkansas in forest management. Both students and instructors lived in tents; classes were conducted in them. [see page 210]

G.A. Pearson was assigned to do a job that had no precedent. Forestry in the United States was in its infancy when he started his work at Fort Valley, its only examples what had been done in Europe and reported in languages other than English. Bessey's forest-planting was still a questionable experiment. Pearson attacked the job with tools he made up as he went along and did the best he could using keen observation to supplement primitive techniques. In the process of blazing trails, he became an authority in his field, a nationally recognized consultant.

During the first year, while he was making domestic arrangements and planning the ranger school, Pearson put two thousand acres of forest into permanent sample plots, "S" plots they were termed, big enough to allow large-scale management experiments. Forty thousand trees were numbered and measured; many were photographed. Every tree was re-measured and the data recorded at five year intervals as long as Pearson was director. [see page 210]

It was ambitious, comprehensive research. In the process, Pearson's men began a study of the relation between climate and forest growth. Weather stations were set up in each tree zone—among juniper–pinon, ponderosa, Douglas fir, and spruce–fir.

Pearson worked in the forest by eye, using what his assistants called "uncanny powers of observation, interpretation and sheer sharp looking." Fritz liked the method.

> Data obtained by measurement were never enough for him. He would stand still, look and ponder, reasoning out the causes and effects. In a few words he would voice his opinions and give his reasons. It was better than a class. His excellent training in botany, physiology, and ecology, together with his powers of observation and interpretation caused him to draw sound conclusions. He would often go "roaming" in the forest, but never aimless wandering, always purposeful, always looking for clues.

Gus Pearson lectured in 1909 at the Fort Valley Ranger School. It was Pearson's custom when speaking to trainees to refer to ponderosa pine as "God's greatest tree."
United States Forest Service

A photograph made in 1921 was the beginning of a study of pine seedling.
G.A. Pearson photograph
Rocky Mountain Forest and Range Experiment Station

The younger men noticed that he recognized they were into something new and needed help. Emanuel Fritz said years later: "I learned to love the old fellow. In fact, he wasn't much older than I was."

> ...Gus Pearson was a tall, raw-boned man; rather quiet and soft-spoken and friendly. Although generally very serious, he had a dry sense of humor. I can still hear him chuckle when something amused him. I never worked under a kinder, fairer or more considerate man. If an assistant made an error, Pearson handled the matter as would a good teacher, part of the job of learning. He encouraged his assistants to look and see for themselves and was happy when he found them investigating a little fact on their own. To research work he applied honesty and his excellent basic knowledge of plant science.

In a foretaste of the future, when youth and hope would turn to bitter isolation, Fritz noticed that Pearson "was often in conflict with administrative officers in Albuquerque and Washington, some of whom had no sympathy for research or had preconceived ideas which their training and experience did not justify."

To the admiration of later foresters, Pearson figured all the problems out the first year, especially the question of the failure of reproduction of the trees. After a full summer's observation, he prepared a Forest Service circular on the subject, the first of nearly one hundred publications during his career.

Logging, he said, which had upset the ancient environmental balance, had been partly responsible for the problem of poor reproduction: heavy cutting handicapped seedlings by allowing too much light to reach them and removing their protection against evaporation and frost. However, the significant reason there were no new trees was weather. Ponderosa could *survive* with scant rainfall, but it couldn't get started. He wrote:

> The spring season from April to July is especially trying, for then the drought is accompanied by severe winds, which blow continuously for many days at a time. The surface soil becomes exceedingly dry, and most of the seeds therefore fail to germinate, and of those which do, only a small proportion succeed in establishing themselves. Practically all of the seedlings start in July and August, after the beginning of the rainy season, and seedlings starting this late are still very tender when the fall frosts come. As a result they are very susceptible to injury. Of the seedlings which sprang up on the Coconino National Forest during August, 1908, at least three-fourths were killed by frost in October.

The trees produced a good crop of seeds not annually, as had been supposed, but only at five-year intervals. That was a second limitation. But even with adequate seed every five years, there might be a long gap between years with sufficient rain to allow trees to become established.

And then, on an average only fifty-nine percent of the seeds produced in any year were viable enough to germinate. They could do so only during the humid days of July and August in warm soils free from competing vegetation. Unless roots managed to penetrate the volcanic ground by at least six inches during the first season, most of the seedlings would die. Less than five percent of the seeds which germinated survived all the injuries to which weather and animals—squirrels, mice, chipmunks, deer—subjected them.

Based on all those factors, the conclusion was that for adequate regeneration, even during a favorable year for rainfall, from four to ten pounds of seeds per acre were required, more than could have been provided by the seed trees that loggers had agreed to leave on Woody Mountain in 1904. Fritz and Pearson's other assistants said that if regeneration worked on the Coconino under such adverse conditions, it could be done anywhere else more easily.

In a circular printed in 1912, when he was thirty-two, Pearson made further observations about the viability of pine seeds, with some unexpected conclusions. The picture was more complicated than Breen's rangers had assumed. First, he said, seed from young trees had a better germination rate than seed from the big mature trees which T.A. had wanted to cut because they provided so much saw timber. (Sixty-eight percent for yellow pine over 140 years old vs. eighty percent for blackjack.)

Second, injuries did not always harm seed quality: mistletoe decreased seed germination by seventeen percent, but, to everybody's surprise, heart rot improved it by three percent and damage to tops by fifteen percent. Pine marked by fire scars also had a germination rate 15% above that of uninjured pines. Basal burns and lightning strikes actually stimulated the tree to production of better seed.

Those figures were of interest to AL&T. T.A. Riordan and Gus Pearson became friendly; both wanted new pines to grow. Pearson was in general a congenial addition to local educated circles. In the little paired communities of Flagstaff and Milton, he and his wife developed friendships with T.A., the Babbitts, the two Slipher brothers at Lowell Observatory, the Coltons of the Museum of Northern Arizona, and with A.E. Douglass whose work on dendrochronology took him all over northern Arizona. Aldo Leopold, legendary pioneer conservationist who was stationed at Albuquerque, was another friend. People in town, especially the ladies, thought Pearson was "just as nice as he could be."

Remembering Professor Bessey's tree nursery in Nebraska, Pearson established one across Fort Valley near Leroux Spring and attempted to grow pine with seed collected from trees the loggers had dropped. T.A. made no freight charge for hauling seed into town on the logging train, asking only "one or two quarts" for planting in Milton.

The Fort Valley foresters hoped to produce stock which could be transplanted, but all attempts at artificial reforestation failed. They found that ponderosa pine was a slow starter even under favorable conditions. Terminal shoots pushed out with the first warm weather, then stopped, and height growth was finished for the year. Seedlings did not take well to transplanting.

Although he believed that foresters should walk if they wanted to see anything, Pearson
had a "touring car" for projects some distance from the station.
Rocky Mountain Forest and Range Experiment Station

Seedlings transplanted in 1917 did not thrive.
Courtesy of Barbara Fritz

For eleven years, until his fortieth birthday, Pearson and his young aides lived with trees and learned about them. During those years Woody Mountain and all the other cut-over land on the Coconino remained stubbornly bare. For eleven years, no matter what they tried, the foresters at Fort Valley couldn't figure out how to make a new forest grow. All the information on what made seeds more viable and the conditions they needed to germinate and thrive didn't result in successful regeneration of the forest, and Pearson continued to investigate the one thing that mattered most: moisture.

> Pine makes its height growth during the period of lowest precipitation in the year. During this period of high activity, the trees are dependent almost entirely upon moisture stored in the soil during the preceding winter and spring...Two inches in April and May are more effective [for tree growth] than two inches from December to March...Spring precipitation with resulting soil moisture also favors the survival of seedlings during the arid fore-summer, when mortality is usually very high.

Distribution and amount of summer rains, when they did come, had to be better than average; really favorable conditions occurred only when showers fell almost every day for a month or more, rather than now and then with intermittent dry weeks. But unless the trees had produced several pounds of seeds the preceding autumn, steady summer rains accomplished little.

With no warning both factors came together. In 1918 ponderosa pines released a heavy seed crop, and that was followed in 1919, to Pearson's joy, by rains in June and exceptionally good summer storms and warm temperatures that guaranteed early germination. He said it was "just like heaven." By spring of 1920 hundreds of thousands of tiny seedlings an inch tall covered bare townships of the Coconino, covered the slopes of Woody Mountain like fuzz, hardly noticeable to anyone but rangers who went up to look around for smoke. They said the little trees were "thick as the hair on a dog's back."

But summer of 1920 was dry, and Pearson's anticipation of a new forest turned to concern. "The outcome still hangs in the balance," he wrote. Late season drought had been aggravated by winter frost heaving and by root competition from grasses that also had germinated during the warm rains of the previous year. Many of those pine seedlings had disappeared.

Through five years mortality continued high. On areas with scattered seed trees, like Woody Mountain, young pines were down from 2800 per acre in 1920 to 1000 in 1921, to 900 in 1922, to 800 in 1923, to 740 in 1924, to 690 in 1929, a death of more than three-fourths within a decade. Many of the gains of 1919, the first real crop of new trees in at least twenty-five years, gradually disappeared, and the estimate was that no more than fifty percent of the cutover land would be restocked.

G.A. Pearson evaluated young pines with apprehension.
United States Forest Service

Pearson began his battle to save the trees in the middle years of his life.
United States Forest Service

As soon as he realized what was happening, Pearson began a long and bitter campaign to save his trees, taking on cattlemen, sheepmen, range technicians in his own organization, even the Chief Forester in Washington. He was a stubborn man when he thought he was right. The result was that a storm of controversy swirled around him for the remaining years of his life and very nearly wrecked his health and his career.

Pearson was forty-five years old by 1925, and he had spent sixteen years at Fort Valley trying to solve the problems of reforestation. Many of them were beyond his control: he couldn't do much about weather or about squirrels and mice that ate the seeds or about deer and antelope that liked the tender new branches. (He had tried to exclude deer from his sample plots and found that they could leap an eight-foot fence.) But he had argued since his days in Oregon that domestic stock were a threat to pine seedlings. As far as he was concerned, there was no question that sheep and cattle grazed so extensively on the primary terminal or "leader," especially during dry seasons, that the trees were stunted or deformed or killed outright and their numbers reduced below requirements for future stands of timber.

As early as 1910 he had said:

> After the seedlings have succeeded in establishing themselves, one of the greatest sources of danger to them is from grazing animals, particularly sheep. They should be excluded on areas where reproduction is desired.

Some of Pearson's sample plots had been left open to grazing animals, some closed, and detailed records kept. He was prepared to prove his claim.

> On approximately 200,000 acres of cut-over land near Flagstaff...reproduction is making unsatisfactory progress. Investigations covering a period of twelve years show that this condition is due primarily to sheep-grazing.

Range and grazing studies, the first in the country, had begun on the Coconino Forest in the summer of 1911. Damage to pine reproduction had been one of the original concerns: ponderosa pine was a cash crop for the Forest Service. However, so was grass in the form of grazing permit fees, which had been sold for a dozen years by then. Pearson argued that pine timber was worth more.

The issue became a source of major contention between livestock interests and the Forest Service. In 1923 Pearson again published an argument that excessive grazing had been the greatest cause of mortality to the 1919 crop and insisted that sheep be excluded from the forest range until the little trees had reached a height which would minimize damage. Gifford Pinchot concurred:

> Great stretches of open forest contain much feed that should not be wasted, provided the ranges are not overstocked and provided again (and this is of the first importance) that when reproduction of the forest is needed, grazing stops. When the young trees are old enough to make it safe, grazing may begin again, but never without careful supervision and control. Exclusion may be necessary for from about a tenth to a fifth of the time it takes to grow a merchantable tree.

Grazing was severely reduced. But sheepmen had battled exclusion for a quarter of a century at that point and had won a round in 1902 during the Roosevelt administration. Politically sophisticated by 1923, they reacted by proposing that the Fort Valley Station be abolished. In 1924 an appropriation cut left Pearson money for only one technical man. Reductions in sheep on the Coconino were postponed temporarily while contending claims could be sorted into a compromise.

In the middle of those political pressures the forest experiment station was expanded to include range and grazing studies as well as silviculture. G.A. Pearson, who had supervised the birth of the station sixteen years earlier for work on trees, was promoted by the Forest Service to the position of director of the expanded scope. The official citation read:

> ...More than any other man [he] has contributed to our scientific knowledge of the forest conditions in these regions. He is a tireless investigator, writes well, and is universally recognized as an authority in his specialty.

He had grown up in Nebraska: his specialty was not grass. He never could accept rangemen as part of his research station. He conceded that the sheepmen had valid interests:

> The sheep industry is dependent upon the national forests for summer range. In order to utilize the range, sheep owners have been obliged to develop water and make other improvements, often at great expense. To deprive them of this range on short notice and without making suitable adjustments would work a serious hardship upon the industry. The Forest Service has deferred extensive exclusion of sheep in the hope of finding a less drastic solution.

He was prepared to blame overstocking and to secure relief with improved range management; otherwise, he wanted sheep excluded for twenty years. Nothing mattered to him as much as his trees. He prepared a manuscript that constituted civil war and, unable to get official approval, published it outside government channels.

The situation was so tense that in the year of Pearson's promotion Chief Forester William Greeley traveled to Flagstaff from Washington to discuss the problem, bringing with him his chief of Grazing and the Regional Forester from Albuquerque. Meetings were held with Coconino officials. Forest Supervisor Edward Miller made a summary:

> We proposed to separate the two industries, cattle and sheep...The sheepmen agreed to have the Forest Service fence National Forest boundaries and to help build the interior fences that would divide cattle and sheep. Col. Greeley agreed that the Forest Service would do its best to dig up some money for fencing purposes although...money for improvements of any kind was scarce. We put on fencing crews, first on exterior boundaries on the east. Then, as fast as funds could be made available from grazing fees, and from money contributed by stockmen, or from improvement funds, the Forest Service built interior fences.

All of Woody Mountain was enclosed by Forest Service field crews. In 1925 more than four miles of fence were strung on the east side, and the next year the south and west sides were closed off. Seven years later, early in the 1930s, two and a half miles of fence on the north completed the circuit. From that time, except for water in Woody Spring, the mountain was closed to domestic stock.

Pines on the mountain were protected, but grazing continued on lower ground outside the wire. Miller wrote:

> We argued that while some reductions in sheep numbers would have to be made, it would be unfair to arbitrarily make heavy reductions overnight. The thing to do was to divide the ranges on an individual basis as far as practicable, then allow each permittee to see what numbers he could graze without serious damage to Yellow Pine reproduction.

The fencing compromise did not end the grazing controversy, which went on in one form or another for two more decades. Even what Pearson called the "divine intervention" of a second good seed crop in the late 1920s was no guarantee of a new forest, given the high mortality rate of pine seedlings, and he felt that success would not be assured in any future he could foresee. He vowed to "fight the issue through to a finish." There were fences, but sheep and cattle were still grazing on the forest, and he was convinced that meant trouble sooner or later.

Many of the men who worked with Pearson early in his career liked him. Emanuel Fritz (until he died at 102 in 1988) remained his friend and would hear no criticism of him. Frank Wadsworth said of him years later: "His nature was gentle but he on occasion displayed understandable wrath, generally with what he considered misguided colleagues." Raymond Kleck worked at the station from 1931 to 1936 and remembered: "He wasn't hard to get along with, just a hard man to understand. He had a sense of humor, but most everybody missed the point."

As Pearson stiffened in his crusade, his nature, at least as people at the station saw it, began to change from that of his youthful enthusiasm to something close to tragic. Sheepmen, of course, had little use for Pearson. It was rumored around the station that one of them had threatened his life. Range specialists who were involved in the grazing controversy found him impossible: "He couldn't get along with people. I don't think he tried. He was just a stubborn Swede. A cranky old man. He always fought about something."

Through all the controversy, which gave him ulcers (he thought it might be stomach cancer and went east to the Mayo Clinic to find out), Pearson continued to publish one technical monograph and article after another on his research. In the *Journal of Forestry* he renewed the attack on sheep, with graphs and tables, under the heading "Recovery of Western Yellow Pine Seedlings from Injury by Grazing Animals." Grazing damage was only one of the lines Pearson followed in his

Seedlings which remained around the stumps of old trees competed with grass
for every drop of rain.
Rocky Mountain Forest and Range Experiment Station

Because Gus Pearson fought to protect them, new pine and oak trees
grew up on the slopes of Woody Mountain.

research on trees, but he returned to the theme again and again, in almost everything he wrote, determined to prove himself right, afraid that his enemy could not be routed.

> Pine seedlings must be carefully guarded against grazing damage until they are at least three years old. After the third year the danger is appreciably less but this should not be interpreted as meaning that grazing can be disregarded because seedlings may be killed even after they are as much as a foot tall. Furthermore, reproduction is seldom complete and therefore there are nearly always small seedlings in need of special protection.

"Grass, Pine Seedlings and Grazing" in the same journal three years later showed him, with more tables, still defending his argument.

> I believe that as a general thing the forest ranges, as well as other ranges in the Southwest, are still too heavily grazed. Pine seedlings are still being damaged too much in many places. After a forest has become well restocked, light and well distributed grazing is the proper course.

Pearson was a partisan of trees who quarreled endlessly with range technicians. Over his protest they had been added to his staff, and he always regarded them as apologists for grazing interests as well as inferior scientists. A pair of them named Cooperrider and Cassidy spent nearly a decade studying the grazing situation.[6] Their conclusion was that pine mortality due to drought, mice, deer, and squirrels rivaled that due to grazing.

The approach recommended by Cooperrider and Cassidy was to regulate but not eliminate sheep and cattle using the forest. Pearson refused to allow publication of their work, charging unsound data. They insisted that he changed his own research data to suit his theories.

It was an impossible situation: bureaucracies survive in the hands of politicians and diplomats, not those of an outspoken and devoted scientist capable of such lines as...

> I used to dream of the day when extensive areas of cutover lands would become waving fields of young pine...Cutover pine lands by millions of acres have restocked under my eyes; I have lived to see the "hoofed locusts" in full retreat before the advancing tide of pine thickets.

G.A. Pearson was released from full management responsibility at Fort Valley in 1935. His new designation was Senior Silviculturist, which meant that he could concentrate on trees and (everyone hoped) ignore grazing issues, but the move was regarded in every office in the building as a demotion. The station had been his from its beginning in 1909, and he was bitterly disappointed by the change.

6 Cooperrider had Ray Kleck on his knees evaluating plots one foot square, brushing away snow, counting seedlings, and listing trees missing since the previous census. Kleck was requested to determine cause of death of the little trees, although sometimes, he said, it was hard to tell.

He was more a pure scientist than a leader anyway, people said, an eccentric, a tree fanatic rather than an all-round government agent. They liked to tell how he would stop his Ford, get out, and roll away rocks that road builders had pushed against young pines, fuming "...no regard for value or beauty!"

Arthur Upson, the new Director, praised Pearson in his first personnel report: "My first inspection of Silvics field work demonstrated, without doubt, that for length of records, careful study over the years, and results to date, his is probably outstanding in forest research."

After he had been at Pearson's old desk for a year, Upson was more candid about personnel relationships which were, he said, not harmonious.

> The long-standing controversy between Pearson and [range] staff and activities
> in general is so deep seated that it is questionable whether it can ever be
> removed...It continues unabated.

It wasn't just range studies: Pearson didn't like statistics either. Educated in the years of forestry's beginnings, he did not trust statistical analysis as a research method and resented its use by younger men. Through the late 1930s he conducted a long quarrel with Fort Valley's statistician, Bert Lexen, a hot-tempered but jolly man with a booming laugh, a scientist of the modern school. Frank Wadsworth, a young forestry aide in 1938, heard the frequent disagreements.

> Near the end of Gus's career the use of statistical methods was introduced to
> forest science. Gus, who had always used plenty of data, but made his greatest
> finds through his eyes out in the forest, did not have an open mind toward the
> impersonal application of sophisticated mathematics to his trees. He once wrote a
> manuscript that started out, "This will be remembered as the age of forestry by
> gadgets."
>
> [He and Lexen] had violent arguments that led [Gus] to ulcers. At times
> they had to go off for a few days to cool off. Bert had a way of asking if something
> Gus stated was "statistically significant." One day Gus responded, "I don't care if
> it is statistically significant, is it *important?*"

When Lexen, in anger and frustration, filed a formal letter of protest detailing his complaints, Pearson's response was blandly self-assured: "The man is crazy."

Lexen said later that he had spent years proving what Gus already knew to be true. But at the time the disagreement escalated into what Upson described as an open break between them. In 1939 he arranged Lexen's transfer to Colorado.

As he grew older, Pearson became more and more contentious. But his anger was directed only toward the men he worked with and stockmen who threatened his trees. Upson was aware of that.

> I want again to record that in discussions with Pearson upon which there is no
> difference of opinion, he is interesting and constructive. In meeting him in the
> office, or in "passing the time of day with him," he is always pleasant. In other
> ways he is considerate of the feelings of others. But when it comes to subjects

upon which he has views that do not agree with those of others or Forest Service policy, or concern the other two lines of research here and one attempts to discuss them with him, he becomes a man with a dual personality.

Matt Black's daughter-in-law, Louise, met Pearson one day in the Monte Vista Hotel and judged: "He was very pleasant...very much a gentleman. He had beautiful manners." (She was surprised later to learn his age; she thought he looked much older than his years.) No one could remember that he had ever used profanity or over-indulged in alcohol. "It was a pleasure to see him," Flagstaff said. "He was intelligent and kind."

Flagstaff's ladies remembered him forty years later as the cleanest man in town. "When Gus Pearson came back in the spring, you knew it was time to spruce up." "He was always in that green uniform with a Forest Service hat, you know, the Smokey Bear kind...very neat and clean." A federal employee, he was expected to wear uniforms on duty, in the forest or in town. Because his work was everything to him, he was in service every day, even on Sundays, even on Christmas, and there was usually a light in his office window at night. He was seldom out of that green uniform.

Florence Cary, Pearson's secretary through the late 1930s, found him "very nice...informal...your friend outside the office." She never used the nickname Gus: "He was too dignified for me to call him that." His son-in-law referred to him as Mr. Pearson and all the other men called him Gus, she said, but his wife didn't care for that at all. Mrs. Pearson pronounced her husband's initials and called him "Gay."

He was not an easy man to work for, definite in his ideas and set in his ways as he grew older, and he demanded that things be done by a routine he liked. He wasn't bossy, Miss Cary remembered. Just set in his ways. And he loved to write. When he was writing, which was much of the time, he was relaxed, calm, easy to get along with, and cheerfully gave her time off. "Except that he kept handing me work. 'Before you go...' he'd say."

It was hard to take dictation from him. As Pearson moved through his fifties, his hearing failed, and finally he couldn't tell whether he was whispering or shouting. Sometimes when he thought he was speaking at a normal level, his secretary couldn't hear what he was saying.

She regarded him as a big-hearted man who loved his family, who tried to be polite and pleasant in social situations. But it was hard for him to carry on a conversation or to laugh readily at jokes he couldn't hear. When he realized how severe his hearing loss was going to be, he went to night school in Tucson to try to learn to lip-read, but it didn't work out. His deafness, which was never total but which affected his speech, embarrassed him.

Ed Groesbeck, Assistant Supervisor of the Coconino National Forest from 1935 to 1943, "a green fashion plate with leather puttees," according to rangers in the field, knew Pearson and liked him.

Gus was a gentleman, always neatly dressed and very courteous and well-mannered. He wore a hearing aid and was quite deaf. It was difficult to talk with him as a result. He seemed to like me and would drop in at my office...I don't think he socialized much with people in Flagstaff. I think because he was so deaf that he avoided groups and public gatherings...One grows to avoid public meetings and gatherings when one cannot hear and understand what people say. It's embarrassing to have people try to talk to you when there are a lot of people or noise around and you can't understand a word they say.

Young foresters, who had not yet thought that they too might be deaf some day, were often amused by Pearson's handicap. A silviculturist named Herman Krauch also was deaf, and the two of them often quarreled, making a din for everyone else. The younger men laughed that when Pearson and Krauch went out into the field, you could hear them a mile away shouting at each other.[7]

As he grew older, Pearson began to talk to himself. Too deaf to realize how loud his voice was, he was a distraction to men trying to work in nearby offices. Finally, as an attempt to ease station tension, he was moved to a remote corner of the building.

He was always busy with his work on trees, continuing his research, writing his controversial opinions, fighting his personal battles. In 1940, at the age of sixty, he published a ten-page article, not approved by Upson, in which he suggested that forest land be classified and each use—timber, grazing, recreation, wildlife, watershed—assigned specific areas for primary use. Thus logging would be restricted in the steep canyons where it was not profitable but which were favored for recreation and wildlife. Pines would be left alone to grow where site, topography, and location made it the use of "maximum yield."

When he was convinced he was right, Pearson was, as they used to say, stubborn as a Forest Service mule. He thought a problem out, made a decision, and stayed with it. In 1941 German divisions invaded Russia, the Japanese were in control of China, Italian occupation forces held Yugoslavia, the British entered Baghdad, and Gus Pearson continued at Fort Valley a long-standing war of his own about damage to trees.

For six years he had battled publication of the Cooperrider–Cassidy argument, "Cattle Grazing on Cutover Timberlands." Disputing their conclusions, he insisted that cattle and sheep should be excluded from the forest until the middle of July and that in some places only yearlings (rather than heavier adult cattle) should be allowed to browse the grass.

---

7 One day in the late 1930s Pearson boxed and sent off to Washington some insects he had found. In an accompanying letter he requested identification, describing them as "large, flying insects with long tongues," and especially wanted to know whether they might damage pines. The return letter soberly gave the Latin name and a formal description and concluded, "In other words, this is a *honey bee*." There was much delight around the station when word got about that Pearson was so single-minded about pines that he didn't know a bee when he saw one.

He was so intemperate as to refer to range research as "an orgy of gross exaggeration and perversion." Insiders called it a situation of "swords point." After a few years of that, Mrs. Pearson and Mrs. Cooperrider, who lived across the road from each other at the station, did not speak.

Pearson aged fast during his long struggle. By 1941 he was firing in all directions, taking on tree specialists at Fort Valley as well as range men, the Chief Forester and head of Grazing in Washington, and anybody who disagreed with him about pine browsing, range management, or watershed protection. Battles raged from room to room at the station with people shouting at each other loudly enough to be heard all over the building. Nobody could get any work done for the quarreling.

Arthur Upson was a good man for the job of director of the research station—intelligent, strict, business-like. He was also a good man in a fight, and faced with Pearson he needed to be. He recognized the older man's value.

> [He is a] pioneer in development of early silvical research technic and prosecution of systematic observations and studies now yielding results indispensable to Region and forestry profession...Credit for his foresight, persistence, and advice is officially acknowledged...Pine research is providing invaluable management data.

He described the old warrior as "...a thorough gentleman and most considerate towards his successor as Director." But he filed criticism in Pearson's official personnel records.

> Complex personality due to a variety of reasons. Stubborn, and when exercised, tactless. With all things silvical, possessive beyond a warranted degree. Thorough investigator of old school; resents application of modern research methods if any chance they will alter his previous findings. Cannot take criticism kindly. Hates domestic livestock. Is firm in his feeling that most all timber regeneration problems and all watershed problems can be laid at door of livestock industry. So biased he will lay failure of early day forest devastated areas to restock wholly to livestock grazing since. Happy in thought some day pine will get better of grass and hence grazing. Can condone or approve little of a range research nature.

Upson tried to handle the problem with diplomacy. Although he found the range men more congenial than Pearson, he forbade anyone on any side of the grazing controversy to publish a statement about it and shelved the Cooperrider–Cassidy report indefinitely. Then he relieved Pearson of responsibility for any silvicultural work at the station except his own, to the relief of other tree men, who had found him difficult.

Speaking carefully, Upson tried to steer Pearson into something safe, something he would like and could do alone: the compilation of "masses of invaluable technical and historical information, not of record any place, which would disappear" at Pearson's death.

> I told him that I felt his greatest value to the Service was to continue exclusively on ponderosa pine research, to get of record in one way or another the great fund of knowledge he had on ponderosa pine, and otherwise to continue undivided attention to the plot measurement and analysis.
>
> I suggested that in his undivided attention on pine he should plan on writing at a fairly early date a comprehensive manuscript...on the history of forest management in the southwest.

Upson hinted that the writing job could better be done away from Fort Valley. Pearson objected to the idea. Furthermore, he said, if he should write a history of silviculture in the Southwest, he would of course have to go fully into the subject of livestock browsing of pine. The discussion grew into what Upson described as "a tirade," and he exploded.

> I told him in no uncertain terms that I was sick and tired of him continuing this controversy...and that I would recommend drastic action if it continued to happen in the future.

The day after the Japanese attack on Pearl Harbor, Upson sent to the Assistant Chief in Washington a seven-page letter headed "Personal and Confidential." In it he recommended that Pearson, whom he described as "a deterrent...unreasonable...blinded to good thinking" be assigned the writing project and then moved away from the station which he had built thirty-two long and productive years earlier.

> Pearson will be 61 years old this month...I do not believe it will be mutually advantageous to either employee or employer that Pearson remain on the active rolls 9 years more...In November of 1943 he should be permanently transferred to Washington where he will continue to work on his [history]...When it is completed, Pearson should be considered for retirement.

No evidence remained that Gus ever saw the letter that urged his exile. He was not moved to Washington.

The Pearsons' daughter, Margaret, met Frank Wadsworth at Fort Valley and married him. Half a century later he remembered that his wife's father had often told him of "his long battle" with stockmen. Wadsworth praised him.

> Gus had a good sense of humor and often gave a sly interpretation to human frailties. However, I think he considered humor a waste of time.
>
> His most outstanding personal trait was the deep loyalty he felt for his employer, the Forest Service. He must have given the government 50% more time than he was paid for...
>
> Professionally he was a giant...What became the Fort Valley Experimental Forest he came to know and love to a degree that seems unique. Over square miles he got to know the history of individual trees by heart.

In 1944, Gus Pearson received an award from the Society of American Foresters for the year's best article on forestry. He retired from active research at sixty-five a year later—just short of thirty-eight years of service. Twenty top men

In 1944, sixty-four years old, G.A. Pearson was still standing in forest sunlight,
holding a sheaf of notes.
Courtesy of Florence Cary Martin

in forest management from seven western states and Washington traveled to Fort Valley to honor him. Gus conducted them through the forest and showed them the trees he had studied for so many years. In the winter there was a party at which Mrs. Pearson received a gardenia corsage and Gus was presented with a bound book of letters from friends and associates. A.E. Douglass was one of the guests.

By the time of his retirement, Pearson was the basic authority, the gospel on ponderosa pine. His reputation was national. Among the tributes paid to him was the recognition that many of his publications had become required reading in college forestry courses. Fifty years later they were still cited as reference.

For the next four years he worked at his office in Tucson on a summary of his life, a major scientific monograph to be titled *Management of Ponderosa Pine in the Southwest*. In a section on regeneration he made one more effort toward vindication in the old controversy.

> During the period 1926 to 1929, large reductions were made in the numbers of livestock on the national forests. In northern Arizona reductions of both cattle and sheep varied by allotments from 25 to as much as 100 percent. A program of fencing forest and allotment boundaries was also completed in 1928. This resulted in control and better distribution of livestock and made possible the segregation of cattle from sheep. The influence of these changes on the severity of browsing damage was pronounced...By 1932 recovery from old injuries was likewise pronounced. The browsing problem was greatly alleviated by 1930, but was not altogether solved.

Pearson did not finish *Management of Ponderosa Pine*. On January 31, 1949, at the age of sixty-nine, he was found at his office desk, dead of a heart attack, his head resting on the manuscript that rounded off his work. Colleagues put the last touches on it for him and prepared it for publication.

He was buried on a cold winter day in the Flagstaff cemetery in Mrs. Pearson's family's plot, where a ponderosa pine tree grew to shade his grave. Five years later a stand of pines near the Fort Valley station was named the G.A. Pearson Natural Area as a memorial to him. The trees on Woody Mountain also stood as a monument to his life. So did every tree in the forest.

On Woody Mountain, mushrooms pushed up through the shallow soil during summer rainy reasons, and Abert squirrels came down from the pines to feed on them as long as they lasted. Then in September the sun moved farther south; so did the sub-tropical high with its moisture from far-away oceans, and summer storms subsided. Autumn was dry and clear; there was usually, only something over an inch of rain in September and October and not much in early November. Shadows of trees and the mountain itself few longer. Aspen and oak leaves turned to yellow and birds began to disappear as earth swung in its orbit around the sun. Wind blew all through the longer nights.

If there had been no late frosts in spring to kill blossoms on the oak, and if summer rains had been ample, acorns were everywhere on the trees. Abert squirrels scrambled among branches to pick them and eat them there on the spot, growing plump and sleek. They needed to be. In the dry Ponderosa forest, winter storms did not last long, and the squirrels that had lived there for thousands of years had never learned to store food in caches.

Truffles, underground mushrooms growing on the shallow subsurface roots of the pines, were the primary source of their winter nutrition—if snow was not so deep that the ground was out of reach. In hard winters the only food available was the inner bark of twigs high in the trees, and those were of such limited nutritional value that the squirrels were often in a state approaching shock by spring.

Chapter Seven
Woody Mountain Wells

1956

Welders built up the drill bit on night shifts.
Courtesy of Lloyd Perry

Flagstaff water distribution between 1883 and 1898 was handled by
direct method—John Yost and his partner.
AHS–Pioneer Museum

Ponderosa pine had learned to adapt to an average annual rainfall of twenty inches. People who settled near the Peaks had not. They could make changes when they had to, but they could not go through dry seasons with the stoicism of the pines. An adequate supply of water, the first necessity for a growing population, was a problem in Flagstaff right from the beginning: the existence of the town, always precarious, was dependent on undependable storms.

For the first fifteen years, drinking, cooking, and washing water for the settlement was hauled from Old Town Spring in buckets and pans or delivered into handed-down whiskey barrels at back doors. There were wells in town, but there were also cesspools and outhouses that drained into them and contaminated the water. The only clean source was springs, here and there, which channeled rain and snow melt down from the mountains.

All her life Mary Annetta Black had vivid memories of those days.

> I remember the water wagon coming once a week. We bought water in barrels at the side of our back steps going up to the back veranda...Our drinking water was brought by Papa who went to the spring with big jugs.

When Old Town Spring went dry occasionally, water was hauled from Leroux Spring, which ran year round, and from Fisher Spring out to the east in Walnut Canyon. Entrepreneurs who carted water the ten miles from Leroux Spring sold it for as much as $1.50 a barrel during the long dry months between March and July. Drinking water from Fisher Spring was carried into town in beer bottles.

Godfrey Sykes told of winter snow being melted on fragments of sheet-iron over wood fires,

> ... and the resultant beverage, with its blended flavours of pitch-wood smoke, iron oxide, and just plain dirt, is an unforgettable memory...Bathtubs, bathrooms, and inside plumbing were of course unattainable luxuries and the town was on a "try-weekly" basis as far as major ablutions were concerned. The routine of this hoped-for Saturday night tubbing...was about as follows: You ambled "down town" and looked into the several saloons, taking note of which of your neighbors were sitting in on any of the games, poker, faro, or roulette, with enough chips in front of them to make it probable that they would stay there for a while. Then you sneaked up to your cabin again, took your two pails and helped yourself to a few gallons of water from their unguarded barrels, heated up your ill-gotten gains on the stove and soon thereafter indulged in a luxurious hot bath of ample volume in the largest available domestic wash-tub.

Sometimes there were a few months of "beautiful weather" that did not provide enough rain or winter snow to keep the springs running. It was a recurrent theme in T.A. Riordan's correspondence: "Those of us who were here in the early days will never forget the scare we used to have over the lack of water." In 1887, only five years after the town was founded, he wrote to a friend:

> Providence has solved the water question by the snow storm which began Saturday, continued all day yesterday at intervals and is threatening still to

continue. We got over six inches of snow and it certainly will prove thousands of dollars benefit to this whole region round about. The cattle were dying already for the want of water to the south and east of us and our own cattle have come in in such a wretchedly poor condition that it looked as if they would be utterly unfit for use this season, and with the strong prospect of there being no grass, the thing did not look very pleasant ahead, but now this timely snow will fix us out in good shape for awhile and probably until the summer rains come. Of course it will cause some temporary inconvenience, such as the preventing of our doing any logging and all that, but that is a very slight matter compared to the vast amount of good that will result.

In January of 1895 Flagstaff was nearly smothered by 126 inches of snow, so slowing work on Emerson School, the Normal School and the county court house that AL&T withdrew its bid for doors and windows. June that year was dry, as usual, and the logging company received from Mrs. M.A. Basset, who lived on the tracks near Mill #2, a request for household water from the trains. T.A. answered: "If you will get three or four barrels and place them alongside the track, we will have the train boys fill them say once every eight or ten days, and do it free of charge."

AL&T, operating steam engines and machinery and constantly threatened by fires, maintained a five hundred gallon water tank near the mill. That summer Flagstaff bought a twelve-man hand pump that could be attached to the tank for fighting fires north of the tracks, an improvement on the old bucket brigade.

Godfrey Sykes went into detail about Flagstaff's fire fighting as manly entertainment:

> As the founder, Chief, and most active and vociferous member of our volunteer Fire Company, [Sandy Donahue] was a great success. His voice alone would have been a notable asset in any Fire Company. Our original equipment consisted of a picturesque old hand-pumper, or "manual," and Sandy's talent for leadership was manifested in the way he kept a copious supply of strong liquor available for the volunteers who worked in relays at the pump-brakes. This operation was known as "priming the pump," and it is obvious how similar it was in principle to some of the modern forms of mass-bribery which are tagged with the same name.
>
> When a fire alarm was sounded, we volunteer firemen jumped out of bed, assembled around our "engine" and lugged it off to the water supply which was closest to the fire. This might be the communal spring, a temporary rain-pond, or even some thrifty citizen's treasured row of water barrels. Then, having dropped the section into the available moisture, we yelled lustily for "more beef" at the brakes and merrily squirted such as came through the machine and hose in the general direction of the blaze. A favourite diversion from the more serious phases of fire-fighting was to let the nozzle "get out of control" of the nozzle man, so that the stream would wet down inquisitive citizens who merely wanted to look on but were not anxious to pull at the brakes. Sandy often encouraged

these mischances by private signals to the hose and nozzle men but was, of course, very apologetic afterwards about them.[1]

But it was obvious that Flagstaff, county seat and site of a new observatory, could not go on getting by with the improvised water system of its first fifteen years. In August of 1895, after two years of "indefinite" discussion by citizens and their town council, the Flagstaff Water Company was finally organized. A survey had estimated that the town's two hundred and fifty houses, five restaurants, seven saloons, three hotels, one brewery, one barber shop, the jail, the courthouse, the schoolhouse, and the Babbitt building could be counted on to subscribe for service. AL&T indicated that Mill Town also expected to be a customer.

Winter and spring of 1896 brought such severe drought that Flagstaff's citizens urged each other to pray for rain. Wells, springs and water holes were nearly dry by early March, with alarm growing for stock as well as people, and Oak Creek was lower than anyone had ever seen it. In mid-May T.A. questioned whether the steam-powered mill, which had been closed all winter, would be able to start for summer operation.

> Everything is drying up rapidly, including the Old Town spring and all the water holes. The railroad people are in as bad shape as anyone else, as they haven't a drop of water at Williams for anything excepting what they hauled from Bellemont...The only consolation in the whole matter is, that there isn't much to do. If there were, a fellow could hardly do it. Sheepmen and cattle men are very much alarmed, and I am told that cattle are dying fast on account of the poor feed and no water. The country is all scorched and dried up, and not a blade of new grass in sight yet. We are having extraordinarily high and dry winds too, nearly every day, and it took the combined force of the company and the town to keep us from burning out a few days ago, as a big fire started in our pasture and another on the Doney quarter one day last week when the wind was blowing a perfect hurricane, and we had the closest call in our history.

Through June, of course, there was no rain. Right on schedule on July 4th it came down in "a perfect flood," filling the Rio de Flag and the pond behind the AL&T dam, and T.A. wrote:

> The rains have changed the entire complexion of the country here. Everything looks bright and fresh and green, and the people are feeling quite jubilant and it has resulted in great relief to everybody.

But weather around Flagstaff was seldom moderate. Rain went on the rest of the summer, "running in torrents down the streets," and "hanging up the loggers completely." By late August T.A. was complaining:

> We are having an awful time here with rain. It seems to never let up...and we have had unusually heavy thunder and lightning showers, so much so that the electric light plant has had to shut down on two or three occasions in the evening

---

1 The Flagstaff Fire Company enlisted fifty-two men in 1895. Among them were three Hochderffers, three Babbitts, two Whipples, Dr. Brannen, banker Puliam, Al Doyle, and Godfrey Sykes's brother Stanley.

and our train and logging operations have been hung up repeatedly as wash-outs and floods would occur at points we never noticed rain before. The bicycle club in town has been making arrangements for a good while for their annual run to the Grand Canyon on their wheels. They got off yesterday morning but heavy rains started in almost after they left town and it has kept it up pretty much ever since so we fear they will have a very hard time of it...

Six years or so before the railroad line had come through, Bear Howard, hunting in the Inner Basin of the Peaks, had followed a stream to its source and found in a deep wash on the south side of the basin a large spring that gushed fifteen gallons of cold water a minute. A few years later Jack Smith located it again, claimed it, and sold a half interest in it to sheep grower Hank Lockett. (Land on which it was located was part of the railroad land grant, but as user of the water, Smith had clear right.)

In July of 1896, with the *Sun* orating that, despite the summer storms, Flagstaff would become "a howling wilderness...a place of destruction from which mankind will flee in terror" if something serious were not done about its water supply, the town council investigated the possibility of piping water up from Oak Creek but decided the cost of getting it out of the canyon would be prohibitive. The council chose instead to pay fourteen hundred dollars for the Jack Smith spring, which was about 2200 feet higher than the houses that needed its water, although there were those who argued that if a break should occur in the pipe line up there in winter "it would take three months to find it." In a letter to his older brother in 1894, T.A. Riordan referred to "that spring up in the mountains" and reported that surveyors were deciding whether they could run a line from it into town east of Mt. Elden, a distance of sixteen miles, or west through Schultz Pass, which would present expensive difficulties but provide a better gravitational fall. Estimated cost of construction: $125,000.

In January of 1897, in response to pressure from the town's representatives, Congress passed and President McKinley signed a bill authorizing the sale of bonds for a real water system in northern Arizona Territory, and the town council began negotiations in St. Louis with the man who had handled its court house bonds. In early May terms were agreed upon: ninety-five cents net and a five per-cent commission. G.S. Sturdevant of Chicago was hired to do the work. That summer pipe was shipped, a wagon road was built into the Inner Basin, and the town was confident that a water system would soon be working, maybe the next year. Through autumn it built a three million gallon reservoir in preparation.

The next year John Woody was town marshall, Julius Abineau was mayor, and local voters passed a bond election to build a flow line from Jack Smith Spring seventeen miles down from the Inner Basin on the Schultz Pass route to the new storage reservoir, with a pipe line into houses in town. It was an ambitious project: there was no automotive equipment, and weather held water-line work on those high slopes to a few months in summer. On warm, dry days wagons carried clay

The railroad created Flagstaff; snow kept it alive.
Special Collections and Archives Department, Cline Library, Northern Arizona University

Mules transported pipe to the Inner Basin.
AHS–Pioneer Museum

pipe and cement and tools as far as they could, and mules took over from there. All labor was done by hand—one hundred and ten to one hundred and thirty men built about sixteen hundred feet of line a day.

But all through spring and summer of 1898 weather was dry again and water was in short supply for the town, the railroad and the lumber mill, and T.A. said, "A heavy shower would be a very welcome thing just now."

> Cooley shut off the town the other day, and they have been hauling water since then by wagon. The probability is that we will have to get water somewhere for the electric light works too. Ed does not think his well will keep the plant going. Unless we get a storm soon the water question is going to be a serious one. The railroad has not been able to keep its trains moving, and yesterday they had to let three trains lie here while the engines went to Bellemont to fill up.

Flagstaff was understandably eager for news about pipe line construction progress. In October, with six miles laid, the engineer promised to put a crew on at both ends and try to get over the Schultz Pass divide by the end of the month and into town by the first of December.

When running water was finally delivered to town, meters were required and rates established. The basic fee for water service, paid in advance on the first of every month, was:

Private family—one faucet . . . .$2.00 per month
each extra faucet 25
bath tub 50
w.c 25
Horse trough or tub on sidewalk 2.50
Saloons 5.00
Laundries 10.00
Livery stables 10.00

While they were at it, the voters organized a sewer corporation as well. Among the sewer rates:

Private houses . . . .$9.00 per month
Barber shops 12.00
Saloons running night and day: 48.00
    in connection with chop houses
    without chop houses [cafes] 24.00

In January of 1899 residents of the West End out toward Mars Hill formed a taxpayers' association as a result of being left out of the contract for the downtown water works. West End citizens held a meeting and appointed neighbor and town marshall John Woody to inquire into the intentions of the council about extending water lines to their homes.

Godfrey Sykes observed that the new system "brought about a remarkable transformation in the habits and appearance of the townsfolk."

> The "try-weekly" baths became an actual weekly function, then semi-weekly, and to some ablutionary enthusiasts a normal daily affair. The domestic washtub was

relinquished for its legitimate use and stationary bath-tubs, selected from the tempting pages of mail-order catalogues, were installed.

The town tried to tap every source. It developed the catch basin formed by Schultz Pass, between the Peaks and Mt. Elden, with pipes in side canyons that drained as much as eight million gallons a day into the reservoir in years of heavy snowfall. In 1900, with money advanced by AL&T and help from the Santa Fe, springs above Jack Smith in the Inner Basin—Bear Paw, Flagstaff, Snowslide, Raspberry—were tied into the system, and the town agreed to deliver to the railroad two hundred thousand gallons of water every twenty-four hours.

But the total flow from all sources wasn't enough to satisfy town and railroad and local industry. Although February of 1901 brought snow of 84.1 inches, overwhelming to a town of unpaved streets and horse transportation, Julius Abineau, who was by then chairman of the city water committee, warned that demand just equalled supply, and supply was beginning to fail: "Your water department has been very liberal in the matter of sprinkling streets, the practicing of fire hose companies, the filling of water ponds and giving undue privileges to consumers." He suggested that tourists be discouraged because Flagstaff didn't have enough water to supply them.

Sometimes, of course, there was too much water. When snow on the Peaks melted quickly and came down all at once, the Rio de Flag overflowed and the dirt streets turned to mud. Now and then summer storms, like those of 1903 and 1904 that complicated logging on Woody Mountain, were altogether too generous. Wooden sidewalks floated out of place, especially over in Milton, and children got onto them and rode them until they grounded. Water at Five Points near the Normal School was occasionally deep enough to float a rowboat.

Through the early twentieth century, the town grew so rapidly that, after only a few years of use, the line from the springs in the Inner Basin needed to be replaced with larger pipe. Eli Giclas, who was town Water Superintendent at the time, had the old Jack Smith cabin repaired to house a work crew and watched over the job, in addition to all his desk responsibilities.

Flagstaff's original water system had cost over one hundred thousand dollars, which had seemed expensive to voters, but in less than a decade it had become inadequate, and it was obvious that, unless townfolks were willing to go back to the old "try-weekly" bathing schedule, a new source of water would have to be found. The lumber mill in Milton was a heavy user, so the Riordans proposed to take responsibility for damming Walnut Creek, where it passed through Clark's Valley, to catch the seasonal flow.

The company obtained permits from the Department of Interior in 1904 to build a dam forty feet high and one thousand feet long across the narrow end of

The Rio de Flag, which flowed six months of the year, was often in flood.
AHS–Pioneer Museum

Eli Giclas was right wheel man on the Milton Fire Hose Team.
AHS–Pioneer Museum

Clark's Valley and lay a pipeline to the city. The cost to AL&T, for what was considered a "drastic measure," was fifty thousand dollars. T.A. named the resulting
seven-mile-long lake, capacity three billion gallons, for his daughter. (It is not Lake
Saint Mary, he lectured the *Sun*.) It helped: Lake Mary saved the town "many a
time."

But it still wasn't enough. Settlers had chosen for their homes a region that
was officially classified as "high desert." Nothing they did provided the amount of
water they wanted to use.

Through dry years and wet, Godfrey Sykes enjoyed the fire hose practice which
Abineau decried.

> The new water supply, now under heavy pressure, revolutionized our Fire
> Department. It was still a volunteer organization and Sandy continued to be its
> Chief, but the hand-power engine was discarded and replaced by two brilliant
> red hose carts—also designed and arranged for human traction. So we formed
> two bitterly rival Companies and we ran "hose races" with each other upon high
> days and holidays, and when called upon to fight fires in blazing shanties we kept
> one eye upon the blaze and the other upon the other Company in order to
> safeguard ourselves against being out-squirted, out-maneuvered, and brought to
> ridicule in the eyes of our neighbors. It is needless to say that the rival Company
> had similar feelings and reactions towards us. Sometimes, in our enthusiasm over
> having high-pressure water to play with we overdid the thing a little and
> drenched and partially wrecked a few of the shanties and other buildings near to
> the blazing one in order "to keep the fire from spreading." Altogether, fire
> fighting was great fun and being a member of a Fire Company exempted one
> from the payment of poll-tax and other irritants.

Every spring across the tracks in Milton, hoses were unrolled and tested to
prove they were in good working condition; once a month all summer, employees
were taken through fire drills on company time. T.A. thought it would be a good
idea to inject "a little friendly competition" into the practice and pitted the departments—the saw mill, the box factory, the yard, the machine shop crew, the car
whackers—against each other. He sent a memo to his superintendent:

> I believe we should try and keep up the old spirit of friendly competition in this
> way and that if you can think of some way to give the boys something that they
> would appreciate, running shoes, and uniform trousers and shirts and caps or
> anything else they might prefer we would be glad to furnish it upon knowing
> what their wishes were.

Within a year, mill competition had grown into a Fourth of July race
between a lumber company team and a hose team from north of the tracks with a
fifty-two dollar prize for the winners. At eleven o'clock, after the morning parade,
the teams lined up with their hose trucks, ready to determine which could get to a
fire in the fastest time.

A water system and racing hose companies were fine and even fun, but they could do nothing to affect drought. In December of 1910 the country was dry again, and T.A. wrote to the Superintendent of the Havasupai Indian School to explain a delay in delivery of lumber:

> We regret exceedingly to have to say that we were notified by the Town Council of Flagstaff that on account of scarcity of water it would be necessary for us to temporarily suspend operations. The water supply of the town has been coming very slowly for a couple of weeks past and it is of course absolutely necessary that the town keep a full reservoir supply on hand for fire and insurance purposes.

Flagstaff survived that early winter emergency and "made do" for another three years, but there was never much surplus water. By October of 1913, after summer storms had failed to develop, the level in the city reservoir was sinking rapidly again, and every water hole in the vicinity was dry. There was some reserve in Lake Mary but, T.A. wrote, "it is out of our reach at present. So we are up against it for water all around."

Officials notified AL&T that the city could continue to supply Milton with domestic water, but the mill would be cut off until weather provided snow melt. T.A. wrote to the general manager of the Santa Fe asking for water to be delivered to the mill in railroad tank cars.

> I thought if, in this emergency, it would be possible for you to give us water at bare cost delivered here, which I suppose would be in the neighborhood of about $1.00 per 1000 gallons, that we might be able to stand this extraordinary expense for fifty to seventy five days to keep things moving. It would take about 45,000 gallons a day to run us, but so long as the town could give us the 15,000 gallons [for drinking water] we could get along with two or three car loads daily, 20,000 to 30,000 gallons.

The general manager of the Santa Fe responded to T.A.'s appeal, and within two weeks details were being arranged.

> I met Mr. Proctor, who indicated that he had been consulted on our water question. He told me there was none to spare at Bellemont or Williams, but that with the recently completed plant at Winslow there was an abundant supply at that point, and that if arrangements could be made for transportation there should be no trouble in getting the water. I suppose your daily short run from Winslow to Flagstaff usually runs light coming this way, and I wish you would let us know if it would not be possible for us to get two or three car loads a day from that point, and if so at what cost.

The Flagstaff City Council offered to supply the Electric Power Plant, which was owned by the Riordans, and keep it running, but T.A. warned:

> On account of the water shortage we will have to begin to cut down in every possible way in the use of water and I think it will be well for you to arrange to

shorten your hours of running the lights to the lowest possible minimum and starting late during the evening and cutting off shortly after day light. If we do not get storms soon I should not be surprised but what before long it will be necessary to cut down to a half night's run of the light plant so you had better begin to consider the matter and be prepared to reduce your running hours as much as possible.

The emergency disappeared within the month, when an early storm and a thaw that melted the snow brought water in the reservoir back up to a safe level.

Winter brought temporary relief to worried citizens. On December 1, 1914, the *Sun* reported: "More snow yesterday...wet and mixed with water." At Christmas: "There continues to be a downfall of wet snow, almost rain, with no signs of the storm clearing up." On January 1, 1915, the newspaper spoke of snow three feet deep on the Tonto road, and in May a spring snow storm dropped eight and a half inches. That took care of things only for a while.

In 1915 the railroad, which needed a reliable water supply every forty miles or so to keep its steam locomotives running, built a fifty million gallon reservoir near the first one and dropped an eight inch line to it from the Inner Basin springs. The town connected to the new reservoir with a cast iron line and felt confident for a while.

But December of 1915 promised to be dangerously dry. In the middle of the month the *Sun* had no holiday storms to describe, although it was hopeful: "The weather has been cool, calm and collected this past week with now and then a slight indication of being precipitate." On Christmas Eve the news was of a holiday rush for incoming mail at the post office, but streets were dry.

A week later in the issue of December 31, 1915, in a box at the top of the front page in one inch high letters, the *Sun* headlined:

MANY BUILDINGS CAVED IN HEAVIEST SNOW STORM IN HISTORY
MAJESTIC THEATER CRUMBLES UNDER WEIGHT OF SNOW
NEARLY FIVE FOOT OF SNOW ON LEVEL AND STILL FALLING

THOUSANDS OF DOLLARS DAMAGE DONE BUT NO CASUALTIES REPORTED
TRAINS NOT BLOCKADED

The Majestic Theatre crumbled to the ground at about 6 o'clock this morning under the weight of snow and is leveled to the ground except a small portion of the front wall.

The box factory roof at the F.L.M. mill caved in during the night. F.E. Brook's warehouse and sheds roof collapsed. Rodriguez dance hall roof caved in during early morning. The roof of a small house owned by W.A. Campbell caved in. H.E. Johnson's carpenter shop on the south side was wrecked. Campbell–Francis Co.'s barns used for their sheep outfit equipment at the corner of Beaver and Birch Avenue gave way and are badly wrecked.

Nearly all business today is given over to shoveling off roofs and breaking open the streets.

In its next week's issue the *Sun* went into detail.

AFTERMATH OF FLAGSTAFF'S HISTORICAL SNOW STORM

The local U.S. weather report for January first says that sixty-one inches of snow fell in the preceding twenty-four hours. In spite of the damage it did, it might have been a whole lot worse. Few residents ever saw a heavier snow fall during one storm in this section of the country, though old timers say there was a similar down fall of the pure white some thirty or thirty-five years ago.

Streets were practically blockaded for a time. Pedestrian and delivery teams were a scarcity, few went out unless compelled to, and businessmen kept shovelers going all day Friday and most of the day Saturday. The streets were broken by means of four-horse teams with drags. The first time around was a very slow process, but by Sunday, going in the main section of town was fairly good, though it looked as though everyone had suddenly took on the war fever and entrenched himself. About all you could see were the heads of people bobbing up and down along behind the snow embankments.

Despite the few hours discomfort and anxiety for heavily laden roofs, it was a beautiful scene and hundreds of photographs were taken by real photographers and snap-shooters, to be retained as souvenirs of the great snow-storm of 1915–1916.

So far as it could be learned the snow was of great value to the stockmen of the north, and no stock were lost in the storm. A few head of drifting stock may have been caught here and there too high up on the mountain, but the loss could not ordinarily be very great.

The days the first of the week were warm and the snow, being heavy, started melting and the big heaps gradually sunk to a reasonable level, though many streets will have to be cleared of snow by hauling it away.

In the forest, logging operations were paralyzed, but rather than close the mill and lay their men off, the Riordans set sawyers and planers to shoveling snow from town sidewalks at AL&T expense. Circumstances were different in the neighborhoods. For a few days Emerson School was closed, for fear the roof would collapse. When it opened again, older children did trail-breaking through snow on the way to school, with the younger ones following in their footsteps. If things were too bad, they turned for home.

That was the year when Charles H. Spencer, a self-educated mining engineer, set about developing what he called "the most remarkable domestic and water power project in the United States," an ambitious scheme to make money by tapping the water held within the porous volcanic rock of the Peaks and piping it into the craters of nearby cinder cones, which he proposed to line with cement to create natural reservoirs. He figured he could collect four billion gallons a year and earn an annual $1,250,000.

At the corner of Aspen and Agassiz men shoveled snow from a roof
on the first day of 1916.
AHS–Pioneer Museum

Homeowners cleared sidewalks on North Leroux.
AHS–Pioneer Museum

First, with money provided by investors in Chicago, he dug west of the Peaks a long ditch that carried water from above Hart Prairie and through a tunnel into Crater Lake. On the east side he projected a tunnel under Lockett Meadow to pipe water into Lennox Crater; 1400 feet of it was completed. But World War I distracted the attention of Spencer's investors, and by 1920 work on the project was stopped and was never resumed.

The town struggled along from flood to drought for another few years of growing population. In 1924 it signed a contract with the Santa Fe for the sale of half a million dollars in bonds to construct a fourteen inch concrete flow line, capacity five million gallons in twenty-four hours, from the springs to a new fifty million gallon reservoir. That gave Flagstaff one hundred and five million gallons of water storage. Trenches were dug through the streets and proper mains were built. The whole system—land, lines, reservoirs—was deeded to the town by the terms of the contract.

Flagstaff sent men up to the line of springs in the Inner Basin in 1929 to put an eight-inch pipe beside the original six inch line at Flagstaff Spring and rework the Raspberry springs. In 1931, with Depression settling in, the intake system at the big Jack Smith Spring was put underground to prevent it from freezing in winter weather, a job that took eighteen men ten days of hand labor. The two miles of connecting pipe from Doyle Spring were buried at the same time.

It wasn't enough. In October of 1931 residents received a postal card from their city.

A Serious Water Shortage Exists

Until Further Notice No Water Will Be Used for Washing Cars, on Lawns, or for Other Unnecessary Purposes.

The flow from springs is less at the present time this year than it has been at any corresponding time of year for many years. This is undoubtedly due to lack of snow and precipitation during the past seasons. The storage in Reservoirs is constantly decreasing—therefore the use of water MUST be curtailed until further notice.

Save Every Drop of Water Possible

BY ORDER OF CITY COUNCIL

In the bleak year of 1934, while the southern plains states were choking with Dust Bowl winds, Flagstaff had its own "Big Drought." Despite Civilian Conservation Corps labor that put in a five mile road and a feeder line to connect Abineau Spring north of the Peaks with the Inner Basin, there simply was not enough water close at hand to supply the town that year.

Residents went with cans to outlying springs, lining up in their cars by the hundreds in the evening, but the springs were soon dry. As available moisture on the range declined, grasses dependent on summer rains became sparse while early seeding varieties like blue grama, which had longer roots and some drought-resistance, actually increased a little. But there wasn't enough grass; hundreds of scrawny cattle were shipped out on the railroad. The Santa Fe again brought water into town in ten thousand gallon tank cars and dumped it into the municipal line. People bathed on days when the water train arrived, and AL&T reclaimed sewer water for mill boilers in order to spare clean water for the city.

Flagstaff continued to hang on, barely, from one storm season to another. On January 1 of 1934, twenty inches of snow fell after 3:00 a.m., and north San Francisco Street was blocked so that children could use it for a sled run. That melted, and another post card went out on September 11, 1934, with an explicit warning.

USE NO MORE WATER ON LAWNS OR FOR UNNECESSARY PURPOSES

We have only 25,000,000 gallons of water in the reservoir.

It is flowing in at the rate of 500,000 gallons a day.

We are using more than 800,000 gallons a day, thus losing 300,000 or more gallons a day.

The in-flow is less than before in 5 years, and is steadily decreasing.

A shortage is inevitable, and unless you save we shall soon be entirely out of water

BY ORDER OF TOWN COUNCIL

Snow in January of 1936 isolated the Experiment Station in Fort Valley, with supplies low and a baby due at the Lexen house, sending Ed Martin skiing into town for a pack of supplies and a book on delivering a baby. The temperature dropped thirty degrees during the day, and he returned home with one hundred pounds on his back and feet so badly frozen that Dr. Sechrist suggested a partial amputation.

The Coconino National Forest was "exceedingly dry" again in summer of 1936, and long strings of tank cars filled with water, clearly labeled to prevent mistakes, came in on the railroad. Residents didn't care much for the taste, but it saved the town.

During heavy snows in 1937, the highway department bought a large rotary snow plow with a blower, but that snow soon melted away into the usual drought of May and June, with low water levels in the reservoirs. Flagstaff was unable to keep even with its climate and its population growth no matter what it did.

An engineer named John Carollo had suggested to Flagstaff a few years earlier that it might be possible to drill deep into the Oak Creek fault east of Woody Ridge and find water. In 1938, desperate, the mayor and city council revived Carollo's idea for wells to tap sub-surface water and requested a geological survey from International Geophysics in Los Angeles. After the California company suggested mapping the Oak Creek fault and putting down a test well on its north end in Fort Valley, the city drew up a lease for Babbitt land and issued a contract to drill a well, but the venture was disappointing. By November everyone concerned conceded that although there was water at shallow levels in Fort Valley, there did not seem to be any further down, at least none above the level of the Supai formation at one thousand feet.[2]

In 1941, with war raging in Europe, Lake Mary was leaking water through its limestone bottom, and University of Arizona geologist Stownoff advised the town to build a second dam higher in Clark's Valley, above the limestone, and create another lake. It too was designated by the name of T.A.'s daughter as Upper Lake Mary.

Water from the new wells was hard and alkaline due to calcium carbonate in the underlying formations, but Flagstaff thought the water problem was finally solved. Climate and population growth simply kept up with developments, making every addition to the water system inadequate before it was paid for, and the pressure increased faster than solutions could be found.

Over and over Flagstaff relearned the same lesson: there isn't much water in the West, not enough to satisfy unlimited human whims. During dry spells in the 1940s householders, having given up on lawns, saved water from washing machines and bathtubs and carried it to their bushes to keep them alive. Trees on the college campus were saved by water hauled in buckets from City Park Lake.

---

2 Water just below the surface in Fort Valley was only eight feet from daylight; a few subsequent small wells were drilled toward the western end by homeowners with post-hole diggers. In 1952, a year before he was elected to the city council, resident Andrew Wolf reached water table at forty-three feet but lost his well into an underground cavity when dynamite used to perforate the pipe lining knocked out the bottom of the hole. Driller Noble Heck plugged it with clay and a small pine tree rammed down into the pipe; the well provided the house with a steady water supply through the rest of the century.

Highest draw on the reservoir was in late spring and early summer, the historical months of no rain, when demand could increase from the half a million gallon a day draw-down of winter to three million gallons a day in June. The importance of winter snows to provide water for spring use was obvious.

But nobody ever knew what kind of weather to expect. In 1948 there was little precipitation in November. Early December was warm and dry with twenty-five-degree-low temperatures, and townsfolk began to worry about another drought until, three days before Christmas, a series of storms began and provided nearly twenty inches of snow before the end of the year.

January of 1949 brought the heaviest snowfall since 1895. The storm started on January 9 with blizzard-force winds that piled up drifts. Rain fell and made snow slushy; then temperatures dropped and froze it, and snow went on falling. By the 14th the *Sun* was calling it a Record Snowfall. On the 21st it reported a total of sixty-one inches since the first of the month, twice the normal amount for January. And snow went on falling.

It built up to window sills, ten feet deep in places. Platt Cline, publisher of the *Sun* in mid-century, said it was deeper than his paper boys were tall. A few small structures caved in. Trains continued to run, thanks to Santa Fe snow plows, but all traffic in town stopped except for emergency vehicles. People were requested to keep their new post-war automobiles off the streets, which were kept open in one-lane trails for emergency vehicles. Flagstaff thought it was fun, for a while, and was glad for the promise of full reservoirs. And snow kept falling.

From January 9 to 23 a total of 100.4 inches of snow fell on Flagstaff, 39.1 inches during one fifty-five hour period. The storms, if you counted those nineteen and some inches in December, broke all official records.

It made problems that were more than the town could handle. Police and businesses struggled to deliver coal and food, to plow paths through snow and remove it from the streets, but they didn't know where to put the stuff. A huge pile of it in the open space between Coconino Street and the railroad tracks was regularly flattened by large caterpillar tractors which moved back and forth across it. There was much discussion about whether plows would be a wise purchase considering that such a storm developed only once every decade, and people were saying the slow debate proved that one way or another, in dealing with water problems, Flagstaff always did too little too late.

The Big Snow of 1949 melted into reservoirs, but a few people were not lulled into forgetting the long-term problem. In the summer of 1951 the superintendent of the city water department, Herman Dunnam,[3] "full-time native" Jimmy Beard,

3 Dunnam's nickname about town was "Flopsie," short for "Cow Flops." Henry Giclas and the other boys ahd called him that because, they said, he walked through manure on his way to school and got it on his shoes. The name persisted the rest of his life.

who would soon succeed him, and city council member Andy Wolf went up into the Inner Basin to evaluate water flow and discuss an idea for increasing it. Sitting on the edge of the collection platform at Strawberry Spring, they decided to request an allocation for digging trenches and placing all spring intakes fifteen feet underground, below the frost line, and wondered whether they could drill wells there in the basin. The City Council approved their plans and their budget: over several summers crews accomplished the work and added to Flagstaff's available water. America's post-war population shift toward the southwest added to Flagstaff's population, negating any gain.

Around the turn of the decade, the El Paso Natural Gas Company, laying a pipeline through northern Arizona and around the south side of the Peaks, had produced water it needed from a well only six hundred feet deep near Leupp, thirty-five miles east of town. The town's suggestion that it drill a well in the same area and use El Paso's ditch to pipe water to Flagstaff was turned down by its bonding company. Leupp was two thousand feet lower; the cost of pumping uphill all that distance was beyond the legal bonding limit. But it was the germ of an idea that took drilling rigs to Woody Mountain two years later.

Ken Switzer was Flagstaff mayor in 1952. At the end of June, "Flops" Dunnam announced that thirty feet of snow had fallen on the Peaks the previous winter, the most since that big storm of 1949. Since there was an ample supply of water at the moment, low rates were to be made available by the city council.

Within two weeks the Coconino Forest had closed watersheds under its control and the council was considering an ordinance to close to public use and camping certain areas along Lake Mary's shores. Tests made in the college swimming pool had revealed that there were problems the Water Purification Plant had not taken care of, and the county Health Department had urged the restrictions to protect Flagstaff's water supply from contamination.

There were problems everywhere the council looked. On a Tuesday afternoon in late July, the town once again had more water than it needed—two-thirds of an inch of rain fell within an hour. Water stood a foot deep on streets near the college campus; a five foot wall of it roared down through Oak Creek Canyon. That kind of storm didn't touch daily use, which had doubled in the past ten years. Insurance companies threatened rising rates unless new lines were installed to bring water in from the reservoirs to provide for fighting fires.

Rainfall for the rest of the winter of 1952 was one-third of normal. Grasses on the forest dried, and by November danger of fires was termed extreme. One foot of snow that fell during the first week the following March was the first major storm of the winter. It was no surprise to anybody when a *Sun* headline in April read "City Council to Seek Additional Water Sources", which meant a proposal to pump water out of Ashurst and Mormon and Kinnikinnik Lakes and into Lake Mary. Local fishermen protested loudly.

However, by 1953 the town realized that Lake Mary was losing a million gallons a day through cracks in the bottom and through evaporation into the dry Arizona air, which was taking a good part of the lake before it could be piped into town. The *Sun* used terms like "urgency of the situation...need for emergency action," and the Kiwanis Club conducted a series of programs on water problems. Talk around town was of a scheme to float whale oil on the surface of the lake to stop evaporation, which provoked both interest and hilarity.

There was no question that still another source of water would have to be provided. People who knew something of geology argued thus:

1. There is quite a lot of rain and snow around here, more than in most places in Arizona.
2. There is very little surface water run-off.
3. Most of our water goes underground through a volcanic cap, limestone, and sandstone with easy access down, due to fracturing and porosity and permeability.
4. Underground water doesn't evaporate.
5. Obviously we need to drill underground for water.

Dunnam suggested that if the city had been interested in pumping water up twenty-six hundred feet from Leupp, maybe it wouldn't object to the idea of drilling down as far right near the need. City Manager Clarence Pulliam agreed.[4]

There were seventy-five thousand dollars in a development fund that had been accumulating since World War II, and the Council agreed to use it either to find underground water or to prove that there wasn't any. A special committee decided that a well near Meteor Crater would cost too much but recommended one that could bring water into town by gravity flow, say from a Riordan sawmill on the railroad line out to the west. Universal opinion was that the town should get Eddie McKee to help locate a site.

As director in charge of research at the Museum of Northern Arizona, McKee was a Flagstaff presence for twelve years. He was credited with the discovery of the "pink" Grand Canyon rattlesnake after he had captured one on the trail and, lacking a container, had carried it to the top in his hands and driven back to the office holding it out the window of his car.

Early in 1952 McKee had moved to Denver and a position with the U.S. Geological Survey. A year later the city council wrote to the U.S.G.S. in Washington and to Senator Goldwater requesting that McKee, the local expert on underground formations, be released briefly to give them advice about where to drill a well.

The moisture situation looked bleak all summer. In June, Barney Pasture was so dry it was closed to the public, temperatures reached a near-record high of

---

4 His name was Clarence, but the town called him "Maggie."

eighty-seven degrees, and a fire caused by a camper burned 100 acres near the highway a few miles to the east of town. There were scattered showers in July, but forests were drier than they had been for a quarter of a century, and all over Arizona they were closed to all users. A heavy storm on August 1 washed out roads without easing the situation much. The headline in the *Sun* was "Committee Urges Development of Additional Water Supplies."

In the forest during one week in early October there were fifteen fires caused by hunters. In November an escaped campfire burned ninety acres near Turkey Butte with flames visible from Sedona and Jerome. Blazes in town destroyed buildings; a child died in a structure fire in mid-November. Winter's first good storm toward the end of the month broke the longest dry spell in ten years.

Snowfall in January and February was above normal, and in mid-March, almost four inches of rain fell in one week, but it was obvious to the Council that delay could just plain endanger the town. On March 13 of 1954 the headline on the front page of the *Sun* was one inch high.

CITY OK'S PROJECT TO LOCATE WELL SITE
SURVEY COSTS ESTIMATED AT ABOUT $4000
SEEK ADDITIONAL MUNICIPAL WATER SUPPLY FOR FLAG

Flagstaff's City Council has taken an important step toward realization of an extensive water development program recommended by a special city committee several weeks ago to augment city supplies.

At a meeting of the council Wednesday, the group approved entering into an agreement with the federal government for geological work in connection with the proposed well-drilling project in the area southwest of here.

The survey would be conducted by the U.S. Coast and Geodetic Survey, experts of which located the water well at Navajo Army Depot.

...Under the survey proposal, the city and federal government would share equally in the estimated $4000 cost of the geological portion of the work. Actual drilling costs would be borne by the city.

City officials report that the federal agencies involved are unable to release Dr. Edwin D. McKee, whose services had been requested for the work, but that other men who have had considerable experience in locating successful wells in this area will be working on the project.

The last sentence was a reference to the man McKee had suggested in his stead, John Harshbarger, District Geologist for the United States Geological Survey and assistant professor of geology at the University of Arizona, who had served as consultant when the Lake Mary wells were drilled. Flagstaff had written to him in early 1953 and asked that he make a survey of possibilities.

Harshbarger was reluctant to take the job. Flagstaff wanted an additional one million gallons a day, which he felt was "quite a bit."

Because of my association with Eddie McKee, I knew somewhat about the difficulties of finding water; that is, water in sufficient quantities for municipal use in this area. Past history...[had] shown it isn't easy to come by. In fact, in the several attempts made, it...proved fruitless. But it was a challenge, so we agreed to

From 1929 to 1940 Ed McKee worked as park naturalist at the Grand Canyon
and made major contributions to the understanding of its geology.
Museum of Northern Arizona

John Harshbarger stood in a lunch line at a geology symposium in 1959.
Museum of Northern Arizona

see what we could do. A cooperative agreement was set up between the Geological Survey and the City of Flagstaff. By that I mean it was cooperatively financed. For every dollar the City put up, the United States Government matched it, dollar for dollar, to make the investigation...The currents and development of water in this area [were] of federal interest as well as of local interest.

He was intrigued by the fault zone, which Carollo had pointed out 20 years earlier, lying east of Woody Ridge and extending south to form Oak Creek Canyon.

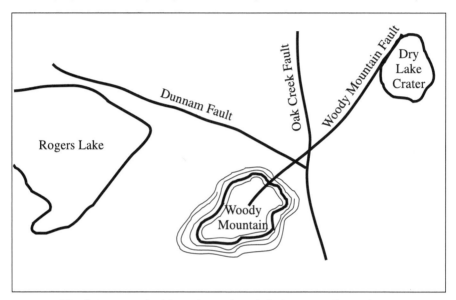

Woody Mountain had formed on a short fault that ran to the northeast, crossing the north–south Oak Creek fault.
From Kent Murray's Geology of the Woody Mountain Volcanic Field

There was a vertical displacement of three hundred feet—that is, the east side was three hundred feet lower than the west—with beds dipping toward the fault zone. It was not a clean-cut plane but a break with a good deal of complementary fracturing, and Harshbarger was interested in the influence that fracturing might have on permeability, on the amount of water that could move through the rock. He suspected that porosity of the upper volcanic layer might be as high as eighty percent because of voids that had developed in cooling lava a few million years earlier.

Speaking to a Flagstaff City Water Conference, Harshbarger described the fault.

It's all busted up—which has proved to be good as far as we are concerned. The drillers [won't] like it worth a darn; it gives them trouble. But as far as getting water is concerned, that's what [we're] looking for.

John Carollo, who was hired by the city to prepare specifications, concurred.

> The effects of faulting on movement of groundwater in the Woody Mountain
> area cannot be overemphasized. Water appears to move readily through rocks
> deformed by faults associated with the "contrary bending" adjacent to the Oak
> Creek faults. Water also appears to move easily along fault planes of Woody
> Mountain, Dunnam, Graben, and other faults...Local recharge enters the
> groundwater system from Rogers Lake, Dry Lake, Sinclair Wash, Woody Wash
> [all drainages of Woody Mountain]...[In other places] the Woody Mountain field
> is recharged from the southwest. Much of the large amounts of precipitation in
> the area enters the groundwater system as recharge through fractures and
> solution openings.

Harshbarger selected a test site half a mile northeast of Woody Mountain
where the fault crossed land held by the state, and the council decided to take the
advice it had paid for. Despite a May Day rainfall of eight inches, it issued a call for
construction bids.[5] On the first of June, a $52,000 contract to drill down as far as
twenty-five hundred feet was issued to Perry Brothers of Winslow.

George, Lloyd, and Don Perry, grandsons of a man who had been involved in
the Lincoln County war, had worked summers with their father on drilling jobs in
New Mexico since they were boys, camping out near the rigs with a milk cow and
chickens. Using the training and advice of their father, who had been in the business for fifty years, they had formed their own company in 1951 and worked on
wells on the Navajo Reservation, at Petrified Forest, all over northern Arizona.
Don was twenty-six when they took the Woody Mountain job, Lloyd twenty-
eight, George forty-two.

The Perry brothers joked that they bid only fifty-two thousand dollars
because they didn't know how hard and tough and full of fractures volcanic rock
could be. They used half their time and most of the money getting through it.

The city acquired a right of way across national forest land for water mains, a
power line and an access road, in addition to the drilling site on the fault line.
Because the land was under sheep grazing permit, the signature of Marianne
Manterola was required before preparation was complete. Drilling with cable tool
rigs started in June.

Harshbarger was on the site and involved in the work.

> We knew we were going to have volcanics, and it was going to be more difficult
> than any of us surmised or thought. There was plenty of trouble...getting
> through the volcanic rocks.

That trouble lasted all summer: the volcanic layer was several hundred feet
deep. The Perry brothers started with a pilot hole which was enlarged to twenty-four

---

5 The urgency was emphasized, after a 200-acre fire near Beaver Creek and another 3600 acre burn at Kelley
  Tank, when the Forest Service declared fire danger extreme on the Coconino and closed to the public
  125,000 acres, including the area around Woody Mountain.

Flanked by drillers, George Perry and city water superintendent Herman Dunnam inspected work at Woody Mountain Well #1. From left to right the men are: unidentified, George Perry, Herman Dunnam, Lloyd Perry, and Perry's brother-in-law Delbert Parnell.
Courtesy of Lloyd Perry

inches, but there were times when the drill advanced less than twelve inches in one eight-hour shift. In mid-July, when they were only one hundred feet down and installing steel casing as they went, they had already run into boulders that made the bit drift off center so that they couldn't keep the hole straight.

The only thing they could see to do was to lower a man down with a jack hammer. From a section of twenty-four-inch casing they made what they called a "cage" with a floor and ceiling welded in and a window cut through the side. For a couple of weeks, well work was done from the cage. Lloyd Perry described it later on:

> I made many trips down that 24 inch hole...We all did, for 30 minutes at a time, and then pulled out and let somebody else have a turn. We was nervous. The air was bad...Cinders rolled down and you thought the hole was caving in...We went down as deep as 200 feet. [see page 256]

The Perrys had rented a hammer from an excavator, Malcolm Mackey, the son of a local dentist. While it was in use, men carried a light cord and a flashlight into the hole, but when they began to place dynamite for blasting, electricity had to be withdrawn for safety. The roof of the casing cage was cut out and large mirrors at the surface reflected sunlight down the hole.

"Flops" Dunnam, interested in every detail, went down in the cage once and came back up to testify he had found a cave underground, part of an ancient lava tube. Dunnam said he had climbed out of the cage and walked around a while with his flashlight but had not cared to explore very far.

Only one man was injured on the job. A driller who was lifting a "boomer" (a chain tightener) attached to one of the guy lines, was struck across the throat when it broke loose and recoiled. Lloyd Perry rushed the unconscious man into the hospital in town and stayed with him until he came around.

When the brothers broke through old lava into the sediment of ancient oceans, Harshbarger was optimistic:

> After [the volcanic layer], the drilling in the limestone and sandstone was relatively easy; although as we got down in the water-bearing formation, we started picking up these subsidiary fractures; and every time we hit one of the subsidiary fractures the drill bit would want to go off toward Venus or somewhere, which of course made the drillers quite unhappy, but it made me smile because we were getting what we were looking for, some fracturing and increased permeability. But there was a little trouble getting a straight hole due to these fracture zones.

Progress on the work was front page news in the *Sun* all summer. On July 24 the newspaper told people in town that drillers were below the 215 foot level; at the end of July it reported that the hole was down to 274 feet. Editors announced cheerfully in the middle of August that Perry Brothers were still enlarging the bore hole. By early September the well had been cased to the five hundred foot level.

Lloyd Perry often went down the hole in a "cage" made from well casing.
Courtesy of Lloyd Perry

But summer precipitation had been far below normal, city storage total was down, and average daily consumption of water in Flagstaff had been two million gallons a day. Despite growing urgency, consulting geologists predicted that water in the Woody Mountain test well would not be reached until the 1250 feet level. Lloyd Perry, remembering the situation thirty-five years later, conceded that the brothers were under pressure.

> The city was runnin' out of water. They was wantin' to reduce the size of the hole...anything to hurry us up...City councilmen came out every week to see how it was going. We had 20 to 30 cars come out visitin' on Sundays, quite a cheering section. Herb Babbitt was there often with a car full of kids.

In September Perry Brothers requested an extension on their drilling contract. Financing was "touch and go," with money to keep the drills going provided by private citizens.

City Councilman Andy Wolf had urged that Flagstaff seek underground water, but he had been dubious about the Woody Mountain site. On the morning of September 18, he met fellow Councilman Jack Knoles on the sidewalk in front of the Weatherford Hotel, and Knoles said, "Have you heard the news? They hit water at Woody Mountain at 1220 feet!" A one-inch headline in the *Sun* that week was: "Drill Hits Water in City Prospect Well."

Water had been found where the geologists had said it would be. The city was so pleased it was already beginning to talk of additional wells in the same area. At the Rotary Club, Ted Spencer poured a symbolic glassful of water from a pitcher to introduce a talk on the history of Flagstaff's water supply.

But trouble wasn't over yet for the Perry Brothers. In early October, a cable broke when a bailer was being brought to the surface, and drillers spent three days fishing for it, recovering it on a Sunday evening at 8:30. Then a drill bit broke off its shaft and lodged at the bottom of the hole for nearly a week until it could be retrieved with a special case-hardened hook. Through October the crew worked on reaming the well out to accommodate a test pump big enough to lift water to the surface, but when they lowered it into the shaft through six inch casing, and started the rig, its gears squealing, the $20,000 pump broke off and jammed in the hole. The Perrys spent several days fishing for it with various devices they invented on the spot and finally admitted "it wouldn't pull." Reluctantly, they put the drill back down and used it to pulverize their pump.

Trouble wasn't over for the city either. Water level in storage reservoirs was still dropping, but before it could be supplemented, a power line had to be built out to Woody Mountain to provide electricity for pumping. Tests showed that the Woody Mountain well might produce 350 gallons a minute, but not yet, not until the following summer at the earliest.

In December the well was tested for seven days at an average rate of 207 gallons pumped per minute while people from town crowded around to watch. After the test week, water level in the well had fallen only sixty-seven feet, which was the encouragement geologists and engineers needed to propose that a field of several wells could be developed in the area. Harshbarger believed it would be capable of putting out as much as ten million gallons a day. But not yet.

Precipitation through the winter was the lightest on record, and water level in storage continued to fall. Lake Mary was nearly dry. By April of 1956 forest fire danger was so near record, the worst in many years, that at the beginning of June, with forty-four fires already burning, the Coconino was closed to campers. Flagstaff's city council asked townfolk to alternate watering days as a preliminary distribution solution.

Woody Mountain Well No. 1 went into production that summer. And just in time. The day the first water went through the line into town was the day pumps sucked mud at Lake Mary. According to councilman Francis Decker, if you compared cost figures for hauling water from Del Rio Springs in Prescott, which the town had done in 1934, the Woody Mountain well paid for itself each thirty days. "Also," Decker said, "there are not any more water tank railroad cars available."

Temperature of the Woody Mountain water was fifty-two degrees Fahrenheit. (Inner Basin water temperature was thirty-nine degrees.) Quality was "good to excellent and satisfactory for domestic use." It contained calcium, magnesium and sodium, but not much iron, copper, manganese, or zinc.

The big problem was that, percolating down through sedimentary deposits as it did, it contained a great deal of sand from ancient ocean beds loosened again from the grip of time and pressure. A sedimentation tank was installed to settle out sand and silt at the surface, but that did not eliminate clogging underground. Submersible electric pumps hanging twelve to fifteen hundred feet down were worn, especially by the fine Coconino Sandstone grains. Sometimes motors overheated and burned out; sometimes a well filled with sand, which buried the motor entirely. It became a long-term concern requiring deepening, lining, servicing, rehabilitation. "Sand production," as the engineers termed it, could not be completely eliminated.

Flagstaff thought it had finally solved its periodic crisis with the Woody Mountain water, but Herman Dunnam warned:

> At the present time the City of Flagstaff has its problem under control, but in
> view of past experience we must realize that water supply will be a continuing
> problem and we must be prepared to meet increased requirements as they arise.

The city went on to develop eight more wells along the Oak Creek fault beside Woody Mountain. Within eight years, with several wells working, almost 386 million gallons annually were pumped to the surface and sent into town through the pipe line.

It was Flagstaff's most expensive source of water. Static level was 1100 to 1250 feet down, requiring pumping to raise water all that distance to the surface and transport it six miles into town. The field never ran dry: its aquifer was dynamic—water flowed through from Rogers Lake and Woody Ridge and country round about—and pumping did not draw it down. However, the cost of providing it to residents made it a resource to use only in emergencies.

Inner Basin springs, high enough for gravity flow, offered a much cheaper and easier supply, but they could be serviced only in summer. Water from Lake Mary wells could be moved to residential taps fairly easily, but they went dry one year in ten. Expensive or not, those wells at Woody Mountain provided a vital back-up. During dry seasons seventy percent of Flagstaff's water came from them.

At a City Water Conference in 1957, Chairman Ralph Bilby agreed that the Council had been right to drill them.

> When you live in an area like Flagstaff where water is as precious to you as it is, you never cease looking for additional supplies and you never quit trying to find ways to improve your water system. And I think that comment applies to every Council the City of Flagstaff has had from 1930 on. They have all had to cope with the problem. I can see a lot of gentlemen here—Mr. Hutchinson, who was Mayor; John Babbitt; and I could probably look around and find others who served on the Council in past years. And they have always had to cope with a water problem, and I am sure they always will.

Seven deep wells were put into place in Lake Mary, with a pumping station that could provide one and a half million gallons each twenty-four hours through a new pipeline to a water treatment plant, but they were not satisfactory. In his report to the mayor and city council in 1961, City Manager Maggie Pulliam, describing an "alarming situation existing...because of little precipitation and resultant snow cover," said: "Should an extremely bad condition continue to exist, the one redeeming factor is our Woody Mountain Wells."

G rasses had finished their annual reproductive cycle by the time autumn arrived. Their narrow, two-ranked leaves were turning pale and brittle again. Deer browsed them until cold weather forced retreat to lower pastures. The little lichen plants that covered rocks and tree trunks, motionless in autumn wind, began to shut down metabolically.

Starting as early as August, ponderosa pine had eased off to nearly nothing such chemical processes as transpiration and photosynthesis. From one season to the next, the pines looked stolid and unchanged, but they cast old needles through the autumn, expelled some water to prevent freezing, and tapered off for the winter. Life on the mountain prepared for the first winter snow, which usually fell a month or so before the shortest day of the year.

Chapter Eight
Lookouts

1910–1986

A-1 fire from the Woody Mountain tower 2:30 p.m. June 12, 1933: with a southwest wind blowing, the fire crowned in the tops of the trees and burned 200 acres.
Courtesy of Stanton Wallace

Fire in the Ponderosa forest left little saleable timber.

Raw frame buildings were just going up in Flagstaff's New Town early in the summer of 1885 when fires began to burn in the dry forest south of town. T.A. Riordan employed in the local lumber company the only organized group large enough to fight them. He sent his crew out and reported the battle to his older brother, Matt.

> ... June 23: Heavy fire in woods south past two days. Began in cutting below pump house. Working up towards our new cutting on [Sections] 5 and 9. Will fight it tonight with six men and hope to get it out without serious damage. High wind from west.

> ... 7 a.m., June 24th: Fought it all night and now have it under control. It extends over four miles of front. Will put our team crew on it today. Nearest point about four miles from mill. Feel sure I can prevent it coming any nearer.

> ... Evening, June 24th: Held the fire under control until 3 p.m. with six men; but at that time the wind caused it to jump, and prospect now is we'll have an all night tussle with entire crew.

> ... June 25: Fought fire all last night and all day today with entire crew in two shifts. Will have to do so tonight and tomorrow. If wind would let up for one day we would be all right, but every time wind freshens it takes new start. Have kept it from advancing northward of Sec. 3 and 5.

> ... June 26: Having got big fire under control, mill was started this morning but had to shut down again at 10:30 to fight new fire about a mile west. Whole crew on both fires this afternoon. I'd like to be able to lay my hands on the man or men who start these fires. Everything dry as tinder.

> ... June 29: We had all fires under control Sat'y night but yesterday had to tackle three new ones. One up near Prentice [north of Woody Mountain], one on pump house road [later I.17], and a third (small) near mill. I do not know that any one has set these fires but I fear so, and have determined to find out if it is so.

Fire in the ten-thousand-year-old forest threatened property and cost money. In August the *Sun* printed a report of new ones.

> During the past week fires have been raging in the vicinity of Dry Lake about three miles west of Flagstaff, and although there was little destruction of timber, the underbrush and fallen trees made an intensely hot fire, and at times there was great danger to the railroad and the...lumber company. During the week the fire broke out in three different places, and in each instance burned about a mile square.
>
> Superintendent Riordan of the mill and a large force of men fought the fire night and day, and only by earnest efforts and hard labor, was the mill company saved from great injury.

Two years later the newspaper reported another big burn, west of town near Woody Mountain, which lasted several days.

> There is a good growth of timber in that direction which will in all probability be destroyed. The origin of the fire is unknown, but is supposed to be the result of

carelessness on the part of someone. Persons traveling through this section of the country at this dry time of year cannot be too careful while camping out, and should take every precaution to see that their camp fires are entirely extinguished before leaving them.

In Wisconsin in 1871 the Peshtigo Fire had burned 1,280,000 acres of forest and killed fifteen hundred people. Other huge fires in timberland in the Lake states had caused government focus on the danger of uncontrolled blazes long before Flagstaff was founded. When Fred Breen got off the train in 1898 to assume responsibility of the new San Francisco Mountain Forest Reserve, his instruction from the head of the General Land Office far away in Washington was specific about priority:

> It is of the first importance to protect the forests from fire...Should prompt action be required on your part at any time to extinguish or prevent the spread of forest fire, and your force of rangers is not available, or it is inadequate, you are authorized in such an emergency to employ assistance, to beat out the fire or get it under control.

There was no special fund available for fighting fires. Breen said: "I was instructed to put forest fires out and keep them under control. That relieved the government of all further responsibility in the matter." The instructions he received about money were hardly helpful:

> You must exercise great caution in employing...assistance, being careful in incurring expenses, which must be kept at the lowest possible figure. Whenever practicable consult by mail or telegraph with the superintendent before incurring such expenditure.

The floor of the pine forest that surrounded the Peaks burned even during rainy seasons; in dry ones fire could race through tree tops, and Breen did not often have time to write to Albuquerque for permission to hire fire crews. He arrived in Flagstaff during one of the country's periodic dry spells.

> During the famous drought from 1898 to 1905 when Mormon Lake was dry and dusty and before Lake Mary was invented by the Arizona Lumber and Timber company dam at this end of Clark's Valley, it wasn't necessary to hunt for forest fires. The country was as dry as a chip with a steady all day forty-mile wind from the southwest, day in and day out...Samples of smoke could be seen in all directions. Our only trouble was to differentiate between forest fire smoke and clouds of dust whipping up into the sky.
>
> They were wonderful years for fires from 1898 to 1905. At one time...I had the best string of forest fires that has existed since the time volcanoes were working in this section. As I remember this hectic season, one fire was burning blithely south of Grand Canyon in the cedars...[In addition there were] a fire north of Bellemont which ran over 50,000 acres; a few neat little fires south of Flagstaff of just a few hundred acres in old slashed-over ground; [a fire that started] over on the Indian reservation with a forty-mile wind behind it struck

our thin streak of forest reserve with an eighteen mile front...A splendid fire [was] working up the Blue River. There may have been a few little hundred acre fires here and there in between those grossing big acreage, but the "office" wasn't interested in small details at that time.

Manpower was spread thin. Just before the creation of the Forest Service, coverage for the unpopulated country on the reserve was only one ranger for the protection of as much as one hundred thousand acres. In addition to supervising loggers, stockmen, and travelers, the ranger was in charge of all fires occurring within his area, and he was expected to stay at the site for as long as it took.

Sparks from logging locomotives were a constant cause of blazes along the tracks. In 1901 Breen issued written warnings to AL&T and accompanied them with a request for help. T.A. answered:

> You may be sure that we will do our share to try and prevent fires spreading in the timber, and that we shall gladly render any service in our power to prevent fires starting and to help extinguish any that may get started from any cause, whether on our lands or not.

He sent a memo off to Ed McGonigle at the mill.

> From this time on...you should put a man to work, at the noon hour, who would have nothing else to do but watch all around the plant for fires.

And he warned contractors in the logging camps.

> There has been a good deal of talk around town about the Government officials issuing a warrant for your arrest for having permitted forest fires in the timber, in and about your camp...Now, of course, I have taken the position that you would not permit any fires to be started there, and that you would put them out if you saw any, and guess we have headed off the warrant being issued.

The problem was worst, of course, before and after the summer rainy season. In April of 1904, as logging was beginning on Woody Mountain, T.A. sent a blizzard of memos to trainmen and logging bosses ordering them to take care along the tracks. To a supervisor in town he wrote:

> During the dry period from now until next winter, we want you to send a trustworthy active man (a Mexican will do) to clean up the right of way on the ground between the Y and Kinney's camp, especially to rake up the needles and make a dead line so the fire cannot spread, and to watch for fires after any locomotive comes out from Kinney's camp. Pick a man who will know how to go after a fire quick when it starts and to prevent it from spreading. He can go down to this work in the mornings always on the first train out to Kinney's.

He advised men at Camp One to take their lunch "and not risk going back to camp at noon" on dry, windy days to minimize the possibility of locomotive sparks in the heat of mid-day.

Fire crews still needed loggers pulled off the job to help the rangers. Breen's scanty personnel seemed to T.A. to offer a convenient solution to another chronic problem: how to respond to the flood of appeals and inquiries he received about work for young men who wanted to come West, "some for their health, others for the finishing touches of their education."

It is a puzzle just how to take care of them...There is very little work in a pioneer country like this of a light nature.

It occurs to me that one of the very best and most healthful positions a young man could take up would be to get on the force as a range rider on the forest reserve. Their duties consist of riding around on horseback and having a general lookout over certain parts of the reservation that is assigned to them, to see that fires do not get started, and that the rules are not infringed on in any way by travelers. As I understand it, the duties are very light and the work ought to be the most healthful in the west.

From town the job looked easier than it was; it came down to hard work, low pay, and infrequent baths for "rope, ride, and shoot" men. F.C.W. Pooler, later District Forester at Albuquerque, went to work for Breen in 1904 at a salary of sixty dollars per month.

My equipment on reporting for duty consisted of a weatherbeaten scale stick, a marking hatchet, a broken-down garden rake, and a two-inch badge; my instructions a small red-covered manual and verbal orders to make myself at home...at whatever point I chose to select for headquarters...There were no headquarters improvements—each ranger made his own arrangements largely to suit himself.

Rangers got only a little more support in 1905 when America's forests were transferred from the General Land Office in Interior over to the 153 professionally trained foresters in what they called "Pinchot's Sweat Shop" in the Department of Agriculture. As part of Roosevelt's conservation revolution, the Bureau of Forestry became the United States Forest Service, with responsibility for territory larger than many European countries, and national reserves became national forests. "Forest engineering," the *Sun* said, "is the new profession." From the Washington office down an elaborate chain of authority to men in the field, it was marked by a feeling of being in at the beginning.

Paul Roberts, supervisor of the Sitgreaves Forest in the 1920s, summarized those first years:

It was a period of tremendous crusading spirit. I don't know whether the Forest Service could ever get that same type of thing going again or not, because a lot of those fellows that had the crusading spirit didn't know anything about forestry. They were ex-cowboys and lumberjacks and all that sort of thing, but they believed in it. Most of 'em went into it because of the spirit of adventure and because it was something worthwhile. It took a hardy breed to do the job and they did it.

Fred Breen (far left) had a crew of rangers in 1898. For fifty dollars a month
they dealt with a generally hostile population.
AHS–Pioneer Museum

Jim Sizer was one of Breen's rangers before he moved to the Apache National Forest.
AHS–Pioneer Museum

With the Forest Service, the federal government became the largest single employer in northern Arizona, and Flagstaff had a new element in its population. In no time, Service people were as numerous as ranchers. The *Sun* began a column headed "Forest News" to report activity of the organization and keep track of personnel, reporting in its "Local and Personal" column doings of men identified as "ranger" or "Forest Supervisor" or "of the Forest Service." It teased the rangers as gleefully as it did everyone else in town.

> Bobby Rhinehart of the Forest Service left Tuesday for Long Beach, California, where he hopes by a rest and change of scene and diet to trade off a stubborn digestion for one a little more to his liking.

Almost everybody in the field was called "ranger." Elliott Barker, later Game Warden of New Mexico and a former ranger himself, said they were ...

> a combination ranch and cowboy type of men, mostly with limited education. They were rugged enough to meet any situation that we had to meet. It was that type of men, believe me, that had to lay the foundation in those rugged conditions in the early days.

The Service looked for western men with outdoor experience, men who could take care of themselves and their horses, stand hardship, live under any conditions, prepare their own food, talk with the locals and fight when they had to. It wanted men "with bark on," as Teddy Roosevelt liked to describe them.

He ordered that Forest Supervisors be allowed to select their own rangers. They promptly ruled that "invalids seeking light out-of-door employment need not apply." The *Forest Use Book*, a manual of instructions produced under Gifford Pinchot, was definite:

> A ranger of any grade must be thoroughly sound and able-bodied, capable of enduring hardships and of performing severe labor under trying conditions. He must be able to take care of himself and his horses in regions remote from settlement and supplies.

Edward Ancona, a forester out of the East, described the demands of service in the West for Edwin Tucker, who compiled *Men Who Matched the Mountains* from his interviews with old-timers.

> I remember getting on a horse that first day in Flagstaff. I had rented a horse, and the Ranger had his horse, of course, and he said, "We're going out to a point east of here—we have some sheep to look over." I came out of the livery stable, and I didn't know how to steer the darned beast. So I sat on top with a pair of reins and used two of them. Well, he didn't know where he wanted to go and neither was I quite sure where I wanted to go. We ended up crossing the street. The horse went up on the sidewalk and mounted part-way up the stairs of the Opera House before I got him turned around and back into the street. In the meantime, the Ranger had jogged off down the street in a typical jog-trot. I think he was pretty disgusted...That was my first horseback ride. I learned though after that, because all of my work was on horses. You just had to adapt yourself to it, or you were sunk.

According to Elliott Barker, if a man couldn't learn to handle a horse it would be "the same as hiring men today who...couldn't learn to drive an automobile."

The Service wanted men between twenty-one and forty years old who could pass a written examination and a field test. When in 1906 the first tests were held all through the West, the *Sun* advertised that Forest Ranger examinations would be given in the sun parlor of the Weatherford Hotel.

Henry Benham, who started work in 1907, passed the examination handily.

> Well, we had a little written test to find out what we knew about surveying, if anything, and mining. It wasn't too big a test. What they wanted to know mostly was whether a man was able to ride the range and see that the cowmen and the sheepmen stayed on their own allotments.
>
> They gave you a paper about the duties of a Forest Ranger, and it was a pretty good description. You had to ride and be able to take care of yourself in the open in all kinds of weather. After they gave me the written test, I had to saddle a horse and ride out a certain distance in a walk, then trot over to another station, then lope back to the starting point. After punching cows for six years, I didn't have any trouble qualifying.
>
> Then they tested to see what you knew about handling a gun, so you didn't go out and shoot somebody with it the first thing. And you had to put a pack on a horse, a bunch of cooking utensils, bedding, bedrolls, and a tarp to cover it with—and a rope to tie it on with.
>
> I'd learned all that before I went into the Forest Service. I didn't have much trouble. Some of the boys had an awful time, winding their ropes under the horse and around his belly.

The ranger's uniform consisted of denim jacket and work pants. Tools were not furnished. According to the *Manual*, rangers were required to provide themselves with "pocket compass, camp outfit, axe, shovel, and pick." Tough and capable, the men spent most of their days riding patrol and being alert to anything that might affect the forest, including timber cutting and cattle grazing. They burned firebreaks, piled brush, built trails and cabins, maintained fences, posted fire warnings—just about anything that needed doing.

It was not considered appropriate work for "the gentler sex," and there were no women rangers. The first female Forest Service employees in the Southwest were clerk stenographers, but that innovation was put into place reluctantly only after paperwork became too heavy for the men.[1]

T.A.'s logging company also held out against hiring women for office work. From the early years of the century, applications regularly arrived from other states and were always answered firmly with "Dear Madam,"

---

1 As late as 1921 a woman on the Santa Fe Forest passed the field exam, but the Regional Office would not approve her appointment because she was "an unattached female."

We never employ women since the conditions here are not exactly suitable for
their employment...Not but that we believe that there are competent lady
stenographers and typewriters; but the position in question has other work
connected with it than the mere taking and writing of letters...This does not mean
that there is any shooting or bloodthirsty methods taking place regularly, but it is
not unusual for us to want the stenographer to ride a rather lively animal out to
one of the logging camps or down town for the mail, or to take his turn helping
out the shipping clerk, or any thing else of the kind that requires main strength
[and] roustabout work...It requires a good deal of rough and tumble speaking and
acting in a lumber office and we find that women are hardly suitable for this
particular kind of work, nor does it make it altogether comfortable for other office
employees to have to submit themselves to the restraints necessary by the reason
of the presence of a woman in the office. We are naturally so bashful that their
presence would interfere with our free swing and besides this the grub would be
intolerable from the standpoint of female digestion.

It wasn't that T.A. fought off all change. He was a dues-paying member of the
American Forestry Association; AL&T was a contributing member of the National
Conservation Association. Riordan was on record as saying: "I feel that every
American citizen is under obligations to those who are behind this great move-
ment...an integral part of the national life and policy."

In Washington, the Congressional Agriculture Committee recommended
cuts in appropriations for fire protection of forests and building of trails and telephone lines, and he promptly fired off letters and telegrams of protest to Senator
Carl Hayden and other representatives from Arizona and New Mexico. When a
Chair of Applied Forestry was established at Yale University, T.A. not only served
on the committee to raise the endowment, he wrote to Fred Breen to ask for a
contribution.

But sometimes agency regulation was too much for his good humor, as
when he was requested by the forest supervisor, who was under local pressure, to
leave trees along a wagon road and preserve its appearance.

These amateur sentimentalists really make one tired. Of course after this timber
is left along the present road it will be changed...leaving good ripe timber to
spoil...If it is not the suffragettes, the Corporation Commission or some other
damn thing that bobs up to help increase your expense and taxes it would be
hopeless, but the good snow we are having this morning and the new
administration at Washington offsets in some measure the pessimistic effect that
comes over one with all the annoyances that are proposed nowadays.

It was in Riordan's interest to encourage the development of a fire organization on the Coconino, and he continued, as he had for years, to offer to Breen all
his resources in cooperation.

We generally work 75 to 125 men in our woods operation and on our logging
road. Of course in any emergency you could depend on us doing what was

possible to help out in fighting fire or anything else where you were interested. Also we would always have plenty of food in our camp which could be used for such purposes...We will make a price of 25 cents per meal for men from your department and 20 cents for horses, and will send instructions to Camp #1 office to establish these prices.

The Forest Service bought such things as axe handles, coal oil, grab hooks, wedges, and lap rings from the AL&T commissary. Rangers in the field stopped by logging camps to pick up potatoes and butter and syrup and condensed milk. Sometimes the Forest Service hired an AL&T team and wagon for heavy hauling. There was ready cooperation between the two groups.

In the first decade of the twentieth century, before lookout points were established on high elevations, loggers found and fought fires (and were paid by government rates) and later informed the forest supervisor in town.

> Some of the boys from Camp One, just in this afternoon, report that a fire started last evening near the Southwest corner of Section 25...The whole crew went out and worked until about ten o'clock last night. They got it under control and left a couple of men in charge during the night and it seemed to be all right this morning.

Woody Mountain had been logged the year before the Forest Service was organized and, with no trees to block the view, it made a handy place from which Breen's men could look the country over. There was no road to the top, no structure of any kind, and no way to communicate. A ranger on patrol in the district just rode his horse up and looked around, and if he saw a fire anyplace, he went and tried to put it out. He hoped other people had seen smoke and were headed for it too, because he had no way to call for help.

If he was lucky, ranchers, farmers, and loggers showed up: people working in the forest on permit were obligated to fight fire whenever their area was threatened. Ed Oldham, ranger on the Flagstaff District, organized settlers into fire crews and ordered them to head for a fire when they saw smoke, without waiting to be notified. Ed Miller, Coconino Supervisor from 1919 to 1935, said in later years:

> I can still see George Moore, with a plow in his wagon [for cutting a fire line], driving his team on a long trot toward a forest fire. You didn't have to send for him; he watched for smokes and was on the way as soon as he saw one.

The first program for organized fire protection for the Southwest, which was developed in 1908, included recommendations for an innovation: lookout stations on peaks and connecting telephone lines to ranger stations. Coconino Supervisor John Guthrie received a letter from the regional office in Albuquerque instructing him to choose lookout peaks and put men on them. It added: "The Section of Engineering will, upon request, furnish designs for lookout stations."

Guthrie was instructed to provide for the construction of telephone lines from such watch posts to ranger's or supervisor's headquarters in order to give prompt notice of fires. While he was at it, he was to see to the construction of a system of trails. As usual, budget was tight and work moved slowly. It was a tough fire year all over the west, but the Forest Service managed to get through it and congratulated itself that "destruction of forest property by fire may be almost entirely prevented by the adoption of a suitable system of patrol."

There was no more talk for a while of lookout sites on the Coconino. However, work continued on the telephone line. In 1909 T.A. proposed to the Forest Supervisor that the Service cooperate with his logging company in the construction of a telephone line into the country west of Woody Mountain and to the new ranger station at Patterson Spring on the west shore of Rogers Lake.

Officially described as the summer headquarters of the Rogers Lake District, Patterson Spring was used by one and at times two of "the special protective force." The first year only a man named J.J. Fisher was in residence; in May of 1910 he was joined by M.O. Dumas. In addition to their other duties, they rode while on patrol up to the top of Woody Mountain to survey the forest, looking for smoke, the first men deputized to do so.

The spring had been developed; rangers had built fences, a house, and a barn, but without a telephone, they were isolated. T.A. was ready with an offer.

> If you will build the line from here to Patterson Springs, and will build around the South end of Rogers Lake instead of the North end, we will continue the line from the Lake to Camp One and maintain that portion of it...Of course Camp One would change about frequently and we would have to take care of moving the line at the woods end from time to time...I am not clear whether or not our line should be connected with Central at Flagstaff...We would expect to talk with our train crews along the line at times and there might be a chance for possible mistakes if the line was open to the public.

Early in 1910 the Coconino Supervisor estimated that the forest had seventy-one miles of telephone lines and needed at least ninety more, but he had no money for construction. In that year—sixty years after an artist, a doctor, and a lieutenant with the Sitgreaves party had climbed up to see the view—he established Woody Mountain as the first lookout position on the north end of the forest, paired with Baker Butte, which covered the south end from its position on the Mogollon Rim. He authorized no structure of any kind to create a facility; it was simply a designated site, one of only two on the Coconino.

Then in the northern Rockies, the summer of 1910 turned into an inferno that wonderfully speeded up the pace of government construction of lookout facilities. Fires broke out in June across Idaho, increased in frequency in July, and exploded into conflagrations in August. The major damage resulted from only fifteen percent of the fires, all of them in remote, rugged locations and all caused by lightning. In the absence of observation posts, communication systems, and trails, the backcountry blazes often had days to become established before anything could be done about them.

Hundreds of fires burned at a time, making runs of several miles in a day, throwing firebrands ten miles in advance of the front and sucking into themselves winds that knocked down trees and almost lifted men out of their saddles. In the middle of August things got worse: the fires "blew up" with whirlwind firestorms and caught thousands of men in the field. Crews evacuated or hid in caves and tunnels and fought the blazes as they could. Eighty-five men died and one hundred others were hospitalized.

When rain in September finally doused the flames, seven to eight billion feet of marketable timber had been destroyed, and three million acres had burned in Idaho and Montana, two million in five other states. The Forest Service submitted to Congress a statement for suppression expenses of 1.1 million 1910 dollars.

Critics complained that ground patrols were obviously not adequate to detect fire in the western mountains and react quickly enough to provide protection. Pinchot was out and Henry Graves in as chief forester in Washington. He declared:

> The necessity of preventing losses from forest fires requires no discussion. It is the fundamental obligation of the Forest Service and takes precedence over all other duties and activities.

Events on Woody Mountain always were connected to concerns somewhere else. Less than a year after the Big Blowup, the telephone line was complete to the ranger station at Rogers Lake, and there was a phone on the old mountain.

Common practice at the time was for a horseman to establish a "tree line" for telephones by paying out small insulated wire from a spool attached to the back of his saddle and using "swinging insulators" to string it from tree to tree. Crews connected the Patterson Spring line at the DK ranch windmill, where they installed a telephone, strung wire on trees down to the ranch in Mill Park, put in another connection at what became Phone Booth Tank, and ran the line on down to Camp One—a total of four miles.

After that there was no need to send a secretary out to camp, and T.A. could write to Willard Drake, Forest Supervisor: "Your letter of the 3rd enclosing check for $22.95 in payment of board and commissary accounts named in your letter, was received. We have telephoned to Camp One and Mr. Murphy says your statement is correct."

The Forest Service added to the telephone system a single line to the top of Woody Mountain, branching off just below the spring to run up the north slope through the trees. Two years after the Southwest was ordered to provide watch points, one year after the mountain's official lookout designation, there was a way to send voices from it for the first time in its several-million-year history. There was no tower, cabin, lean-to, or shelter of any kind—just an iron, hand-crank, wall-type telephone hung on a pole on top of the bare mountain. It was powered by batteries, which were removed at the end of each fire season and stored in the ranger station for the winter.

George Foster and Fred W. Croxen were assigned to the Patterson Spring station in May of 1911 and given responsibility for the country roundabout. Croxen claimed the distinction of being the first official lookout, specifically assigned to the job, on both the Coconino and on Woody Mountain.[2]

Croxen was a farm boy from Iowa who had come west for the excitement of it. His son, later Flagstaff City Magistrate Fred Croxen II, said in memory that he had "some of the romantic that's in everyone. The West was still opening up. He heard the call of adventure and followed it." In the process he became the very model of a westerner, the kind of man on whom legends were founded. He worked as a cowboy on a ranch in Wyoming, drove sway mules in mining camps in Nevada, pitched alfalfa in California, worked on a newspaper in Tonopah.

> It had always been my desire to live and work in what some people call "the big open spaces."…All these forest rangers were fulfilling their duties on saddle animals and pack horse outfits. After meeting and talking with the men in regards to their duties, my desire to become a forest ranger was first in my thoughts.

In 1909 he moved to Flagstaff, and after a year as a city street superintendent, then as a limber and oiler with Greenlaw Lumber, and a blacksmith swinging a twelve pound hammer ten hours a day for AL&T, he joined the new Forest Service.

> I had taken the Forest Ranger examination the fall before—in the fall of 1910— and received notice in April that I had passed the examination. Of course I was a tickled kid. Willard M. Drake was Forest Supervisor. I went down to his house and talked to him one Sunday morning. He put me on the Coconino.

He was twenty-three. John Woody was serving his last summer as Deputy Sheriff. Bear Howard, who had gone to live with his daughter beyond Mingus Mountain on the edge of Lonesome Valley, died that year at the age of ninety-three. But Fred Croxen was young.

> I moved out to Woody Mountain as lookout. I'm sure I was the first forest officer to be assigned as a permanent lookout during a fire season in [the Southwest Region]. I was issued a Forest Service badge, compass, telescope, shovel, rake and ax. When I was drawing my tools, I drew a 5-pound double-bitted axe. [Three and a half pounds was standard.] Everybody laughed at me, but it seemed awful light to me after swinging a 12-pound hammer.

2 His son Charles said: "Dad mentioned to me a couple of times in the past that he was the first fire lookout in the state of Arizona. This was on Woody Mountain in 1911 or 1912. I've also heard it told that George Crosby of Greer has also claimed to have been the first lookout in the state, probably on the Apache National Forest. Maybe we should give them both the credit."

Fred W. Croxen was the first official lookout on Woody Mountain.
Courtesy of his son Fred Crozen II

Three mules, C.R. "Pat" Duke, Carl Riblett, Ben G. Maxwell, Will J. Brown,
Jesse Bushnell, and Fred Croxen (far right) worked on a telephone construction crew
on the Coconino in 1915.
Courtesy of Charles Croxen

Croxen provided his own horse and bedroll for the job on Woody Mountain, which was referred to as a "riding lookout." Every day he rode to the top of the mountain, scrambled up a tree fitted out with pegs, and scanned the area with a monocular glass.

> Jerry Fisher, one of the old rangers [the first man assigned to the Patterson Spring ranger station in 1909], had two large staffs put up side-by-side, about the size of telephone poles. We painted a wagon sheet black and would run it up there. If [other people] would see the sheet, they would know there was a fire.

Croxen lived in the log cabin in the aspen down at Woody Spring and rode daily up a trail to the top.

> I had my saddle horse down there and I was supposed to go to any fire within a reasonable distance. Fortunately I didn't have to go to but two fires.

One of those fires was a one hundred and eighty acre burn that he fought with only one other man until loggers arrived in a buckboard.

After summer rains began, Croxen was detailed to the area north of the Peaks to post sheep allotment boundaries. The next year he went on to Sedona to do the assortment of jobs that a ranger did.

> Each spring, it was the duty of the district ranger and his assistant to go over and repair [telephone] tree lines. Considerable damage was usually done by high winds and winter snows, causing broken tree limbs to fall across the lines. The rangers indeed acquired creditable skill as linesmen, and in repairing the wall telephones at each ranger station and guard camp, lookouts and field phones, throughout the forest.

As lookout on Woody Mountain, Croxen had a map and could make a rough estimate about the location of smoke, but he did not have an Osborne Fire-finder. W.B. Osborne, a forester from Yale, had invented the fire-finder in the winter of 1910 in the basement shop of his home in Portland, Oregon. It was a simple device, on the principle of a surveyor's transit and plane table, with a sighting rod that turned through a 360-degree protractor marked with compass bearings and mounted above a map of the forest. It enabled a lookout to establish on a line the location of sighted smoke.

When a fire was visible from two or more sites equipped with the device, the location could be stated precisely for ground crews at the point where lookout lines crossed. Machine manufacture of the instrument was planned in 1913; Woody Mountain probably had one by 1915.

There was no road to the top of Woody Mountain when Fred Croxen was lookout. Travel all over the northern part of the state was still forbiddingly primitive. Horses could go almost anywhere, but roads were necessary for men who owned cars, and T.A. couldn't use his Overland much: "If we had any sort of decent roads the year round I think I would like to have a Packard car but we do not care enough about motors or motoring under our conditions to take it very seriously."

In 1913 he wrote to Arizona Secretary of State Sydney Osborne to ask about the unheard-of possibility of there being government regulation.

> I have just been informed that it is necessary for one to have a state license for an automobile and also a chauffeur. I am unable to find out just how to go about this so write you to say that I want to have whatever the law requires. I have a four cylinder Overland car and a chauffeur by name Caspar Seitz. If you will send me whatever I should have for the machine and for the man, together with bill for the same I will remit.

Change was everywhere. After Arizona became a state in 1912, the legislature sent male voters a referendum to decide whether women should be allowed to vote. The men, Flagstaff's rangers among them, approved it by a two-to-one margin.

Another state action took away from Flagstaff's incredulous men for the first time in the town's history the right to drink beer in the saloons on Front Street after January 1, 1915. The *Sun* reported the last night of 1914:

> The closing scenes of the old year were numerous and varied. There was mingled joy, sorrow and exhilaration in quantities all over the downtown district until promptly 12 o'clock, when all saloons refused to sell another drop...There was no fuss or grandstand play made such as hanging out "for rent" signs or boarding up fronts. It was closing time as usual at that hour, except that this closing hour was more definite and enduring.

Along Front Street, concrete sidewalks replaced the old board walks. A Music and Sociability Club met in the home of Carolyn and Fred Breen, who owned the *Sun* by then, and Flagstaff got its first gasoline-powered fire truck. But amenities hadn't changed the town's spirit. On flat ground south of the tracks and east of Milton, where the Northern Arizona University stadium would later be built, there were noisy races between locals driving horses and buggies.

Because most transportation was still horse-drawn, little building had been done outside the fairly even land near the railroad tracks. Up two steep inclines north of town on rocky Knob Hill, the Forest Service owned 320 acres on which it maintained a storehouse and a pasture for the horses of local rangers. There was a cow in town every couple of blocks in those years, and every day the Switzer sisters drove their cow and those of their neighbors to graze on Knob Hill, which they described as "way up there."

The development of a lookout station on Woody Mountain was an indication of slowly growing sophistication of Forest Service approach to fire suppression. An addition to the telephone and firefinder was built in 1916—a four-strand barbed wire fence to enclose a ten-acre pasture "for holding a lookout man's horse while he is using the lookout." Cost of wire, staples, and five days of labor by Patterson

Springs ranger Henry Deutsch was $31.90. He circled the whole top of the mountain, about ten acres, on an irregular course with four strands of wire.

Deutsch had trouble about that fence even before he finished building it, according to an August memorandum to Forest Supervisor Guthrie.

> Riblett was in at noon—having returned from Woody Lookout—and told me
> that the posts at the Woody Lookout pasture were set only about one foot deep
> and they can be pushed over with one hand and not tamped good. About 50 posts
> have been set. Tried to get Deutsch over phone but could not raise him.

The fence-post memo was signed by the deputy forest supervisor, who had ridden up on an inspection. He reported that the mountain top pasture was "full of logs and brush" and recommended that the "Lookoutman" remove them. He also did not like the trail, which he termed "very steep," especially near the summit, and proposed laying out a series of switchbacks to ease the climb.

He added, "The timber on the crest has been cut and...an excellent view can be had." His major recommendation was for "a shelter cabin hexagon in shape with windows wherein the protractor and telephone are placed, thus affording shelter for the lookout man and his equipment." Early experience had shown that the usefulness of Osborne's fire-finder was hampered by weather—by rain or strong winds or the fierce hail that pounded the mountain at intervals in summer—but the supervisor wrote at the bottom of the report, "I do not consider a watch box is needed." Europe was at war in 1916, and the Forest Service was keeping a wary eye on budget.

That year there were 194 fires on the Coconino between March 18 and November 25. Logging engines started fifty-one of them. Rangers fumed that the trail of one cattle roundup could be followed by forest fires that started from cigarettes and matches thrown into dry grass. In spring of the next year *Arizona* magazine informed its readers that the rangers' fire-fighting work had been recognized.

> Notice was received at the Flagstaff Forest [Supervisor's Office] on January 22,
> 1917, that the Coconino National Forest has been awarded the forest fire prize
> for the season of 1916. The prize, established by the district forester's office in
> Albuquerque, N.M., is awarded annually to the National Forest in Arizona and
> New Mexico making the best record for the discovery and suppression of forest
> fires.

A year later the decision not to build a shelter on Woody Mountain was reversed. The forest examiner rode up for an inspection in the company of Walter Mickelson, who had replaced Deutsch at Patterson Spring, and reported his opinion.

> This lookout seems to have gained the idea that it was useless, but from our
> observation it seems to be one of the best lookouts on this end of the forest. A
> good view of the Barney Pasture country and country to the southeast can be
> gained from this lookout.
> The only thing that is needed for adequate services on this lookout is a small
> hexagonal shaped shelter with windows wherein the protractor and telephone are

placed, thus affording shelter for the lookout man and his equipment. This shelter I do not think should cost over $25 and is needed badly as it is almost impossible on windy days such as we have during the fire season for the lookout man to telephone. A shelter of this sort would make a very good addition to this lookout. This shelter should be placed on as soon as possible if any funds are available for such purposes.

Edward Miller, who was the new forest supervisor, approved the suggestion. He wrote large across the heading, "This looks OK—we have the money—go to it," and signed his initials. As Supervisor of the Coconino, Miller authorized construction of three different lookout structures on Woody Mountain.[3]

It was 1918. The nation was at war when Woody Mountain rang with the sounds of hammers, as a work crew built the little hexagon. News came into town in the spring that people on the east coast were ill: the Spanish influenza epidemic, which killed half a million Americans, was beginning to spread. When it broke out in Flagstaff and across the tracks in Milton, there was sickness in every family and death of someone every day. The local Public Health Service took over Emerson School, removed the desks, and turned the school into an infirmary. After it was full, rooms were used in the Ideal Hotel.

People stopped holding "socials." They didn't gather at the news stand on Front Street or come in from outlying ranches with their teams and wagons. Local women tried home remedies: mustard plaster, castor oil, Epsom salts. Mrs. Switzer scrubbed her house daily with Lysol. But there was no known cure for the disease, and treatment was guesswork. The death toll was high in the little town; at makeshift mortuaries, coffins were in short supply.

In the early years of the 1920s there were tentative steps toward what would become strong movements—an amendment to the national constitution gave women the right to vote in presidential elections and the first small government actions were taken, here and there, to preserve wilderness in the West. But the same old problems hung on: the *Sun* was full of items about fire problems.

> ... A tourist was arrested and taken to Williams on Tuesday, where he was fined $10 for not extinguishing his camp fire...He had been warned by a forester to put it out before moving on and had agreed to.

> ... The Forest Service officials are finding it necessary to put fire lookouts [back on], as underbrush is drying out in the mountains, and as it is feared some hunters will show carelessness with campfires and with the throwing away of lighted matches.

---

3 During his years in Flagstaff, his wife died, and his young children visited the woman who had been their kindergarten teacher to tell her that they needed a mother and ask her to marry their daddy. She did.

Momentum in Forest Service fire organizations had picked up speed since the Big Blowup in Idaho in 1910 and been given boosts in 1914, 1917, and again in 1920 with fires on 1.4 million acres. Early in 1920 there was another chief forester in Washington, William Greeley, who had been regional forester for the northern Rockies in 1910 and who said that the experience had burned into him the conviction that "fire prevention is the No. 1 job of American foresters." During the eight years of his tenure no aspect of fire prevention was neglected.

Therefore, within four years of its construction, the little hexagon on Woody Mountain was replaced by a second structure, a wooden tower with short legs and a ladder for access. And in January of 1922, fifteen years after the Use Book called for rangers "capable of enduring hardships," Miller asked permission of the Regional Office to spend two hundred dollars to add a twelve by fourteen foot frame cabin to the facility and called it a "protective improvement."

> At present a good tower and shelter exists at Woody Lookout and with the addition of a small cabin near the tower this lookout will give entire satisfaction for several years to come.

The expenditure was approved, and Arizona Lumber and Timber was directed to "deliver this material on your log train to the foot of Woody Mountain" on the first of May. The train, running nearly empty on the morning trip out of town, paused not far from the spring long enough for building supplies to be unloaded, and Forest Service men carried lumber to the top. Living in tents while they did the job, they built a tidy cabin that stood through weather for sixty years.

The year the first cabin and tower were built on Woody Mountain, John Weatherford was half finished building his toll road that would allow motorists to drive, he said, "all the way to the top" of the Peaks. He called it San Francisco Peaks Boulevard. Local opinion was that John "was gonna make a mint."

The town was no longer removed by the length of a train ride from the American scene: in November "complete election returns" were available by wire at Starkey's Pool Hall. The first airplane landed at Flagstaff that year, in the Babbitt pasture northeast of town and went up again several times, taking any Flagstaff citizen who was willing to pay for the ride. One of his passengers was Mrs. T.A. Riordan. In November Doolittle made the first flight across the continent; three years later Charles Lindbergh flew to Paris.

Transportation was as essential a theme in the Forest Service story as it was of the town: it was the job of rangers to cover a lot of ground. From its first years, while they were patrolling the Coconino on horses, the Service had made appropriations for the necessary roads and trails, and as early as 1903 a rutted wagon road climbed up to Flagstaff out of lower Oak Creek Canyon on Schnebly Hill. But war intervened, and after it was over, the only graded road on the forest was a strip fourteen feet wide and partly paved with cinders that eased travel between Flagstaff and Williams. Roads in the forests all over the Southwest were mostly "natural" ones that could be traveled only in dry weather.

Construction of the first tower and cabin on Woody Mountain in 1922
was done when the new pines were still small.
Coconino National Forest

After the war the Service resumed plans for building "truck trails," and the Flagstaff Chamber of Commerce asked it to extend its influence and financial cooperation to help build a direct route south to the head of Oak Creek Canyon. In 1922 the *Sun* reported:

> The Forest Service is figuring on doing some extensive road work between Mormon Lake and Double Cabin Park this spring and summer...Forest Supervisor Miller says there is a section of road in that district that needs attention badly, tourists being constantly marooned there. He has seen as high as 29 cars stuck there.

They went on to build a road to the top of Woody Mountain. That memorandum of 1916 proposing switchbacks on the trail testified to there being no road up the mountain at that time. Henry Giclas saw no sign of one to the top when he rode out to the spring with his father in 1920. But if a track was not roughed in to transport materials for the construction of the cabin in 1922, it was two years later in 1924. Evidence for the date remained in a letter from Ed Miller, dated July 8, 1924, to Ranger Oscar McClure:

> Dear Mr. McClure: We are setting up an allotment of $125 for the construction of the Woody cistern. In case this amount will not cover the project we shall be able to set up a few dollars additional. Mr. Lochman will handle the construction work, but we shall depend upon you to see that the materials are laid down on the ground.

Lumber to build a shelter, a tower, and a cabin could have been packed up on mules, but not water to mix cement for a cistern. There was a truck road spiraling up the sides of Woody Mountain no later than 1924. It was primitive—there was no available construction equipment heavier than a plow. [see page 284]

The road cut through the network of grass rhizomes and the decaying roots of trees that had been gone for eighteen years. On the east side, it blasted into an extrusion of lava and exposed ten vertical feet of twisted rock that had disappeared from sunlight more than a million years earlier. It circled the mountain in a raw gash from top to bottom.

Lichen fastened onto new footholds provided by the road. Wind took dust stirred by the wheels of Forest Service trucks and blew it away. Earth no longer held in place by roots was washed down by rain and by the fast-melting snow of April, which softened the surface of the new road and etched it with rivulet patterns. The road to the tower made summer easier for lookouts stationed on top of Woody Mountain. It also accelerated by several hundred thousand years the busy, impersonal work of erosion, which labored endlessly to erase mountains and make all the earth flat.

When there was a road, a Forest Service crew under the supervision of a man named Lochman built an octagonal storage cistern five feet deep and four feet in diameter. Rainwater drained down to it from the cabin roof through a clay pipe and was dipped out by a bucket.

With shelter and a cistern, the Woody Mountain station passed from being a "riding lookout" to a residential installation manned consistently through the fire season. For the first time in all its history the old mountain had a human presence at the top for months at a time, someone who worked and ate and slept there. And produced garbage—empty bean cans and syrup cans shaped like log cabins—and threw it down the slope. A lookout worked straight through the fire season in those years with no days off; he had no time to carry trash away.[4]

4 The Forest Service had begun to hire women lookouts in other places by 1920, but there was no evidence that they were employed either on the Coconino or on Woody Mountain, and plenty of evidence in Western attitudes that they were not. Mary Sweitzer was emphatic: "It never would have been a woman."

Down in the town that supplied the new Woody Mountain lookout station, there were four black families. Charlie Johnson, a plasterer and construction worker, was there with his wife Hattie and their two boys. The Davises had two children in school, Orluff and his sister. Walter Garrison, a pipe fitter and plumber, worked under Eli Giclas at AL&T. He and his family lived next door to Mr. Horne, janitor at the Normal School, his wife who was cook/housekeeper for I.B. Koch, and their son, who taught cornet lessons. (Henry Giclas and his friends thought it a wonderful joke that Horne played the horn.)

Chinese wives had arrived in Flagstaff by then, and there were two Chinese families with children in the schools. Japanese were farming out on the road to Fort Valley. There were no Indian children in town; there were no Indian families in town. An occasional Hopi or Navajo man was employed by a local business, but most came in now and then for supplies and went back out again.

Flagstaff was a lively little town all through the Roaring Twenties, prosperous and booming like the rest of the country and ready for progress. Public dances were held on Saturday nights in a pavilion downtown, and people danced the Charleston and sang Irving Berlin songs, "Indian Love Call," "What'll I Do?"

Horsemen in town were gone by the middle of the decade. Two blocks along Railroad Avenue were paved; the other streets still turned to mud after rains. Wooden sidewalks were gradually replaced by concrete, and children used them for roller skating, which had been impossible on the old boardwalks. Recognizing reality, Milton joined Flagstaff legally, and a higher civic tone was achieved when Railroad Avenue/Front Street was renamed Santa Fe.

The town was in a building mood in those years. Houses constructed by Flagstaff's pioneers were pulled down and new ones took their places. In 1926 the *Sun* announced the organization of the Museum of Northern Arizona, which took up residence in the Women's Club Building while Harold Colton negotiated an option to build on the old McMillan ranch northwest of town. A new train depot opened on a Tuesday afternoon in January of that year, and all Flagstaff was invited. The town was, in Breen's words, "darn proud."

The "progress" of the '20s touched Woody Mountain: it was listed in 1927 by the U.S. Coast and Geodetic Survey in the North American Datum, to which all coordinates for horizontal points were referenced. The NAD included all survey data available at the time.

The twenties were the years of national Prohibition, which Flagstaff adjusted to with the determination shown by the rest of the country. Druggists provided Virginia Dare wine only once a month to a customer, as a tonic, and kept lists of all alcohol sold. However, it was no secret that stronger liquor could be bought in town. There were distilleries in Sycamore Canyon; kegs were sent up the trail on the backs of sheep. Kendrick Park was full of stills and bootleggers. The south side of Flagstaff had its Bootleg Row, where anybody with money could buy "home hooch" and wild berry wine from the mountain.

Building roads on the Coconino was mule-and-plow work in the 1920s.
AHS–Pioneer Museum

As part of the fun during those years, the Elks took on the job of staging the town's Fourth of July celebration. In 1929 Gladwell Richardson and local businessmen suggested the startling idea of inviting Indians to come into town on the Fourth for a community party, with free food and a chance for games and races and dances. It was the beginning of Flagstaff's All-Indian Pow Wow, which was the town's big show for forty years.

The pace of change picked up until it felt like frenzy to older folks. In 1929 T.A. Riordan wrote to Arizona's Senator Henry Ashurst: "Dozens of planes were passing over our very house here for several days, and it begins to make us feel that there is no escape from the advance that transportation methods are making."

In 1929 Carolyn Breen died of cancer, "only a shadow of her former self." Sandy Donahue was admitted to the Arizona Pioneers Home in Prescott. And the stock market collapsed. Then it was Depression and soup lines in Flagstaff.

The Forest Service, the only source of steady income for a few local men once the mill closed, continued to function during the hard times. It used the old post office building for headquarters—the ranger station on Knob Hill was too far out of town to be a central location.

Half of Flagstaff owned stock in the new Community Hotel, which was named
Monte Vista after a spirited contest. Stockholders lined the sidewalk
to watch construction in 1926.
AHS–Pioneer Museum

Flagstaff's rangers drank as much bootleg whiskey as any other respectable
men in town, but the resistance they had faced through early years had faded and
they maintained an acceptable reputation. Billie Yost, who went to work for the
Sun in the middle of the decade, confirmed their position in the community.

> When you work in a newspaper office you hear all the bad things. I never heard
> anything derogatory about the Forest Service, never any scandal. Personnel were
> looked up to with high regard. They carried out their orders to the letter. All
> through the years they were substantial, honest, credible people of integrity.
> They had steady jobs during the Depression. They were accepted, and besides,
> they had to be there.

With the Depression, the boom had gone out of beleaguered western business. Nevertheless Ed Miller, working from his downtown office in 1931, issued an
administrative withdrawal that closed Woody Mountain to all forms of commercial use, saying, "While there is very little danger of mining claims on this
Forest, it seems to me that we would be safer if we would withdraw and post at
least 40 acres."

By that action of Miller's the whole top of the mountain, occupied as it was by "capital improvements," was removed under law from settlement, sale, mining, location, entry, and all forms of appropriation, and reserved "for a particular public purpose or program" which could not be "protected by any other means." That did not create a recreation site on the narrow summit. The Service reservation was for the sole purpose of protecting a working station.

In 1932 Fred Breen died, and the spirit of high humor that had been part of Flagstaff from the beginning dimmed a little. Franklin Roosevelt was elected president of the country. When the Twenty-first Amendment was ratified in 1933, Flagstaff's illicit stills moved into the past. Saloons opened again the day it was legal, and a blackface box on the front page of the *Sun* heralded the event.

Beer Ban Lifts Today

A beer-laden motor truck is speeding from California today, rushing a cargo of 3.2 per cent beverage to Flagstaff as the government ban is lifted throughout the country. One local merchant expects to offer beer for sale here tomorrow, but the majority said their shipments are not due until early next week.

But there was still depression. On March 4, 1933, F.D. Roosevelt took office, and within a month the C.C.C., the Civilian Conservation Corps, went into effect "for the relief of unemployment through the performance of useful public work." The first federal recovery program, the Three Cs made as great an impact on the Forest Service as had the 1910 fire season in Idaho.

The president directed that a quarter of a million unemployed young men (average age eighteen to twenty-three) be at work in the forests by early summer, approximately the number of men enlisted nationally during the Spanish-American War. Those plans stunned Forest Service people, who were going to have to supervise the work of a sudden flood of city kids inexperienced with the out-of-doors and tools and, for that matter, books. Many could barely read. Edward Miller, still supervisor on the Coconino, was informed by telegram that six hundred C.C.C. enrollees would be assigned to his forest and was advised to be prepared to take care of them, which meant equipping tent camps or wooden barracks for housing and field kitchens for feeding. It was a staggering supply responsibility. The new people were not the old-fashioned rangers who could be directed to provide their own shovels and cook their own meals in the field.

In addition, Miller was going to have to find some "useful public work" for them to do. Three camps of some two hundred men each were thrown up on the forest—at Mormon Lake and Woods Spring and in the Flagstaff area on the Shultz Pass road. Miller said:

By the time the enrollees showed up, our boys had installed water mains, storage tanks, had made some clearings, and were ready for the CCC camps to be established...We started on some fencing work, some erosion control work like building little checkerdams in some of the arroyos...We also started in on some recreation improvements.

Cracks in the bottom of Lake Mary were filled; campgrounds in Oak Creek Canyon were developed with fireplaces, tables and water lines; stream bottoms in Long Valley were fenced and checkdams built. For the first time the forest had manpower in quantities adequate to tackle major tasks and money to go with it. Roads, trails, telephone lines, fuel breaks, guard stations, recreation sites—anything that looked to be needed was proposed for the C.C.C. men to work on. Their motto was "We Can Do It."

But the young C.C.C. men did not work as fire watch. In 1933 and 1934, when the relief agency was getting organized, the lookout on Woody Mountain was a local man, Stanton Wallace, grandson of the "Spud" Anderson who had arrived in Flagstaff in 1882. Stan Wallace had gone to work for the Forest Service at the age of seventeen over on the Mormon Lake Lookout to pay for his college education and his teacher's degree and moved to Woody Mountain after graduation.

He was twenty-four and twenty-five the two summers he worked on Woody Mountain, at a salary of $125 a month. One third of America's work force was unemployed by then and flat broke. For a young teacher just out of school that $125 a month was more than a lot of men had.

> The lookout jobs were very good summer jobs for me while I was in high school and college and at Woody it was during summer vacation the two years I taught school.[5] The salary was about comparable with day labor at that time, except a laborer may have had Sundays off. It was a 24 hour a day job and one was supposed to be available at all times.

He found that the unfiltered water in the cistern on the mountain had a distinct taste of wood shingles.

> I would hike down to Woody Spring about a half mile north of the tower once or twice a week and carry back a couple of gallon canteens of spring water. On one of my trips, as I was returning I found bear tracks on top of tracks I had made going down.

Wallace's fire communication was over the one-wire, tree-line telephone that hung on the wall. It was "generally pretty good" except that lightning strikes on trees along the line made the phone ring.

> Of course when the lightning hit the line near the tower or hit the tower at Turkey Butte and knocked the telephone off the wall, that stopped communication with Turkey Butte until the telephone was replaced.

The telephone number for the lookout, which was listed in the Flagstaff phone book, was 1-R11.

---

5 During the winters, Wallace was principal and junior-high teacher in Sedona.

C.C.C. enrollees worked in the tree nursey at For Valley. In addition to pines, they grew blue spruce which they balled and took into town and gave to residents.
U.S. Forest Service

The track to the top of the mountain, narrow and rocky in those years, branched off the main road west of the spring and wound upward. Wallace found it passable: "We never had any difficulty driving to the Lookout. My barber even drove out once or twice and cut my hair in 1934."

After the fire season ended, he did graduate work in Forestry and Range Management at Colorado State College in Fort Collins and, in the spring of 1935, took and passed both the Junior Forester and Junior Range Examinations. On July 1, 1935, he returned to the Coconino as assistant ranger under Ed Oldham on the Flagstaff district.

Down in Flagstaff, life moved faster as the years went on into the thirties. Four passenger trains a day went through the little western town. Once in a great while ranchers drove in with horses and wagons, but Model Ts and Dodges were more common in the streets, where cattle still wandered loose, as they had twenty years earlier when John Woody had been town marshall.

Roads to the western section of the Navajo reservation had been paved by then, but few Indians visited Flagstaff except for the Fourth of July All-Indian Pow Wow, which attracted people of different tribes from all over the northern part of the state. It had been half a century since Flagstaff's settlers had seriously proposed fencing the reservation to keep Navajos in.

Margaret Schnebly, daughter of Sedona Sechebly, visited Wallace on
Woody Mountain when she was home on vacation from nurse's training.
In 1934 they were married.
Courtesy of Stanton Wallace

They came into town in wagons and trucks and camped at Thorpe Park,
crowded into every available space, prepared their food over fires. Navajo women
hung rugs from ropes strung between the trees and draped them over the tailgates
of trucks. Jewelry and all kinds of crafts were displayed for sale along the road. The
town required no business license from the Indians: "That was their four days."

A parade started at 11:00 each morning. After dark there were ceremonial
dances lit by camp fires, but the big events were the rodeos at 1:30 each afternoon
in the stadium at city park. There was bronc riding, of course, and steer riding and
calf roping and bulldogging, with saddles and boots and even cash as prizes.
Tourists who crowded the bleachers liked the wild cow milking, tug-of-war games
between women of different tribes, Hopi stick-and-stone races, and the sack pull
that the men played from the backs of fast-moving horses.

By 1936, after three years of working out-of-doors, the C.C.C. boys were young, brown, and hard as the Indians. Lookout towers were on the list of their approved project work—they put up seven new ones that year in Arizona—and the Coconino saw an opportunity. The pines on Woody Mountain were growing and blocking the view from the little wooden tower, which was not holding up well in the weather. The Coconino's acting supervisor wrote to the regional forester in Albuquerque:

> We are planning to build a 48-ft. steel tower (we would like to have an inside
> ladder or steps) on Woody Mountain this year to replace the old wooden tower.
> We shall appreciate your ordering this tower for us. The old tower is in very bad
> shape so we should get the new one as soon as possible.

The chief of maintenance in Albuquerque responded: "The price will be about $350 delivered in Flagstaff. Let us know your desires."

As arrangements were being made, it was apparent that the forest hoped to use C.C.C. money and C.C.C. labor to erect the new steel tower, but authorization was questionable. Next spring Ed Miller was gone and Ralph W. Hussey was the new forest supervisor. In April of 1936 the *Sun* ran two separate side-by-side columns to report work planned on the forest for the summer.

HEAVY SCHEDULE LAID
OUT FOR THIS SUMMER
Two CCC camps will move into Coconino
National Forest within 10 days,
providing weather permits, and begin
a heavy schedule of twig blight
eradication, forest culture,
recreational area improvements and
road maintenance work that has been
outlined by the Forest Service for
this summer...Twig blight will take
up considerable of the CCC men's
activity this summer...every effort
will be made to eradicate the blight
before it spreads.

FOREST PLANNING MUCH
NEW WORK
Besides the regular schedule of
fire protection work, grazing
supervision forest culture and
recreation grounds improvements,
Coconino National Forest office
is planning quite a program of
new lookout tower construction.
A new steel tower will be built
this season at Woody Mountain and
new towers with living quarters
on Turkey Butte, Baker's Butte
and Hutch Mountain southeast of
Mormon Lake.

Despite those right-hand column plans, C.C.C. workmen constructed a tower on Turkey Butte in 1937. No records preserved evidence of whether they did the work on Woody Mountain in 1936, although years later everybody was "pretty sure" they did.

Max Castillo was a teen-aged orphan and high school dropout when he enrolled in the C.C.C. in 1934. In 1985 he was seventy years old and living in the Verde Valley. He was proud to have been in the corps, said he had learned how to work because of it, how to operate a jack hammer. It had been a good four years with a lot of fun, grief, and fights, and he didn't regret any of it. "We could work in our skin if we wanted to. We built wherever they told us."

He worked out of the Schultz Pass camp on a crew of twelve to fifteen from all over, from Arizona, a few from Texas, some Indians from Oklahoma. Using jackhammers to drill rocks and powder to blast them out of the way because they had no tractor, they built a good road all the way to Turkey Butte and East Pocket Knob. He remembered that "the road was just a trail until then." In 1937 five of them camped at Turkey Butte in a tent and replaced an "old short rickety wooden" tower with a new steel one. "We were all over that thing like a buncha monkeys."

Castillo didn't work on Woody Mountain the previous year, although he drove to the top once. "You could drive up, but it was kinda rough. We went up in a truck." He didn't know who improved the road to the top or when.[6]

He didn't know who put up the tower. But he did know who bossed the job: Dutch Lochman, the Coconino construction superintendent, who traveled in an old Dodge truck from one district to another to take care of building and repair. Castillo's crew of "four or five guys" got stuck one day in mud and Dutch came along and pulled them out; his Dodge truck was equipped with a block and tackle.

Charles N. Lochman had been in the Forest Service almost from its beginning. He was identified in an issue of the *Sun* in 1917 as a "riding patrolman," which might have meant that he was one of three motorcycle patrolmen hired on the forest that year. Forest Service records put him on the Beaver Creek District in 1918. The memo that ordered the cistern on Woody Mountain in 1926 said: "Mr. Lochman will handle the construction work." The 1929 Flagstaff city directory included Lochman as "Sr. Forest Ranger."

Stanton Wallace had worked with Lochman in 1929 on a telephone line to Mormon Lake.

> I do not know when Charley Lochman went to work on the Coconino. He was the construction and maintenance man for many years, I would guess 25 years or more. On many projects he worked alone or like the telephone line construction he had a small crew. I would guess he was in his fifties when I worked with him...The retirement age for the Forest Service at that time was 62 years and with few exceptions you retired.

Lochman was sixty or so years old in 1936. He was a broad-shouldered, heavy-muscled man of 160 pounds, about 5 foot 8 or 10 inches. Strong as a mule, he could work all day without tiring. He and George Hochderffer understood each other: both spoke with strong German accents.

---

6 Later everybody assumed the C.C.C., but it would have been late in the decade that the work was done. Frances McAllister and her husband, who had recently bought the ranch on Sinclair Wash, had a new Buick in which they explored all over the country. In 1936 they drove it, very slowly, to the top of Woody Mountain. It was a rugged trip, she said, but "the car was pretty tough."

Wallace treated him with the respect due to an older man of intimidating habits.

He was one of two men with whom I worked who took a big swig of Bootleg whiskey about the first thing after he got out of bed. That helped me to be pretty much of a teetotaler. I just could not fathom a drink like that on an empty stomach and so early in the morning. To my knowledge he never drank on the job.

Charley chewed or ate Mail Pouch and Muleshoe tobacco, the shredded kind that came in quarter-pound paper pouches. He would take a handful and stuff it in his mouth and get on with his work. If he ran out of tobacco he was cranky and difficult to get along with until the supply was replenished.

From his many stories he was quite a rounder in his younger days. He like too many of our time had to experiment on drugs having "Hit the Pipe" in China Town in San Francisco and told of the pleasant reaction.

Many people referred to Charley as Dutch, but he was always Mr. Lochman or Charley to me. He was a man I was happy to work with.

Much of the time Lochman worked alone. During the early years when he handled construction of ranger stations, logging camps, telephone lines, and lookout towers, he lived in a small cabin on the south side of town, out toward the mill, and had a fair-sized work and tool and material shed.

In the 1930s, nearly sixty years old, he married a woman decades younger than he was. According to gossip, Lochman was very drunk one day, as he often was, in the section on San Francisco Street two blocks south of the tracks where the bawdy houses were located. He spoke to a woman who ignored him, and he stormed, "I'll marry the next woman who talks to me." At that moment a girl leaned out of the lower window of one of the houses and greeted him. Lochman lifted her bodily out the window and took her away to a judge. She was willing: she said she'd had about all of that life she wanted. The neighbors said they "never saw a truer woman" than Mrs. Lochman.

As a married man, finally, Dutch built himself a house on South Beaver Street. When he was ready to pour cement for the foundation, he hired Don Shanks, a fourteen-year-old from across the street, to help. The boy thought Lochman was "a crabby old Dutchman."

The Coconino's building boss, Lochman probably was responsible for the first tower and the cabin on Woody Mountain. After his marriage, he went on building for the Forest Service for a few years, long enough to put up the second tower. Pacific Coast Steel Company manufactured the components and sent along detailed blueprints to direct Lochman's assembly. By 1936, with the logging trains gone, the Forest Service trucked steel girders to the top of the mountain. A crew of half a dozen would have been sufficient to do the construction—setting up supports, clinging to girders in the wind, hoisting sections, and bolting them together.

Early summer that year was hot and dry, as usual. District Ranger Ed Oldham warned that dry conditions had raised fire danger. In June the *Sun* reported that

The tower framework was all made of steel.

Assistant Ranger Stanton Wallace drove a truck that had been assigned to
Supervisor Miller after Miller transferred to the Regional Office.
Courtesy of Stanton Wallace

only the "alertness of lookouts" had kept eleven forest fires to a total of three acres. On July 1 the forest declared emergency conditions and prohibited fireworks.

Storms the remainder of the summer slowed construction work.

> July 24, 1936: Lightning fires over Sunday and Monday kept forest service men busy in the Rogers Lake district. They were handled mainly by men stationed in that area, Stanton Wallace going from here to direct the work...Though the fires were quickly controlled and only two reached an approximate size of a quarter acre, the men were fatigued by having to move rapidly from place to place to fight the small blazes that kept bobbing up, and Tuesday Lloyd Wall of the forest office sent 10 CCC men into the area to give the regular crews a rest.

During a storm Saturday of the next week, lightning hit in the top of a big pine near the Lowell Observatory building, but did no damage, the *Sun* said, except to the tree. July rains were above normal. In August, with frequent rain, hail and lightning, the Rio de Flag was one hundred yards wide through town and dammed near Fort Valley by debris carried down by rain. More rain was reported in September, but not lightning; erection of the tower may have been saved for that month.

It was late September, warm in the afternoons and dry, when the crew formed a cement pad at the foot of the tower stairs. Telephone line was fed through a hole drilled in the wooden fir slabs of the floor and attached to the old hand-crank phone in the northeast corner. Then Dutch Lochman sent the C.C.C. crew away and did the carpentry work himself, cut the boards for landings, attached stair steps, fitted hand rails.

The new tower gave Woody Mountain official significance. In the Depression year when it was built, the U.S. Coast and Geodetic Survey established the apex of its roof as a third order horizontal control point, an intersection station that could be observed from other monumented points. At the same time, the U.S. Geological Survey designated the site of the tower as a bench mark and placed an identifying disk on the ground below it. In government archives it was, like respectable women down in town, "accepted."

The last known grizzly was shot in Arizona the year before the tower was built. The last jaguar was killed along about then, and wolves were going under. It was no longer the country the settlers had come into.[7] Flagstaff residents barely noticed that the old pioneer town was nearly gone.

Official records of seasonal fire employees also disappeared, probably because the paychecks had been met by cooperative funds from both the state and the Forest Service. Fifty years later nobody could remember who was lookout on Woody Mountain the twenty-two years between Fred Croxen and Stanton Wallace. Summer people had left less impression on the slopes than fires had.

---

7 But "sportsmen" had to have something to shoot at. Wild turkeys, long-since erased from the area, were brought back into Arizona in the 1930s and released on the Coconino Forest.

Neither was anybody sure about the first man to use the new steel tower. Probably it was a long-time fire guard ready to retire, "just an old cowboy type of man," who needed a job that wasn't too hard on his knees. Joe Robinson down at the DK Ranch remembered that his name was Oscar Denny. [see page 296]

According to Dean Cutler, who was on the district between 1936 and 1940, he was a big man and a sociable one.

> Denny never let the phone ring without listening. We thought that he was afraid that Bill Pratt, the LO on Elden, might report a fire around Woody Mountain first. Everybody knew that Denny was listening. One day Mrs. Miller, the wife of the rancher at the DK ranch, made an appointment with her hairdresser in Flagstaff and forgot the time. She called Denny and asked him and he told her exactly.

Denny kept an eye on the DK ranch and sometimes answered the DK signal— four rings—to tell callers, "Mr. Miller went into town an hour ago." Once he chatted for a while with a girl who had called for Duane, telling her his place was "the ranch in the sky." He wasn't the only curious man on the line: everybody listened. As each person picked up the phone, voices became dimmer and harder to hear.

Sometimes Mrs. Denny "spelled" her husband during the late 1930s, which made her the first female lookout of record on Woody. The Miller boys called her the Wild Woman of the Mountain. She was a large, strong person who wore a bonnet and drove a black Chevy flivver remodeled as a fire truck and stocked with axes and tools.

Her special peeve was drivers of the logging trucks who thought they owned the road, and one of them ran her off into a ditch once too often. He stopped to see whether she was injured. According to the story the Miller boys loved to tell, she waited until he got close, climbed out of her flivver, grabbed an axe from the trunk, and took out after that driver. Two laps around his truck she chased him with the axe until he got far enough ahead of her to get back in and lock the door.

After the Dennys, the next lookout to learn the heat of morning sun through the glass and the sound of wind beating against the tower and the way it shook in a summer storm was Don Shanks, the boy who had helped Dutch Lochman build his house five years earlier. Like other lookouts in those years, he lived in the 1922 cabin through the season and did not leave the mountain. His parents brought groceries out to him. There was "lotsa night lightning" in 1940, and part of Shanks's duty was to figure and list the locations where it struck. "Many's the time," he said, "when I set up there all night recording strikes."

Lookouts still had no communication with field crews. They watched fires and advised the dispatcher on the hand-crank phone how the smoke was doing— and sometimes went down and poured water on the ground around the telephone connection to make it work better.

The Dennys lived on a homestead down in the draw west of the mountain, where they raised rabbits in a hutch bigger than their house. Fifty years later all that remained was a pile of boards on the ground and one old bedspring and a broken washtub.

Oscar Denny was probably the first lookout to climb Dutch Lochman's stairs.

In June of 1940 one dry lightning storm started 110 fires on the Long Valley ranger district. Smoke was so dense that lookouts couldn't see ten miles. Helpless in locating fires, they were called off their towers to fight "smokes" wherever they found them.

It was the last year of peace for a while. The summer that led into the second world-wide war, there was another old-timer as lookout on Woody Mountain, David Lonze Joy. Born sixty-five years earlier in Texas, he had arrived in Springerville, Arizona, in 1900 with his two brothers. All his life he was a bachelor, a bowlegged cowboy with a big hat and boots and a game leg because of a horse that threw him when he was a kid riding saddle broncs, he said, in Madison Square Garden. When the war started he had been a fixture on the Flagstaff district for years. Ed Groesbeck knew him:

> Ranger Ed Oldham used to hire Dave Joy, an old broken-down cowpuncher, as [patrol and fire guard and] Lookout down at Fernow in the Barney Pasture. Dave was a good lookout all right, and a character besides. Ed would send Dave out there a week or two ahead of time to clear out the fire roads before fire season.
>
> One Spring Dave came upon a big pine snag about three feet in diameter that had fallen diagonally across the road out toward East Pocket Knob. Dave must have spent a couple of days sawing out a section across the road with an old two-man saw. Instead of sawing at right angles to the tree, he had sawed parallel to the road which involved about 50 percent more sawing. Duncan Lang and I were out there later in the summer and stopped by Fernow. Dunc asked Dave why he had sawed that big snag off that way. Old Dave said, "Well, you see, the darn thing fell down loblong and I had to cut it off loblong."

He was a country boy who had worked on the Loy and Mooney trails and never learned to drive an automobile: he walked to all fires in his vicinity leading his old horse, which carried the tools and supplies. It wasn't often he could go into town from Barney Pasture, but when he got near Black's Bar on Santa Fe after being out for six months, "he really whooped and hollered." Not that he ever caused any trouble when he was drunk, beyond an occasional fight with three or four men at a time. He just "wavered three feet in every direction—how he ever stood up nobody could figure." Harlow Yeager, who knew him in the 1940s, said it took three days to get him sobered up and out of jail.

Groesbeck remembered him by smell.

> At the end of the summer Dave would come to town with his summer's wages and go down to the store and buy enough supplies to last him through the winter, then proceed to get drunk with the rest of his money. Along with the whiskey he drank, he would get a few sacks of garlic bulbs which he would eat like onions. One fall the weather turned dry again and Ed had to send Dave back out to Fernow for a while. I was going out that way and Ed asked me if I would

take Dave along. Boy, the smell of that stale whiskey, along with the garlic he had eaten, was something! I had to ride with my head out of the window most of the way in order to stay in the same car with him.

Dave was a small man, five foot six inches or so. Once in fire camp down in Barney Pasture, Mrs. Denny wrestled him to the ground and sat on him, to the laughter of the other men.

The thing everybody remembered about him was that he was a talker: "you couldn't hardly get a word in on him." "He could talk the leg off of any Forest Service mule," they said, "talk faster than a dog could trot." "You couldn't read around him, and you had to cover your ears if you wanted to sleep." "He was the only man I ever knew who was talking when he came into view, talking as you passed him, and still talking till he was out of sight."

He often kept the other men on the phone. Stanton Wallace recalled:

> We had a fire one time Dave was on Turkey Butte. Oscar McClure went to it but was having a hard time finding it so hooked his portable telephone to the "tree line." He could not contact either of the lookouts but heard us talking. Dave said it looked like Oscar was adding fuel to the fire so he knew it was still burning and took off again and located the fire.

Everybody laughed that "after Dave picked up a smoke he would spend so much time telling the dispatcher how to get a crew in to it the fire would grow fairly large during the instructions."

He wasn't content with listening in on conversations like everybody else. Dave joined right in. First he might chuckle if something amused him, then it wasn't long, another sentence or two, before he began to add comments. The other men didn't object. That was just how Dave was.

They liked him, indulgently, and remembered him with grins years later. Ed Miller praised him.

> Someone asked us in the office at Flagstaff over 30 years ago if local Forest officers were erosion-minded; whether they actually saw what was taking place. I told him that I thought all of us were learning. I took him in the [Barney] pasture country—at that time a part of the Rogers Lake Ranger District—and showed him some of the work that Dave Joy, our old-time fireman and trail maintenance man, was doing.
>
> When the Fernow guard camp and ranger station was established the Valley, bordered by fine pine timber, was a dust heap. There had been a potato patch there in the old days. Maybe Old Barney himself raised spuds there, I'm not sure. We turned Old Dave loose at odd times, when there was little fire danger, and had him fell some trees, upstream; he got all the brush that he could find; reseeded with different grasses including Kentucky bluegrass, and by 1935 the old dust heap was completely sealed over.
>
> Dave would gather seed from the grasses within the guard camp pasture...He would carry that seed around with him and as he walked to and from trail work he would scatter seed along the arroyos and around an old burn

that had occurred as I recall about 1917. This Researcher from Utah was amazed and told me afterwards that Dave Joy, who never went to school above the second or third grade, was the most practical erosion-control man he had ever met in the Forest Service.

There was a promontory out on the rim, between South Pocket and Little Round Mountain (overlooking what was later the Red Rock-Secret Mountain Wilderness) that Oldham and Miller named for Dave. It pleased the old man to move his finger solemnly across a map and say, "... and this is Rattlesnake Mesa and this is South Pocket and this is Dave Joy Point and this is Little Round Mountain and this is Round Top Mountain ..."

As Dave grew older, he couldn't get around a fire so well any more with that game leg, so they put him up on Woody Mountain to work during the war. He had white hair to his shoulders by then. Keith Hunter, who had traveled to Arizona to work for the C.C.C., had worked with Dave for several seasons on the ground.

> I caught the tail of his career. I was just a kid—twenty—and he was in his sixties. I used to go up to Woody sometimes to relieve him, maybe seven or eight days all told, so he could go into town and get drunk. Lookouts had no days off then, no sick leave. They worked seven days a week, and their food was delivered. You married the Forest Service in those days.

In 1942, when Dave Joy was on Woody Mountain, the last wolf was shot in the country north of the Mogollon Rim.

Joy was Woody lookout during the war years between 1941 and 1946, when troop trains went through town constantly, and T.A. Riordan, nearing eighty-three, was on the Flagstaff Housing Authority Board. Because of the war, the Army built an ordnance depot ten miles west along the railroad line at Bellemont for the storage of ammunition. Most of the men who constructed and worked at the facility were Indians; the post was named for them. With the establishment of the Navajo Ordnance Depot, Hopi and Navajo families moved to the Indian Village on the base and to Flagstaff in sizable numbers for the first time.[8]

With so few men left around during the war, the Forest Service decided to pay wives of fire guards to help chase smokes and found that they could do most of the job as men did it. They watched for "widowmakers," built line, mopped up, did the usual hard, dirty work of fighting fire. The Service also began hiring women for summer lookout work. Some were teachers up from Phoenix who stayed with the job three or four years before moving on.

But the names of the first full-time women on Woody Mountain were thrown out with old paperwork. So were the names of most of the men. Forty years later a list of lookouts prepared by the district had more gaps than entries.

---

8 By 1950, Indians made up 3.4% of the Flagstaff population.

They still used a telephone to talk to town and to each other and had no communication with fire crews on the ground. Even after radios were available, they were heavy things with forty-pound batteries, impossible to carry to an off-road burn. Keith Hunter, who began a legendary ("There'll never be another like him") twenty-five-year career as Coconino fire dispatcher in 1946, worked the job from an office on Knob Hill virtually blind.

> Each pick-up had what we called a "portable." All units also had a ground rod. When a group [of fire fighters] arrived at a fire, a man was sent to the nearest telephone line and connected in. All the dispatcher could do was ask the nearest lookout what the fire looked like. A dispatcher sending men to a fire had no idea of when they arrived or its condition, other than a lookout's report.

Crews lit green branches to put up thick white smoke as a signal to lookouts that a fire was in hand.

Most of the people who had settled Flagstaff in the 1880s were gone by the time the war was over. One by one the old-timers had dropped away into the stillness of the cemeteries. Life in the little town went past them, leaving their names to fade into places: Lockett Meadow, the Weatherford road, Hochderffer Hill, the Oldham Trail. Flagstaff lost a long-prominent citizen when T.A. Riordan died in 1946 at the age of eighty-seven of cancer of the stomach. He was buried in Flagstaff's Catholic cemetery beside his wife, near his brother and his little grandson and his daughter Anna.

The Emerson School where people had lain dying of influenza in 1918 had been replaced by a bigger building. Cattle still wandered loose in the streets of Flagstaff; in summer police drove them from the college campus. Bill Moyer still drove into town with a team and wagon, and Pete Michelbach drove his horses in all the way from Hart Prairie. But the old frontier days were gone like a drowned city, covered by the rising years, and new people who moved to town were blithely unaware of them.

A second order horizontal control point was established on Woody Mountain in 1952, by the U.S. Coast and Geodetic Survey, on the north side of the mountain within DK land. It was used as an instrument set up point for various control surveys. But no one ever went to the mountain to stay, not even the lookouts. Young men just out of college, old men ready to retire, school teachers and, after the war, women—a procession of people served a season or two in the tower and moved on, and none of them remembered Fred Croxen, Dutch Lochman, Stanton Wallace, Dave Joy, or Mrs. Denny.

Through all the years of the twentieth century, the mountain stood silent on Flagstaff's horizon. Some years were drier than others. Sometimes a late spring freeze killed bloom on the oak, which meant no acorns for the few squirrels in autumn. The mountain wore away inexorably with summer rain, and no one stayed long enough to notice.

Trees grew up around Dutch Lochman's tower in the 1950s.

Lookouts no longer needed horses.
Courtesy of Allan and Dotty Wing

Allan and Dotty Wing were on the mountain one summer early in the 1950s. They lived in the cabin and kept food cool in a fifty-gallon drum that had been sunk into the ground among oak saplings a few yards from the door. Allan was twenty-seven, his wife twenty-five. [see page 301]

> We lived in a one room cabin on Woody. Our water supply was a cistern that collected water from the roof of the cabin...We had few visitors, mostly friends and relatives. Dotty liked animals and promptly adopted a skunk, a porcupine, and a huge snowshoe hare. The skunk and the porky followed her around like puppies. Rogers Lake was often covered with large herds of elk, and we saw deer, turkey, and a bear came around at night sometimes. I was off on small fires most of the time while Dotty manned the tower. It was a good way of life for a young couple, but there was no future for us. We eventually found career jobs.

Over in Prescott at the Pioneer's Home at the end of the summer the Wings were on the mountain, Dave Joy died. A little old bowlegged cowboy seventy-seven years old and quiet at last, he was buried in the Pioneer's Cemetery. The only possessions he left behind were his rifle and a .38.

The phone line over which he and Oscar Denny and Stanton Wallace had talked was gone the next season. The last year of a listing in the Flagstaff phone book for the Woody Mountain lookout was 1955. After that, the Coconino communicated with portable, two-way radios, and everybody on the forest could listen in on lookout conversations.

In February of 1956 the Coconino sold two and a half miles of the phone line to the Millers at Rogers Lake for $12.50. The bill of sale stated: "After wide solicitation, no other party interested in this line." Sale involved wires, crossarms or brackets and other hardware "as is and where is." The single wire grounded circuit line that had served some forty years to the top of Woody Mountain was removed. Here and there high in a pine an old glass insulator was all that was left.

The Millers tried to repair the line for their own communication with town. But it buzzed, and hunters thought it was funny to shoot at the glass insulators, which had to be replaced every spring. After five years of annoyance, the Millers took down the wire.

For five summers in the mid-1950s Roy and Clea Beach and their children lived on Woody Mountain. Clea, who was afraid of high places, worked as primary lookout in the tower and learned to go up and down the stairs, both arms loaded, without holding onto the hand rails. She stored cases of groceries on a wooden deck behind the cabin, prepared meals on a small wood cook stove, dipped water from Dutch Lochman's cistern.

Roy was a fire guard in a pick-up truck with the new two-way radio, fighting fires, setting up road blocks, and patrolling Barney Pasture. When fire danger was

The older Beach children (left to right) Jane, Polly, Roland, and Janell, felt that
Woody Mountain belonged to them in the 1950s.
AHS–Pioneer Museum

Through the weather of five summers, the Beach family lived in the little cabin
and in a sixteen-foot camp trailer parked outside.
Courtesy of Roy Beach

high, Keith Hunter called Roy in to Knob Hill to work as dispatcher until late in the evenings. During big fires in 1956 he was in charge of fire camps for...

> the big crews that came into Flagstaff to fight the fires. This task involved making arrangements at restaurants for meals while they were in town and ordering sack lunches to put on the buses taking them to the fire camp. The fire camp was set up to feed the crews as they reported in and rotated to the fire and back to camp for rest, sometimes as many as 150 men at a time.

Often, with Tex Wright as pilot, he flew air patrol surveys, locating fires or talking crews into them.

Thirty-five years later he reminisced:

> The kids had "a ball" each day, and got so dirty that visitors to the tower must have wondered about their nationality. The Beach family had many exciting experiences during the five summers, such as finding a huge rat in the water collection system coming from the roof of the cabin; Ross, a two year old, getting lost for a couple of hours; several severe lightning storms with lightning hitting the tower and shaking things up while the family was in the cabin; a hail storm, so heavy that Clea, on the tower could not hear the radio with Knob Hill calling her. [I] happened to be on the radio at Knob Hill and could see the severe storm over Woody Mountain but couldn't get a response from Clea for 30 minutes; driving up the steep road to the tower during a rainstorm and the car sliding off the road into the deep barpit and having to walk up the hill to the cabin; and a hail storm so heavy that it piled up deep around the cabin and the kids made a small snowman. Also, some memorable experiences with ladybugs, porcupines, skunks, and a rare assortment of tourists.

Time removed old landmarks in Flagstaff and added others while the character of the growing community changed. On May 29, 1961, the AL&T sawmill on U.S. 66 burned down, and the land on which it had stood for eighty years was sold to the Holiday Inn Corporation. In 1965 a U.S. Geological Survey facility was built on a hill that had once been too high and far out of town for travel in a horse and buggy. There were new people: in January of 1966 the *Sun* said that almost half of the students in Flagstaff schools were bilingual. A ski facility, which had been established up on the Peaks for twenty years by then, attracted a few hardy athletes up from Phoenix. There were a good many buildings at the institution south of the tracks that had once been called the Normal School and was soon to be elevated from Arizona State College to Northern Arizona University.

Up on Woody Mountain, the Geological Survey cemented still another marker disk into a boulder directly under the tower. It established an instrument set-up point for a horizontal control survey. That made no difference to the tower, which stood through the seasons. Winter did no damage. Summer lightning strikes never really hurt it; people did. Vandalism grew all over the forest with the growing Arizona population.

In 1970, Coconino employees returned to open the tower for another summer and found that someone had cut the lock and fired twenty-eight times into

Coconino NF Engineering

windows, the roof, the map board—from the inside. After that, according to Van Bateman, who worked as relief lookout:

> ... when you looked inside it, you could discover nuts and bolts through holes in
> the walls that were not holding anything up. They were from bullet shots.
> Whenever one was discovered, someone would lean outside and put a bolt
> through it.

A new kind of outdoorsman had replaced the dedicated rangers of 1910. A few years after the tower was savaged, all the windows in the cabin were blown out by shotgun blasts during the fall and winter off season. Bullets were fired through the outdoor privy.

During the worst years of vandalism, the man who had been Woody Mountain's first official lookout followed Dave Joy and all the others into silence. Fred Croxen had worked for the Forest Service for twenty years, one of a number of early rangers who went armed. In 1921 he had shot and killed a rancher in a gun fight the latter had provoked. He had fought smugglers as a horse-mounted Border Patrol officer and managed the Navajo Police Patrol at Window Rock. He died in Flagstaff in 1977, three weeks short of his ninetieth birthday, and was buried a few yards from G.A. Pearson. [see page 306]

Like outdoorsmen, lookout personnel had changed since Croxen's day. The new breed were specialists who did not go down to fight the fires they spotted; their job

In his last years Croxen wrote articles on Arizona history, in which
he had played a significant part.
AHS–Pioneer Museum

was just to look around and report. Inactive and restless in a seven by seven tower, few of them stayed long enough to learn the landscape the way the old-timers had known it, and they usually left for other jobs after a season.

Through the 1950s, 1960s, and 1970s from two to ten percent of fires on the Coconino were reported from Woody Mountain, depending on the alertness of the current lookout. Roseanna Finley, who worked the tower for three seasons in the 1970s, held the record ten percent. [see page 308]

At 11:52 on the hot, dry Friday morning of June 17, 1977, with a Red Flag wind blowing, Finley reported the first lookout sighting of the Radio Fire burning on the western slope of Mt. Elden. East Pocket lookout crossed her azimuth reading. The first Forest Service patrol on the scene was Maureen Gallagher, who found "not just an escaped campfire; it was *walls* of flame."

By 2:00 p.m. the fire reached the top of Elden, burning the tower, from which the lookout had fled, and all radio and electronic equipment established there. A total of 1382 people fought it for three days, including pilots of air tankers, operators of forty ground tankers, and thirty-six crews with hand tools. Final size was 4594 acres; cost of suppression was $1,424,542.

At the same time, other crews were fighting a large fire burning near the Baker Butte lookout tower and a smaller blaze at Yellow Jacket Spring northeast of Mormon Lake, and there was a fire on the North Rim of the Grand Canyon. It was a major organizational crisis for the fire resources of northern Arizona and for Coconino dispatchers Hub Harris, Johnny Chavez, and Amos Coochyouma.[10] Because relay equipment was put out of service by the fire on Mt. Elden, radio traffic on the Coconino for a while went from Johnny Chavez, sitting on the roof of the Supervisor's Office with a portable unit, through Finley on Woody Mountain. She worked thirty-six consecutive hours with no relief and was up all night relaying messages.

The Woody Mountain tower was threatened by fire the summer after the big Radio burn when the Metz fire started four miles upwind off to the south and west. On the radio district fire boss Ki Porter warned: "Roseanna, if we can't catch this one at the road, we won't catch it short of the mountain. Pack up." She hurried to gather everything. Then Porter called again. "We got it, Roseanna. You can unpack."

Wooden structures on the mountain lasted longer than the people who used them, but they aged as inevitably. After forty-three years, the floor Dutch Lochman had built for the tower was weak and full of dry rot. In spring of 1979, with no oak leaves out yet and Rogers Lake full of water, a new floor was put into the old tower by patrolmen Paul Boucher, Dana Schmidt, and Kurt Winchester. They lifted the massive firefinder base on two legs and, balanced over empty air,

10 Coochyouma, a Hopi born on First Mesa, had grown up at Keams Canyon and had been crew boss for the Happy Jack Hot Shot firefighters for three seasons. Ninety years had gone by since Flagstaff's first settlers had arrived afraid of Indians; here and there the Forest Service had them in charge.

If fire records were any guide, Roseanna Finley was the best of the late-century lookouts
on Woody Mountain. The only fall ever recorded from the tower was that of Finley's dog.
Asleep on the top landing, the dog shifted position, rolled off, fell forty-five feet, and
hit the ground with a thud. Roseanna rushed to the ground. Eyes glazed, gums white,
the dog stood up with tail wagging. Roseanna went out of service and took the dog
to the vet. When it had recovered, it climbed to the top again.
Courtesy of Roseanna Finley

installed tongue-and-groove on the joists and covered that with heavy plywood.
They considered it "a monumental task, took a coupla days."

At the same time the district contracted a "cherry picker" to mop and broom
trailer sealant on the roof, which was leaking. A few years later Tom Gross built
wooden panels that fitted around the inside walls to cover the bullet holes. Those
remodeling carpenters represented a new kind of Forest Service employee—field
men with handy skills and university degrees in forestry and other science. The days
of the "old cowboy" types were gone as surely as Navajo wagons down in town.

The cabin built when the trees were small stood through the years until it
was so rickety and full of mice that lookouts drove out from town every day rather
than live there. It was finally destroyed in 1981, by winter lightning, according to
the carefully phrased report. Secretaries and clerks stood in the parking lot at the
Knob Hill Ranger Station to watch black smoke rise from the top of the mountain.

A forest service crew built a 12 x 16 foot cabin on Woody Mountain in 1982.
Courtesy of Lynn Bleeker

Through the cold months that winter a new cabin was constructed in the fire barn at Knob Hill. When snow melted it was taken apart, trucked to the mountain, and reassembled. The job was finished in July.[11]

The superficial marks humans had made on the mountain were erased one by one as years went by, with no sign of them left for future lookouts to see. New marks took their place, and then access itself changed. The Forest Service had built its road to the top long before the Millers had taken control of the DK Ranch. For the first half mile it crossed their private quarter section, passing near the spring that was the sole source of water for the ranch. When Cecil Miller fenced his land, he allowed the Forest Service to continue to use the road to the tower, asking that lookouts entering and leaving keep the gate closed. The arrangement was satisfactory for a few years, but city vandals out for a frolic were persistent. In 1982 the Millers legally closed the road that led across their land and put their own lock on the gate.

Lookouts were excluded as completely as Manterola sheep. Lynn Bleeker worked on top at the time. The Millers notified the district ranger and went up

11 There was also change for a close neighbor that year, Frances McAllister incorporated at her ranch, a little over a mile away on Sinclair Wash, an arboretum for the promotion of research, education, and the conservation of native plants of the area.

Lynn Bleeker was Woody Mountain lookout when the access was changed.
Courtesy of Lynn Bleeker

from the ranch to warn Bleeker of the pending closure. But the date was only "pretty soon," and the district made no plans. One day she finished a day's work and found that the gate was locked and she couldn't get out:

> Roseanna was on patrol that year. I cross-countried it as far as I could west toward Rogers Lake and called her on the radio. She came by and picked me up. Ed Piper found an old skid road that I could get up the rest of the season. Just two tracks through the trees. The rest of the summer I drove a four-wheel truck to work.

Using heavy equipment, the Coconino built in one summer a new road to Woody Mountain, across a section owned by the state. For good measure, it installed a locked gate half a mile below the tower as its own deterrent to vandals.[12] After that about all that was left on the mountain from the early days were a piece of C.C.C. road, a cement cistern locked shut for safety, and a battered old tower.

When the new cabin replaced the old one on the mountain, Flagstaff had just passed its centennial mark, proud to be forward-looking. The last of the children were gone from the high-ceilinged classrooms and wide wooden staircases of the

---

12 Gates were also installed at Turkey Butte and East Pocket. Shirley Pierce, longtime lookout at Turkey Butte, approved of the new gates: "You know, a drunk won't walk very far *uphill*."

second Emerson School. Plans had been drawn up to demolish it and build a fine new city library to replace the old green one that stood where the Babbitt house had once been, across the street from the Catholic church. The home Fred Breen had owned had made way for a city park. No sign was left of the house where John and Ella Woody had lived for nearly four years, and the college library covered what had once been T.A. Riordan's golf course. The old Knob Hill Ranger Station was being destroyed so that a new city hospital could be built in its place.

The tower on Woody Mountain neared its half century mark as the oldest full-season fire tower still in use on the Coconino. Instead of pulling it down, the ranger district decided to give the old structure a fiftieth anniversary party. During the summer of 1986, while a search went out for people who had worked as lookouts in the past, prevention personnel built a concrete base to hold a commemorative plaque.

A small metal marker was chosen after debate by office clerks.

> Dedicated to the men and women
> who have served since 1910 as
> WOODY MOUNTAIN LOOKOUT
> and to Charles N. Lochman
> who in 1936 supervised
> construction of this tower.
> September 1986

Bill Hill, Mike Rabe, and Debbie Binnewies had shoveled cement into a form at the foot of the tower stairs.

Pat Stein from the forest archaeology division brought in an old firefinder with a hand-crank telephone attached to the pole, like the one that had been on Woody Mountain in 1915.

Debbie Binnewies escorted Smokey Bear to the party. People who wore the costume had limited vision: they needed an escort.

The date for the anniversary party on the mountain was set for September 24, when Coconino weather was usually bright blue and gold, air transparently clear, oak and aspen turning color. The district's three remaining horses were promised, with mounted rangers to be on the road welcoming old-timers back. Fire crews arranged to burn piles of worn tires in the vicinity so that former lookouts could report one more smoke from Woody Mountain. Smokey Bear was invited; a 1922 Dodge Forest Service truck was moved over from Springerville; a 1915 firefinder with a hand-crank telephone was loaned by Sharlot Hall Museum in Prescott.

Then two tropical storms met above Arizona and clouds lowered until the mountain was shrouded in fog. At daybreak on the morning of the 24th, snow was falling. Riding rangers and burning tires were canceled. Working feverishly until the last minute, patrolmen moved the party into town to the conference room in the Supervisor's Office, where people who had known Woody Mountain through the years shared their stories. Most of them had never met.

Fred Croxen II, hoilding a photograph of his father, talked with Stanton Wallace.

Karen Smith,
Woody Mountain lookout,
1975, laughed at the story
of Mrs. Denny and the
driver of the logging truck.

Van Bateman,
relief lookout, 1970s,
admitted that he had been
too tall to see out the
tower windows while
he was standing up.

Later a cavalcade of Forest Service fire trucks drove to the top of Woody Mountain with Stanton and Margaret Wallace in the lead in a two-hundred-gallon tanker truck. Snow had stopped falling, but wind was cold and fog still blew through the trees. Former lookouts were photographed at the tower stairs. One hundred and thirty five years earlier almost to the month Woodhouse and Kern and Park had also stood there.

On December 29, 1987, after surveys conducted by the Coconino under direction of the Department of Agriculture, the fire tower on Woody Mountain was placed on the National Register of Historic Places by the United States Department of the Interior. And in the summer of 1991 a second historical plaque was cemented into a base under the old tower to inform visitors of its status in human affairs.

Allan and Dotty Wing stood on Woody Mountain thirty-two years after they had left it. By then Dotty was an employee of Mountain Bell in Prescott, Allan a commander of the patrol division, with the rank of lieutenant, of the Prescott Police Department.

The plaques at the base of the Woody Mountain tower.

Stanton Wallace and the Woody Mountain tower,1986.
Photograph by Laurie Smith, Arizona Daily News

More than half of the moisture that fell on Woody Mountain was snow from late November to April. Then clouds slid past low and dark, moving fast. The black, wet trunks of pines looked grey from twenty feet as they receded down the slopes into mist, and flakes fell silently, building into pillows on the branches. Most life on the mountain retreated to a six-month refuge, grasses and oaks into their roots, rodents into burrows.

Abert squirrels were awake through the cold months. They stayed close to their nests, curled inside during storms for a week at a time, but they did not hibernate. Winter was a hard season for the squirrels. If storms were light and widely spaced, they foraged on the ground for pine seeds and acorns and truffles. But if snow was heavy all winter and piled deep between the trees, the squirrels bit off the ends of pine branches, peeled back the outer covering, and ate the inner bark. Reduced to such food, they lost as much as one-fourth of their body weight. Depending on snow storms, from twenty-two to sixty percent of the squirrels died during winter because of malnutrition. It was the single greatest factor in their mortality.

Chapter Nine
The Mountain

Woody Mountain, to the right of the Oak Creek Fault, from Hart Prairie.

The Grand Canyon that tourists traveled through Flagstaff to see made visible so much time that time became just a word. One could only repeat numbers. Seventeen million years in the past there had been a mountain range twenty thousand feet high on that spot. Deep in the canyon, below the sediment left by seas that washed ancient shores before the time of the dinosaurs, evidence was exposed that twice mountains had risen there, when no life existed anywhere on the planet, and had worn away at the rate of no more than six inches in a thousand years.

Those mountains may have extended ninety miles to the southeast. Under the silt of oceans, their roots probably lay deep beneath Woody Mountain, hidden from the sun for millions upon millions of years. The molten rock that had formed the mountain had come up through them and who knew what other rock-written history, buried far below.

Erosion had been a persistent force. The old mountains were gone. Woody too was not what it had been a million years earlier. Its eastern wall had worn slowly away with each season until dirt washed down to the Oak Creek fault was eighteen feet deep on underlying lava. When John Woody arrived, the mountain was already worn and wrinkled, scarred where water draining from its flanks had cut ravines. Trees, grasses, lichen, wind, weather—all had been busy for centuries at their work of breaking basalt into dust. In the one hundred and some years after the mountain received a name, what with logging and road building and rain storms, more of it had disappeared.

Given the earth's actively moving nature, ten million years in the future the Grand Canyon will no longer exist. Neither will Woody Mountain. Through future aeons, as the planet's rotation slows and the sun itself grows dimmer, the old volcano will be carried away grain by grain. Ravines that drain east and west will erode the saddle, where the crater once was, and cut the mountain in half, and then the two halves will wear away. The Peaks, Mt. Elden, and O'Leary will also be cut into two parts by erosion.

In some distant time, Dutch Lochman's tower will topple and vanish with Henry Deutsch's fence, and the C.C.C. road will disappear. Particles from Woody Mountain will be carried down to fill Rogers Lake, burying the bones of Inemacio Valdez ever deeper, and seep into the Oak Creek fault, filling the Perry Brothers' well, and sift farther east to cover the grave of Dr. Raymond. Gus Pearson's pines will probably be long gone by then. The spring Eli Giclas and Cecil Miller's boys worked on will be gone too.

With dust from the Peaks and Mt. Elden, Woody Mountain will move down to cover the graves of Ella Woody, of Matt Black and James Vail and their babies, of T.A. Riordan and Fred Croxen and Fred Breen and their wives, of John Weatherford and Jack Crabb and "Spud" Anderson and "Maggie" Pulliam, of the Locketts and the Babbitts and the Hochderffers and the people they knew. All trace of Flagstaff's settlers will vanish under the dust of mountains.

Flagstaff Citizens Cemetery

In the long view of geology, they had been only a moment in the mountain's story. Like the town they founded, they will succumb to the laws of the earth, which include Leaving Behind. The first building of the Normal School will go under, and so will the county court house and Lowell Observatory and the Pioneer Museum. Like Woody Mountain, they will all disappear some day into the earth's silence.

Someday the spot will be someplace else on the globe. It may be that the plateau will subside, and an ocean will flood in again. Perhaps the continents in their endless drifting will push up new mountain ranges or form new volcanos where the old ones stood, to be named in their turn by whatever people come to live among them. No one then will care that on Woody Mountain, winter of the year 2741 had been hard, and all the squirrels had died.

Sources

Chapter One

Published:

Andrews, Henry N. Jr. *Ancient Plants*. Ithaca, New York: Comstock Publishing Co., Inc., 1947.

Arnold, Chester. *An Introduction to Paleontology*. New York: McGraw-Hill Co. Inc., 1947.

Breed, Bill. "The Mountains of Fire," *Arizona Highways*. July 1978.

Breed, Bill and Evelyn Roat, editors. *Geology of the Grand Canyon*. Flagstaff: Museum of Northern Arizona, 1976.

Brown, Lauren. *Grasslands*. New York: Alfred A. Knopf, 1946.

Colton, Harold S. *An Archaeological Survey of Northwestern Arizona*. Flagstaff: Museum of Northern Arizona Bulletin #l6, Northern Arizona Society of Science and Art, June 1939.

Colton, Harold S. *Cinder Cones and Lava Flows*. Flagstaff: Museum of Northern Arizona, 1967.

Crampton, C. Gregory. *Land of Living Rock*. New York: Alfred A Knopf, 1972.

Darrah, William C. *Principles of Paleobotany*. New York: The Ronald Press Company, 1900.

Futuyma, Douglas J. *Evolutionary Biology*. Sunderland, Massachusetts: Sinauer Associates, Inc., 1986.

Macdonald, Gordon A. *Volcanos*. Englewood Cliffs, New Jersey: Prentice-Hall, Inc., 1972.

Martin, Paul and Fred Plog. *The Archaeology of Arizona*. Garden City, New York: American Museum of Natural History, Doubleday/Natural History Press, 1973.

McKee, Edwin D. *Ancient Landscapes of the Grand Canyon*. Flagstaff: U.S. Geological Survey, 1931.

Pewe, Troy L. and Randall Updike. *San Francisco Peaks, a Guidebook to the Geology*. Flagstaff. Museum of Northern Arizona, 1976.

Phillips, Allan, Joe Marshall, and Gale Monson. *The Birds of Arizona*. Tucson: University of Arizona Press, 1978.

Retkevich, Ronald Paul. *Dinosaurs of the Southwest*. Albuquerque: University of New Mexico Press, 1976.

Romer, Alfred Sherwood. *Vertebrate Paleontology*. Chicago: University of Chicago Press, 1974.

Seward, A.C. *Plant Life Through the Ages*. Cambridge: Cambridge University Press, 1941.

Shugart, Herman, H. *A Theory of Forest Dynamics, the Ecological Implications of Forest Succession Models*. New York: Springer–Verloy, 1984.

Smathers, Garrett A., and Dieter Mueller-Dombois. *Invasion and Recovery of Vegetation after a Volcanic Eruption in Hawaii.* National Park Service Scientific Monograph Series #5, 1974.

Stanley, Steven M. *Extinction.* New York: Scientific American Library, 1987.

Stewart, Wilson S. *Paleobotany and the Evolution of Plants.* Cambridge: Cambridge University Press, 1983.

Walton, John. *An Introduction to the Study of Fossil Plants.* London: Adam and Charles Black, 1953.

Primary:

Held in the Cline Library of Northern Arizona University:

    Alexander, William J. *Reconnaissance Geology and Geomagnetics of Western Flagstaff.* Thesis for Master of Science degree in Geology, Northern Arizona University, 1974.

    Carollo, John. *Woody Mountain Aquifer Report.* Presented to the City of Flagstaff, 1976.

    Murray, Kent Stephens. *Geology of the Woody Mountain Volcanic Field.* Thesis for a Master of Science degree in Geology, Northern Arizona University, 1973.

    ——— *Geology of Northern Arizona.* Geological Society of America, Rocky Mountain Section Meeting, Flagstaff, 1974.

Lectures:

    Colbert, Dr. Edwin H. "Ancient Dinosaurs of the Colorado Plateau," Museum of Northern Arizona, 1987.

    Morales, Dr. Michael. "Paleontological Research in the Painted Desert," Museum of Northern Arizona, 1987.

Conversations with:

    Jerry Bradley, Range specialist, Coconino National Forest
    Mike Landram, Timber specialist, Coconino National Forest
    Peter Pilles, Archaeologist, Coconino National Forest
    Marvin Puyama, Technician, Coconino National Forest
    Linda Farnsworth, Archaeologist, Coconino National Forest
    Greg Haynes, Archaeologist, Kenlani

Chapter Two

Published:

Byrkit, James W. *The Overland Road: An Important Historic Arizona Trail on the Kaibab National Forest.* USFS Kaibab National Forest, January 1988.

Cline, Platt. *They Came to the Mountain.* Flagstaff: Northland Press, 1976.

Colton, Harold S. "Samuel Washington Woodhouse," *Museum Notes.* Flagstaff: Northern Arizona Society of Science and Art, Museum of Northern Arizona, July 1932.

Cooper, Charles F. "Changes in vegetation, structure, and growth of southwest pine forests since white settlement," *Ecological Monographs.* 1960.

Davis, Goode P. Jr. *Man and Wildlife in Arizona.* Arizona Game and Fish Department, 1982.

Fuchs, James R. *A History of Williams, Arizona*. Tucson: University of Arizona Social Science Bulletin #23, University of Arizona Press, 1955.

McKee, Edwin D. "Distribution of the Tassel-eared Squirrels," *Plateau*. Flagstaff: Museum of Northern Arizona, July 1941.

Mumey, Nolie. *John Williams Gunnison (1812–1853): The Last of the Western Explorers; A History of the Survey Through Colorado and Utah with a Biography and Details of His Massacre*. Denver: Artcraft Press, 1955.

Palmer, General William J. *Report on Surveys Across the Continent in 1867–1868 on the 35th and 32nd Parallels for a Route Extending the Kansas Pacific Railway to the Pacific Ocean at San Francisco and San Diego*. Philadelphia: W.B. Selheimer (printer), 1869.

Parkhill, Forbes. *The Blazed Trail of Antoine Leroux*. Los Angeles: Westernlore Press, 1965.

Sherburne, John P. *Through Indian Country to California*. Edited by Mary McDougal Gordon. Stanford: Stanford University Press, 1988.

Sitgreaves, Captain Lorenzo. To the 33rd Congress *Report of an Expedition down the Zuni and Colorado Rivers*. Washington: 1853.

Smith, Jack. *A Guide to the Beale Wagon Road Through Flagstaff, Arizona*. Flagstaff: Tales of the Beale Road Publishing Company, 1984.

Sutton, Ann and Myron. "Arizona's Tassel-Eared Clowns," *Arizona Highways*. June 1955.

Wallace, Andrew. "Across Arizona to the Big Colorado; the Sitgreaves Expedition of 1851," *Arizona and the West, A Quarterly Journal of History*, Volume 26 #4. Tucson: University of Arizona Press, Winter 1984.

Primary:

Kern, Richard. "Field Notes of a Reconnaissance of the Zuni, Little and Big Colorado Rivers Under the Command of Captain L. Sitgreaves," 1851, held in The Huntington Library and Art Gallery, San Marino, California.

Park, Lieutenant John Grubb. *Zuni Diary*. Held in the United States Military Academy at West Point. A transcript was made on permission of the owner by Dr. Andrew Wallace of Northern Arizona University, who made it available to the author.

Woodhouse, Samuel Washington. *Zuni Expedition, Aug 13th 1851 to Nov.15*. (Collection 387, Academy of Natural Sciences of Philadelphia Library, Manuscript/Archives), Vol. 3, pp. 130–137. A transcript was made on permission of the Academy of National Sciences by Dr. Andrew Wallace of Northern Arizona University, who made it available to the author.

Chapter Three

Published:

Ashurst, Henry Fountain. "Senator Ashurst Recalls Fond Memories," *Arizona Sheriff*. June 1975.

Bader, Lou. *In the Shadow of the San Francisco Peaks: Frontier Adventures*. Sedona, Arizona: Light Technology Publishing, 1988.

Barney, James M. "Flagstaff Beginnings," *Arizona Municipalities*. July 1940.

Bowen, William A. *The Willamette Valley.* Seattle: University of Washington Press, 1978.

Bryant, Keith L., Jr. *History of the Atchison, Topeka and Santa Fe Railroad.* New York: Macmillan Publishing Co., 1974.

Cline, Platt. *They Came to the Mountain.* Flagstaff: Northland Press, 1976.

The Flagstaff Cook Book. Flagastaff: Published by the Ladies' Aid Society of the Methodist Episcopal Church in 1896, republished in 1976 by the Northern Arizona Pioneer's Historical Society.

Fong, Lawrence Michael. "Sojourners and Settlers, the Chinese Experience in Arizona," *Journal of Arizona History.* Tucson: Arizona Historical Society, Autumn 1980.

Giclas, Henry L. "Stanley Sykes," *Journal of Arizona History.* Tucson: Arizona Historical Society, Summer 1985.

Gould, Frank W. *Grasses of the Southwestern United States.* Tucson: University of Arizona Press, 1977.

Granger, Byrd. *X Marks the Place.* Tucson: Falconer Publishing, 1983.

Hochderffer, George. *Flagstaff, Whoa!* Flagstaff: Museum of Northern Arizona with Northland Press, 1965.

Keller, Helen Rex. *The Dictionary of Dates.* New York: Harper Publishing, 1971.

Murphy, Merwin L. *W.J. and the Valley.* Alhambra, California: Published by Merwin Murphy, 1975.

Potter, Miles F. *Oregon's Golden Years.* Caldwell, Idaho: The Caxton Printers Ltd., 1976.

Recorded Marks and Brands of Live Stock for Arizona. Phoenix: Arizona Livestock and Sanitary Board with McNeil Company, 1908.

Roberts, Paul H. *Hoof Prints on Forest Ranges.* San Antonio, Texas: Naylor Co., 1963.

Smith, Dean. *Brothers Five: The Babbitts of Arizona.* Tempe: Arizona Historical Foundation, 1989.

Stemmer, Charles C. *A Brand From the Burning: From the Depths of Despair to the Gates of Heaven.* Boston: The Christopher Publishing House, 1959.

Sykes, Godfrey. *A Westerly Trend...Being a Veracious Chronicle of More Than Sixty Years of Joyous Wanderings, Mainly in Search of SPACE AND SUNSHINE.* Tucson: Arizona Pioneers Historical Society, 1944.

Tinker, George H. *Northern Arizona and Flagstaff in 1887.* Glendale, California: Arthur H. Clark Company, 1969.

Way, Thomas E. *The Parker Story.* Prescott: Prescott Graphics, 1981.

———*Sgt. Fred Platten's Ten Years on the Trail of Redskins.* Williams, Arizona: Williams News Press, 1963.

Primary:

Special Collections and Archives Department, Cline Library, Northern Arizona University:

Arizona Lumber and Timber Company Collection, AHS–Pioneer Museum Manuscript Collection #47: Outgoing Correspondence, Cartons 200 to 215; Financial Ledgers 2, 8, 9, 10, 20, 21, and 22.

George Hochderffer Collection, AHS–Pioneer Museum Manuscript Collection #3: Series I and IIA, Box 2, Folder 91.

Black, Mary Annetta, "I Remember When: Memories of Early Flagstaff," unpublished manuscript.

Minutes of the Pioneers' Society of Northern Arizona, Arizona Historical Society Manuscript Collection #1: Box 3.

Flagstaff City/Coconino County Library Oral History Project; Tape Collection #28: Michelbach sisters, Kathryn Rucker, Platt Cline, Bill Wong.

Gladwell Richardson Collection, AHS–Pioneer Museum Manuscript Collection #48.

Justice of the Peace Records Collection 1889–1890, Docket of J.W. Weatherford, Justice of the Peace, AHS–Pioneer Museum Manuscript Collection #18: Book 2.

Flagstaff, Arizona Police Journal Collection 1895–1898, AHS–Pioneer Museum Manuscript Collection #17.

Smith, Miriam. "Riordan Brothers". Unpublished manuscript.

Microfilm of Arizona newspapers: *Arizona Champion, Coconino Sun, Flagstaff Gem, Arizona Republican, Weekly Arizona Democrat.*

University of Arizona's Special Collections Library:

Miscellaneous papers in the A.E. Douglass Collection, Boxes 155–159, Personal Material (Various).

City of Flagstaff Records:

Minutes of the Common Council

Citizens' Cemetery

City Planning Office

Tax and Licenses

City Water

Sanborn Fire Inspection Maps

Yavapai County Arizona Records:

Clerk of the Superior Court

County Recorder's Office

Fresno County, California, Records:

Microfilm of 1892 *Great Register of Voters*

Coconino County Arizona Records:

Minutes of the Board of Supervisors

Duplicate Tax

County Recorder's Office: *Great Register of Voters, Book 1; Deed Records, Books 4, 9, 10, 37, 38, and 42; Records of Leases, Book 1; Transactions, Township 20 North to Township 22 North, Bills of Sale.*

Office of the Clerk of the Superior Court: *Register of Civil Actions, Marriage License Register, Register of Probate, Register of Divorces, Index to Wills.*

State of Arizona Records, supplied by:

Lynn Reyes, Public Contact Assistant, Arizona Bureau of Land Management

Carol Downey, Department of Library, Archives, and Public Records

Federal Records:

Coconino National Forest Supervisor's Office: maps and records, *Classification Extensive.*

United States Census microfilms for: Oregon, 1860; Arizona, 1880 and 1910; Flagstaff, 1900.

Lowell Observatory Library:
>
> Sykes, Glenton G. "Scraps from the Past". Unpublished manuscript, 1967.

Conversations with:

> Pinky Wong, Flagstaff businesswoman
> Louise Black, daughter-in-law of a Flagstaff settler
> Henry Giclas, son of a Flagstaff settler
> Lillian Hall, Coconino County Treasurer
> Mary Sweitzer, daughter of a Flagstaff settler
> John Irwin, Flagstaff City –Coconino County Public Library
> Joe Meehan, AHS Pioneer Museum
> Bonnie Greer, Archivist, AHS Pioneer Museum
> Stella Sandoval, Coconino County Supervisor's Office
> Margaret Fiche, Flagstaff District Clerk, US Forest Service
> Elizabeth Dobrinsky, granddaughter of a Flagstaff settler
> Dr. James Rominger, Northern Arizona University
> Platt Cline, Flagstaff historian

Correspondence with:

> Henry Giclas, son of a Flagstaff settler
> Mary Annetta Black, daughter of a Flagstaff settler
> Richard Barney, grandson of a Flagstaff settler
> Laura McBride, great-granddaughter of J.J. "Bear" Howard
> Della Greenwell, great-granddaaughter of J.J. Howard.

Chapter Four

Published:

Guidebook of the Western United States. Washington, D.C.: United States Geological Survey, 1915.

Harper, Kinball T., Fred J. Wagstaff, and Lynn M. Kunzler. *Biology and Management of the Gambel Oak Vegetation Type: A Literature Review.* Ogden, Utah: U.S.D.A. Forest Service IF and RES, General Technical Report INT-179, March 1985.

Harrington, Michael G. *Phytotoxic Potential of Gambel Oak on Ponderosa Pine Seed Germination and Potential Growth.* Fort Collins, Colorado: U.S.D.A. Forest Service Research Paper RM-277, 1987.

Leiberg, John B., Theodore F. Rixon, and Arthur Dodwell. *Forest Conditions in the San Francisco Mountains Forest Reserve, Arizona.* Washington: United States Geological Survey, 1904.

Lucia, Ellis. *The Big Woods.* Garden City, New York: Doubleday & Co., 1975.

Neilson, Ronald R. and L.H. Wullstein. "Microhabitat affinities of Gambel Oak seedlings," *Great Basin Naturalist.* April 1986.

Patton, David R., Richard L. Wadleigh, and Howard G. Hudak. "The Effects of Timber Harvesting on the Kaibab Squirrel," *Journal of Wildlife Management.* 1985.

Pinchot, Gifford. *Breaking New Ground.* Seattle: University of Washington Press, 1947.

Prouty, Andrew Mason. *More Deadly Than War: Pacific Coast Logging, 1827–1981.* New York: Garland Publishing, 1985.

Robbins, William G. *Lumberjacks and Legislatures.* Texas A. & M. University Press, 1982.

Wells, Robert W. *Daylight in the Swamp.* Garden City, New York: Doubleday, 1978.

Primary:

Held in the Cline Library, Northern Arizona University:

Beard, Christine. "The Flim Flam: A Geographic and Historic Survey." An unpublished manuscript prepared for the Department of Anthropology, Northern Arizona University, 1984.

Bryant, Keith L., Jr. *History of the Atchison, Topeka and Santa Fe Railroad in Northern Arizona.* Thesis for a Master of Arts degree in History, Northern Arizona University, 1971.

Garnett, Henry. *The Forests of the United States.* Extract from the 19th Annual Report of the USGS Survey 1897–1898, Part V: Forest Reserves, Serial Set No. 3763, Department of the Interior.

LaBoone, Ken. *The Arizona Lumber and Timber Company, 1881–1981.* Flagstaff: Copyright by the Arizona Lumber and Timber Company, 1981.

Matheny, Robert Lavesco. *The History of Lumbering in Arizona Before World War II.* Dissertation for a Doctor of Philosophy degree in History, University of Arizona, 1975.

Murray, Kent Stephens. *Geology of the Woody Mountain Volcanic Field.* Thesis for a Master of Science degree in Geology, Northern Arizona University, 1973.

Wahmann, Russell. *The Historical Geography of the Santa Fe Railroad in Northern Arizona.* Thesis for a Master of Arts degree in History, Northern Arizona University, 1971.

Special Collections and Archives Department, Cline Library, Northern Arizona University:

"Frederick Breen," NAU Vertical File

Arizona Lumber and Timber Company Collection, AHS–Pioneer Museum Manuscript Collection #47: Outgoing Correspondence, Cartons 200 to 215; Financial Ledgers; Footage Records, Volume #6.

Blanche Riordan Chambers Collection, AHS–Pioneer Museum #4, Correspondence, Box #4, Book #7.

Gladwell Richardson Collection, ANS–Pioneer Museum Manuscript Collection #48

Microfilms of Arizona Newspapers: *Coconino Sun, Prescott Courier, Flagstaff Gem, Williams News.*

Federal Records:

United States Geological Survey of 1908

Depository of Federal Records in Denver: Coconino National Forest USFS; Agency Container #9, FRC Container #743932; Agency Container #7, FRC Container #3743932.

Coconino National Forest Records: *Land Status Book,* maps and records in the Forest Archaeology Department.

Miscellaneous documents at Riordan State Historical Park, Flagstaff.

Conversations with:

Lillian Hall, Coconino County Treasurer
Joe Mehan, Arizona Historical Society Pioneer Museum
Stanton Wallace, U.S. Forest Service (retired)
Duane Miller, Coconino Cattle Company
Bruce Greco, Silviculturist, Coconino National Forest
Mike Landram, Timber, Coconino National Forest
Scott Ewers, Timber, Coconino National Forest
Bonnie Greer, Archivist, AHS Pioneer Museum
Mary Sweitzer, daughter of a Flagstaff Pioneer
Bob Munson, Riordan State Park
Mary Malmgren, granddaughter of T.A. Riordan
Rita Gannon, granddaughter of T.A. Riordan
Helen McPherson, granddaughter of T.A. Riordan
Malcolm Mackey, Flagstaff native

Correspondence with:

Mary Malmgren, granddaughter of T.A. Riordan
Duane Miller, Coconino Cattle Company
Naomi Kuhn, wife of Millard Kuhn
Bruce Greco, Silviculturist, Coconino National Forest

Chapter Five

Published:

Arizona Revised Statutes, Annotated. Prepared under Legislative Authority, Volume 8A, Title 23, Title 24. St. Paul, Minnesota: West Publishing Co., 1977.

Arizona Water: The Management of Scarcity. Research report prepared by the University of Arizona, Tucson, for the 31st Arizona Town Hall, 1977.

Barstad, Jan. *The Verde River Sheep Bridge and the Sheep Industry in Arizona.* Phoenix: Gerald A. Doyle and Associates, P.C., sponsored by the United States Department of Agriculture, Forest Service, Tonto National Forest, 1988.

Brands and Marks of Cattle, Horses, Sheep, Goats and Hogs. Phoenix: Livestock Sanitary Board of Arizona with the Press of the McNeil Co., 1908.

Calef, Wesley. *Private Grazing and Public Lands: Studies of the Local Management of the Taylor Grazing Act.* Chicago: University of Chicago Press, 1960.

Cline, Platt. *They Came to the Mountain.* Flagstaff: Northland Press, 1976.

Coolidge, Dane. *Arizona Cowboys.* New York: E.P. Dutton and Company, 1938.

Dedera, Don. *A Little War of Our Own.* Flagstaff: Northland Press, 1988.

Dittmer, Howard J. "Vegetation of the Southwest—Past and Present," *The Texas Journal of Science.* September 1951.

Douglass, William A. and Jon Bilbao. *Amerikanuak: Basques in the New World.* Reno: University of Nevada Press, 1975.

"E.H. Crabb," *Arizona Cattlelog.* Arizona Cattle Growers' Association, October 1948.

Embach, Harry B. "Jose Antonio Manterola—A Real Sheepman," *Arizona Stockman.* 1950.

Fausold, Martin L. *Gifford Pinchot: Bull Moose Progressive*. New York: Syracuse University Press, 1961.

Fuchs, James R. *A History of Williams*. Tucson: Social Sciences Bulletin No. 23, University of Arizona, 1953.

Granger, Byrd. *X Marks the Place*. Tucson: Falconer Publishing, 1983.

Greever, William S. *Arid Domain: the Santa Fe Railway and Its Western Land Grant*. Stanford: Stanford University Press, 1954.

Haskett, Bert. "History of the Sheep Industry in Arizona," *Arizona Historical Review*. Tucson: Arizona Pioneer Historical Society and the University of Arizona, July 1936.

———"History of the Sheep Industry in Arizona," *Arizona: the New State Magazine*. Phoenix: October 1912.

"Hurley Death Closes Noted Pioneer Career", *Phoenix Gazette*, June 24, 1946.

"Hurley Family Came Early, Liked It—They're Still Here," *Arizona Republic*, August 7, 1966.

Keith, Abbie W. "Arizona Heritage," *Outlook*. Arizona Cattle Growers' Association, August 1984.

Kupper, Winifred. *The Golden Hoof*. New York: Alfred A. Knopf, 1945.

Mangam, William David. *The Clarks of Montana*. New York: The Silver Bow Press, 1939.

Mann, Dean E. *The Politics of Water in Arizona*. Tucson: University of Arizona Press, 1963.

McGavock, E.H., T.W. Anderson, Otto Moosburner, and Larry J. Mann. *Water Resources of Southern Coconino County, Arizona*. Tucson: Geological Survey, United States Department of the Interior, 1986.

McGeary, M. Nelson. *Gifford Pinchot: Forester–Politician*. Princeton: Princeton University Press, 1960.

Mercer, Lloyd J. *Railroads and Land Grant Policy: A Study in Government Intervention*. New York: Academic Press, Harcourt Brace Jovanovich Publishers, 1982.

Peterson, Sue. "Shepherds of the Open Range," *Arizona Highways*. August 1978.

Phillips, Arthur M., Dorothy House, and Barbara G. Phillips. "Expedition to the San Francisco Peaks", *Plateau*. Museum of Northern Arizona, Northern Arizona Society of Sciences and Art, Inc., 1989.

Pinchot, Gifford. *Breaking New Ground*. Seattle: University of Washington Press, 1947.

Portrait and Biographical Record of Arizona. Chicago: Chapman Publishing Company, 1901.

Powell, John Wesley. *Report on the Lands of the Arid Region of the United States*. Washington, D.C.: U.S. Geographical and Geological Survey, Department of the Interior, D.C., 1878.

Revised Statutes of Arizona Territory. Columbia, Missouri: Press of E.W. Stephens, 1901.

Richardson, Gladwell (alias Maurice Kildare). "Rogers Lake Loot," *Treasure Trails Old West*. Conroe, Texas: True Treasure Publications, Inc., Summer 1973.

Roberts, Paul H. *Hoof Prints on Forest Ranges: The Early Years of National Forest Range Administration*. San Antonio, Texas: The Naylor Company, 1963.

Schmidt, Elain F. "Basque Shepherds in Arizona," *Outdoor Arizona*. November 1976.

Smith, H.V. *The Climate of Arizona*. Tucson: University of Arizona College of Agriculture Bulletin No. 130, 1930.

The Taming of the Salt: a collection of biographies of pioneers who contributed significantly to water development in the Salt River Valley. Salt River Project, 1971.

Taylor, Zeke. *Reflections of the Past As It Rolled Along.* Humbolt, Arizona: printed by John Kennedy, 1987.

The Use of the National Forest Reserves. Washington, D.C.: United States Forest Service, 1906.

Those Early Days…Old Timers' Memoirs; Oak Creek, Sedona and the Verde Valley Region of Northern Arizona. Sedona Westerners, 1975.

Viele, Cathy. "Basques in Northern Arizona: A Quiet Strength Gone Quieter," *Northlander.* September 1975.

Voigt, William Jr. *Public Grazing Lands.* New Brunswick, New Jersey: Rutgers University Press, 1976.

Wentworth, Edward Norris. *America's Sheep Trails.* Ames, Iowa: Iowa State College Press, 1948.

Wilkinson, Charles F. and H. Michael Anderson. *Land and Resource Planning in the National Forests.* Washington, D.C.: Island Press, 1987.

Wilson, Roscoe G. *Pioneer Cattlemen of Arizona.* Phoenix: Valley National Bank, 1951.

———"They Died by Thousands," *Arizona.* November 17, 1968.

———"Sheep Raising Now in Hands of Basques," *Arizona Republic.* August 9, 1953.

Woody, Clara and Milton L. Schwartz. "War in Pleasant Valley: The Outbreak of the Graham–Tewksbury Feud", *The Journal of Arizona History.* Tucson: Arizona Historical Society, Spring 1977.

Primary:

Held in the Cline Library, Northern Arizona University:

McCarger, Dennis. *The Arizona Cattle Growers: The Pre-Corporate Years, 1903–1923.* Unpublished manuscript, Arizona Cattle Growers Association Collection #7, folder #1.

Ruisnek, Walter. *The Sanction for Overdrafts: Arizona Groundwater Policy, 1948–1980.* Thesis for a Master's Degree in History, Northern Arizona University, 1980.

Wisbey, Herbert Andrew Jr. *A History of the Santa Fe Railroad in Arizona to 1917.* Thesis for a Master's Degree in History, University of Arizona, 1946.

Special Collections and Archives Department, Cline Library, Northern Arizona University:

AHS–Pioneer Manuscript Collection #47: Outgoing Correspondence, 1929. A–I, Annual Report to the Arizona Corporation Commission 1931; Report to the Bureau of Labor Statistics 1931.

Gladwell Richardson Collection, AHS Pioneer Museum Manuscript Collection #47: statement by George McCormick in 1928, L.P. Brown folder

Black family genealogy

AHS Pioneer Museum Manuscript Collection #47: Interview with Millard Kuhn, Howard Sheep Company Collection

Babbitt Brothers Trading Company Collection #83: *Minutes Book of Glendale Stock Farms.*

Microfilms of Arizona Newspapers: *Coconino Sun, Phoenix Gazette, Arizona Republic.*

Jerome News (held in the office of the Jerome Historical Society).

Coconino County Records:

Recorder's Office: *Index to Deeds, Index to Leases, Great Register of Voters, Articles of Incorporation, Water Rights*

Treasurer's Office: *Duplicate Tax Records*

Clerk of the Superior Court: *Index to Probate*

Yavapai County Records:

Recorder's Office: *Index to Deeds, Great Register of Voters*

Miller Brothers Archives:

Minutes Book of the Board of Directors of the Coconino Cattle Company, Minutes Book of the Board of Directors of Hampshire Farms

Archives of the Rocky Mountain Forest and Range Experimental Station, Flagstaff

Conversations with:

Lillian Hall, Coconino County Treasurer
Louise Black, daughter-in-law of a Flagstaff pioneer
Bonnie Greer, Archivist, AHS Pioneer Museum
Duane Miller, Coconino Cattle Company
Cecil Miller jr., Coconino Cattle Company
Platt Cline, Flagstaff historian
Joe Hancock, Pioneer rancher near Sedona
Frank Auza, Basque sheepman in Coconino County
Sylvia Manterola, daughter of a Basque sheepman

Correspondence with:

Thomas C. Buckley, Manager—Public Relations, Santa Fe–Southern Pacific Corporation, Los Angeles, California
Lynn Reyes, United States Department of the Interior, Bureau of Land Management, Arizona.
Ricky Curcio, State Examiner, Surface Water Section of the Arizona Department of Water Resources, Phoenix
Carol Downey, Reference Librarian, Arizona Department of Library, Archives and Public Records, Phoenix
Earl Van Deren, son of settlers near Sedona
Henry Giclas, son of a Flagstaff settler
Della Greenwell, great-granddaughter of J.J. Howard

Chapter Six

Published:

"Anders Peter Pearson, Pioneer of Phelps County," *Holdrege (Nebraska) Progress,* November 14, 1912.

Ball, Phyllis. *A Photographic History of the University of Arizona.* Tucson: Isbell Printing Company, 1986.

Colley, Charles C. *The Century of Robert H. Forbes.* Tucson: Arizona Historical Society, 1977.

Dietrich, John H. *Chimney Spring Forest Fire History*. Research paper RM-220, Rocky Mountain Forest and Range Experiment Station, USDA Forest Service, September 1980.

Everett, Dick. *The Old Sod House Frontier*. Lincoln, Nebraska: Johnson Publishing Company, 1954.

———*Conquering the Great American Desert*. Lincoln, Nebraska: Nebraska State Historical Society, 1975.

Fritz, Emanuel. "Recollections of Fort Valley, 1916–1917," *Forest History*. Fall 1964.

Gaines, Edward M. and Elmer W. Shaw. *Half a Century of Research: Fort Valley Experimental Forest, 1908–1958*. Rocky Mountain Forest and Range Experiment Station Paper No. 38, USDA Forest Service, October 1958.

Giclas, Henry. "Stanley Sykes," *The Journal of Arizona History*. Tucson: Arizona Historical Society, Summer 1985.

History of the State of Nebraska. Chicago: The Western Historical Company, 1882.

Hochderffer, George. *Flagstaff, Whoa!* Flagstaff: Museum of Northern Arizona with Northland Presss, 1965.

Hoyt, William Graves. *Lowell and Mars*. Tucson: University of Arizona Press, 1976.

Leonard, Louise. *Percival Lowell: an Afterglow*. Boston: The Gorham Press, 1921.

Lowell, Abbott Lawrence. *Biography of Percival Lowell*. New York: Macmillan, 1935.

Madson, John. "Nebraska's Sand Hills," *National Geographic*. October 1978.

Manley, Robert N. *Centennial History of the University of Nebraska; I. Frontier University, 1869–1919*. Lincoln, Nebraska: University of Nebraska Press, 1969.

Merriam, Dr. C. Hart. "General Results of a Biological Survey of the San Francisco Mountain Region in Arizona, With Special Reference to the Distribution of Species," *North American Fauna*. 1890.

Mumey, Nolie. *John Williams Gunnison (1812–1853) The Last of the Western Explorers; A History of the Survey Through Colorado and Utah with a Biography and Details of his Massacre*. Denver: Artcraft Press, 1955.

Nicoll, Bruce. *Nebraska: A Pictorial History*. Lincoln, Nebraska: University of Nebraska Press, 1967.

Pearson, G.A. *Timber Growing and Logging Practice in the Southwest and in the Black Hills Region*. Technical Bulletin No. 480, USDA Forest Service, October 1935.

———*Reproduction of Western Yellow Pine in the Southwest*. Forest Service Circular 174, 1910.

———"The Relation Between Spring Precipitation and Height Growth of Western Yellow Pine Saplings in Arizona," *Journal of Forestry*. October 1918.

———"Recovery of Western Yellow Pine Seedlings from Injury by Grazing Animals," *Journal of Forestry*. October 1931.

———*Management of Ponderosa Pine in the Southwest: As Developed by Research and Experimental Practice*. USDA Forest Service Agriculture Monograph No. 6.

———"Making a Permanent Resource Out of the Forest of the Southwest," *The Southern Lumberman*. Nashville, Tennessee: March 26, 1921.

———"Grass, Pine Seedlings and Grazing," *Journal of Forestry*. 32(5), 1934.

———*The Influence of Age and Condition of the Tree Upon Seed Production in Western Yellow Pine*. USDA Forest Service Circular 196, 1912.

——"Forest Land Use," *Journal of Forestry*. 38(3), 1940.

——*Forest Planting in Arizona and New Mexico*. Fort Valley Experimental Station, 1914.

Pinchot, Gifford. *Breaking New Ground*. Seattle: University of Washington Press, 1947.

Price, Raymond. *History of Forest Service Research in the Central and Southern Rocky Mountain Regions, 1908–1975*. USDA Forest Service General Technical Report RM-27, August 1976.

Ringland, Arthur C. with Fern Ingersoll. "Pioneering in Southwest Forestry," *Forest History*. April 1973.

The University of Nebraska; Semi-Centennial Anniversary Book. by the University, 1919.

Trefil, James S. "Concentric Clues from Growth Rings Unlock the Past," *Smithsonian*. July 1985.

Webb, George Ernest. *Tree Rings and Telescopes*. Tucson: University of Arizona Press, 1983.

Who Was Who in America, Vol. 2, 1943–1950. Chicago: A.N. Marquis Company, 1966.

Wigdore, David. *Roscoe Pound*. Westport, Connecticut: Greenwood Press, 1974.

Primary:

Special Collections and Archives Department, Cline Library, Northern Arizona University:
  AHS–Pioneer Museum Hochderffer Collection, Series A Box 11, folder 30.
  AHS–Pioneer Museum Manuscript Collection #47: Outgoing Correspondence.
  Microfilms of Arizona Newspapers: *Coconino Sun*, 1894, 1901.
University of Arizona's Special Collections Library: Miscellaneous papers in the A.E. Douglass Collection, Boxes 155–159, Personal Material (Various).
Federal Records:
  USFS: unpublished research notes for *Men Who Matched the Mountains*, Region 3, Supervisor's office, Albuquerque, New Mexico.
Private Archives:
  Lowell Observatory, Flagstaff
  U.S. Naval Observatory, Flagstaff
  Rocky Mountain Forest and Range Experiment Station, Flagstaff
University of Nebraska Special Collections Library:
  Pearson–Bessey correspondence from the Bessey Collection

Conversations with:

  Pat Heideman, Rocky Mountain Forest and Range Experiment Station
  Steve Sackett, Rocky Mountain Forest and Range Experiment Station
  John Dietrich, Rocky Mountain Forest and Range Experiment Station (retired)
  Gorden Bade, U.S. Forest Service (retired)
  Norman Borg, U.S. Forest Service (retired), brother-in-law of Bert Lexen
  Florence Martin, U.S. Forest Service (retired), former secretary to G.A. Pearson
  Henry Giclas, Lowell Observatory
  Dottie Brumbaugh, Lowell Observatory Librarian
  Peter Pilles, Archaeology, Coconino National Forest
  Mary Malmgren, granddaughter of T.A. Riordan
  Lillian Hall, Flagstaff native

Isabella Wallace, Flagstaff native
Frank Ronco, Rocky Mountain Forest and Range Experiment Station (retired)
John Irwin, alumnus, Nebraska Wesleyan University
Jerry Bradley, Range, Coconino National Forest

Correspondence with:

Edward Groesbeck, U.S. Forest Service (retired)
Frank Wadsworth, son-in-law of G.A. Pearson
Bruce Greco, Silviculturist, Coconino National Forest
John S. Hall, U.S. Navy astronomer (retired)
E.M. Hornibrook, Rocky Mountain Forest and Range Experiment Station (retired)
Laboratory of Tree Ring Research, Tucson
Barbara Fritz, daughter of Emanuel Fritz
Joseph Svoboda, Archivist, Special Collections Library, University of Nebraska
Malcolm Mackey, Flagstaff native

Chapter Seven

Published:

Bader, Lou. *In the Shadow of the San Francisco Peaks: Frontier Adventures.* Sedona, Arizona: Light Technology Publishing, 1988.

Colton, Harold S. "Early Failure to Solve the Water Shortage." *Plateau.* Museum of Northern Arizona, Northern Arizona Society of Sciences and Art, Inc., October 1956.

Weaver, J.E. and F.W. Albertson. "Nature and Degree of Recovery from the Great Drought of 1933 to 1940," *Ecological Monographs* 14:393–479. October 1944.

Owen-Joyce, Sandra J. and C.K. Bell. *Appraisal of Water Resources in the Upper Verde River Area, Yavapai and Coconino Counties, Arizona.* Phoenix: Geological Survey, United States Department of the Interior, March 1983.

Water System Improvement Program, City of Flagstaff. Tucson: Brown and Caldwell Consulting Engineers, November 1980.

Primary:

Held in the Cline Library, Northern Arizona University:

Farrar, Christopher D. *Ground Water Potential in the Middle Paleozoic Carbonate Rocks, Flagstaff Area, Coconino County.* Thesis for Master of Science at Northern Arizona University, May 1980.

Woody Mountain Aquifer Report to the City of Flagstaff, Arizona, Harshbarger and Associates in Tucson, John Carollo Engineers, Phoenix 1973.

Special Collections and Archives Department, Cline Library, Northern Arizona University:

"Flagstaff, Arizona—Water Supply"; Vertical file.

Notes of the Flagstaff Water Conference. City Hall, February 13, 1957.

Souvenir of the Dedication of the New Half Million Dollar Community Water System, Flagstaff, June 18, 1926.

Flagstaff City/Coconino County Library Oral History Project, Tapes #28-2 to 29-4-5: Mary Sala, Eva Cavanessa, Dr. Martin Fronske, Elizabeth Dobrinski, Switzer sisters, Platt Cline, Billie Yost, Louise Black, Kathryn Rucker, Bill Wong.

Pulliam–Marshall Collection #225.

Frances Decker Collection, Northern Arizona University's Manuscript Collection #13: Folder 52.

AHS–Pioneer Museum Manuscript Collection #36: Flagstaff Fire Company

Microfilms of Arizona Newspapers: *Coconino Sun*

Private archives:

Unpublished papers on water sites prepared in 1967 by James Beard, City of Flagstaff water consultant; held by Lloyd Perry.

Conversations with:

Louise Black, longtime Flagstaff resident
Andrew Wolf, Flagstaff City Council, 1952–1958
Lloyd Perry of Perry Brothers
Bruce Moseley, Superintendent of Flagstaff Water Systems
Don Perry, son of Lloyd Perry
Malcolm Mackey, Flagstaff native
Henry Giclas, Flagstaff native

Chapter Eight

Published:

Ames, Charles R. "A History of the Forest Service," *Smoke Signal*. Fall 1967.

Arizona Death Records. Tucson: Arizona State Genealogical Society, 1976.

Baker, Robert D., Robert S. Maxwell, Victor H. Treat and Henry C. Dethloff. *Timeless Heritage: A History of the Forest Service in the Southwest*. United States Department of Agriculture, Forest Service, August 1988.

Brown, Arthur A. and Kenneth P. Davis. *Forest Fire Control and Use*. New York: McGraw-Hill, 1959.

Chandler, Craig, Phillip Cheney, Philip Thomas, Louis Trabaud, and Dave Williams. *Fire in Forestry*. New York: John Wiley and Sons, 1983.

Cook, James E. "Forest-fire battles burned into memory," *The Arizona Republic*. June 19, 1988.

———— "Conservation Corps answered call to duty," *The Arizona Republic*. April 10, 1988.

Corning, Howard McKinley. "The Lookout's Mechanical Eye," *American Forests*, Vol. 58, No. c., March 1952

Downum, Garland. *A Flagstaff Heritage: The Federated Community Church*. Flagstaff: The Federated Community Church, 1983.

Fincher, Jack. "America's Deadly Rendezvous with the 'Spanish Lady'," *Smithsonian*. January 1989.

Groesbeck, Edward C. *Events in the Life of a Timber Beast*. Steamboat Springs, Colorado: The Steamboat Pilot, 1976.

Kelly, Roger E. and John O. Cramer. *American Indians in Small Cities: A Survey of Urban Acculturation in Two Northern Arizona Communities.* Flagstaff: Rehabilitation Monographs No. 1, Department of Rehabilitation, Northern Arizona University, 1966.

Lacy, Leslie Alexander. *The Soil Soldiers.* Radnor, Pennsylvania: Chilton Book Co., 1976.

Nash, Gerald D. "Bureaucracy and Reform in the West," *Western Historical Quarterly.* July 1971.

Pyne, Stephen J. *Fire in America: A Cultural History of Wildland and Rural Fire.* Princeton: Princeton University Press, 1982.

Reid, Megan. "Fowler Makes First Landing in Territory," *Arizona History.* Tucson: The Arizona Historical Society, May/June 1988.

Sentries on the Summit. Prepared by the Forest Service, Southwestern Region, August 1984.

Spring, Ira and Byron Fish. *Lookouts.* Seattle: The Mountaineers, 1981.

Steen, Harold K. *The United States Forest Service: A History.* Seattle: University of Washington, 1976.

Stevens, Jan. "Fifty Years of Winter Fun," *Discover Flagstaff.* Winter/Spring 1988.

Tucker, Edwin and George Fitzpatrick. *Men Who Matched the Mountains.* Washington, D.C.: U.S.D.A. Forest Service, 1972.

Zimmerman. "The Evolution of the Lookout Tower," *Forest Fire Detection.* Washington, D.C.: U.S. Forest Service, U.S. Government Printing Office, January 1969.

Primary:

Flagstaff City-Coconino County Public Library:

> Cummings, William H. *A History of the Flagstaff Public Schools.* 1987. Bound but unpublished

Held in the Cline Library, Northern Arizona University:

> Sawyer, Gregg S. *The History of Fire Control on the Coconino National Forest.* Thesis for a degree of Master of Arts, Northern Arizona University, 1976.

Special Collections and Archives Department, Cline Library, Northern Arizona University:

> AHS–Pioneer Museum Manuscript Collection #47: Outgoing Correspondence.

> John W. Weatherford Collection, AHS–Pioneeer Museum Manuscript Collection #7.

> Flagstaff City/Coconino County Library Oral History Project, Northern Arizona University's Tape Collection #28: Dr. Martin Fronske, Kathryn Rucker, Mary Sweitzer, Elizabeth Dobrinski, Switzer sisters, Mary Sala and Eva Cavaness (Michelbach sisters), Bill Wong, Louise Black, Platt Cline.

Newspapers—*Coconino Sun* Historical edition

Federal records:

> Unpublished notes for *Men Who Matched the Mountains*; Region 3 Supervisor's Office, Albuquerque, New Mexico

> Depository of Federal Records, Denver: Coconino National Forest USFS; Agency Container #9, FRC Container #743932; Agency Container #7, FRC Container #3743932.

> 1960 Inventory of towers in Region 3, Regional Supervisor's Office in Albuquerque

Conversations with:

Laura McBride, granddaughter of J.J. Howard
Louise Black, long-time Flagstaff resident
Isabella Wallace, granddaughter of a Flagstaff settler
Mary Sweitzer, long-time Flagstaff resident
Billie Yost, long-time Flagstaff resident
Helen Sandoval, long-time Flagstaff resident
Max Castillo, veteran of the Civilian Conservation Corps
Frank Auza, Basque sheepman
Joe Robinson, Arizona cowboy
Alice Etter, granddaughter of a Flagstaff pioneer
Duane Miller, Coconino Cattle Company
Henry Giclas, Flagstaff native
Andy Wolf, former member of Flagstaff City Council
Cecil Miller Jr., Coconino Cattle Company
Keith Hunter, Coconino National Forest Fire Dispatcher, 1946–1970 (retired)
Milford Suida, Coconino National Forest Dispatcher
Amos Coochyouma, Coconino National Forest Dispatcher
Stanton Wallace, Woody Mountain Lookout (retired)
Don Shanks, Woody Mountain Lookout (retired)
Roseanna Finley, Woody Mountain Lookout
Lynn Bleeker, Woody Mountain Lookout
Maureen Gallagher, Coconino National Forest
Shirley Pierce, Turkey Butte Lookout
Frances McAllister, long-time Arizona resident

Correspondence with:

Barbara Abels, Public Affairs Office, Federal Aviation Administration, Los Angeles
Stanton Wallace, Lookout on Woody Mountain, 1933–1934
N.E. Johnson, veteran of the Civilian Conservation Corps
Dean D. Cutler, USFS Flagstaff District, 1936–1940
Aida L. Papp, Prescott Pioneer's Home
Elizabeth B. Wade, Horizontal Network Branch, National Geodetic Survey
John Tompkins, Federal Aviation Administration
Dean Gossard, Flagstaff District Ranger, 1958–1961
Al Bell, Coconino National Forest fire dispatcher (retired)
Harlow A. Yeager, Coconino National Forest, 1941 (retired)
Allan Wing, Woody Mountain Lookout (retired)
Roy Beach, Woody Mountain Lookout (retired)

Chapter Nine

Published:

Redfern, Ron. *Corridors of Time*. New York: New York Times Books, 1980.

Index